Third Editi

IT STRATEGY:

ISSUES AND PRACTICES

James D. McKeen
Queen's University

Heather A. Smith
Queen's University

PEARSON

Boston Columbus Indianapolis New York San Francisco Upper Saddle River
Amsterdam Cape Town Dubai London Madrid Milan Munich Paris Montréal Toronto
Delhi Mexico City São Paulo Sydney Hong Kong Seoul Singapore Taipei Tokyo

Editor in Chief: Stephanie Wall
Acquisitions Editor: Nicole Sam
Program Manager Team Lead: Ashley Santora
Program Manager: Denise Vaughn
Editorial Assistant: Kaylee Rotella
Executive Marketing Manager: Anne K. Fahlgren
Project Manager Team Lead: Judy Leale
Project Manager: Thomas Benfatti
Procurement Specialist: Diane Peirano
Cover Designer: Lumina Datamantics
Full Service Project Management: Abinaya Rajendran at Integra Software Services, Pvt. Ltd.
Cover Printer: Courier Companies, Inc.
Composition: Integra Software Services, Pvt. Ltd.
Printer/Binder: Courier Companies, Inc.
Text Font: 10/12 Palatino LT Std

Credits and acknowledgments borrowed from other sources and reproduced, with permission, in this textbook appear on appropriate page within text.

Library of Congress Cataloging-in-Publication Data

McKeen, James D.
   IT strategy in action/James D. McKeen, Heather A. Smith.—3rd ed.
    p. cm.
   ISBN–13: 978-0-13-354424-4
   ISBN–10: 0-13-354424-9
   1. Information technology—Management.   I. Mckeen, James D.   II. Smith, Heather A.
   HD30.2.M3987 2008
   004.068—dc22

                                   2007048123

10 9 8 7 6 5 4 3 V092 15

ISBN–10:   0-13-354424-9
ISBN–13: 978-0-13-354424-4

IT STRATEGY:

ISSUES AND PRACTICES

CONTENTS

PREFACE

Today, with information technology (IT) driving constant business transformation, overwhelming organizations with information, enabling 24/7 global operations, and undermining traditional business models, the challenge for business leaders is not simply to *manage* IT, it is to *use* IT *to deliver business value*. Whereas until fairly recently, decisions about IT could be safely delegated to technology specialists *after* a business strategy had been developed, IT is now so closely integrated with business that, as one CIO explained to us, "We can no longer deliver business solutions in our company without using technology so IT and business strategy must constantly interact with each other."

What's New in This Third Edition?

* Six new chapters focusing on current critical issues in IT management, including IT shared services; big data and social computing; business intelligence; managing IT demand; improving the customer experience; and enhancing development productivity.
* Two significantly revised chapters: on delivering IT functions through different resourcing options; and innovating with IT.
* Two new mini cases based on real companies and real IT management situations: Working Smarter at Continental Furniture and Enterprise Architecture at Nationstate Insurance.
* A revised structure based on reader feedback with six chapters and two mini cases from the second edition being moved to the Web site.

All too often, in our efforts to prepare future executives to deal effectively with the issues of IT strategy and management, we lead them into a foreign country where they encounter a different language, different culture, and different customs. Acronyms (e.g., SOA, FTP/IP, SDLC, ITIL, ERP), buzzwords (e.g., asymmetric encryption, proxy servers, agile, enterprise service bus), and the widely adopted practice of abstraction (e.g., Is a software monitor a person, place, or thing?) present formidable "barriers to entry" to the technologically uninitiated, but more important, they obscure the importance of teaching students how to make *business* decisions about a key organizational resource. By taking a critical issues perspective, *IT Strategy: Issues and Practices* treats IT as a tool to be leveraged to save and/or make money or transform an organization—not as a study by itself.

As in the first two editions of this book, this third edition combines the experiences and insights of many senior IT managers from leading-edge organizations with thorough academic research to bring important issues in IT management to life and demonstrate how IT strategy is put into action in contemporary businesses. This new edition has been designed around an enhanced set of critical real-world issues in IT management today, such as innovating with IT, working with big data and social media, enhancing customer experience, and designing for business intelligence and introduces students to the challenges of making IT decisions that will have significant impacts on how businesses function and deliver value to stakeholders.

IT Strategy: Issues and Practices focuses on how IT is changing and will continue to change organizations as we now know them. However, rather than learning concepts "free of context," students are introduced to the complex decisions facing real organizations by means of a number of mini cases. These provide an opportunity to apply the models/theories/frameworks presented and help students integrate and assimilate this material. By the end of the book, students will have the confidence and ability to tackle the tough issues regarding IT management and strategy and a clear understanding of their importance in delivering business value.

Key Features of This Book

- A focus on IT *management* issues as opposed to *technology* issues
- Critical IT issues explored within their organizational contexts
- Readily applicable models and frameworks for implementing IT strategies
- Mini cases to animate issues and focus classroom discussions on real-world decisions, enabling problem-based learning
- Proven strategies and best practices from leading-edge organizations
- Useful and practical advice and guidelines for delivering value with IT
- Extensive teaching notes for all mini cases

A DIFFERENT APPROACH TO TEACHING IT STRATEGY

The real world of IT is one of issues—critical issues—such as the following:

- How do we know if we are getting value from our IT investment?
- How can we innovate with IT?
- What specific IT functions should we seek from external providers?
- How do we build an IT leadership team that is a trusted partner with the business?
- How do we enhance IT capabilities?
- What is IT's role in creating an intelligent business?
- How can we best take advantage of new technologies, such as big data and social media, in our business?
- How can we manage IT risk?

However, the majority of management information systems (MIS) textbooks are organized by system *category* (e.g., supply chain, customer relationship management, enterprise resource planning), by system *component* (e.g., hardware, software, networks), by system *function* (e.g., marketing, financial, human resources), by system *type* (e.g., transactional, decisional, strategic), or by a combination of these. Unfortunately, such an organization does not promote an understanding of IT management in practice.

IT Strategy: Issues and Practices tackles the real-world challenges of IT management. First, it explores a set of the most important issues facing IT managers today, and second, it provides a series of mini cases that present these critical IT issues within the context of real organizations. By focusing the text as well as the mini cases on today's critical issues, the book naturally reinforces problem-based learning.

IT Strategy: Issues and Practices includes thirteen mini cases—each based on a real company presented anonymously.[1] Mini cases are *not* simply abbreviated versions of standard, full-length business cases. They differ in two significant ways:

1. *A horizontal perspective.*   Unlike standard cases that develop a single issue within an organizational setting (i.e., a "vertical" slice of organizational life), mini cases take a "horizontal" slice through a number of coexistent issues. Rather than looking for a *solution* to a specific problem, as in a standard case, students analyzing a mini case must first *identify and prioritize* the issues embedded within the case. This mimics real life in organizations where the challenge lies in "knowing where to start" as opposed to "solving a predefined problem."
2. *Highly relevant information.*   Mini cases are densely written. Unlike standard cases, which intermix irrelevant information, in a mini case, each sentence exists for a reason and reflects relevant information. As a result, students must analyze each case very carefully so as not to miss critical aspects of the situation.

Teaching with mini cases is, thus, very different than teaching with standard cases. With mini cases, students must determine what is really going on within the organization. What first appears as a straightforward "technology" problem may in fact be a political problem or one of five other "technology" problems. Detective work is, therefore, required. The problem identification and prioritization skills needed are essential skills for future managers to learn for the simple reason that it is not possible for organizations to tackle all of their problems concurrently. Mini cases help teach these skills to students and can balance the problem-solving skills learned in other classes. Best of all, detective work is fun and promotes lively classroom discussion.

To assist instructors, extensive teaching notes are available for all mini cases. Developed by the authors and based on "tried and true" in-class experience, these notes include case summaries, identify the key issues within each case, present ancillary information about the company/industry represented in the case, and offer guidelines for organizing the classroom discussion. Because of the structure of these mini cases and their embedded issues, it is common for teaching notes to exceed the length of the actual mini case!

This book is most appropriate for MIS courses where the goal is to understand how IT delivers organizational value. These courses are frequently labeled "IT Strategy" or "IT Management" and are offered within undergraduate as well as MBA programs. For undergraduate juniors and seniors in business and commerce programs, this is usually the "capstone" MIS course. For MBA students, this course may be the compulsory core course in MIS, or it may be an elective course.

Each chapter and mini case in this book has been thoroughly tested in a variety of undergraduate, graduate, and executive programs at Queen's School of Business.[2]

---

[1] We are unable to identify these leading-edge companies by agreements established as part of our overall research program (described later).

[2] Queen's School of Business is one of the world's premier business schools, with a faculty team renowned for its business experience and academic credentials. The School has earned international recognition for its innovative approaches to team-based and experiential learning. In addition to its highly acclaimed MBA programs, Queen's School of Business is also home to Canada's most prestigious undergraduate business program and several outstanding graduate programs. As well, the School is one of the world's largest and most respected providers of executive education.

These materials have proven highly successful within all programs because we adapt how the material is presented according to the level of the students. Whereas undergraduate students "learn" about critical business issues from the book and mini cases for the first time, graduate students are able to "relate" to these same critical issues based on their previous business experience. As a result, graduate students are able to introduce personal experiences into the discussion of these critical IT issues.

ORGANIZATION OF THIS BOOK

One of the advantages of an issues-focused structure is that chapters can be approached in any order because they do not build on one another. Chapter order is immaterial; that is, one does not need to read the first three chapters to understand the fourth. This provides an instructor with maximum flexibility to organize a course as he or she sees fit. Thus, within different courses/programs, the order of topics can be changed to focus on different IT concepts.

Furthermore, because each mini case includes multiple issues, they, too, can be used to serve different purposes. For example, the mini case "Building Shared Services at RR Communications" can be used to focus on issues of governance, organizational structure, and/or change management just as easily as shared services. The result is a rich set of instructional materials that lends itself well to a variety of pedagogical applications, particularly problem-based learning, and that clearly illustrates the reality of IT strategy in action.

The book is organized into four sections, each emphasizing a key component of developing and delivering effective IT strategy:

- **Section I: Delivering Value with IT** is designed to examine the complex ways that IT and business value are related. Over the past twenty years, researchers and practitioners have come to understand that "business value" can mean many different things when applied to IT. Chapter 1 (Developing and Delivering on the IT Value Proposition) explores these concepts in depth. Unlike the simplistic value propositions often used when implementing IT in organizations, this chapter presents "value" as a multilayered business construct that must be effectively managed at several levels if technology is to achieve the benefits expected. Chapter 2 (Developing IT Strategy for Business Value) examines the dynamic interrelationship between business and IT strategy and looks at the processes and critical success factors used by organizations to ensure that both are well aligned. Chapter 3 (Linking IT to Business Metrics) discusses new ways of measuring IT's effectiveness that promote closer business–IT alignment and help drive greater business value. Chapter 4 (Building a Strong Relationship with the Business) examines the nature of the business–IT relationship and the characteristics of an effective relationship that delivers real value to the enterprise. Chapter 5 (Communicating with Business Managers) explores the business and interpersonal competencies that IT staff will need in order to do their jobs effectively over the next five to seven years and what companies should be doing to develop them. Finally, Chapter 6 (Building Better IT Leaders from the Bottom Up) tackles the increasing need for improved leadership skills in all IT staff and examines the expectations of the business for strategic and innovative guidance from IT.

In the mini cases associated with this section, the concepts of delivering value with IT are explored in a number of different ways. We see business and IT executives at Hefty Hardware grappling with conflicting priorities and perspectives and how best to work together to achieve the company's strategy. In "Investing in TUFS," CIO Martin Drysdale watches as all of the work his IT department has put into a major new system fails to deliver value. And the "IT Planning at ModMeters" mini case follows CIO Brian Smith's efforts to create a strategic IT plan that will align with business strategy, keep IT running, and *not* increase IT's budget.

- **Section II: IT Governance** explores key concepts in how the IT organization is structured and managed to effectively deliver IT products and services to the organization. Chapter 7 (IT Shared Services) discusses how IT shared services should be selected, organized, managed, and governed to achieve improved organizational performance. Chapter 8 (A Management Framework for IT Sourcing) examines how organizations are choosing to source and deliver different types of IT functions and presents a framework to guide sourcing decisions. Chapter 9 (The IT Budgeting Process) describes the "evil twin" of IT strategy, discussing how budgeting mechanisms can significantly undermine effective business strategies and suggesting practices for addressing this problem while maintaining traditional fiscal accountability. Chapter 10 (Managing IT-based Risk) describes how many IT organizations have been given the responsibility of not only managing risk in their own activities (i.e., project development, operations, and delivering business strategy) but also of managing IT-based risk in *all* company activities (e.g., mobile computing, file sharing, and online access to information and software) and the need for a holistic framework to understand and deal with risk effectively. Chapter 11 (Information Management: The Nexus of Business and IT) describes how new organizational needs for more useful and integrated information are driving the development of business-oriented functions within IT that focus specifically on information and knowledge, as opposed to applications and data.

  The mini cases in this section examine the difficulties of managing complex IT issues when they intersect substantially with important business issues. In "Building Shared Services at RR Communications," we see an IT organization in transition from a traditional divisional structure and governance model to a more centralized enterprise model, and the long-term challenges experienced by CIO Vince Patton in changing both business and IT practices, including information management and delivery, to support this new approach. In "Enterprise Architecture at Nationstate Insurance," CIO Jane Denton endeavors to make IT more flexible and agile, while incorporating new and emerging technologies into its strategy. In "IT Investment at North American Financial," we show the opportunities and challenges involved in prioritizing and resourcing enterprisewide IT projects and monitoring that anticipated benefits are being achieved.

- **Section III: IT-Enabled Innovation** discusses some of the ways technology is being used to transform organizations. Chapter 12 (Innovation with IT) examines the nature and importance of innovation with IT and describes a typical innovation life cycle. Chapter 13 (Big Data and Social Computing) discusses how IT leaders are incorporating big data and social media concepts and technologies to successfully deliver business value in new ways. Chapter 14 (Improving the Customer Experience: An IT Perspective) explores the IT function's role in creating and improving an organization's customer experiences and the role of technology in helping companies to understand and learn from their customers' experiences. Chapter 15 (Building Business Intelligence) looks at the nature of business intelligence and its relationship to data, information, and knowledge and how IT can be used to build a more intelligent organization. Chapter 16 (Enabling Collaboration with IT) identifies the principal forms of collaboration used in organizations, the primary business drivers involved in them, how their business value is measured, and the roles of IT and the business in enabling collaboration.

The mini cases in this section focus on the key challenges companies face in innovating with IT. "Innovation at International Foods" contrasts the need for process and control in corporate IT with the strong push to innovate with technology and the difficulties that ensue from the clash of style and culture. "Consumerization of Technology at IFG" looks at issues such as "bring your own device" (BYOD) to the workplace. In "CRM at Minitrex," we see some of the internal technological and political conflicts that result from a strategic decision to become more customercentric. Finally, "Customer Service at Datatronics" explores the importance of presenting unified, customer-facing IT to customers.

- **Section IV: IT Portfolio Development and Management** looks at how the IT function must transform itself to be able to deliver business value effectively in the future. Chapter 17 (Application Portfolio Management) describes the ongoing management process of categorizing, assessing, and rationalizing the IT application portfolio. Chapter 18 (Managing IT Demand) looks at the often neglected issue of demand management (as opposed to supply management), explores the root causes of the demand for IT services, and identifies a number of tools and enablers to facilitate more effective demand management. Chapter 19 (Creating and Evolving a Technology Roadmap) examines the challenges IT managers face in implementing new infrastructure, technology standards, and types of technology in their real-world business and technical environments, which is composed of a huge variety of hardware, software, applications, and other technologies, some of which date back more than thirty years. Chapter 20 (Enhancing Development Productivity) explores how system development practices are changing and how managers can create an environment to promote improved development productivity. And Chapter 21 (Information Delivery: IT's Evolving Role) examines the fresh challenges IT faces in managing the exponential growth of data and digital assets; privacy and accountability concerns; and new demands for access to information on an anywhere, anytime basis.

The mini cases associated with this section describe many of these themes embedded within real organizational contexts. "Project Management at MM" mini case shows how a top-priority, strategic project can take a wrong turn when project management skills are ineffective. "Working Smarter at Continental Furniture" mini case follows an initiative to improve the company's analytics so it can reduce its environmental impact. And in the mini case "Managing Technology at Genex Fuels," we see CIO Nick Devlin trying to implement enterprisewide technology for competitive advantage in an organization that has been limping along with obscure and outdated systems.

SUPPLEMENTARY MATERIALS

Online Instructor Resource Center

The following supplements are available online to adopting instructors:

- PowerPoint Lecture Notes
- Image Library (text art)
- Extensive Teaching Notes for all Mini cases
- Additional chapters including Developing IT Professionalism; IT Sourcing; Master Data Management; Developing IT Capabilities; The Identity Management Challenge; Social Computing; Managing Perceptions of IT; IT in the New World of Corporate Governance Reforms; Enhancing Customer Experiences with Technology; Creating Digital Dashboards; and Managing Electronic Communications.
- Additional mini cases, including IT Leadership at MaxTrade; Creating a Process-Driven Organization at Ag-Credit; Information Management at Homestyle Hotels; Knowledge Management at Acme Consulting; Desktop Provisioning at CanCredit; and Leveraging IT Vendors at SleepSmart.

For detailed descriptions of all of the supplements just listed, please visit http://www.pearsonhighered.com/mckeen.

CourseSmart eTextbooks Online

CourseSmart is an exciting new choice for students looking to save money. As an alternative to purchasing the print textbook, students can purchase an electronic version of the same content and save up to 50 percent off the suggested list price of the print text. With a CourseSmart etextbook, students can search the text, make notes online, print out reading assignments that incorporate lecture notes, and bookmark important passages for later review. www.coursesmart.com.

THE GENESIS OF THIS BOOK

Since 1990 we have been meeting quarterly with a group of senior IT managers from a number of leading-edge organizations (e.g., Eli Lilly, BMO, Honda, HP, CIBC, IBM, Sears, Bell Canada, MacDonalds, and Sun Life) to identify and discuss critical IT management issues. This focus group represents a wide variety of industry sectors (e.g., retail, manufacturing, pharmaceutical, banking, telecommunications, insurance, media, food processing, government, and automotive). Originally, it was established to meet the companies' needs for well-balanced, thoughtful, yet practical information on emerging IT management topics, about which little or no research was available. However, we soon recognized the value of this premise for our own research in the rapidly evolving field of IT management. As a result, it quickly became a full-scale research program in which we were able to use the focus group as an "early warning system" to document new IT management issues, develop case studies around them, and explore more collaborative approaches to identifying trends, challenges, and effective practices in each topic area.[3]

---

[3] This now includes best practice case studies, field research in organizations, multidisciplinary qualitative and quantitative research projects, and participation in numerous CIO research consortia.

As we shared our materials with our business students, we realized that this issues-based approach resonated strongly with them, and we began to incorporate more of our research into the classroom. This book is the result of our many years' work with senior IT managers, in organizations, and with students in the classroom.

Each issue in this book has been selected collaboratively by the focus group after debate and discussion. As facilitators, our job has been to keep the group's focus on IT management issues, not technology per se. In preparation for each meeting, focus group members researched the topic within their own organization, often involving a number of members of their senior IT management team as well as subject matter experts in the process. To guide them, we provided a series of questions about the issue, although members are always free to explore it as they see fit. This approach provided both structure for the ensuing discussion and flexibility for those members whose organizations are approaching the issue in a different fashion.

The focus group then met in a full-day session, where the members discussed all aspects of the issue. Many also shared corporate documents with the group. We facilitated the discussion, in particular pushing the group to achieve a common understanding of the dimensions of the issue and seeking examples, best practices, and guidelines for dealing with the challenges involved. Following each session, we wrote a report based on the discussion, incorporating relevant academic and practitioner materials where these were available. (Because some topics are "bleeding edge," there is often little traditional IT research available on them.)

Each report has three parts:

1. A description of the issue and the challenges it presents for both business and IT managers
2. Models and concepts derived from the literature to position the issue within a contextual framework
3. Near-term strategies (i.e., those that can be implemented immediately) that have proven successful within organizations for dealing with the specific issue

Each chapter in this book focuses on one of these critical IT issues. We have learned over the years that the issues themselves vary little across industries and organizations, even in enterprises with unique IT strategies. However, each organization tackles the same issue somewhat differently. It is this diversity that provides the richness of insight in these chapters. Our collaborative research approach is based on our belief that when dealing with complex and leading-edge issues, "everyone has part of the solution." Every focus group, therefore, provides us an opportunity to explore a topic from a variety of perspectives and to integrate different experiences (both successful and otherwise) so that collectively, a thorough understanding of each issue can be developed and strategies for how it can be managed most successfully can be identified.

ABOUT THE AUTHORS

James D. McKeen is Professor Emeritus at the Queen's School of Business. He has been working in the IT field for many years as a practitioner, researcher, and consultant. In 2011, he was named the "IT Educator of the Year" by ComputerWorld Canada. Jim has taught at universities in the United Kingdom, France, Germany, and the United States. His research is widely published in a number of leading journals and he is the coauthor (with Heather Smith) of five books on IT management. Their most recent book—*IT Strategy: Issues and Practices* (2nd ed.)—was the best-selling business book in Canada (*Globe and Mail*, April 2012).

Heather A. Smith has been named the most-published researcher on IT management issues in two successive studies (2006, 2009). A senior research associate with Queen's University School of Business, she is the author of five books, the most recent being *IT Strategy: Issues and Practices* (Pearson Prentice Hall, 2012). She is also a senior research associate with the American Society for Information Management's Advanced Practices Council. A former senior IT manager, she is codirector of the IT Management Forum and the CIO Brief, which facilitate interorganizational learning among senior IT executives. In addition, she consults and collaborates with organizations worldwide.

ACKNOWLEDGMENTS

The work contained in this book is based on numerous meetings with many senior IT managers. We would like to acknowledge our indebtedness to the following individuals who willingly shared their insights based on their experiences "earned the hard way":

Michael Balenzano, Sergei Beliaev, Matthias Benfey, Nastaran Bisheban, Peter Borden, Eduardo Cadena, Dale Castle, Marc Collins, Diane Cope, Dan Di Salvo, Ken Dschankilic, Michael East, Nada Farah, Mark Gillard, Gary Goldsmith, Ian Graham, Keiko Gutierrez, Maureen Hall, Bruce Harding, Theresa Harrington, Tom Hopson, Heather Hutchison, Jim Irich, Zeeshan Khan, Joanne Lafreniere, Konstantine Liris, Lisa MacKay, Mark O'Gorman, Amin Panjwani, Troy Pariag, Brian Patton, Marius Podaru, Helen Restivo, Pat Sadler, A. F. Salam, Ashish Saxena, Joanne Scher, Stewart Scott, Andy Secord, Marie Shafi, Helen Shih, Trudy Sykes, Bruce Thompson, Raju Uppalapati, Len Van Greuning, Laurie Schatzberg, Ted Vincent, and Bond Wetherbe.

We would also like to recognize the contribution of Queen's School of Business to this work. The school has facilitated and supported our vision of better integrating academic research and practice and has helped make our collaborative approach to the study of IT management and strategy an effective model for interorganizational learning.

James D. McKeen
Kingston, Ontario

Heather A. Smith
School of Business
June 2014

SECTION I

Delivering Value with IT

1

Developing and Delivering on the IT Value Proposition[1]

It's déjà vu all over again. For at least twenty years, business leaders have been trying to figure out exactly how and where IT can be of value in their organizations. And IT managers have been trying to learn how to deliver this value. When IT was used mainly as a productivity improvement tool in small areas of a business, this was a relatively straightforward process. Value was measured by reduced head counts—usually in clerical areas—and/or the ability to process more transactions per person. However, as systems grew in scope and complexity, unfortunately so did the risks. Very few companies escaped this period without making at least a few disastrous investments in systems that didn't work or didn't deliver the bottom-line benefits executives thought they would. Naturally, fingers were pointed at IT.

With the advent of the strategic use of IT in business, it became even more difficult to isolate and deliver on the IT value proposition. It was often hard to tell if an investment had paid off. Who could say how many competitors had been deterred or how many customers had been attracted by a particular IT initiative? Many companies can tell horror stories of how they have been left with a substantial investment in new forms of technology with little to show for it. Although over the years there have been many improvements in where and how IT investments are made and good controls have been established to limit time and cost overruns, we are still not able to accurately articulate and deliver on a value proposition for IT when it comes to anything other than simple productivity improvements or cost savings.

Problems in delivering IT value can lie with how a value proposition is conceived or in what is done to actually implement an idea—that is, selecting the right project and doing the project right (Cooper et al. 2000; McKeen and Smith 2003; Peslak 2012). In addition, although most firms attempt to calculate the expected payback of an IT investment before making it, few actually follow up to ensure that value has been achieved or to question what needs to be done to make sure that value will be delivered.

---

[1] This chapter is based on the authors' previously published article, Smith, H. A., and J. D. McKeen. "Developing and Delivering on the IT Value Proposition." *Communications of the Association for Information Systems* 11 (April 2003): 438–50. Reproduced by permission of the Association for Information Systems.

This chapter first looks at the nature of IT value and "peels the onion" into its different layers. Then it examines the three components of delivering IT value: value identification, conversion, and value realization. Finally, it identifies five general principles for ensuring IT value will be achieved.

PEELING THE ONION: UNDERSTANDING IT VALUE

Thirty years ago the IT value proposition was seen as a simple equation: Deliver the right technology to the organization, and financial benefits will follow (Cronk and Fitzgerald 1999; Marchand et al. 2000). In the early days of IT, when computers were most often used as direct substitutes for people, this equation was understandable, even if it rarely worked this simply. It was easy to compute a bottom-line benefit where "technology" dollars replaced "salary" dollars.

Problems with this simplistic view quickly arose when technology came to be used as a productivity support tool and as a strategic tool. Under these conditions, managers had to decide if an IT investment was worth making if it saved people time, helped them make better decisions, or improved service. Thus, other factors, such as how well technology was used by people or how IT and business processes worked together, became important considerations in how much value was realized from an IT investment. These issues have long confounded our understanding of the IT value proposition, leading to a plethora of opinions (many negative) about how and where technology has actually contributed to business value. Stephen Roach (1989) made headlines with his macroeconomic analysis showing that IT had had absolutely no impact on productivity in the services sector. More recently, research shows that companies still have a mixed record in linking IT to organizational performance, user satisfaction, productivity, customer experience, and agility (Peslak 2012).

These perceptions, plus ever-increasing IT expenditures, have meant business managers are taking a closer look at how and where IT delivers value to an organization (Ginzberg 2001; Luftman and Zadeh 2011). As they do this, they are beginning to change their understanding of the IT value proposition. Although, unfortunately, "silver bullet thinking" (i.e., plug in technology and deliver bottom-line impact) still predominates, IT value is increasingly seen as a multilayered concept, far more complex than it first appeared. This suggests that before an IT value proposition can be identified and delivered, it is essential that managers first "peel the onion" and understand more about the nature of IT value itself (see Figure 1.1).

What Is IT Value?

Value is defined as the worth or desirability of a thing (Cronk and Fitzgerald 1999). It is a subjective assessment. Although many believe this is not so, the value of IT depends very much on how a business and its individual managers choose to view it. Different companies and even different executives will define it quite differently. Strategic positioning, increased productivity, improved decision making, cost savings, or improved service are all ways *value* could be defined. Today most businesses define *value* broadly and loosely, not simply as a financial concept (Chakravarty et al. 2013). Ideally, it is tied to the organization's business model because adding value with IT should enable a firm to do its business better. In the focus group (see the Preface), one company sees value

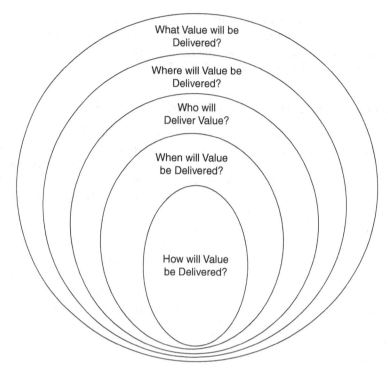

FIGURE 1.1   IT Value Is a Many-Layered Concept

resulting from all parts of the organization having the same processes; another defines value by return on investment (ROI); still another measures it by a composite of key performance indicators. In short, there is no single agreed-on measure of IT value. As a result, misunderstandings about the definition of *value* either between IT and the business or among business managers themselves can lead to feelings that value has not been delivered. Therefore, a prerequisite of any IT value proposition is that everyone involved in an IT initiative agree on what value they are trying to deliver and how they will recognize it.

Where Is IT Value?

Value may also vary according to where one looks for it (Davern and Kauffman 2000; Oliveira and Martins 2011). For example, value to an enterprise may not be perceived as value in a work group or by an individual. In fact, delivering value at one level in an organization may actually conflict with optimizing value at another level. Decisions about IT value are often made to optimize firm or business process value, even if they cause difficulties for business units or individuals. As one manager explained, "At the senior levels, our bottom-line drivers of value are cost savings, cash flow, customer satisfaction, and revenue. These are not always visible at the lower levels of the organization." Failure to consider value implications at all levels can lead to a value proposition that is counterproductive and may not deliver the value that is anticipated. Many executives take a hard line with these value conflicts. However, it is far more desirable to aim for a value that is not a win–lose proposition but is a win–win at all levels. This can leverage overall value many times over (Chan 2000; Grant and Royle 2011).

Who Delivers IT Value?

Increasingly, managers are realizing that it is the *interaction* of people, information, and technology that delivers value, not IT alone.[2] Studies have confirmed that strong IT practices *alone* do not deliver superior performance. It is only the combination of these IT practices with an organization's skills at managing information and people's behaviors and beliefs that leads to real value (Birdsall 2011; Ginzberg 2001; Marchand et al. 2000). In the past, IT has borne most of the responsibility for delivering IT value. Today, however, business managers exhibit a growing willingness to share responsibility with IT to ensure value is realized from the organization's investments in technology. Most companies now expect to have an executive sponsor for any IT initiative and some business participation in the development team. However, many IT projects still do not have the degree of support or commitment from the business that IT managers feel is necessary to deliver fully on a value proposition (Peslak 2012).

When Is IT Value Realized?

Value also has a time dimension. It has long been known that the benefits of technology take time to be realized (Chan 2000; Segars and Chatterjee 2010). People must be trained, organizations and processes must adapt to new ways of working, information must be compiled, and customers must realize what new products and services are being offered. Companies are often unprepared for the time it takes an investment to pay off. Typically, full payback can take between three and five years and can have at least two spikes as a business adapts to the deployment of technology. Figure 1.2 shows this "W" effect, named for the way the chart looks, for a single IT project.

Initially, companies spend a considerable amount in deploying a new technology. During this twelve-to-sixteen-month period, no benefits occur. Following implementation, some value is realized as companies achieve initial efficiencies. This period lasts for about six months. However, as use increases, complexities also grow. Information overload can occur and costs increase. At this stage, many can lose faith in the initiative. This is a dangerous period. The final set of benefits can occur only by making the business simpler and applying technology, information, and people more effectively. If a business can manage to do this, it can achieve sustainable, long-term value from its IT investment (Segars and Chatterjee 2010). If it can't, value from technology can be offset by increased complexity.

Time also changes perceptions of value. Many IT managers can tell stories of how an initiative is vilified as having little or no value when first implemented, only to have people say they couldn't imagine running the business without it a few years later. Similarly, most managers can identify projects where time has led to a clearer

---

[2] These interactions in a structured form are known as *processes*. Processes are often the focus of much organizational effort in the belief that streamlining and reengineering them will deliver value. In fact, research shows that without attention to information and people, very little value is delivered (Segars and Chatterjee 2010). In addition, attention to processes in organizations often ignores the informal processes that contribute to value.

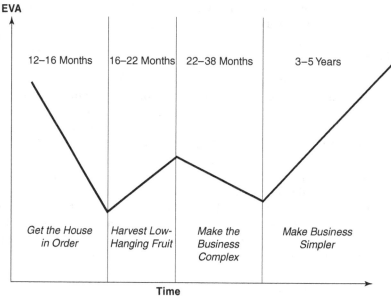

EVA

| 12–16 Months | 16–22 Months | 22–38 Months | 3–5 Years |

| Get the House in Order | Harvest Low-Hanging Fruit | Make the Business Complex | Make Business Simpler |

Time

FIGURE 1.2 The 'W' Effect in Delivering IT Value (Segars & Chatterjee, 2010)

understanding of the potential value of a project. Unfortunately, in cases where antici-pated value declines or disappears, projects don't always get killed (Cooper et al. 2000).

Clarifying and agreeing on these different layers of IT value is the first step involved in developing and delivering on the IT value proposition. All too often, this work is for-gotten or given short shrift in the organization's haste to answer this question: How will IT value be delivered? (See next section.) As a result, misunderstandings arise and tech-nology projects do not fulfill their expected promises. It will be next to impossible to do a good job developing and delivering IT value unless and until the concepts involved in IT value are clearly understood and agreed on by both business and IT managers.

THE THREE COMPONENTS OF THE IT VALUE PROPOSITION

Developing and delivering an IT value proposition involves addressing three compo-nents. First, potential opportunities for adding value must be identified. Second, these opportunities must be converted into effective applications of technology. Finally, value

Best Practices in Understanding IT Value

- Link IT value directly to your business model.
- Recognize value is subjective, and manage perceptions accordingly.
- Aim for a value "win–win" across processes, work units, and individuals.
- Seek business commitment to all IT projects.
- Manage value over time.

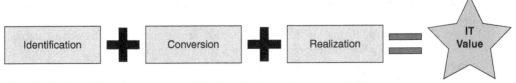

FIGURE 1.3 The Three Components of the IT Value Proposition

must be realized by the organization. Together, these components comprise the fundamentals of any value proposition (see Figure 1.3).

Identification of Potential Value

Identifying opportunities for making IT investments has typically been a fairly informal activity in most organizations. Very few companies have a well-organized means of doing research into new technologies or strategizing about where these technologies can be used (McKeen and Smith 2010). More companies have mechanisms for identifying opportunities within business units. Sometimes a senior IT manager will be designated as a "relationship manager" for a particular unit with responsibility for working with business management to identify opportunities where IT could add value (Agarwal and Sambamurthy 2002; Peslak 2012). Many other companies, however, still leave it up to business managers to identify where they want to use IT. There is growing evidence that relegating the IT organization to a passive role in developing systems according to business instructions is unlikely to lead to high IT value. Research shows that involving IT in business planning can have a direct and positive influence on the development of successful business strategies using IT (Ginzberg 2001; Marchand et al. 2000). This suggests that organizations should establish joint business–IT mechanisms to identify and evaluate both business and technical opportunities where IT can add value.

Once opportunities have been identified, companies must then make decisions about where they want to focus their dollars to achieve optimal value. Selecting the right projects for an organization always involves balancing three fundamental factors: cash, timing, and risk (Luehrman 1997). In principle, every company wants to undertake only high-return projects. In reality, project selection is based on many different factors. For example, pet or political projects or those mandated by the government or competitors are often part of a company's IT portfolio (Carte et al. 2001). Disagreement at senior levels about which projects to undertake can arise because of a lack of a coherent and consistent mechanism for assessing project value. All organizations need some formal mechanism for prioritizing projects. Without one, it is very likely that project selection will become highly politicized and, hence, ineffective at delivering value. There are a variety of means to do this, ranging from using strictly bottom-line metrics, to comparing balanced scorecards, to adopting a formal value-assessment methodology. However, although these methods help to weed out higher cost–lower return projects, they do not constitute a foolproof means of selecting the right projects for an organization. Using strict financial selection criteria, for example, can exclude potentially high-value strategic projects that have less well-defined returns, longer payback periods, and more risk (Cooper et al. 2000; DeSouza 2011). Similarly, it can be difficult getting important infrastructure initiatives funded even though these may be fundamental to improving organizational capabilities (Byrd 2001).

Therefore, organizations are increasingly taking a portfolio approach to project selection. This approach allocates resources and funding to different types of projects, enabling each type of opportunity to be evaluated according to different criteria (McKeen and Smith 2003; Smith and McKeen 2010). One company has identified three different classes of IT—infrastructure, common systems, and business unit applications—and funds them in different proportions. In other companies, funding for strategic initiatives is allocated in stages so their potential value can be reassessed as more information about them becomes known. Almost all companies have found it necessary to justify infrastructure initiatives differently than more business-oriented projects. In fact, some remove these types of projects from the selection process altogether and fund them with a "tax" on all other development (McKeen and Smith 2003). Other companies allocate a fixed percentage of their IT budgets to a technology renewal fund.

Organizations have come a long way in formalizing where and how they choose to invest their IT dollars. Nevertheless, there is still considerable room for judgment based on solid business and technical knowledge. It is, therefore, essential that all executives involved have the ability to think strategically and systematically as well as financially about project identification and selection.

Effective Conversion

"Conversion" from idea/opportunity to reality has been what IT organizations have been all about since their inception. A huge amount of effort has gone into this central component of the IT value proposition. As a result, many IT organizations have become very good at developing and delivering projects on time and on budget. Excellent project management, effective execution, and reliable operations are a critical part of IT value. However, they are not, in and of themselves, sufficient to convert a good idea into value or to deliver value to an organization.

Today managers and researchers are both recognizing that more is involved in effective conversion than good IT practices. Organizations can set themselves up for failure by not providing adequate and qualified resources. Many companies start more projects than they can effectively deliver with the resources they have available. Not having enough time or resources to do the job means that people are spread too thin and end up taking shortcuts that are potentially damaging to value (Cooper et al. 2000). Resource limitations on the business side of a project team can be as damaging to conversion as a lack of technical resources. "[Value is about] far more than just sophisticated managerial visions.... Training and other efforts ... to obtain value from IT investments

---

Best Practices in Identifying Potential Value

- Joint business–IT structures to recognize and evaluate opportunities
- A means of comparing value across projects
- A portfolio approach to project selection
- A funding mechanism for infrastructure

are often hamstrung by insufficient resources" (Chircu and Kauffman 2000). Inadequate business resources can lead to poor communication and ineffective problem solving on a project (Ginzberg 2001). Companies are beginning to recognize that the number and quality of the staff assigned to an IT project can make a difference to its eventual outcome. They are insisting that the organization's best IT and businesspeople be assigned to critical projects.

Other significant barriers to conversion that are becoming more apparent now that IT has improved its own internal practices include the following:

- *Organizational barriers.*   The effective implementation of IT frequently requires the extensive redesign of current business processes (Chircu and Kauffman 2000). However, organizations are often reluctant to make the difficult complementary business changes and investments that are required (Carte et al. 2001). "When new IT is implemented, everyone expects to see costs come down," explained one manager. "However, most projects involve both business and IT deliverables. We, therefore, need to take a multifunctional approach to driving business value." In recognition of this fact, some companies are beginning to put formal change management programs in place to help businesses prepare for the changes involved with IT projects and to adapt and simplify as they learn how to take advantage of new technology.
- *Knowledge barriers.*   Most often new technology and processes require employees to work differently, learn new skills, and have new understanding of how and where information, people, and technologies fit together (Chircu and Kauffman 2000; Perez-Lopez and Alegre 2012). Although training has long been part of new IT implementations, more recently businesses are recognizing that delivering value from technology requires a broader and more coordinated learning effort (Smith and McKeen 2002). Lasting value comes from people and technology working *together* as a system rather than as discrete entities. Research confirms that high-performing organizations not only have strong IT practices but also have people who have good information management practices and who are able to effectively use the information they receive (Beath et al. 2012; Marchand et al. 2000).

Realizing Value

The final component of the IT value proposition has been the most frequently ignored. This is the work involved in actually realizing value *after* technology has been implemented. Value realization is a proactive and long-term process for any major initiative. All too often, after an intense implementation period, a development team is disbanded to work on other projects, and the business areas affected by new technology are left to

Best Practices in Conversion

- Availability of adequate and qualified IT and business resources
- Training in business goals and processes
- Multifunctional change management
- Emphasis on higher-level learning and knowledge management

sink or swim. As a result, a project's benefits can be imperfectly realized. Technology must be used extensively if it is to deliver value. Poorly designed technology can lead to high levels of frustration, resistance to change, and low levels of use (Chircu and Kauffman 2000; Sun et al., 2012).

Resistance to change can have its root cause in an assumption or an action that doesn't make sense in the everyday work people do. Sometimes this means challenging workers' understanding of work expectations or information flows. At other times it means doing better analysis of where and how a new process is causing bottlenecks, overwork, or overload. As one manager put it, "If value is not being delivered, we need to understand the root causes and do something about it." His company takes the unusual position that it is important to keep a team working on a project until the expected benefits have been realized. This approach is ideal but can also be very costly and, therefore, must be carefully managed. Some companies try to short-circuit the value management process by simply taking anticipated cost savings out of a business unit's budget once technology has been implemented, thereby forcing it to do more with less whether or not the technology has been as beneficial as anticipated. However, most often organizations do little or no follow-up to determine whether or not benefits have been achieved.

Measurement is a key component of value realization (Thorp 1999). After implementation, it is essential that all stakeholders systematically compare outcomes against expected value and take appropriate actions to achieve benefits. In addition to monitoring metrics, a thorough and ongoing assessment of value and information flows must also be undertaken at all levels of analysis: individual, team, work unit, and enterprise. Efforts must be taken to understand and improve aspects of process, information, and technology that are acting as barriers to achieving value.

A significant problem with not paying attention to value recognition is that areas of unexpected value or opportunity are also ignored. This is unfortunate because it is only after technology has been installed that many businesspeople can see how it could be leveraged in other parts of their work. Realizing value should, therefore, also include provisions to evaluate new opportunities arising through serendipity.

FIVE PRINCIPLES FOR DELIVERING VALUE

In addition to clearly understanding what value means in a particular organization and ensuring that the three components of the IT value proposition are addressed by every project, five principles have been identified that are central to developing and delivering value in every organization.

Best Practices in Realizing Value

- Plan a value-realization phase for all IT projects.
- Measure outcomes against expected results.
- Look for and eliminate root causes of problems.
- Assess value realization at all levels in the organization.
- Have provisions for acting on new opportunities to leverage value.

Principle 1. Have a Clearly Defined Portfolio Value Management Process

Every organization should have a common process for managing the overall value being delivered to the organization from its IT portfolio. This would begin as a means of identifying and prioritizing IT opportunities by potential value relative to each other. It would also include mechanisms to optimize *enterprise* value (e.g., through tactical, strategic, and infrastructure projects) according to a rubric of how the organization wants to allocate its resources.

A portfolio value management process should continue to track projects as they are being developed. It should ensure not only that projects are meeting schedule and budget milestones but also that other elements of conversion effectiveness are being addressed (e.g., business process redesign, training, change management, information management, and usability). A key barrier to achieving value can be an organization's unwillingness to revisit the decisions made about its portfolio (Carte et al. 2001). Yet this is critically important for strategic and infrastructure initiatives in particular. Companies may have to approve investments in these types of projects based on imperfect information in an uncertain environment. As they develop, improved information can lead to better decision making about an investment. In some cases this might lead to a decision to kill a project; in others, to speed it up or to reshape it as a value proposition becomes clearer.

Finally, a portfolio value management process should include an ongoing means of ensuring that value is realized from an investment. Management must monitor expected outcomes at appropriate times following implementation and hold someone in the organization accountable for delivering benefits (Smith and McKeen 2010).

Principle 2. Aim for Chunks of Value

Much value can be frittered away by dissipating IT investments on too many projects (Cho et al. 2013; Marchand et al. 2000). Focusing on a few key areas and designing a set of complementary projects that will really make a difference is one way companies are trying to address this concern. Many companies are undertaking larger and larger technology initiatives that will have a significant transformational and/or strategic impact on the organization. However, unlike earlier efforts, which often took years to complete and ended up having questionable value, these initiatives are aiming to deliver major value through a series of small, focused projects that, linked together, will result in both immediate short-term impact and long-term strategic value. For example, one company has about three hundred to four hundred projects underway linked to one of a dozen major initiatives.

Principle 3. Adopt a Holistic Orientation to Technology Value

Because value comes from the effective interaction of people, information, and technology, it is critical that organizations aim to optimize their ability to manage and use them together (Marchand et al. 2000). Adopting a systemic approach to value, where technology is not viewed in isolation and interactions and impacts are anticipated and planned, has been demonstrated to contribute to perceived business value (Ginzberg 2001). Managers should aim to incorporate technology as an integral part of an overall program of business change rather than dealing with people and information management as afterthoughts to technology (Beath et al. 2012). One company has done this by taking a single business objective (e.g., "increase market penetration by 15 percent over five years") and designing a program around it that includes a number of bundled technology projects.

Principle 4. Aim for Joint Ownership of Technology Initiatives

This principle covers a lot of territory. It includes the necessity for strong executive sponsorship of all IT projects. "Without an executive sponsor for a project, we simply won't start it," explained one manager. It also emphasizes that all people involved in a project must feel they are responsible for the results. Said another manager, "These days it is very hard to isolate the impact of technology, therefore there must be a 'we' mentality." This perspective is reinforced by research that has found that the quality of the IT–business relationship is central to the delivery of IT value. Mutual trust, visible business support for IT and its staff, and IT staff who consider themselves to be part of a business problem-solving team all make a significant difference in how much value technology is perceived to deliver (Ginzberg 2001).

Principle 5. Experiment More Often

The growing complexity of technology, the range of options available, and the uncertainty of the business environment have each made it considerably more difficult to determine where and how technology investments can most effectively be made. Executives naturally object to the risks involved in investing heavily in possible business scenarios or technical gambles that may or may not realize value. As a result, many companies are looking for ways to firm up their understanding of the value proposition for a particular opportunity without incurring too much risk. Undertaking pilot studies is one way of doing this (DeSouza 2011). Such experiments can prove the value of an idea, uncover new opportunities, and identify more about what will be needed to make an idea successful. They provide senior managers with a greater number of options in managing a project and an overall technology portfolio. They also enable potential value to be reassessed and investments in a particular project to be reevaluated and rebalanced against other opportunities more frequently. In short, experimentation enables technology investments to be made in chunks and makes "go/no go" decisions at key milestones much easier to make.

Conclusion

This chapter has explored the concepts and activities involved in developing and delivering IT value to an organization. In their efforts to use technology to deliver business value, IT managers should keep clearly in mind the maxim "Value is in the eye of the beholder." Because there is no single agreed-on notion of business value, it is important to make sure that both business and IT managers are working to a common goal. This could be traditional cost reduction, process efficiencies, new business capabilities, improved communication, or a host of other objectives. Although each organization or business unit approaches value differently, increasingly this goal includes much more than the simple delivery of technology to a business unit. Today technology is being used as a catalyst to drive many different types of organizational transformation and strategy. Therefore, IT value can no longer be viewed in isolation from other parts of the business, namely people and information. Thus, it is no longer adequate to focus simply on the development and delivery of IT projects in order to deliver value. Today delivering IT value means managing the entire process from conception to cash.

References

Agarwal, R., and V. Sambamurthy. "Organizing the IT Function for Business Innovation Leadership." Society for Information Management Advanced Practices Council Report, Chicago, September 2002.

Beath, C., I. Becerra-Fernandez, J. Ross, and J. Short. "Finding Value in the Information Explosion." *MIT Sloan Management Review* 53, no. 4 (2012): 18–20.

Birdsall, W. "Human Capabilities and Information and Communication Technology: The Communicative Connection." *Ethics and Information Technology* 13, no. 2 (2011): 93–106.

Byrd, T. A. "Information Technology, Core Competencies, and Sustained Competitive Advantage." *Information Resources Management Journal* 14, no. 2 (April–June 2001): 27–36.

Carte, T., D. Ghosh, and R. Zmud. "The Influence of IT Budgeting Practices on the Return Derived from IT Investments." CMISS White Paper, November 2001.

Chakravarty, A., R. Grewal, and V. Sambamurthy. "Information Technology Competencies, Organizational Agility, and Firm Performance: Enabling and Facilitating Roles." *Information Systems Research* 24, no. 4 (2013): 976–97, 1162–63, 1166.

Chan, Y. "IT Value: The Great Divide Between Qualitative and Quantitative and Individual and Organizational Measures." *Journal of Management Information Systems* 16, no. 4 (Spring 2000): 225–61.

Cho, W., M. Shaw, and H. Kwan. "The Effect of Synergy Enhancement on Information Technology Portfolio Selection." *Information Technology and Management* 14, no. 2 (2013): 125–42.

Chircu, A., and R. J. Kauffman. "Limits to Value in Electronic Commerce-Related IT Investments." *Journal of Management Information Systems* 17, no. 2 (Fall 2000): 59–80.

Cooper, R., S. Edgett, and E. Kleinschmidt. "New Problems, New Solutions: Making Portfolio Management More Effective." *Research Technology Management* 43, no. 2 (March/April 2000): 18–33.

Cronk, M., and E. Fitzgerald. "Understanding 'IS Business Value': Derivation of Dimensions." *Logistics Information Management* 12, no. 1–2 (1999): 40–49.

Davern, M., and R. Kauffman. "Discovering Potential and Realizing Value from Information Technology Investments." *Journal of Management Information Systems* 16, no. 4 (Spring 2000): 121–43.

DeSouza, K. *Intrapreneurship: Managing Ideas in Your Organization.* Toronto: University of Toronto Press, 2011.

Ginzberg, M. "Achieving Business Value Through Information Technology: The Nature of High Business Value IT Organizations." Society for Information Management Advanced Practices Council Report, Chicago, November 2001.

Grant, G. L., and M. T. Royle. "Information Technology and Its Role in Creating Sustainable Competitive Advantage." *Journal of International Management Studies* 6, no. 1 (2011): 1–7.

Luehrman, T. A. "What's It Worth? A General Manager's Guide to Valuation." *Harvard Business Review* (May–June 1997): 131–41.

Luftman, J., and H. S. Zadeh. "Key Information Technology and Management Issues 2010–2011: An International Study." *Journal of Information Technology* 26, no. 3 (2011): 193–204.

Marchand, D., W. Kettinger, and J. Rollins. "Information Orientation: People, Technology and the Bottom Line." *Sloan Management Review* (Summer 2000): 69–80.

McKeen, J. D., and H. A. Smith. *Making IT Happen.* Chichester, England: John Wiley & Sons, 2003.

McKeen, J. D., and H. A. Smith. "Application Portfolio Management." *Communications for the Association of Information Systems* 26, Article 9 (March 2010), 157–70.

Oliveira, T., and M. F. Martins. "Literature Review of Information Technology Adoption Models at Firm Level." *Electronic Journal of Information Systems Evaluation* 14, no.1 (2011): 110–21.

Perez-Lopez, S., and J. Alegre. "Information Technology Competency, Knowledge Processes and Firm Performance." *Industrial Management and Data Systems* 112, no. 4 (2012): 644–62.

Peslak, A. R. "An Analysis of Critical Information Technology Issues Facing Organizations." *Industrial Management and Data Systems* 112, no. 5 (2012): 808–27.

Roach, S. "The Case of the Missing Technology Payback." Presentation at the Tenth International Conference on Information Systems, Boston, December 1989.

Segars, A. H., and D. Chatterjee. "Diets That Don't Work: Where Enterprise Resource Planning Goes Wrong." *Wall Street Journal*, August 23, 2010. online.wsj.com/article/SB100014240527 48703514404574588060852535906.html.

Smith, H., and J. McKeen. "Instilling a Knowledge Sharing Culture." Presentation at the KM Forum, Queen's School of Business, Kingston, Ontario, Canada, 2002.

Smith, H., and J. McKeen. "Investment Spend Optimization at BMO Financial Group." *MISQ Executive* 9, no. 2 (June 2010): 65–81.

Sun, Y., Y. Fang, K. Lim, and D. Straub. "User Satisfaction with Information Technology Service Delivery: A Social Capital Perspective." *Information Systems Research* 23, no. 4 (2012): 1195–211.

Thorp, J. "Computing the Payoff from IT." *Journal of Business Strategy* 20, no. 3 (May/June 1999): 35–39.

2 Developing IT Strategy for Business Value[1]

Suddenly, it seems, executives are "getting" the strategic potential of IT. Instead of being relegated to the back rooms of the enterprise, IT is now being invited to the boardrooms and is being expected to play a leading role in delivering top-line value and business transformation (Korsten 2011; Luftman and Zadeh 2011; Peslak 2012). Thus, it can no longer be assumed that business strategy will naturally drive IT strategy, as has traditionally been the case. Instead, different approaches to strategy development are now possible and sometimes desirable. For example, the capabilities of new technologies could shape the strategic direction of a firm (e.g., mobile, social media, big data). IT could enable new competencies that would then make new business strategies possible (e.g., location-based advertising). New options for governance using IT could also change how a company works with other firms (think Wal-Mart or Netflix). Today new technologies coevolve with new business strategies and new behaviors and structures (see Figure 2.1). However, whichever way it is developed, if IT is to deliver business value, IT strategy must always be closely linked with sound business strategy.

Ideally, therefore, business and IT strategies should complement and support each other relative to the business environment. Strategy development should be a two-way process between the business and IT. Yet unfortunately, poor alignment between them remains a perennial problem (Frohman 1982; Luftman and Zadeh 2011; McKeen and Smith 1996; Rivard et al. 2004). Research has already identified many organizational challenges to effective strategic alignment. For example, if their strategy-development processes are not compatible (e.g., if they take place at different times or involve different levels of the business), it is unlikely that the business and IT will be working toward the same goals at the same time (Frohman 1982). Aligning with individual business units can lead to initiatives that suboptimize the effectiveness of corporate strategies (McKeen and Smith 1996). Strategy implementation must also be carefully aligned to

---

[1] This chapter is based on the authors' previously published article, Smith, H. A., J. D. McKeen, and S. Singh. "Developing IT Strategy for Business Value." *Journal of Information Technology Management* XVIII, no. 1 (June 2007): 49–58. Reproduced by permission of the Association of Management.

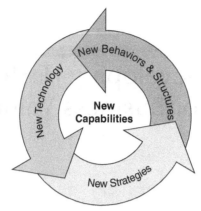

FIGURE 2.1   Business and IT Strategies Co-evolve to Create New Capabilities

ensure the integration of business and IT efforts (Smith and McKeen 2010). Finally, companies often try to address too many priorities, leading to an inadequate focus on key strategic goals (Weiss and Thorogood 2011).

However, strategic *alignment* is only one problem facing IT managers when they develop IT strategy. With IT becoming so much more central to the development and delivery of business strategy, much more attention is now being paid to strategy *development* than in the past. What businesses want to accomplish with their IT and how IT shapes its own delivery strategy are increasingly vital to the success of an enterprise. This chapter explores how organizations are working to improve IT strategy development and its relationship with business strategy. It looks first at how our understanding of business and IT strategies has changed over time and at the forces that will drive even further changes in the future. Then it discusses some critical success factors for IT strategy development about which there is general consensus. Next it looks at the different dimensions of the strategic use of IT that IT management must address. Finally, it examines how some organizations are beginning to evolve a more formal IT strategy-development process and some of the challenges they are facing in doing so.

BUSINESS AND IT STRATEGIES: PAST, PRESENT, AND FUTURE

At the highest level, a strategy is an approach to doing business (Gebauer 1997). Traditionally, a competitive business strategy has involved performing different activities from competitors or performing similar activities in different ways (Porter 1996). Ideally, these activities were difficult or expensive for others to copy and, therefore, resulted in a long-term competitive advantage (Gebauer 1997). They enabled firms to charge a premium for their products and services.

Until recently, the job of an IT function was to understand the business's strategy and figure out a plan to support it. However, all too often IT's strategic contribution was inhibited by IT managers' limited understanding of business strategy and by business managers' poor understanding of IT's potential. Therefore, most *formal* IT plans were focused on the more tactical and tangible line of business needs or opportunities for operational integration rather than on supporting enterprise strategy (Burgelman and Doz 2001). And projects were selected largely on their abilities to affect the short-term bottom line rather than on delivering top-line business value. "In the past IT had to be a strategic incubator because businesspeople simply didn't recognize the potential of technology," said a member of the focus group.

As a result, instead of looking for ways to be different, in the past much business strategy became a relentless race to compete on efficiencies with IT as the primary means of doing so (Hitt et al. 1998; Porter 1996). In many industries, companies' improved information-processing capabilities have been used to drive down transaction costs to near zero, threatening traditional value propositions and shaving profit margins. This is leading to considerable disruption as business models (i.e., the way companies add value) are under attack by new, technology-enabled approaches to delivering products and services (e.g., the music industry, bookselling). Therefore:

> Strategists [have to] honestly face the many weaknesses inherent in [the] industrial-age ways of doing things. They [must] redesign, build upon and reconfigure their components to radically transform the value proposition. (Tapscott 1996)

Such new business strategies are inconceivable without the use of IT. Other factors, also facilitated by IT, are further influencing the relationship between the business and IT strategy. Increasingly, globalization is altering the economic playing field. As countries and companies become more deeply interrelated, instability is amplified. Instead of being generals plotting out a structured campaign, business leaders are now more likely to be participating in guerilla warfare (Eisenhardt 2002; Friedman 2005). Flexibility, speed, and innovation are, therefore, becoming the watchwords of competition and must be incorporated into any business or IT strategy–development process.

These conditions have dramatically elevated the business's attention to the value of IT strategy (Korsten 2011; Weiss and Thorogood 2011). As a result, business executives recognize that it was a mistake to consider technology projects to be solely the responsibility of IT. There is, thus, a much greater understanding that business executives have to take leadership in making technology investments in ways that will shape and/or complement business strategy. There is also recognition at the top of most organizations that problems with IT strategy implementation are largely the fault of leaders who "failed to realize that adopting … systems posed a business—not just a technological—challenge" and didn't take responsibility for the organizational and process changes that would deliver business value (Ross and Beath 2002).

Changing value models and the development of integrated, cross-functional systems have elevated the importance of both a *corporate* strategy and a technology strategy that crosses traditional lines of business. Many participants remarked that their executive teams at last understand the potential of IT to affect the top line. "IT recently added some new distribution channels, and our business has just exploded," stated one manager. Others are finding that there is a much greater emphasis on IT's ability to grow revenues, and this is being reflected in how IT budgets are allocated and projects prioritized. "Our executives have finally recognized that business strategy is not only enabled by IT, but that it can provide new business opportunities as well," said another manager. This is reflected in the changing position of the CIO in many organizations over the past decade. "Today our CIO sits on the executive team and takes part in all business strategy discussions because IT has credibility," said a group member. "Our executives now want to work closely with IT and understand the implications of technology decisions," said another. "It's not the same as it was even five years ago." Now CIOs are valued for their insight into business opportunities, their perspective across the entire organization, and their ability to take the long view (Korsten 2011).

However, this does not mean that organizations have become good at developing strategy or at effectively integrating business and IT strategies. "There are many inconsistencies and problems with strategy development," said a participant. Organizations have to develop new strategy-making capabilities to cope in the future competitive environment. This will mean changing their current top–down method of developing and implementing strategy. If there's one thing leading academics agree on, it's that future strategy development will have to become a more dynamic and continuous process (Casadesus and Ricart 2011; Eisenhardt 2002; Kanter 2002; Prahalad and Krishnan 2002; Quinn 2002; Weill et al. 2002). Instead of business strategy being a well-crafted plan of action for the next three to five years, from which IT can devise an appropriate and supportive technology strategy, business strategy must become more and more evolutionary and interactive with IT. IT strategy development must, therefore, become more dynamic itself and focused on developing strategic *capabilities* that will support a variety of changing business objectives. In the future, managers will not align business strategy and IT at particular points in time but will participate in an organic process that will address the need to continually evolve IT and business plans in concert with each other (Casadesus and Ricart 2011).

FOUR CRITICAL SUCCESS FACTORS

Each focus group member had a different approach to developing IT strategy, but there was general agreement that four factors had to be in place for strategy development to be effective.

1. *Revisit your business model.* The worlds of business and IT have traditionally been isolated from each other, leading to misaligned and sometimes conflicting strategies. Although there is now a greater willingness among business managers to understand the implications of technology in their world, it is still IT that must translate their ideas and concepts into business language. "IT must absolutely understand and focus on the business," said a participant.

   Similarly, it is essential that all managers thoroughly understand how their business as a whole works. Although this sounds like a truism, almost any IT manager can tell "war stories" of business managers who have very different visions of what they think their enterprise should look like. Business models and strategies are often confused with each other (Osterwalder and Pigneur 2010). A business model explains how the different pieces of a business fit together. It ensures that everyone in an organization is focused on the kind of value a company wants to create. Only when the business model is clear can strategies be developed to articulate how a company will deliver that value in a *unique* way that others cannot easily duplicate (Osterwalder and Pigneur 2010).

2. *Have strategic themes.* IT strategy used to be about individual projects. Now it is about carefully crafted *programs* that focus on developing specific business

capabilities. Each program consists of many smaller, interrelated business and IT initiatives cutting across several functional areas. These are designed to be adapted, reconfigured, accelerated, or canceled as the strategic program evolves. Themes give both business and IT leaders a broad yet focused topic of interest that challenges them to move beyond current operations (Kanter 2002). For example, one retail company decided it wanted to be "a great place to work." A bank selected mobile banking as a critical differentiator. Both firms used a theme to engage the imaginations of their employees and mobilize a variety of ideas and actions around a broad strategic direction. By grouping IT and business programs around a few key themes, managers find it easier to track and direct important strategic threads in an organization's development and to visualize the synergies and interdependencies involved across a variety of projects spread out across the organization and over time.

3. *Get the right people involved.*   One of the most important distinguishing factors between companies that get high business value from their IT investment and those that don't is that senior managers in high-performing companies take a leadership role in IT decision making. Abdication of this responsibility is a recipe for disaster (Ross and Beath 2002). "In the past it was very hard to get the right people involved," said a focus group member. "Now it's easier." Another noted, "You don't send a minion to an IT strategy meeting anymore; it's just not done." In this type of organization, the CIO typically meets regularly with the president and senior business leaders to discuss both business and IT strategies.

   Getting the right people involved also means getting business managers and other key stakeholders involved in strategy as well. To do this, many companies have established "relationship manager" positions in IT to work with and learn about the business and bring opportunities for using technology to the table. Research shows that the best strategies often stem from grassroots innovations, and it is, therefore, critical that organizations take steps to ensure that good ideas are nurtured and not filtered out by different layers of management (DeSouza 2011). "We have two levels of strategy development in our organization," said a focus group participant. "Our relationship managers work with functional managers and our CIO with our business unit presidents on the IT steering committee." This company also looks for cross-functional synergies and strategic dependencies by holding regular meetings of IT account managers and between account managers and infrastructure managers.

4. *Work in partnership with the business.* Successful strategy demands a true *partnership* between IT and the business, not just use of the term. Strategy decisions are best made with input from both business and IT executives (Ross and Beath 2002). The focus group agreed. "Our partnerships are key to our success," stated a manager. "It's not the same as it was a few years ago. People now work very closely together." Partnership is not just a matter of "involving" business leaders in IT strategy or vice versa or "aligning" business and IT strategies. Effective strategizing is about continuous and dynamic synchronization of capabilities (Smith and McKeen 2010). "Our IT programs need synchronizing with business strategy—not only at a high level, but right down to the individual projects and the business changes that are necessary to implement them properly," explained another participant.

THE MANY DIMENSIONS OF IT STRATEGY

One of the many challenges of developing effective IT strategy is the fact that technology can be used in so many different ways. The opportunities are practically limitless. Unfortunately, the available resources are not. Thus, a key element of IT strategy is determining how best to allocate the IT budget. This issue is complicated by the fact that most businesses today require significant IT services just to operate. Utility and basic support costs eat up between 30 and 70 percent of the focus group members' budgets. That's just the cost of "keeping the lights on"—running existing applications, fixing problems, and dealing with mandatory changes (e.g., new legislation). IT strategy, therefore, has two components: how to do more with less (i.e., driving down fixed costs) and how to allocate the remaining budget toward those projects that will support and further the organization's business strategy.

With occasional exceptions, CIOs and their teams are mostly left alone to determine the most cost-effective way of providing the IT utility. This has led to a variety of IT-led initiatives to save money, including outsourcing, shared services, use of software-as-a-service (SaaS), global sourcing, and partnerships. However, it is the way that IT spends the rest of its budget that has captured the attention of business strategists. "It used to be that every line of business had an IT budget and that we would work with each one to determine the most effective way to spend it," said a manager. "Now there is much more recognition that the big opportunities are at the enterprise level and cut across lines of business."

Focus group members explained that implementing a strategic program in IT will usually involve five types of initiatives. Determining what the balance among them will be is a significant component of how IT strategy delivers business value. Too much or too little emphasis on one type of project can mean a failure to derive maximum value from a particular strategic business theme:

1. *Business improvement.* These projects are probably the easiest to agree on because they stress relatively low-risk investments with a tangible short-to-medium-term payback. These are often reengineering initiatives to help organizations streamline their processes and save substantial amounts of money by eliminating unnecessary or duplicate activities or empowering customers/suppliers to self-manage transactions with a company. Easy to justify with a business case, these types of projects have traditionally formed the bulk of IT's discretionary spending. "Cost-reduction projects have and always will be important to our company," stated one member. "However, it is important to balance what we do in this area with other types of equally important projects that have often been given short shrift."

2. *Business enabling.* These projects extend or transform how a company does business. As a result, they are more focused on the top-line or revenue-growing aspects of an enterprise. For example, a data warehouse could enable different parts of a company to "mine" transaction information to improve customer service, assist target marketing, better understand buying patterns, or identify new business opportunities. Adding a new mobile channel could make it easier for customers to buy more or attract new customers. A customer information file could make it more enjoyable for a customer to do business with a company (e.g., only one address change) and also facilitate new ways of doing business.

Often the return on these types of projects is less clear, and as a result it has been harder to get them on the IT priority list. Yet many of these initiatives represent the foundations on which future business strategy will be built. For example, one CIO described the creation of a customer information file as "a key enabler for many different business units.... It has helped us build bench strength and move to a new level of service that other companies cannot match" (Smith 2003).

3. *Business opportunities.*   These are small-scale, experimental initiatives designed to test the viability of new concepts or technologies. In the past these types of projects have not received funding by traditional methods because of their high-risk nature. Often it has been left up to the CIO to scrounge money for such "skunkworks." There is a growing recognition of the potential value of strategic innovation projects in helping companies to learn about and prepare for the future. In some companies the CEO and CFO have freed up seed money to finance a number of these initiatives. However, although there is considerably more acceptance for such projects, there is still significant organizational resistance to financing projects for which the end results are unpredictable (Quinn 2002; Weiss and Thorogood 2011). In fact, it typically requires discipline to support and encourage innovation experiments, which, by definition, will have a high number of false starts and wrong moves (DeSouza 2011). The group agreed that the key to benefiting from them is to design them for learning, incorporate feedback from a variety of sources, and make quick corrections of direction.

4. *Opportunity leverage.*   A neglected but important type of IT project is one that operationalizes, scales up, or leverages successful strategic experiments or prototypes. "We are having a great deal of success taking advantage of what we have learned earlier," said one manager. Coming up with a new strategic or technological idea needs a different set of skills than is required to take full advantage of it in the marketplace (Charitou and Markides 2003; DeSouza 2011). Some companies actually use their ability to leverage others' ideas to their strategic advantage. "We can't compete in coming up with new ideas," said the manager of a medium-sized company, "but we can copy other peoples' ideas and do them better."

5. *Infrastructure.*   This final type of IT initiative is one that often falls between the cracks when business and IT strategies are developed. However, it is clear that the hardware, software, middleware, communications, and data available will affect an organization's capacity to build new capabilities and respond to change. Studies have found that most companies feel their legacy infrastructure can be an impediment to what they want to do (Peslak 2012; Prahalad and Krishnan 2002). Research also shows that leading companies have a framework for making targeted investments in their IT infrastructure that will further their overall strategic direction (Weill et al. 2002). Unfortunately, investing in infrastructure is rarely seen as strategic. As a result, many companies struggle with how to justify and appropriately fund it.

Although each type of project delivers a different type of business value, typically IT strategy has stressed only those initiatives with strong business cases. Others are shelved or must struggle for a very small piece of the pie. However, there was a general recognition in the group that this approach to investment leads to an IT strategy with a heavy emphasis on the bottom line. As a result, all participating companies were looking at new ways to build a strategy-development process that reflects a more appropriate balance of all dimensions of IT strategy.

TOWARD AN IT STRATEGY-DEVELOPMENT PROCESS

Strategy is still very much an art, not a science, explained the focus group. And it is likely to remain so, according to strategy experts. Strategy will never again be a coherent, long-term plan with predictable outcomes—if it ever was. "Leaders can't predict which combinations [of strategic elements] will succeed [and] they can't drive their organizations towards predetermined positions" (Quinn 2002). This situation only exacerbates the problem that has long faced IT strategists—that is, it is difficult to build systems, information, and infrastructure when a business's direction is continually changing. Yet this degree of flexibility is exactly what businesses are demanding (Chakravarty et al. 2013; Luftman and Zadeh 2011; Korsten 2011). Traditional IT planning and budgeting mechanisms done once a year simply don't work in today's fast-paced business environment. "We always seem to lag behind the business, no matter how hard we try," said a manager.

Clearly, organizations need to be developing strategy differently. How to do this is not always apparent, but several companies are trying ways to more dynamically link IT strategy with that of the business. Although no one company in the focus group claimed to have *the* answer, they did identify several practices that are moving them closer to this goal:

- *"Rolling" planning and budget cycles.* All participants agreed that IT plans and budgets need attention more frequently than once a year. One company has created an eighteen-month rolling plan that is reviewed and updated quarterly with the business to maintain currency.
- *An enterprise architecture.* This is an integrated blueprint for the development of the enterprise—both the business and IT. "Our enterprise architecture includes business processes, applications, infrastructure, and data," said a member. "Our EA function has to approve all business and IT projects and is helpful in identifying duplicate solutions." In some companies this architecture is IT initiated and business validated; in others it is a joint initiative. However, participants warned that an architecture has the potential to be a corporate bottleneck if it becomes too bureaucratic.
- *Different funding "buckets."* Balancing short-term returns with the company's longer-term interests is a continual challenge. As noted earlier, all five types of IT projects are necessary for an effective IT strategy (i.e., business improvement, business enabling, business opportunities, opportunity leverage, and infrastructure). In order to ensure that each different type of IT is appropriately funded, many companies are allocating predetermined percentages of their IT budget to different types of projects (Smith and McKeen 2010). This helps keep continual pressure on IT to reduce its "utility costs" to free up more resources for other types of projects. "Since we implemented this method of budgeting, we've gone from spending 70 percent of our revenues on mandatory and support projects to spending 70 percent on discretionary and strategic ones," said a manager. This

is also an effective way to ensure that IT infrastructure is continually enhanced. Leading companies build their infrastructures not through a few large investments but gradually through incremental, modular investments that build IT capabilities (Weill et al. 2002).

- *Relationship managers.*   There is no substitute for a deep and rich understanding of the business. This is why many companies have appointed IT relationship managers to work closely with key lines of business. These managers help business leaders to observe their environments systematically and identify new opportunities for which IT could be effective. Furthermore, together relationship managers can identify synergies and interdependencies among lines of business. One organization holds both intra- and interfunctional strategy sessions on a regular basis with business managers to understand future needs, develop programs, and design specific roadmaps for reaching business goals. "Our relationship managers have been a significant factor in synchronizing IT and business strategies," said its manager.

- *A prioritization rubric.*   "We don't do prioritization well," said one participant. IT managers have long complained that it is extremely difficult to justify certain types of initiatives using the traditional business case method of prioritization. This has led to an overrepresentation of business improvement projects in the IT portfolio and has inhibited more strategic investments in general capabilities and business opportunities. This problem is leading some companies to adopt multiple approaches to justifying IT projects (Chakravarty et al. 2013; Ross and Beath 2002). For example, business-enabling projects must be sponsored at a cross-functional level on the basis of the capabilities they will provide the enterprise as a whole. Senior management must then take responsibility to ensure that these capabilities are fully leveraged over time. Infrastructure priorities are often left up to IT to determine once a budget is set. One IT department does this by holding strategy sessions with its relationship and utility managers to align infrastructure spending with the organization's strategic needs. Unfortunately, no one has yet figured out a way to prioritize business opportunity experiments. At present this is typically left to the "enthusiasms and intuitions" of the sponsoring managers, either in IT or in the business (DeSouza 2011). "Overall," said a manager, "we need to do a better job of thinking through the key performance indicators we'd like to use for each type of project."

Although it is unlikely that strategy development will ever become a completely formalized process, there is a clear need to add more structure to how it is done. A greater understanding of how strategy is developed will ensure that all stakeholders are involved and a broader range of IT investments are considered. The outcomes of strategy will always be uncertain, but the process of identifying new opportunities and how they should be funded must become more systematic if a business is going to realize optimum value from its IT resources.

CHALLENGES FOR CIOs

As often happens in organizations, recognition of a need precedes the ability to put it into place. IT leaders are now making significant strides in articulating IT strategy and linking it more effectively with business strategy. Business leaders are also more open to a more integrated process. Nevertheless, some important organizational barriers that inhibit strategy development still remain.

A supportive governance structure is frequently lacking. "Now that so many strategies are enterprisewide, we need a better way to manage them," explained one manager. Often there are no formal structures to identify and manage interdependencies between business functions and processes. "It used to be that everything was aligned around organizational boundaries, but strategy is now more complex since we're working on programs with broader organizational scope," said another. Similarly, current managerial control systems and incentives are often designed to reward thinking that is aligned to a line of business, not to the greater organizational good. Enterprisewide funding models are also lacking. "Everything we do now requires negotiation for funding between the lines of business who control the resources," a third stated. Even within IT, the group suggested it is not always clear who in the organization is responsible for taking IT strategies and turning them into detailed IT plans.

Traditional planning and budgetary practices are a further challenge. This is an often-neglected element of IT strategy. "Our business and IT strategies are not always done in parallel or even around the same time," said a participant. As a result, it is not easy to stay aligned or to integrate the two sets of plans. Another commented, "Our business plans change constantly. It is, therefore, common for IT strategies to grow farther and farther apart over time." Similarly, an annual budgeting process tends to lock an organization into fixed expenditures that may not be practical in a rapidly changing environment. IT organizations, therefore, need both a longer-term view of their resourcing practices and the opportunity to make changes to it more frequently. Even though rolling budgets are becoming more acceptable, they are by no means common in either IT or the business world today.

Both business and IT leaders need to develop better skills in strategizing. "We've gotten really good at implementing projects," said an IT manager. "Strategy and innovation are our least developed capabilities." IT is pushing the business toward better articulation of its goals. "Right now, in many areas of our business, strategy is not well thought through," said another manager. "IT is having to play the devil's advocate and get them to think beyond generalities such as 'We are going to grow the business by 20 percent this year.'" With more attention to the process, it is almost certain to get better, but managers' rudimentary skills in this area limit the quality of strategy development.

Over and over, the group stressed that IT strategy is mainly about getting the balance right between conflicting strategic imperatives. "It's always a balancing act

Barriers to Effective IT Strategy Development

- Lack of a governance structure for enterprisewide projects
- Inadequate enterprisewide funding models
- Poorly integrated processes for developing IT and business strategies
- Traditional budget cycles
- Unbalanced strategic and tactical initiatives
- Weak strategizing skills

between our tactical and operational commitments and the work that builds our long-term capabilities," said a participant. Deciding how to make the trade-offs between the different types of IT work is the essence of effective strategy. Unfortunately, few businesses do this very well (Burgelman and Doz 2001; Luftman and Zadeh 2011). According to the focus group, traditional business thinking tends to favor short-term profitability, while IT leaders tend to take a longer-term view. Making sure some types of IT work (e.g., infrastructure, new business opportunities) are not underfunded while others (e.g., utility, business improvement) are not overfunded is a continual challenge for all IT and business leaders.

Conclusion

Effective strategy development is becoming vital for organizations. As the impact of IT has grown in companies, IT strategy is finally getting the attention it deserves in business. Nevertheless, most organizations are still at the earliest stages of learning how to develop an effective IT strategy and synchronize it with an overall business strategy. Getting the balance right between the many different ways IT can be used to affect a business is a constant challenge for leaders and one on which they do not always agree. Although there is, as yet, no well-developed IT strategy–development process, there appears to be general agreement on certain critical success factors and the key elements involved. Over time, these will likely be refined and better integrated with overall business strategy development. Those who learn to do this well without locking the enterprise into inflexible technical solutions are likely to win big in our rapidly evolving business environment.

References

Burgelman, R., and Y. Doz. "The Power of Strategic Integration." *MIT Sloan Management Review* 42, no. 3 (Spring 2001): 28–38.

Casadesus-Masanell, R., and J. Ricart. "How to Design a Winning Business Model." *Harvard Business Review* 89, nos. 1–2 (January–February 2011): 100–107.

Chakravarty, A., R. Grewal, and V. Sambamurthy. "Information Technology Competencies, Organizational Agility, and Firm Performance: Enabling and Facilitating Roles." *Information Systems Research* 24, no. 4 (December 2013): 976–97.

Charitou, C., and C. Markides. "Responses to Disruptive Strategic Innovation." *MIT Sloan Management Review* (Winter 2003): 55–63.

DeSouza, K. *Intrapreneurship: Managing Ideas in Your Organization.* Toronto: University of Toronto Press, 2011.

Eisenhardt, K. "Has Strategy Changed?" *MIT Sloan Management Review* 43, no. 2 (Winter 2002): 88–91.

Friedman, T. *The World is Flat: A Brief History of the Twenty-First Century.* New York: Farrar, Strauss and Giroux, 2005.

Frohman, A. "Technology as a Competitive Weapon." *Harvard Business Review* (January–February 1982): 80–94.

Gebauer, J. "Virtual Organizations from an Economic Perspective." *Communications of the ACM* 40 (September 1997): 91–103.

Hitt, M., B. Keats, and S. DeMarire. "Navigating in the New Competitive Landscape: Building Strategic Flexibility." *Academy of Management Executive* 12, no. 4 (1998): 22–42.

Kanter, R. "Strategy as Improvisational Theater." *MIT Sloan Management Review* (Winter 2002): 76–81.

Korsten, P. "The Essential CIO." *IBM Institute for Business Value.* Somers, NY: IBM Global Business Services, 2011.

Luftman, J., and H. S. Zadeh. "Key Information Technology and Management Issues 2010–2011: An International Study." *Journal of Information Technology* 26, no. 3 (2011): 193–204.

McKeen, J., and H. Smith. *Management Challenges in IS: Successful Strategies and Appropriate Action.* Chichester, England: John Wiley & Sons, 1996.

Osterwalder, A., and Y. Pigneur. *Business Model Generation.* Hoboken, NJ: John Wiley & Sons, 2010.

Peslak, A. R. "An Analysis of Critical Information Technology Issues Facing Organizations." *Industrial Management and Data Systems* 112, no. 5 (2012): 808–27.

Porter, M. "What Is Strategy?" *Harvard Business Review* (November–December 1996): 61–78.

Prahalad, C., and M. Krishnan. "The Dynamic Synchronization of Strategy and Information Technology." *MIT Sloan Management Review* (Summer 2002): 24–33.

Quinn, J. "Strategy, Science, and Management." *MIT Sloan Management Review* (Summer 2002): 96.

Rivard, S., B. Aubert, M. Patry, G. Pare, and H. Smith. *Information Technology and Organizational Transformation: Solving the Management Puzzle.* New York: Butterworth Heinemann, 2004.

Ross, J., and C. Beath. "Beyond the Business Case: New Approaches to IT Investment." *MIT Sloan Management Review* (Winter 2002): 51–59.

Smith, H. A. "The Best of the Best: Part II." *CIO Canada,* October 1 (2003).

Smith, H., and J. McKeen. "Investment Spend Optimization at BMO Financial Group." *MISQ Executive* 9, no. 2 (June 2010): 65–81.

Tapscott, D. *The Digital Economy: Promise and Peril in the Age of Networked Intelligence.* New York: McGraw-Hill, 1996.

Weill, P., M. Subramani, and M. Broadbent. "Building IT Infrastructure for Strategic Agility." *MIT Sloan Management Review* (Fall 2002): 57–65.

Weiss, J., and A. Thorogood. "Information Technology (IT)/Business Alignment as a Strategic Weapon: A Diagnostic Tool." *Engineering Management Journal* 23, no. 2 (June 2011): 30–41.

3 Linking IT to Business Metrics[1]

From the first time IT started making a significant dent in corporate balance sheets, the holy grail of academics, consultants, and business and IT managers has been to show that what a company spends on IT has a direct impact on its performance. Early efforts to do this, such as those trying to link various measures of IT input (e.g., budget dollars, number of PCs, number of projects) with various measures of business performance (e.g., profit, productivity, stock value) all failed to show any relationship at all (Marchand et al. 2000). Since then, everyone has properly concluded that the relationship between what is done in IT and what happens in the business is considerably more complex than these studies first supposed. In fact, many researchers would suggest that the relationship is so filtered through a variety of "conversion effects" (Cronk and Fitzgerald 1999) as to be practically impossible to demonstrate. Most IT managers would agree. They have long argued that technology is not the major stumbling block to achieving business performance; it is the business itself—the processes, the managers, the culture, and the skills—that makes the difference. Therefore, it is simply not realistic to expect to see a clear correlation between IT and business performance at any level. When technology is successful, it is a *team* effort, and the contributions of the IT and business components of an initiative cannot and should not be separated.

Nevertheless, IT expenditures must be justified. Thus, most companies have concentrated on determining the "business value" that specific IT projects deliver. By focusing on a goal that matters to business (e.g., better information, faster transaction processing, reduced staff), then breaking this goal down into smaller projects that IT can affect directly, they have tried to "peel the onion" and show specifically how IT delivers value in a piecemeal fashion. Thus, a series of surrogate measures are usually used to demonstrate IT's impact in an organization. (See Chapter 1 for more details.)

More recently, companies are taking another look at business performance metrics and IT. They believe it is time to "put the onion back together" and focus on what

---

[1] This chapter is based on the authors' previously published article, Smith, H. A., J. D. McKeen, and C. Street. "Linking IT to Business Metrics." *Journal of Information Science and Technology* 1, no. 1 (2004): 13–26. Reproduced by permission of the Information Institute.

really matters to the enterprise. This perspective argues that employees who truly understand what their business is trying to achieve can sense the right ways to personally improve performance that will show up at a business unit and organizational level. "People who understand the business and are informed will be proactive and ... have a disposition to create business value every day in many small and not-so-small ways" (Marchand et al. 2000). Although the connection may not be obvious, they say, it is there nevertheless and can be demonstrated in tangible ways. The key to linking what IT does to business performance is, therefore, to create an environment within which everyone thoroughly understands what measures are important to the business and is held accountable for them. This point of view does not suggest that all the work done to date to learn how IT delivers value to an organization (e.g., business cases, productivity measures) has been unnecessary, only that it is incomplete. Without close attention to business metrics *in addition,* it is easy for IT initiatives and staff to lose their focus and become less effective.

This chapter looks at how these controversial yet compelling ideas are being pursued in organizations to better understand how companies are attempting to link IT work and firm performance through business metrics. The first section describes how business metrics themselves are evolving and looks at how new management philosophies are changing how these measures are communicated and applied. Next it discusses the types of metrics that are important for a well-rounded program of business measurement and how IT can influence them. Then it presents three different ways companies are specifically linking their IT departments with business metrics and the benefits and challenges they have experienced in doing this. This section concludes with some general principles for establishing a business measurement program in IT. Finally, it offers some advice to managers about how to succeed with such a program in IT.

BUSINESS MEASUREMENT: AN OVERVIEW

Almost everyone agrees that *the* primary goal of a business is to make money for its shareholders (Goldratt and Cox 1984; Haspeslagh et al. 2001; Kaplan and Norton 1996). Unfortunately, in large businesses this objective frequently gets lost in the midst of people's day-to-day activities because profit cannot be measured directly at the level at which most employees in a company work (Haspeslagh et al. 2001). This "missing link" between work and business performance leads companies to look for ways to bridge this gap. They believe that if a firm's strategies for achieving its goal can be tied much more closely to everyday processes and decision making, frontline employees will be better able to create business value. Proponents of this value-based management (VBM) approach have demonstrated that an explicit, firmwide commitment to shareholder value, clear communication about how value is created or destroyed, and incentive systems that are linked to key business measures will increase the odds of a positive increase in share price (Haspeslagh et al. 2001).

> Measurement counts. What a company measures and the way it measures influence both the mindsets of managers and the way people behave. The best measures are tied to business performance and are linked to the strategies and business capabilities of the company. (Marchand et al. 2000)

Although companies ascribe to this notion in theory, they do not always act in ways that are consistent with this belief. All too often, therefore, because they lack clarity about the links between business performance and their own work, individuals and even business units have to take leaps of faith in what they do (Marchand et al. 2000).

Nowhere has this been more of a problem than in IT. As has been noted often, IT investments have not always delivered the benefits expected (Bensaou and Earl 1998; Holland and Sharke 2001; Peslak 2012). "Efforts to measure the link between IT investment and business performance from an economics perspective have... failed to establish a consistent causal linkage with sustained business profitability" (Marchand et al. 2000). Value-based management suggests that if IT staff do not understand the business, they cannot sense how and where to change it effectively with technology. Many IT and business managers have implicitly known this for some time. VBM simply gives them a better framework for implementing their beliefs more systematically.

One of the most significant efforts to integrate an organization's mission and strategy with a measurement system has been Kaplan and Norton's (1996) balanced scorecard. They explain that competing in the information age is much less about managing physical, tangible assets and much more about the ability of a company to mobilize its intangible assets, such as customer relationships, innovation, employee skills, and information technology. Thus, they suggest that not only should business measures look at how well a company has done *in the past* (i.e., financial performance), but they also need to look at metrics related to customers, internal business processes, and learning and growth that position the firm to achieve *future* performance. Although it is difficult putting a reliable monetary value on these items, Kaplan and Norton suggest that such nonfinancial measures are critical success factors for superior financial performance in the future. Research shows that this is, in fact, the case. Companies that use a balanced scorecard tend to have a better return on investment (ROI) than those that rely on traditional financial measures alone (Alexander 2000).

Today many companies use some sort of scorecard or "dashboard" to track a variety of different metrics of organizational health. However, IT traditionally has not paid much attention to business results, focusing instead on its own internal measures of performance (e.g., IT operations efficiency, projects delivered on time). This has perpetuated the serious disconnect between the business and IT that often manifests itself in perceptions of poor alignment between the two groups, inadequate payoffs from IT investments, poor relationships, and finger-pointing (Holland and Sharke 2001; Peslak 2012; Potter 2013). All too often IT initiatives are conceived with little reference to major business results, relying instead on lower-level business value surrogates that are not always related to these measures. IT organizations are getting much better at this bottom-up approach to IT investment (Smith and McKeen 2010), but undelivered IT value remains a serious concern in many organizations. One survey of CFOs found that only 49 percent felt that their ROI expectations for technology had been met (Holland and Sharke 2001). "Despite considerable effort, no practical model has been developed to measure whether a company's IT investments will definitely contribute to sustainable competitive advantage" (Marchand et al. 2000). Clearly, in spite of significant efforts over many years, traditional IT measurement programs have been inadequate at assessing business value. Many IT organizations believe, therefore, that it is time for a different approach to delivering IT value, one that holds IT accountable to the same measures and goals as the rest of the business.

KEY BUSINESS METRICS FOR IT

No one seriously argues that IT has no impact on an organization's overall financial performance anymore. There may be disagreement about whether it has a positive or a negative impact, but technology is too pervasive and significant an expense in most firms for it not to have some influence on the corporate bottom line. However, as has been argued earlier, we now recognize that neither technology nor business alone is responsible for IT's financial impact. It is instead a joint responsibility of IT *and* the business. This suggests that they need to be held accountable *together* for its impact. Some companies have accepted this principle for individual IT projects (i.e., holding business and IT managers jointly responsible for achieving their anticipated benefits), yet few have extended it to an enterprise level. VBM suggests that this lack of attention to enterprise performance by IT is one reason it has been so hard to fully deliver business value for technology investments. Holding IT accountable for a firm's performance according to key financial metrics is, therefore, an important step toward improving its contribution to the corporate bottom line.

However, although financial results are clearly an important part of any measurement of a business's success today, they are not enough. Effective business metrics programs should also include nonfinancial measures, such as customer and employee satisfaction. As already noted, because such nonfinancial measures are predictive of future performance, they offer an organization the opportunity to make changes that will ultimately affect their financial success.

Kaplan and Norton (1996) state "the importance of customer satisfaction probably cannot be overemphasized." Companies that do not understand their customers' needs will likely lose customers and profitability. Research shows that merely adequate satisfaction is insufficient to lead to customer loyalty and ultimately profit. Only firms where customers are completely or extremely satisfied can achieve this result (Heskett et al. 1994). As a result, many companies now undertake systematic customer satisfaction surveys. However, in IT it is rare to find external customer satisfaction as one of the metrics on which IT is evaluated. While IT's "customers" are usually considered to be internal, these days technology makes a significant difference in how external customers experience a firm and whether or not they want to do business with it. Systems that are not reliable or available when needed, cannot provide customers with the information they need, or cannot give customers the flexibility they require are all too common. And with the advent of online business, systems and apps are being designed to interface directly with external customers. It is, therefore, appropriate to include external customer satisfaction as a business metric for IT.

Another important nonfinancial business measure is employee satisfaction. This is a "leading indicator" of customer satisfaction. That is, employee satisfaction in one year is strongly linked to customer satisfaction and profitability in the next (Koys 2001). Employees' positive attitudes toward their company and their jobs lead to positive behaviors toward customers and, therefore, to improved financial performance

(Rucci et al. 1998; Ulrich et al. 1991). IT managers have always watched their own employee satisfaction rate intently because of its close links to employee turnover. However, they often miss the link between IT employee satisfaction and customer satisfaction—both internal customer satisfaction, which leads to improved general employee satisfaction, and external customer satisfaction. Thus, only a few companies hold IT managers accountable for general employee satisfaction.

Both customer and employee satisfaction should be part of a business metrics program for IT. With its ever-growing influence in organizations, technology is just as likely to affect external customer and general employee satisfaction as many other areas of a business. This suggests that IT has three different levels of measurement and accountability:

1. *Enterprise measures.*   These tie the work of IT directly to the performance of the organization (e.g., external customer satisfaction, corporate financial performance).
2. *Functional measures.*   These assess the internal work of the IT organization as a whole (e.g., IT employee satisfaction, internal customer satisfaction, operational performance, development productivity).
3. *Project measures.*   These assess the performance of a particular project team in delivering specific value to the organization (e.g., business case benefits, delivery on time).

Functional and project measures are usually well addressed by IT measurement programs today. It is the enterprise level that is usually missing.

DESIGNING BUSINESS METRICS FOR IT

The firms that hold IT accountable for enterprise business metrics believe this approach fosters a common sense of purpose, enables everyone to make better decisions, and helps IT staff understand the implications of their work for the success of the organization (Haspeslagh et al. 2001; Marchand et al. 2000; Potter 2013; Roberts 2013). The implementation of business metrics programs varies widely among companies, but three approaches taken to linking IT with business metrics are distinguishable.

1. *Balanced scorecard.*   This approach uses a classic balanced scorecard with measures in all four scorecard dimensions (see the "Sample Balanced Scorecard Business Metrics" feature). Each metric is selected to measure progress against the entire enterprise's business plan. These are then broken down into business unit plans and appropriate submetrics identified. Individual scorecards are then developed with metrics that will link into their business unit scorecards. With this approach, IT is treated as a separate business unit and has its own scorecard linked to the business plan. "Our management finally realized that we need to have everyone thinking in the same way," explained one manager. "With enterprise systems, we can't have people working in silos anymore." The scorecards are very visible in the organization with company and business unit scorecards and those of senior executives posted on the company's intranet. "People are extremely interested in seeing how we're doing. Scorecards have provided a common framework for our entire company." They also provide clarity for employees about their roles in how they affect key business metrics.

Sample Balanced Scorecard Business Metrics

- Shareholder value (financial)
- Expense management (financial)
- Customer/client focus (customer)
- Loyalty (customer)
- Customercentric organization (customer)
- Effectiveness and efficiency of business operations (operations)
- Risk management (operations)
- Contribution to firmwide priorities and business initiatives (growth)

Although scorecards have meant that there is better understanding of the business's drivers and plans at senior management levels, considerable resistance to them is still found at the lower levels in IT. "While developers see how they can affect our customers, they don't see how they can affect shareholder value, profit, or revenue, and they don't want to be held accountable for these things," stated the same manager. She noted that implementing an effective scorecard program relies on three things: good data to provide better metrics, simplicity of metrics, and enforcement. "Now if someone's scorecard is not complete, they cannot get a bonus. This is a huge incentive to follow the program."

2. *Modified scorecard.* A somewhat different approach to a scorecard is taken by one company in the focus group. This firm has selected five key measures (see the "Modified Scorecard Business Metrics" feature) that are closely linked to the company's overall vision statement. Results are communicated to all staff on a quarterly basis in a short performance report. This includes a clear explanation of each measure, quarterly progress, a comparison with the previous year's quarterly results, and a "stretch" goal for the organization to achieve. The benefit of this approach is that it orients all employees in the company to the same mission and values. With everyone using the same metrics, alignment is much clearer all the way through the firm, according to the focus group manager.

In IT these key enterprise metrics are complemented by an additional set of business measures established by the business units. Each line of business identifies one or two key business unit metrics on which they and their IT team

Modified Scorecard Business Metrics

- *Customer loyalty index.* Percentage of customers who said they were very satisfied with the company and would recommend it to others.
- *Associate loyalty index.* Employees' perception of the company as a great place to work.
- *Revenue growth.* This year's total revenues as a percentage of last year's total revenues.
- *Operating margin.* Operating income earned before interest and taxes for every dollar of revenue.
- *Return on capital employed.* Earnings before interest and tax divided by the capital used to generate the earnings.

will be measured. Functional groups within IT are evaluated according to the same metrics as their business partners as well as on company and internal IT team performance. For example, the credit group in IT might be evaluated on the number of new credit accounts the company acquires. Shared IT services (e.g., infrastructure) are evaluated according to an average of all of the IT functional groups' metrics.

The importance the company places on these metrics is reflected in the firm's generous bonus program (i.e., bonuses can reach up to 230 percent of an individual's salary) in which all IT staff participate. Bonuses are separate from an individual's salary, which is linked to personal performance. The percentage influence of each set of business measures (i.e., enterprise, business unit, and individual/team) varies according to the level of the individual in the firm. However, all staff have at least 25 percent of their bonus linked to enterprise performance metrics. No bonuses are paid to anyone if the firm does not reach its earnings-per-share target (which is driven by the five enterprise measures outlined in the "Modified Scorecard Business Metrics" feature). This incentive system makes it clear that everyone's job is connected to business results and helps ensure that attention is focused on the things that are important to the company. As a result, interest is much stronger among IT staff about how the business is doing. "Everyone now speaks the same language," said the manager. "Project alignment is much easier."

3. *Strategic imperatives.* A somewhat different approach is taken by a third focus group company. Here the executive team annually evaluates the key environmental factors affecting the company, then identifies a number of strategic imperatives for the firm (e.g., achieve industry-leading e-business capability, achieve 10–15 percent growth in earnings per share). These can vary according to the needs of the firm in any particular year. Each area of the business is then asked to identify initiatives that will affect these imperatives and to determine how they will be measured (e.g., retaining customers of a recent acquisition, increased net sales, a new product). In the same way, IT is asked to identify the key projects and measures that will help the business to achieve these imperatives. Each part of the company, including IT, then integrates these measures into its variable pay program (VPP).

The company's VPP links a percentage of an individual's pay to business results and overall business unit performance. This percentage could vary from a small portion of one's salary for a new employee to a considerable proportion for senior management. Within IT, the weight that different measures are accorded in the VPP portion of their pay is determined by a measurement team and approved by the CIO and the president. Figure 3.1 illustrates the different percentages allocated to IT's variable pay component for a typical year. Metrics can change from year to year depending on where management wants to focus everyone's attention. "Performance tends to improve if you measure it," explained the manager. "Over the years, we have ratcheted up our targets in different areas. Once a certain level of performance is achieved, we may change the measure or change the emphasis on this measure."

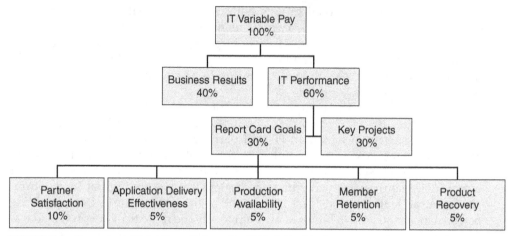

FIGURE 3.1   Percentage Weightings Assigned to IT Variable Pay Components for a Particular Year

An important difference from the scorecard approach is the identification of key IT projects. "These are not all IT projects, but a small number that are closely aligned with the strategic business imperatives," stated the manager. "Having the success of these projects associated with their variable pay drives everyone's behavior. People tend to jump in and help if there's a problem with one of them." The goal in this process is for everyone to understand the VPP measures and to make them visible within IT. Targets and results are posted quarterly, and small groups of employees meet to discuss ideas about how they can influence business and IT goals. "Some amazing ideas have come out of these meetings," said the manager. "Everyone knows what's important, and these measures get attention. People use these metrics to make choices all the time in their work."

Each of these business measurement programs has been implemented somewhat differently, but they all share several key features that could be considered principles of a good business metrics program for IT:

1. *Focus on overall business performance.*   These programs all focus employees on both financial and nonfinancial enterprise performance and have an explicit expectation that everyone in the organization can influence these results in some way.
2. *Understanding is a critical success factor.*   If people are going to be held accountable for certain business results, it is important that they understand them. Similarly, if the organization is worried about certain results, this must be communicated as well. Holding regular staff meetings where people can ask questions and discuss results is effective, as is providing results on a quarterly basis. Understanding is the goal. "If you can ask … a person programming code and they can tell you three to four of their objectives and how those tie into the company's performance and what the measures of achieving those objectives are, you've got it" (Alexander 2000).
3. *Simplicity.*   Successful companies tend to keep their measures very simple and easy to use (Haspeslagh et al. 2001). In each approach already outlined, a limited number of measures are used. This makes it very easy for employees to calculate

their bonuses (or variable pay) based on the metrics provided, which further strengthens the linkage between company performance and individual effort.

4. *Visibility.*   In each of the programs already discussed, metrics were made widely available to all staff on a quarterly basis. In one case they are posted on the company's intranet; in another they are distributed in a printed report; in a third they are posted in public areas of the office. Visibility encourages employee buy-in and accountability and stimulates discussion about how to do better or what is working well.

5. *Links to incentive systems.*   Successful companies tend to include a much larger number of employees in bonus programs than unsuccessful ones (Haspeslagh et al. 2001). Extending incentive schemes to all IT staff, not just management, is important to a measurement program's effectiveness. The most effective programs appear to distinguish between fair compensation for individual work and competencies and a reward for successfully achieving corporate objectives.

ADVICE TO MANAGERS

The focus group had some final advice for other IT managers who are thinking of implementing a business metrics program:

- *Results will take time.*   It takes time to change attitudes and behavior in IT, but it is worth making the effort. Positive results may take from six months to a year to appear. "We had some initial pushback from our staff at the beginning," said one manager, "but now the metrics program has become ingrained in our attitudes and behaviors." Another manager noted, "We had a few bumps during our first year, but everyone, especially our executives, is getting better at the program now [that] we're in our third year. It really gets our staff engaged with the business." If there has been no dramatic difference within three years, management should recognize that it is either using the wrong measures or hasn't got employee buy-in to the program (Alexander 2000).

- *Have common goals.*   Having everyone measured on the same business goals helps build a strong team at all levels in the organization. It makes it easier to set priorities as a group and collaborate and share resources, as needed.

- *Follow up on problem areas.*   Companies must be prepared to take action about poor results and involve staff in their plans. In particular, if companies are going to ask customers and employees what they think, they must be prepared to act on the results. All metrics must be taken seriously and acted on if they are to be used to drive behavior and lead to continuous improvement.

- *Be careful what you measure.*   Measuring something makes people pay attention to it, particularly if it is linked to compensation. Metrics must, therefore, be selected with care because they will be a major driver of behavior. For example, if incentives are solely based on financial results, it is probable that some people may be so driven that they will trample on the needs and interests of others. Similarly, if only costs are measured, the needs of customers could be ignored. Conversely, if a metric indicates a problem area, organizations can expect to see a lot of ingenuity and support devoted to addressing it.

- *Don't use measurement as a method of control.* A business metrics program should be designed to foster an environment in which people look beyond their own jobs and become proactive about the needs of the organization (Marchand et al. 2000). It should aim to communicate strategy and help align individual and organizational initiatives (Kaplan and Norton 1996). All managers should clearly understand that a program of this type should not be used for controlling behavior, but rather as a motivational tool.

Conclusion

Getting the most value out of IT has been a serious concern of business for many years. In spite of considerable effort, measurement initiatives in IT that use surrogates of business value or focus on improving internal IT behavior have not been fully successful in delivering results. Expecting IT to participate in achieving specific enterprise objectives—the same goals as the rest of the organization—has been shown to deliver significant benefits. Not only are there demonstrable financial returns, but there is also considerable long-term value in aligning everyone's behavior with the same goals; people become more supportive of each other and more sensitive to the greater corporate good, and decisions are easier to make. A good business metrics program, therefore, appears to be a powerful component of effective measurement in IT. IT employees may initially resist accountability for business results, but the experiences of the focus group demonstrate that their objections are usually short lived. If a business measurement program is carefully designed, properly linked to an incentive program, widely implemented, and effectively monitored by management, it is highly likely that business performance will become an integral part of the mind-set of all IT staff and ultimately pay off in a wide variety of ways.

References

Alexander, S. "Business Metrics." *Computerworld* 34, no. 24 (2000): 64.

Bensaou, M., and M. Earl. "The Right Mind-Set for Managing Information Technology." *Harvard Business Review* 76, no. 5 (September–October 1998): 110–28.

Cronk, M., and E. Fitzgerald. "Understanding 'IS Business Value': Derivation of Dimensions." *Logistics Information Management* 12, no. 1–2 (1999): 40–49.

Goldratt, E., and J. Cox. *The Goal: Excellence in Manufacturing.* Croton-on-Hudson, NY: North River Press, 1984.

Haspeslagh, P., T. Noda, and F. Boulos. "Managing for Value: It's Not Just About the Numbers." *Harvard Business Review* (July–August 2001): 65–73.

Heskett, J., T. Jones, G. Loveman, E. Sasser, and L. Schlesinger. "Putting the Service Profit Chain to Work." *Harvard Business Review* (March–April 1994): 164–74.

Holland, W., and G. Sharke. "Is Your IT System VESTed?" *Strategic Finance* 83, no. 6 (December 2001): 34–37.

Kaplan, R., and D. Norton. *The Balanced Scorecard.* Boston: Harvard Business School Press, 1996.

Koys, D. "The Effects of Employee Satisfaction, Organizational Citizenship Behavior, and Turnover on Organizational Effectiveness: A Unit-Level, Longitudinal Study." *Personnel Psychology* 54, no. 1 (Spring 2001): 101–14.

Marchand, D., W. Kettinger, and J. Rollins. "Information Orientation: People, Technology and the Bottom Line." *Sloan Management Review* (Summer 2000): 69–89.

Peslak, A. R. "An Analysis of Critical Information Technology Issues Facing Organizations." *Industrial Management and Data Systems* 112, no. 5 (2012): 808–27.

Potter, K. "Business Key Metrics Data: Accelerate the IT Value Journey." Gartner Group, ID: G00256958, October 16, 2013.

Roberts, J. P. "Define Strategic IT Metrics as Part of Your IT Strategy." Gartner Group, ID: G0025861, November 5, 2013.

Rucci, A., S. Kirn, and R. Quinn. "The Employee-Customer-Profit Chain at Sears." *Harvard Business Review* 76 (January/February 1998): 82–97.

Smith, H., and J. McKeen. "Investment Spend Optimization at BMO Financial Group." *MISQ Executive* 9, no. 2 (June 2010): 65–81.

Ulrich, D., R. Halbrook, D. Meder, M. Stuchlik, and S. Thorpe. "Employee and Customer Attachment: Synergies for Competitive Advantage." *Human Resource Planning* 14 (1991): 89–103.

4 Building a Strong Relationship with the Business[1]

There is no doubt that a strong business–IT relationship is now critical to the success of an organization's successful and effective use of IT (Bassellier and Benbasat 2004; Kitzis and Gomolski 2006). With the rapid evolution of IT in business, simply "keeping the lights on" and delivering systems on time and on budget are not enough. Today, IT's ability to deliver value is closely linked with the nature of its relationship with a large number of business stakeholders. Recognizing this, many IT functions have tried to become "partners" with the business at the most senior strategic levels, but with limited success (Gordon and Gordon 2002). It has become clear from these initiatives that business–IT interactions are more complex and highly resistant to change than first assumed and that building a strong relationship with business is a major challenge for most IT leaders.

We know that the nature and quality of the business–IT relationship are affected by many factors such as the subfunction of IT involved (e.g., operations, application development), the business unit involved, the management levels involved, changing expectations, and general perceptions of IT (McKeen and Smith 2008). However, research suggests that IT managers are still somewhat naïve about how relationships work in business and that interpersonal interaction and clear communication are often missing between the groups. We have also learned that perceptions of the value IT delivers are correlated with how well IT is perceived to understand and identify with the business (Anonymous 2002; Gold 2006; Tallon et al. 2000).

Nevertheless, we still know very little about the elements that contribute to a "strong relationship" between IT and business, nor even about how to characterize such a relationship (Day 2007). This chapter first looks at the nature of the business–IT relationship and how an effective relationship could be characterized. Then it examines in turn each of the four foundational elements of a strong, positive relationship, making suggestions for how IT managers could strengthen them.

---

[1] This chapter is based on the authors' previously published article, Smith, H. A., and J. D. McKeen. "Building a Strong Relationship with the Business." *Communications of the Association for Information Systems* 26, Article 19 (April 2010): 429–40. Reproduced by permission of the Association for Information Systems.

THE NATURE OF THE BUSINESS–IT RELATIONSHIP

"The IT-business relationship is a set of beliefs that one party holds about the other and how these beliefs are formed from the interactions of...individuals as they engage in tasks associated with an IT service" (Day 2007). The business–IT relationship in organizations tends to span the full range of relationship possibilities. Some members of the focus group felt they had generally healthy and positive relationships, and others labeled them negative or ineffective. Overall, "there's still a general perception that IT is slow, expensive, and gets in the way," said one manager. Even the focus group member with the most positive business–IT relationship admitted it was "not easy," and one set of researchers has described it as typically "arduous" (Pawlowski and Robey 2004).

Although "you can't have a one-sided relationship," as one focus group manager remarked, agreement is almost universal that IT needs to change if it is to improve. Literally dozens of articles have been written about what IT *should* be doing to make it better. For example, IT should better understand the fundamentals of business and aim to satisfy the "right" customers (Kitzis and Gomolski 2006); act as a knowledge broker (Pawlowski and Robey 2004); get involved in the business and be skilled marketers (Schindler 2007); manage expectations (Ross 2006); convince the business that it understands its goals and concerns and communicate in business language (Bassellier and Benbasat 2004); and demonstrate its competencies (Day 2007). In short, "IT has to keep proving itself" to the business to demonstrate its value (Kaarst-Brown 2005). Thus, practitioners and researchers both consistently stress that cultivating a strong business–IT relationship is "a continuous effort" (a focus group member); "ongoing" (Luftman and Brier 1999); a "core IT skill" (Feeny and Willcocks 1998); and "emergent" (Day 2007).

On the business side of the relationship, two features stand out. First, business managers are often disengaged from IT work, according to both the focus group and researchers (Ross and Weill 2002). For example, in some cases in the focus group, IT staff have taken on business roles in projects in order to get them done. Second, it is clear that what business wants from this relationship is continually changing. "The business–IT relationship is cyclical," explained one manager. "The business goes back and forth about whether it wants IT to be an order taker or an innovator. Every time the business changes what it wants, the relationship goes sour."

So what *do* we know about the business–IT relationship in organizations? First, we know it is a multifaceted interaction of people and processes. It is unfortunately true that the existence of positive relationships between individual business and IT professionals does not necessarily mean that interactions will be positive on a particular development project, with the IT help desk, with an individual business unit, or between IT and the business as a whole (McKeen and Smith 2008). Because relationships manifest themselves in so many ways—formal and informal, tacit and explicit, procedural and cultural—we must recognize that their complexity means that they don't lend themselves to simplistic solutions (Day 2007; Guillemette et al. 2008; Ross 2006).

Second, we know difficult, complex relationships often exhibit lack of clarity around expectations and accountabilities and difficulty communicating (Galford and Drapeau 2003; Pawlowski and Robey 2004). This, in turn, leads to lack of trust. In the business–IT relationship, "complexity often arises when expectations differ in various parts of an organization, leaving a CIO with the difficult task of reconciling them and elucidating exactly what the IT function's mission and strategic role should be"

(Guillemette et al. 2008). Several focus group members complained that different parts of their business expected different things from IT. "In some parts of our business, they want IT to be an order-taker; in others, they want us to be thought leaders and innovators," stated one manager. Another noted, "We live in an age of unmet expectations. There's never enough resources to do everything the business wants us to do."

Third, assumptions by the business about IT tend to cluster into patterns. One researcher has identified five sets of assumptions: (1) IT is a necessary evil, (2) IT is a support, not a partner, (3) IT rules, (4) business can do IT better, and (5) business and IT are equal partners. Business leaders who espouse one of these sets will tend to have similar ideas about who should control IT's direction, how central IT is to business strategy, the value of IT skills and knowledge, how to justify IT investments, and who benefits from IT (Kaarst-Brown 2005). Building on this idea, another study has also shown that business–IT relationships tend to vary along similar patterns. Different organizations tend to adopt one of five IT value profiles and expect IT to behave in accordance with the profile selected (see Appendix A). Problems arise when the assumptions and value profiles espoused by IT conflict with those of the organization or a specific part of the organization. As a result, many "disconnects" are often present in the relationship. For example, although IT organizations often seek to be a business partner, their participation in this way is not always welcomed by the business (Pawlowski and Robey 2004).

Focus group members defined a strong business–IT relationship in ways that recognize each of these factors. To them, it should include the following:

- Clearly defined expectations, governance models, and accountabilities.
- Trust between the two groups.
- Articulation and incorporation of corporate and client values and priorities in all IT work.
- A blurred line between business and IT (i.e., no "us vs. them").
- IT dedicated to business success.
- IT serving as a trusted advisor to the business.
- Mutual recognition of IT value.

In short, a strong business–IT relationship is one where realistic, mutual expectations are clearly articulated and communicated through individual and procedural interactions and where both groups recognize that all facets of this relationship are important to the successful delivery of IT value.

Characteristics of the Business–IT Relationship

- IT has to keep proving itself.
- The business is often disengaged from IT work.
- Business expectations of IT change continually.
- The relationship is affected by the interaction of many people and processes at multiple levels.
- Clarity is often lacking around expectations and accountabilities.
- Business assumptions of IT tend to cluster.
- There are many "disconnects" between the two groups.

THE FOUNDATION OF A STRONG BUSINESS–IT RELATIONSHIP

Strong relationships do not simply happen. They are built over time and, if they are to deliver value for the organization, they must be built to endure (Day 2007). The focus group told several stories of how the business–IT relationship in their organization had deteriorated when a business or IT leader changed or when a project wasn't delivered on time. Because it can so easily become dysfunctional, constant attention and nurturing are needed at all levels, said the focus group. However, building a strong relationship is not easy to do. Although there is no shortage of prescriptions, the sustained nature of problems in this relationship suggests that some underlying root causes need to be addressed (Appendix B provides one organization's view of what is needed in this relationship).

We have suggested previously that four components must be in place in order to deliver real business value with IT: competence, credibility, interpersonal interaction, and trust. The focus group reviewed these components and agreed that they also form the foundation of a successful and effective business–IT relationship. The focus group saw that developing, sustaining, and growing a strong business–IT relationship in each of these areas is closely intertwined with IT's ability to deliver value with technology. Therefore, a consistent and structured initiative to strengthen the business–IT relationship in these dimensions will also lead to an improved ability to deliver value successfully (see Figure 4.1). In the remainder of this chapter, we look at these four components in turn, discussing in detail how each acts as an important building block of a strong business–IT relationship and suggesting how each could be strengthened.

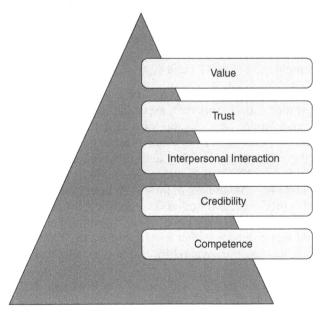

FIGURE 4.1 Strong Relationships are Built on a Strong Foundation

Building Block #1: Competence

Although a competent IT organization that consistently delivers cost-efficient and reliable services is the bare minimum for an IT function, businesses today expect a great deal more of both their IT organizations and their IT professionals. Although many IT organizations have adopted an internal service model in order to "operate IT like a business" and have demonstrated that they can provide services as effectively as external service providers, these competencies fall short of what business now expects of IT (Kitzis and Gomolski 2006). Over the last decade, researchers and practitioners have identified a number of new competencies that are now required—to a greater or lesser extent—from all IT professionals.

First and foremost, IT staff need *business knowledge*. This goes beyond basic knowledge of a single business unit to include the "big picture" of the whole organization. IT personnel need to understand the business context in which their technologies are deployed, including organizational goals and objectives, capabilities, critical success factors, environment, and constraints. At all levels, they need to be able to "think about and understand the development of the business as [any other business] member would and participate in making [it] successful in the same way" (Bassellier and Benbasat 2004). Furthermore, they need to be able to apply their business understanding to help the organization visualize the ways in which "IT can contribute to organizational performance and look for synergies between IT and business activities" (Bassellier and Benbasat 2004). In this regard, an important competence an IT department and its staff can bring to an organization is cross-domain and cross-functional business knowledge (Kitzis and Gomolski 2006; Wailgum 2008a).

Developing business knowledge does not mean that IT staff should become businesspeople but that they should be able to demonstrate they understand the business's goals, concerns, language, and processes and are working to help achieve them (Feeny and Willcocks 1998). One focus group organization surveyed its senior managers about IT and found that these managers felt IT staff had a poor understanding of the business; as a result, they didn't trust IT's ideas.

Other key competencies that IT must cultivate include the following:

- *Expertise.*   This includes having up-to-date knowledge, being able to support a technical recommendation, applying expertise to a particular business situation, and offering wise advice on risks, options, and trade-offs, as well as the ability to bring useful new ideas and external information (e.g., about new technologies or what the competition is doing with technology) to the business (Joni 2004; Pawlowski and Robey 2004).
- *Financial Awareness.*   Awareness of how IT delivers value and the ability to act in accordance with this value is a rare and prized skill (Mahoney and Gerrard 2007). All the focus group members felt pressure to continually demonstrate the business value of IT and recognized a strong need to make all IT staff more aware of such concepts as ROI, total cost of ownership, and how IT affects the bottom line and/or business strategy.
- *Execution.*   It is not enough to understand the business and develop a vision; IT must also operationalize them. Since much of the business–IT relationship is dynamic—that is, continually being re-created—every IT action speaks about its competence. It is well known that the inability to deliver an individual project on

time and within budget will undermine the business's view of IT's overall competence. However, it is also the case that the actions of IT operations, the help desk, and other IT subfunctions will also be held up to similar scrutiny. As one focus group manager stated, "Poor delivery of *any* type can break a relationship."

In short, if the IT function is not seen to be competent at executing basic IT services or able to communicate in business terms, it will simply not be given an opportunity to participate in higher-order business activities, such as planning and strategy development (Gerrard 2006).

STRENGTHENING COMPETENCE

- *Find ways to develop business knowledge in all IT staff.*   Focus group members use "lunch and learn" sessions, job shadowing, and short-term assignments in the business to accomplish this, but they recognize that more needs to be done to develop this competence.
- *Link IT's success criteria to business metrics.*   This not only lifts IT's perspective to larger business concerns, but it also introduces all IT staff to the key financial and other measures that drive the rest of the organization.
- *Make business value an explicit criteria in all IT decisions.*   Asking why the business should care about a particular IT decision, and how it will affect the business in both the long and short terms, changes the focus of IT professionals in a subtle but very effective way, enabling them to communicate even technical decisions in business terms.
- *Ensure effective execution in all IT activities.*   This ensures that IT sends a consistent message of competence to all parts and levels of the organization.

Building Block #2: Credibility

Credibility is the belief that others can be counted on to do what they say they will do. It is built in many ways. Keeping agreements and acting with integrity, honesty, and openness are essential behaviors, whereas lack of timely and substantive responses and failure to observe deadlines can undermine it (Feeny et al. 1992; Greenberg et al. 2007). Focus group managers concurred that credibility is very important to the business–IT relationship. Although in earlier days, credibility was largely about the ability to deliver systems on time and budget, now earning and maintaining credibility with the business has become more complex. Today's IT projects often involve many more elements (e.g., multiple platforms, risk management, adherence to laws and standards) and stakeholders than in the past, and the methods and tools of delivery are constantly changing. Furthermore, research shows that it is often the "little things" that can be most significant in undermining credibility and that people often make decisions based on IT's attention or inattention to such details (Buchanan 2005). One study concluded that "each and every IT service incident and event must be considered for its long-term influence" (Day 2007).

IT staff often assume that because they are *competent* they will be *credible*, but this is an invalid assumption. Thus, for example, a survey of CIOs found that they wished their developers "didn't appear so clueless to the rest of the organization" (Wailgum 2008b). It is essential, therefore, that competence be *demonstrated* for others to feel someone is credible (Ross 2006). This is especially important in relationships where there is little face-to-face interaction. In these cases in particular, work must be visible and communication constant in order to demonstrate credibility (Hurley 2006).

STRENGTHENING CREDIBILITY

- *Communicate frequently and explicitly.* Make progress and accomplishments visible in clear and nontechnical ways. Focus group members found that when difficult decisions are planned together and clearly articulated in advance, much less tension develops in the relationship.
- *Pay attention to the "little things."* Wherever possible, take steps to provide prompt feedback and responses to queries and to ensure consistently high-quality service encounters.
- *Utilize external cues to credibility.* Examples include awards, endorsements from third parties, and the experience and background of IT staff. These specifics can be very useful when starting a new relationship with the business.
- *Assess all business touch points.* All focus group members stressed the need to really listen to what the business says about its expectations and the problems it feels exist in the relationship. Just the effort alone sends a strong and positive message about the importance of this relationship, said a manager. However, he also stressed that undertaking such a review creates expectations that changes will be made, so regular reports back to the business about what is being done to improve things are especially important.

Building Block #3: Interpersonal Interaction

The business–IT relationship is shaped by the development of mutual understanding, interests, and expectations, which are formed and shaped during a wide variety of interpersonal interactions (Gold 2006). Business–IT interactions must be developed and nurtured at many different levels in the business–IT relationship, said focus group managers, and although CEO–CIO interactions can set the tone for the relationship, the connections at multiple touch points contribute to its overall quality (Flint 2004; Prewitt 2005). The following are the four significant dimensions of interpersonal interaction:

- *Professionalism.* This is the unarticulated set of working behaviors, attitudes, and expectations that serves as the glue that keeps teams of diverse individuals working together toward the same goal. These behaviors are not only carefully watched by the business, they are also just as important *within* IT, said the focus group. Members noted that difficult internal IT relationships can lead to problems delivering effective IT services. Five sets of attitudes and behaviors contribute to developing IT professionalism: (1) comportment (i.e., appearance and manners on the job), (2) preparation (i.e., displaying competence and good organization), (3) communication skill (i.e., both clarity and etiquette), (4) judgment (i.e., the ability to make right choices for the organization), and (5) attitude (i.e., caring about doing a job well and about doing the right thing for the company) (McKeen and Smith 2008).
- *Nontechnical communication.* Over and over, research has found that the inability to communicate clearly with the business in its own terms can undermine the

business–IT relationship (Bassellier and Benbasat 2004; Kitzis and Gomolski 2006). Today, because IT staff work across many organizational boundaries, they must also be effective at translating and interpreting needs, not only from business to technology and vice versa, but also between business units, in order to enable members of different communities to understand each other (Wailgum 2008a). Increasingly, as IT programs and services are delivered collaboratively *by* external partners and *to* external partners, clarity in communication is becoming mission critical.

- *Social skills.* The social dimension of the business–IT relationship is often ignored by both sides, leading to misunderstandings and lack of trust (Day 2007). Social bonds help diverse groups build trust and develop a common language, both of which are essential to a strong relationship. Socialization also helps build mutual understanding, enabling all parties to get comfortable with one another and uncovering hidden assumptions, which may become obstacles to success (Kaarst-Brown 2005). Socialization also develops empathy and facilitates problem solving (Feeny and Willcocks 1998).

Unfortunately, many IT organizations are structured in ways that create barriers between business and IT. For example, the use of "relationship managers" to act as interfaces between IT and the business is a mixed blessing. Although individually, these managers may be skilled and viewed positively by the business, focus group members noted that their position often leads them to act as gatekeepers to the business. One manager mentioned being hauled on the carpet to explain his lunch with a business manager (a personal friend), which hadn't been approved by the relationship manager! "We need a broad range of social interactions with the business," said another manager. "We use account managers, but we also encourage interactions through such things as lunches and social events." Ongoing, face-to-face interaction is the ideal, but with today's virtual teams and global organizations, other forms of social interaction, such as networking and collaboration tools, are being introduced to help bridge gaps in this area. Social bonds can be created in a virtual environment, but these take longer and are harder to develop although they are, if anything, more important than in a more traditional workplace (Greenberg et al. 2007).

- *Management of politics and conflict.* The business–IT relationship can be turbulent, and IT personnel are not noted for their skills in dealing with the conflicts and challenges involved. Furthermore, conflict and politics tend to be exacerbated by the types of projects most commonly undertaken by IT—that is, those that cross internal and external organizational boundaries (Weiss and Hughes 2005). As a result, IT functions and personnel need ways to effectively address conflict and use it to deliver creative solutions. All too often, conflict is avoided or treated as a "hot potato" to be tossed up the management hierarchy (Weiss and Hughes 2005). Straight talk and the development of a healthy give-and-take attitude are fundamental to dealing with conflict at its source. Experts also recommend the development of transparent processes for managing disagreements and frank discussions of the trade-offs involved in dealing with problems (Pascale et al. 1997). These not only help stop damaging escalation and growing uncertainty but also help to model conflict-resolution skills for the staff involved.

As well, failure to understand the role of politics in a particular organization makes IT personnel less effective in their business interactions because they cannot craft "win–win" solutions. Thus, all IT staff need to understand something about politics and how they can affect their work. At more senior levels, it is imperative that IT professionals learn how to act "wisely and shrewdly in a political environment" (Kitzis and Gomolski 2006). Since politics are part of every business relationship and cannot be avoided, IT personnel must learn how to work with them, said focus group members, even if they are trying to avoid them as much as possible.

STRENGTHENING INTERPERSONAL INTERACTIONS

- *Expect professionalism.* IT managers must not only articulate professional values and behaviors, they must also *live* them and measure and reward them in their staff.
- *Promote a wide variety of social interactions at all levels.* Whether face-to-face or virtual, sharing information about each other's background and interests is an important way to bolster working relationships at all levels. Therefore, even where formal relationship managers are in place, IT leaders should encourage all IT staff to connect informally with their business colleagues. "Social interaction facilitates quick problem ownership and resolution and helps to develop a common language," said a focus group participant. Although the need for socialization increases as one moves up the organizational hierarchy, even at the lowest levels staff should be expected to spend about 10 percent of their time in this type of interaction (Kitzis and Gomolski 2006).
- *Develop "soft skills" in IT staff.* Although the need for interpersonal skills in IT has never been greater, many companies still give their development short shrift, preferring instead to stress technical competencies. In developing interpersonal skills, formal training should be only one component. It is even more important that IT managers take time to develop such skills in their staff through mentoring and coaching. Many focus group members have implemented "soft" skills development initiatives informally, but they have also admitted that the pressure to be instantly productive often detracts from both business and IT participation in them.

Building Block #4: Trust

Effective interpersonal interactions, a belief that the job at hand will get done and get done right, and demonstrated business and technical competence are all required to facilitate trust that IT can be a successful partner with the business. But *even if* these are in place, proactive measures are still needed to actually *build* trust between the two groups. In many firms, an underlying sense of distrust of IT *as a whole* remains:

> IT's processes are notoriously convoluted and bureaucratic, leaving the business unsure of how to accomplish their business strategies with IT. From strategy alignment to prioritization to budgeting and resourcing to delivering value to managing costs, it must be clear that what IT is doing is for the benefit of the enterprise, not itself. (McKeen and Smith 2008)

The most important way to build trust at this level is through effective governance. The story of how one CIO managed to transform the business–IT relationship at Farm Credit Canada illustrates its importance:

> [At FCC, when Paul MacDonald became CIO], IT was considered a necessary evil. Business people were afraid of it and wished it would just go away.... [Transforming this relationship] was a very difficult and complex job—especially for cross-functional processes. Clear responsibilities and accountabilities had to be defined.... "It's all about clarity of roles and responsibilities," MacDonald said. The new IT governance model was validated and refined through sessions with key business stakeholders. "These sessions were important to demonstrate that we weren't just shuffling the boxes around in IT," [MacDonald] said.... MacDonald also made sure that the new model actually worked the way it was supposed to. "There were cases where it didn't ... and with these, we made changes in our processes." He attributes his willingness to make changes where needed to his ability to make the new model actually function the way it was supposed to....
>
> "Today, at FCC user satisfaction is very high and IT is seen as being indispensable.... [MacDonald] stressed that it is important to review and refine the new governance model continually." "There were some things that just didn't work," he said. "We are still constantly learning." (Smith and McKeen 2008)

Effective governance should be designed to build common business goals and establish a good decision-making process (Gerrard 2006). Mature processes in IT and transparency about costs develop trust (Levinson and Pastore 2005; Overby 2005). A focus group manager stated succinctly, "[M]ore transparency equals fewer surprises and you get transparency through governance." Aspects of governance that have enhanced trust in focus group organizations include integrated planning, defined accountabilities, a clear picture of mandates and authorities, and clarity around how work gets done.

Another focus group manager explained the importance of governance in this way:

> *In the past, we couldn't break the trust barrier. Now, [with an effective governance structure] we are more proactive and are fighting fewer fires. Our processes ensure proper escalation and a new focus on value. In short, governance captures the value of a good relationship and good fences make good neighbours.*

Trust is essential for both superior performance and for developing the collaborative relationships that lead to success (Greenberg et al. 2007). It is developed through consistency, clear communication, willingness to tackle challenges, and owning up to and learning from mistakes (Upton and Staats 2008). Both inconsistent messages to stakeholders and inconsistent processes and standards can seriously undermine trust (Galford and Drapeau 2003).

Nevertheless, it must be stressed that there is no optimal form of governance (Gordon and Gordon 2002). The key is to develop a model of IT governance that addresses the business's *expectations* of its IT function. Thus, an IT organization can best build trust if it clearly understands the organization's priorities for IT and designs its governance model to match (Guillemette et al. 2008).

STRENGTHENING TRUST

- *Design governance for clarity and transparency.* IT leaders should assess how the business views IT processes—from the help desk on up. It is important to recognize that all processes play a very visible role in how IT is viewed in the organization and that clear, effective, and fair processes are needed to break the "trust barrier" between business and IT at all levels.
- *Mandate the relationship.* Although it may seem counterintuitive, companies have had success from strictly enforcing relationship basics such as formal roles and responsibilities, joint scorecards, and the use of common metrics. Such structural measures can ensure that common expectations, language, and goals are developed and met.
- *Design IT for business expectations.* Clearly understanding the *primary* value the business wants IT to deliver can help IT understand how to focus its process and governance models (see Appendix A).

Conclusion

There is clearly no panacea for a strong business–IT relationship. Yet, the correlation between a good relationship and the ability to deliver value with IT makes it imperative that leaders do all they can to develop effective interpersonal and interfunctional business–IT relations. It is unfortunately still incumbent on IT leadership to take on the bulk of this task, if only because it will make IT organizations more effective. Business–IT relationships are complex, with interactions of many types, at many levels, and between both individuals and across functional and organizational entities. This chapter has not only identified and explored what a strong business–IT relationship should look like in its many dimensions but also has described the four major components needed to build it: competence, credibility, interpersonal skills, and trust. Unfortunately, business–IT relationships still leave a lot to be desired in most organizations. Recognizing that what it takes to build a strong business–IT partnership is also closely related to what is needed to deliver IT value may help to focus more attention on these mission-critical activities.

References

Anonymous. "Senior IT People Excluded from IT Decision-Making." *Career Development International* 7, no. 6/7 (2002).

Bassellier, G., and I. Benbasat. "Business Competence of Information Technology Professionals: Conceptual Development and Influence on IT-Business Partnerships." *MIS Quarterly* 28, no. 4 (December 2004).

Buchanan, L. "Sweat the Small Stuff." *Harvard Business Review* (April 2005). hbr.org/2005/04/sweat-the-small-stuff/ar/1 (accessed March 10, 2011).

Day, J. "Strangers on the Train: The Relationship of the IT Department with the Rest of the Business." *Information Technology and People* 20, no. 1 (2007).

Feeny, D., B. Edwards, and K. Simpson. "Understanding the CEO/CIO Relationship." *MIS Quarterly* 16, no. 4 (1992).

Feeny, D., and L. Willcocks. "Core IS Capabilities for Exploiting Information Technology." *Sloan Management Review* 39, no. 3 (Spring 1998).

Flint, D. "Senior Executives Don't Always Realize the True Value of IT." Gartner Inc., ID Number: COM-22-5499, June 21, 2004.

Galford, R., and A. Drapeau. "The Enemies of Trust." *Harvard Business Review* #R0302G (February 2003).

Gerrard, M. "Three Critical Success Factors in the Business/IT Relationship." Gartner Inc., ID Number: G00143352, October 18, 2006.

Gold, R. "Perception *Is* Reality: Why Subjective Measures Matter and How to Maximize Their Impact." *Harvard Business School Publishing Balanced Scorecard Report* (July–August 2006).

Gordon, S., and J. Gordon. "Organizational Options for Resolving the Tension Between IT Departments and Business Units in the Delivery of IT services." *Information Technology and People* 15, no. 4 (2002).

Greenberg, P., R. Greenberg, and Y. Antonucci. "Creating and Sustaining Trust in Virtual Teams." *Business Horizons* 50 (2007).

Guillemette, M., G. Paré, and H. Smith. "What's Your IT Value Profile?" *Cahier du GReSI #08-04.* Montréal, Canada: HEC Montréal, November 2008.

Hurley, R. "The Decision to Trust." *Harvard Business Review* #R0609B (September 2006).

Joni, S. "The Geography of Trust." *Harvard Business Review* #R0403F (March 2004).

Kaarst-Brown, M. "Understanding an Organization's View of the CIO: The Role of Assumptions About IT." *MIS Quarterly Executive* 4, no. 2 (June 2005).

Kitzis, E., and B. Gomolski. "IT Leaders Must Think Like Business Leaders." Gartner Inc., ID Number: G00143430, October 26, 2006.

Levinson, M., and R. Pastore. "Transparency Helps Align IT with Business." *CIO Magazine* (June 1, 2005).

Luftman, J., and T. Brier. "Achieving and Sustaining Business–IT Alignment." *California Management Review* 41, no. 1 (Fall 1999).

Mahoney, J., and M. Gerrard. "IT Value Performance Tools Link to Business–IT Alignment." Gartner Inc., ID Number: G00152551, November 2, 2007.

McKeen, J., and H. Smith. *IT Strategy in Action.* Upper Saddle River, NJ: Pearson-Prentice Hall, 2008.

Overby, S. "Turning IT Doubters into True Believers: Executive Summary." *CIO Research Reports* (June 1, 2005).

Pascale, R., M. Millemann, and L. Gioja. "Changing the Way We Change." *Harvard Business Review* (November–December 2007).

Pawlowski, S., and D. Robey. "Bridging User Organizations: Knowledge Brokering and the Work of Information Technology Professionals." *MIS Quarterly* 28, no. 4 (2004).

Prewitt, E. "The Communication Gap." *CIO Magazine* (June 1, 2005).

Ross, J. "Trust Makes the Team Go 'Round.'" *Harvard Management Update* 11, no. 6 (June 2006): 3–6.

Ross, J., and P. Weill. "Six IT Decisions Your IT People Shouldn't Make." *Harvard Business Review* #R0211F (November 2002).

Schindler, E. "What IT Can Learn from the Marketing Department." CIO Web 2.0 Advisor, September 21, 2007. advice.cio.com/esther_schindler/what_it_can_learn_from_the_marketing_department (accessed March 10, 2011).

Smith, H., and J. McKeen. "Creating a Process-Centric Organization at FCC: SOA from the Top Down." *MIS Quarterly Executive* 7, no. 2 (June 2008): 71–84.

Tallon, P., K. Kramer, and V. Gurbaxani. "Executives' Perceptions of the Business Value of Information Technology: A Process-Oriented Approach." *Journal of Management Information Systems* 16, no. 4 (Spring 2000).

Upton, D., and B. Staats. "Radically Simple IT." *Harvard Business Review* R0803 (March 2008).

Wailgum, T. "Why Business Analysts Are So Important for IT and CIOs." *CIO Magazine* (April 16, 2008a).

Wailgum, T. "Eight Reasons Why CIOs Think Their Application Developers Are Clueless." *CIO Magazine* (September 3, 2008b).

Weiss, J., and J. Hughes. "Want collaboration? Accept—and Actively Manage—Conflict." *Harvard Business Review* #R0503F (March 2005).

APPENDIX A

The Five IT Value Profiles

Each of the following profiles is a unique way for IT to contribute to an organization. One is not "better" than the other, nor is one profile more or less mature than any other. Each represents a different, consistent way of organizing IT to deliver value. Each is different in five ways: main activities, dominant skills and knowledge, the business–IT relationship, governance and decision-making, and accountabilities.

Profile A: Project Coordinator

This type of IT function coordinates IT activities between the business and outsourcers. Therefore, the primary value it delivers is organizational flexibility through the IT outsourcing strategy it establishes and through promoting informed IT decision making in the business units. The Project Coordinator function works with the business units, helping them formalize their requirements, and then finds an outsourcer to develop and implement what is needed. The Project Coordinator also manages the relationships between vendors and business units, not only with the organization's current activities but also in planning for the future by developing strategic partnerships.

Profile B: Systems Provider

The primary mission of the Systems Provider is to provide the organization with quality information systems at the lowest possible cost. Strategically, the Systems Provider uses the organization's business plans to set IT's goals, prepare budgets, and determine the resources needed to implement the organization's strategy for the required systems development projects.

Profile C: Architecture Builder

The primary mission of this type of IT function is to link the firm's various business units by integrating computerized systems, data, and technological platforms. The Architecture Builder seeks to design a flexible architecture and infrastructure that will meet the company's needs. The architecture builder typically receives broad strategic direction from the organization and designs an architecture and infrastructure with which the organization can implement its strategy.

Profile D: Partner

The main objective of the Partner IT function is to create IT-enabled business capabilities to support current business strategies. IT and the business collaborate to achieve a two-way strategic alignment that is developed iteratively and reciprocally over time. The Partner is a catalyst for change in business processes and seeks to improve organizational efficiency. As guardian of the organization's business processes, the Partner's mission therefore extends far beyond its technological tools.

Profile E: Technological Leader

The Technological Leader tries above all to use innovation to transform the organization's strategy. IT's main objective is therefore to identify opportunities, find innovative organizational applications for technology that will enable the organization to secure a significant competitive advantage, and then implement such applications.

Source: Guillemette et al. 2008.

APPENDIX B

Guidelines for Building a Strong Business–IT Relationship

The following was provided by a focus group member and is an excerpt from a company memo on improving the business–IT relationship.

Now more than ever, we must truly understand the business transformation agenda. This will require us to potentially interact differently than in the past or in a mode beyond what our executives may be looking for. We must

- Stop acting as and being viewed as order takers once IT projects have been identified.
- Develop an understanding of business improvement ideas before they become initiatives or projects.
- Be prepared to offer alternative perspectives on business solutions.
- Be part of the strategic equation and have "feet on the street."
- Engage early before ideas and issues turn into projects.
- Continue to shape the solution during pre-concept and concept phases.

To develop a relationship with the business units where we are viewed as a trusted advisor and as adding value, we need to truly be part of their decision-making process and team. We must ask ourselves the following questions:

- Are we considered a member of the business's senior leadership team?
- Are we consulted before decisions are made or just asked to execute what has already been decided?
- Are we involved in shaping the content of the strategic agenda not just its schedule?

Creating a consistent forum for one-on-one strategic interaction should allow us to rise above the normal churn of issues, projects, or other regularly scheduled meetings and be positioned to truly start understanding where our help is needed. Potential short-term next steps include the following:

- Get invited to each business unit's leadership team meetings.
- Schedule a monthly one to one strategy meeting with no set agenda.

CHAPTER

5 Communicating with Business Managers[1]

At an IT governance meeting, attended by all our business executives,
our IT architect was asked to discuss IT security and what steps
needed to be taken to improve it. The architect proceeded to bombard
the executives with extremely low-level details—an oversaturation of
information, which they did not understand—and he lost their attention
in very short order. What he did not do was deliver information in a
positive manner geared to his audience. As a result, there was diminished
business interest and understanding about this topic and a slowed-down
budget for needed upgrades, which also affected other projects.

—(Senior IT manager in a global retail organization)

A s this true story illustrates, the ability to communicate with the business in business terms does not appear to be a current IT strength. This is a serious problem for IT managers because as IT and business grow more entwined, IT staff are going to need to be increasingly organization savvy and possess greater business and interpersonal competencies (Basselier and Benbasat 2004; Karlsen et al.; 2008; Mingay 2005). Yet, despite consistent complaints from both business and IT leaders about how IT staff lack business and communication skills, it seems that many IT departments still hire largely for technical competencies and have little budget available for "soft skills" development (Cukier 2007). Problems communicating with business continue to play a significant part in today's poor perceptions of IT in organizations and inhibit what IT is able to do *for* the organization (McKeen and Smith 2009). IT managers often bemoan the fact that IT-based initiatives—for example, to implement new technologies or establish

---

[1] This chapter is based on the authors' previously published article, Smith, H. A., and J. D. McKeen. "How to Talk so Business Will Listen...and Listen so Business Can Talk." *Communications of the Association for Information Systems* 27, Article 13 (August 2010): 207–16. Reproduced by permission of the Association for Information Systems.

a standard infrastructure—which they believe could have significant benefits for their organizations are not funded. Many of the reasons for this lie in IT's inability to explain the value of such investments in terms the business will understand.

In short, one of the most important skills all IT staff need to develop today is how to communicate effectively with business. "Effective communication between IT . . . and its stakeholders has never been so important . . . so complex or so difficult to get right." (Mingay 2005). Over and over, research has shown that if IT and business cannot speak the same language, focus on the same issues, and communicate constructively, they cannot build a trusting relationship (Karlsen et al. 2008). And business is consistently more negative than IT about IT's abilities in communicating effectively. In fact, even while IT collaboration is improving, business's assessment of IT's communication skills is declining (Willcoxson and Chatham 2004).

Much attention has been paid to organizational alignment between IT and business (e.g., governance, structure), while very little has been paid to the nature and impact of the social dimension of alignment, a big element of which involves communication (Reich and Benbasat 2000). This chapter explores the business and interpersonal competencies that IT staff will need in order to do their jobs effectively over the next five to seven years and what companies should be doing to help develop them. It begins by characterizing the state of communication in the business–IT relationship and why "good communication" is becoming increasingly important. Then, it explores what is meant by "good communication" in this relationship and looks at some of the inhibitors of effective communication between these groups. Finally, it discusses the key communication skills that need to be developed by IT staff and makes recommendations for how organizations can improve or develop communication in the business–IT relationship.

COMMUNICATION IN THE BUSINESS–IT RELATIONSHIP

"Poor communication is a constant source of irritation, confusion, and animosity," said one focus group manager. Another agreed: "So many of our IT staff don't understand organizational dynamics. They say and do things that would be completely inappropriate anywhere else in our company." There is general agreement between practitioners and researchers that poor business–IT communication is the source of poor relationships and alignment between these groups (Bittler 2008; Reich and Benbasat 2000). One study noted:

> Many IT people have "turned off" their business peers with too much technical jargon. This is one reason why the number of IT people that are "allowed" to speak with business people has been deliberately limited in many organizations. (Bittler 2008)

Communication is both an enabler and an inhibitor of a good business–IT relationship. On one hand, poor communication tends to be persistent and of lasting concern to practitioners (Coughlan et al. 2005). Often, IT personnel are perceived to live in an "ivory tower," disengaged from the needs of the business (Burton et al. 2008). Typically, these problems are described as a communication or a cultural "gap" between the two groups and are considered a major cause of systems development failures (Coughlan et al. 2005; Reich and Benbasat 2000). "We struggle with communication gaps and challenges," said a manager. "There's a lot of IT arrogance we need to deal with." Another commented, "IT doesn't listen and doesn't talk the talk."

On the other hand, there is broad recognition that good communication is essential for many reasons. First, it is fundamental to building a strong, positive business–IT relationship. "When business people believe IT people 'get it,' the relationships are always improved" (Bittler 2008). Second, it helps set sensible expectations of IT and helps IT to manage how it is perceived in business (Day 2007). Third, it is an essential element of building trust and partnership, which in turn help drive the delivery of business value (McKeen and Smith 2012). Fourth, it is essential to conveying the business value of IT (Hunter 2007). And finally, it is critical to understanding the priorities and pressures of the business. Focus group managers spoke of the need for staff who would listen and look for new opportunities to deliver business value. In short, good communication is widely seen as being critical for IT to deliver successful projects, effective performance, and value (Karlsen et al. 2008; Reich and Benbasat 2000; Willcoxson and Chatham 2004).

As a result, improving communication is increasingly recommended as a top priority for IT managers (Burton et al. 2008; Mingay 2005). Several managers stated that they are working on building communication into their annual goals and into their expectations of staff. What is missing, however, is a better understanding of the nature of good business–IT communication and some of the obstacles IT managers face in improving it (Coughlan et al. 2005). Thus, poor communication continues to be the norm in most organizations (Pawlowski and Robey 2004).

WHAT IS "GOOD" COMMUNICATION?

Unfortunately, there is no magic formula for defining and teaching "good" communication since it is a complex concept that has many dimensions. There are, however, some principles that are recognized as important elements of effective communication which can be used as guidelines for those who wish to assess their communication performance.

- *Principle 1: The effectiveness of communication is measured by its outcomes.* Communication is successful when it achieves the outcomes we desire (Gilberg 2006). However, all too often we measure communication by our intentions rather than its outcomes. The problem with that is this: "Communication is in the ear of the beholder," and even the most direct, clear, understandable, and consistent message can therefore get distorted through such filters as politics, culture, and personal points of view. As messages get passed along to others, they get further distorted, much like in the children's game of "Telephone." One study showed that although 97 percent of managers believed their own communication was clear, only 25 percent of the same people believed that the communication they received from their direct superior was clear and effective (Martin 2006). Another study showed that IT managers feel their communication is more effective than business managers feel it is (Willcoxson and Chatham 2004).
- *Principle 2: Communication is social behavior.* Communication not only transmits ideas but also negotiates relationships. Thus, *how* you say what you mean is

just as important as *what* you say (Tannen 1995). This is an especially important principle for IT staff to learn because, as teams become increasingly diverse and virtual, many of the traditional nonverbal signals that we instinctively rely on to provide meaning are lost. A host of factors act as a social subtext to our communication: tone of voice, rate of speed, degree of loudness, and pacing and pausing. These are all culturally learned signals that affect how we evaluate each other as people (Tannen 1995). Gender and culture are key social filters that all of us use. For example, the degree of directness and indirectness in communication has often been a source of significant misunderstandings. Women learn to be more indirect when telling others what to do so as not to be perceived as "bossy"; men are indirect when admitting to fault or weakness. In short, there is no one "right" way to speak, but speakers and listeners need to become more aware of the power of different linguistic styles, and managers must learn to use and take advantage of these styles in different communication situations (Tannen 1995).

- *Principle 3: Shared knowledge improves communication.* It is all too well known that many IT people don't "speak the language of the business." As one manager stated, "Many IT staff think they've 'communicated' by explaining a technology need or a technology decision, instead of ensuring that everyone understands the business implications of what's involved." Studies show that the more IT staff learns about the business, the better communication becomes (Reich and Benbasat 2000). This is true not only because IT people understand business better but also because shared knowledge leads to increased *frequency* of communication and greater *mutual understanding*, both of which lead to more success in implementation, which in turn leads to more communication and improved relationships (Reich and Benbasat 2000). Thus, the creation of shared knowledge can be the beginning of a "virtuous circle" of continuously improving communication (see Figure 5.1).

- *Principle 4: Mature organizations have better communication.* Although communication is a social process, it is also embedded within and fundamental to organizational processes (Coughlan et al. 2005). Organizational maturity plays a significant part in the effectiveness of business–IT communication because strong practices support and reinforce good interpersonal communication. "You can't be a partner unless you're a mature IT organization," explained one manager. The research supports this contention, showing that high-performing IT functions have a strong foundation of communication (Peppard and Ward 1999; Reich and Benbasat 2000). Thus, successful IT organizations embed appropriate communication in their processes and consider this to be a significant component of IT's work (Mingay 2005). This work is even more important in times of organization transformation. "We are quite good about communicating operationally," said a manager, "but we need to improve when talking with our business executives about strategy." Another commented, "we need better skills to move up the 'run, change, innovate' curve, and we need the organizational maturity to do this." The focus group identified some of the areas where improved maturity could help communication: developing business cases; assessing risk; integrating with the "big picture"; and communicating across business silos. In short, although communication is often seen as an individual competency, it should be viewed and managed as an IT functional competency at all levels.

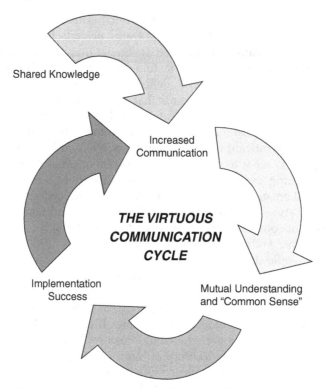

Shared Knowledge

Increased
Communication

*THE VIRTUOUS
COMMUNICATION
CYCLE*

Implementation
Success

Mutual Understanding
and "Common Sense"

FIGURE 5.1   Shared Knowledge Leads to Improved Communication

OBSTACLES TO EFFECTIVE COMMUNICATION

Why is it so difficult to achieve effective business–IT communication? The principles haven't changed much over time, but they have often not been applied, or they have been forgotten or ignored as busy IT managers focus on tight timelines and major deliverables (Mingay 2005). However, in addition to these considerations, some other obstacles to effective communication can hinder or prevent communication from occurring. These include the following:

*   *The changing nature of IT work.*   There is no question that IT work has become more complex over time. Increasingly, IT staff are intermediaries between third-party contract staff, global staff, or external stakeholders and vendors as well as traditional business users. When multiple cultures, different political contexts, diverse time zones, and virtual relationships are added into the mix, communication simply becomes more multifaceted and challenging. Furthermore, organizations are expecting IT to do more for them. Transformation, innovation, or simply bigger and more visible projects all require *more* communication than the norm and therefore more management attention (Mingay 2005). "We must take a broader view of communication," stated an IT manager. "And we need conversations at many levels." Thus, although IT may have adopted communication solutions that meet the needs of the past, these are inadequate for present and future needs.

- *Hiring practices.* "IT organizations can no longer support smart, super-talented, but socially disruptive people who cannot work well with a team or with the business," said one manager. The group concurred that IT skills are changing to become more consultative and collaborative. Yet, frequently their organizations still hire for technology skills, rather than the "softer" skills, such as communication, which are essential for success these days. One study found that there is serious misalignment in hiring between "the skills needed for a job (which heavily emphasize communication and general business skills...) [and] the job requirements that are... advertised (which tend to emphasize formal technical training)" (Cukier 2007).

- *IT and business organization structures.* A few years ago, many IT functions attempted to deal with their communication problems by creating relationship managers. These were skilled IT individuals whose job was to bridge the business and IT organizations and thus act as a communication conduit between the two groups. Unfortunately, relationship managers have become a mixed blessing at best and an obstacle at worst, restricting contact between the two groups and thereby limiting the development of shared knowledge and mutual understanding. "Relationship managers appear to do more to exacerbate rather than ameliorate," found one study (Coughlan et al. 2005). A focus group manager agreed, "You can't partner if your only contact is through a relationship manager." Furthermore, business silos can make communication about enterprise issues extremely challenging for IT staff, who can be expected to play a "knowledge broker" role, not only between IT and business but also between business units (Pawlowski and Robey 2004).

- *Nature and frequency of communication.* It's a bit of a chicken-and-egg situation: More frequent contact with business leads to improved communication, but IT's communication is often so full of jargon, technocentric, and inappropriate that many organizations have sought ways to limit the amount and nature of communication between the two groups. One study found that about one-third of IT staff simply did not speak to the business at all (Basselier and Benbasat 2004). However, some of the focus group stated that, even when they are not restricted, IT staff often have trouble getting business to take the time to sit with them. Researchers have pointed out that it is the sharing of tacit and unstructured knowledge, which takes place in low-risk and informal settings, that contributes most to effective communication and mutual understanding (Basselier and Benbasat 2004; Dunne 2002; Kitzis and Gomolski 2006). Limiting one's focus to formal interactions (e.g., through IT governance processes) has been shown to be the *least* effective way of communicating successfully (Dunne 2002).

- *Attitude.* Finally, IT's attitude can be a huge obstacle to good communication. It was surprising to hear this complaint from so many in the focus group. "Our IT staff think their work is about IT. They don't understand that we're here to deliver business value with technology," one manager stated. One manager described IT staff as "crotchety"; another as "obtuse"; and several stated IT staff are "defensive." It is not surprising that if this is the case, a negative attitude on the part of an IT worker toward his or her work, business, or employer ends up being reflected in communication and how it is perceived (McKeen and Smith 2012). In turn, this can color how the communication is received (Anonymous 2005; Martin 2006).

Unfortunately as well, many IT staff are motivated by the desire to be right rather than the desire to communicate effectively (Gilberg 2006). "We definitely need a 'we' attitude in IT," said a manager, "not an 'us–them' attitude."

Overcoming these obstacles will require a combination of management attention to all dimensions of business–IT communication and the development of critical communication skills in IT staff. The next two sections of this chapter address these issues.

"T-LEVEL" COMMUNICATION SKILLS FOR IT STAFF

Although IT workers' communication skills need upgrading, there is no one-size-fits-all strategy for doing this (Kalin 2006). Nor do lists of communication competencies move us much further forward in clarifying exactly what IT workers are doing wrong and what needs to change in their communication style (see Appendix A for a sample list). It has been suggested that as business becomes more complex, it really needs more T-shaped professionals who are not only deep problem solvers in their home discipline but also capable of interacting with and understanding others from a wide range of disciplines and functional areas (Ding 2008). People possessing these skills are able to shape their knowledge to fit problems and apply synergistic thinking (Leonard-Barton 1995). Unfortunately, most IT organizations encourage I-shaped skills—that is, deep functional expertise. As a result, the individual is driven ever deeper into his or her specialized set of skills (Leonard-Barton 1995).

Developing T-shaped IT staff addresses the concern some in the focus group expressed that emphasizing the development of "soft skills" could come at the expense of the excellent technology skills still needed by the organization. "You don't want your staff becoming disconnected from their technological capabilities," said one. "Connecting the dots" between the group's comments and the research on communication shows that four communication skills form the horizontal bar of the "T" for IT professionals (the vertical one being the professionals' technology skills and knowledge):

1. *Translation.* IT staff typically fail miserably at translating IT issues and concerns into business impacts—as illustrated by the story at the beginning of this chapter. Eliminating jargon is the first step. "Too often our IT population speaks in nano-words and gigabits, instead of using the English language," said a manager. However, translation requires more than this because it requires the ability to understand *how* IT initiatives will affect the business or deliver value to it. To communicate effectively about IT's value, IT managers "must translate IT's operational performance into business performance...and drive home the message that all IT initiatives are business initiatives" (Hunter 2007). It is not often recognized that IT staff are effectively knowledge brokers and that translation is a critical part of their work (Pawlowski and Robey 2004). As a result, bridging and translation skills are still rare in IT, agreed the focus group.

   The work involved in translation can be characterized as a four-step process where IT staff move from the world of technology into the world of business to discuss problems in terms of business impact and possible business solutions and then *back* into IT to translate these solutions into technological reality (see Figure 5.2). "In the end," said a manager, "we must be able to translate what the business knows and wants into actionable IT proposals."

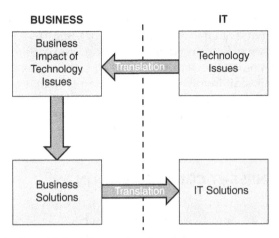

FIGURE 5.2   Communicating with Business Involves Translation

2. *Tailoring.*   IT staff also need to adapt their communication to the needs of their audience. This involves two skills. First, IT workers need to know their audience—understanding *their* needs, *their* agendas, and *their* politics—so that they communicate in ways the business needs and wants to hear (Burton et al. 2008). Second, all IT personnel need to know how to choose communication methods appropriately. For example, bad news is best delivered in face-to-face meetings, not in reports or e-mails (as some in the focus group reported); and presentations to executives are not the place to expound on one's technology expertise (Martin 2006).

3. *Transparency.*   Transparency is a cornerstone of trust in the business–IT relationship (Smith and McKeen 2007), and IT managers should not assume that success speaks for itself. The business needs to see what is being done in IT and what it costs. In fact, it has been suggested that transparency is the key to changing the business's perception of IT's value (Levinson and Pastore 2005). At an individual level, one member of the focus group defined transparency as communication that is "honest, accurate, ethical, and respectful." "We need honesty and openness," stated another. Transparency also means involving the right people in making decisions and recognizing that the goal is to get the communication process flowing both ways (Burton et al. 2008; Dunne 2002). Other ways to promote transparent communication include checking assumptions, clarifying goals, stating intentions up front, and asking for feedback on understanding (Dunne 2002; Gilberg 2006).

4. *Thinking, talking, and listening.*   An important communication skill that is increasingly valued by business is the ability to "think outside the box" and to challenge the status quo, albeit diplomatically and responsibly. Focus group managers suggested that IT staff need to think "horizontally" across the enterprise in order to do what is best for the business. Communicating innovative ideas effectively involves "getting inside the head of the business," they explained. In the future, the ideal IT manager will "think and talk like a business person with a strong background in technology" (Kitzis and Gomolski 2006). Thinking, however, does not mean simply blurting out ideas; it means understanding how and where to speak and how to listen to others. Learning to listen can be a challenge

for IT staff who tend to be impatient with politics and the process of coming to a solution that everyone can live with (Dunne 2002). Similarly, IT staff can underestimate the importance of listening to nonverbal communication or the "noise" of the context in which communication takes place (Anonymous 2005; Coughlan et al. 2005). In short, this skill involves more than simply "talking and waiting to talk" but also incorporates a more sophisticated and nuanced awareness of the *process* of communication, recognizing that *how* one reaches a decision is as important to the success of communication as the actual decision itself.

IMPROVING BUSINESS–IT COMMUNICATION

The focus group managers were the first to admit that much more needs to be done in their own organizations to improve communication between IT and the business at all levels. However, they were also implementing a number of practices that they believed would promote the development of good communication skills among their staff and also as an IT function. Their recommendations included the following:

- *Make the importance of effective communication visible.*   It is well accepted that if you want people to pay attention to something, you need to measure and incentivize for it. Several managers felt that good communication skills should be expected of every IT staff member. "These are now baseline expectations for us," said one. A key way to get staff to pay attention is to incorporate communication skills into performance appraisals. One company makes it clear that specialized "niche" skills are more likely to be outsourced and that those who understand and can work with the business are more likely to have a long-term career in its organization.
- *Work with HR to develop new skills expectations and roles.*   Several firms are incorporating specific communication competencies into staff role descriptions. One is even trying to create jobs that have titles which reflect the types of competencies needed, such as "senior business consultant," "technology relationship manager," and "business technology specialist." Another is trying to make it easier for IT staff to transfer laterally into the business for a period of time.
- *Develop communication skills both formally and informally.*   To support these new expectations, some firms offer formal training in communication skills in areas such as making presentations, communication styles, and negotiations. Incorporating communication skills into personal development plans is one way some managers tailor formal skills development for personal needs. However, the effectiveness of formal training is "mixed," said many managers, and some firms don't offer it at all, or only as part of management development. More informal approaches include mentoring, lunch-and-learn sessions, and self-assessment tools.
- *Increase the nature and frequency of communication.*   Although not an initiative of any of the focus groups, the research is clear that creating a "virtuous communication cycle" starts with creating shared knowledge between the two groups all levels. There are few "quick fixes" to the communication problem, but the importance of regular communication between IT and business at all levels cannot be overemphasized (Reich and Benbasat 2000). Wherever possible, priority should be given to informal communication and social interaction as these are the best ways to build up shared language and understanding (Burton et al.; 2008;

Dunne 2002). These types of interactions are particularly important when face-to-face communication is irregular or impossible (Greenberg et al. 2007). Recognizing this, one company that makes extensive use of global, virtual teams encourages socialization, and even virtual parties, through its social networking technologies.

- *Spend more time on communication.*   Most important, IT leaders at all levels need to spend more time on communication—not only in what and how they communicate personally but, rather, in learning how their staff and organizations communicate. They need to seek out and remove obstacles to communication, coach their staff, become sensitized to their organization's communication processes (both formal and informal), and do whatever it takes to develop a shared understanding and language with the business. Although the initial investment of time may be high, it is certain to pay off in terms of an improved relationship with business and greater perceptions of IT value.

Conclusion

"What we have here is a failure to communicate" is a famous (and sarcastic) movie quote that is nevertheless an extraordinarily accurate description of the business–IT relationship. Although many words and documents may flow between the two groups, it is fair to say that often little true communication is occurring. This has resulted in misunderstandings, dysfunctional behavior, and, above all, a failure to deliver value to the organization. This chapter has examined the difficult and complex challenges facing IT leaders as they attempt to improve their function's communication with the business. It demonstrated that good communication has both social and organizational dimensions, both of which need to be appropriately managed. It also showed that there is a "virtuous circle" of communication, which is associated with improved IT performance and perceptions of IT value. In short, good communication *is* important to the successful implementation of IT in business, and developing it is therefore worth more time and attention than most managers currently pay to it. This chapter has focused on the IT side of the communication equation—since it is usually held to be the culprit in the sometimes nasty war of words that ranges back and forth between the two groups. There is much that can be done within IT to improve communication skills—without losing technology capabilities—but it nevertheless behooves business managers to explore ways in which they can assist IT in doing this. Most important, they can make the time and effort to ensure that IT staff are well educated in how their business works. If they do, business leaders just might find that many of IT's "communication problems" disappear.

References

Anonymous. "The Tone of Communication." *CIO Magazine* (July 8, 2005).

Basselier, G., and I. Benbasat. "Business Competence of Information Technology Professionals: Conceptual Development and Influence on IT–Business Partnerships." *MIS Quarterly* 28, no. 4 (December 2004).

Bittler, R. "Align Enterprise Architecture to the Top 2008 CIO Priorities." Gartner Inc., ID Number: G00159369, September 2, 2008.

Burton, B., D. Weiss, and P. Allega. "Q&A: Architects Must Advocate, Evangelize and Educate." Gartner Inc., ID Number: G00155902, March 11, 2008.

Coughlan, J., M. Lycett, and R. Macredie. "Understanding the Business–IT Relationship." *International Journal of Information Management* 24, no. 4 (2005).

Cukier, W. "Diversity—The Competitive Edge: Implications for the ICT Labour Market." Information and Communications Technology Council, Ottawa, Canada, March 2007.

Day, J. "Strangers on the Train: The Relationship of the IT Department with the Rest of the Business." *Information Technology & People* 20, no. 1 (2007).

Ding, David. "T-Shaped Professionals, T-Shaped Skills, Hybrid Managers." *Coevolving Innovations in Business Organizations and Information Technologies*, September 6, 2008. coevolving.com/blogs/index.php/archive/t-shaped-professionals-t-shaped-skills-hybrid-managers.

Dunne, D. "Q&A with the Wharton School's Richard Shell: Communication." *CIO Magazine* (March 1, 2002).

Gilberg, D. "A CIO's Guide to Communication Basics." *CIO Magazine* (June 14, 2006).

Greenberg, P., R. Greenberg, and Y. Antonucci. "Creating and Sustaining Trust in Virtual Teams." *Business Horizons* 50 (2007).

Hunter, R. "Executive Summary: Business Performance Is the Value of IT." Gartner Inc., ID Number: G00148820, April 1, 2007.

Information and Communications Technology Council (ICTC). *ICT Competency Profiles: A Framework for Developing Tomorrow's ICT Workforce.* Ottawa, Canada: ICTC. www.ictc-ctic.ca, 2009.

Leonard-Barton, D. *Wellsprings of Knowledge: Building and Sustaining the Sources of Innovation.* Boston: Harvard Business School Press, 1995.

Kalin, S. "Tools and Tactics for Communicating IT's Value to the Business." *CIO Magazine* (August 1, 2006).

Karlsen, J., K. Graee, and M. Massaoud. "Building Trust in Project-Stakeholder Relationships." *Baltic Journal of Management* 3, no. 1 (2008).

Kitzis, E., and B. Gomolski. "IT Leaders Must Think Like Business Leaders." Gartner Inc., ID Number: G00143430, October 26, 2006.

Levinson, M., and R. Pastore. "Transparency Helps Align IT with the Business." *CIO Magazine* (June 1, 2005).

Martin, C. "Check What Was Heard, Not What Was Said." *CIO Magazine* (December 28, 2006).

McKeen, J., and H. Smith. *IT Strategy in Action.* Upper Saddle River, NJ: Pearson-Prentice Hall, 2009.

McKeen, J., and H. Smith. *IT Strategy: Issues and Practices.* Upper Saddle River, NJ: Pearson-Prentice Hall, 2012.

Mingay, S. "Effective Communication Between IT Leaders and Stakeholders Must Be Structured and Contextual." Gartner Inc., ID Number: G00130023, 2005.

Pawlowski, S., and D. Robey. "Bridging User Organizations: Knowledge Brokering and the Work of Information Technology Professionals." *MIS Quarterly* 28, no. 4 (December 2004).

Peppard, J., and J. Ward. "Mind the Gap: Diagnosing the Relationship Between the IT Organization and the Rest of the Business." *Journal of Strategic Information Systems* 8, no. 2 (1999).

Reich, B., and I. Benbasat. "Factors That Influence the Social Dimension of Alignment Between Business and Information Technology Objectives." *MIS Quarterly* 24, no. 1 (March 2000).

Smith, H., and McKeen, J. "Managing Perceptions of IS." *Communications of the Association for Information Systems* 20, Article 47 (November 2007): 760–73.

Tannen, D. "The Power of Talk: Who Gets Heard and Why." *Harvard Business Review* (September–October 1995).

Willcoxson, L., and R. Chatham. "Progress in the IT/Business Relationship: A Longitudinal Assessment." *Journal of Information Technology* 19, no. 1 (March 2004).

APPENDIX A

IT Communication Competencies

Level 1
Listens and clearly presents information

- Listens/pays attention actively and objectively (Persons with hearing impairments may lip-read.)
- Presents information and facts in a logical manner, using appropriate phrasing and vocabulary
- Shares information willingly and on a timely basis
- Communicates with others honestly, respectfully, and sensitively
- Recognizes and uses nonverbal communications

Level 2
Fosters two-way communication

- Recalls others' main points and takes them into account in own communication
- Checks own understanding of others' communication (e.g., paraphrases, asks questions)
- Elicits comments or feedback on what has been said
- Maintains continuous, open, and consistent communication with others, considering nonverbal messaging as required

Level 3
Adapts communication

- Tailors communication (e.g., content, style, and medium) to diverse audiences
- Reads cues from diverse listeners to assess when and how to change planned communication approach to effectively deliver message
- Communicates equally effectively with all organizational levels and sells ideas and concepts
- Understands others' complex or underlying needs, motivations, emotions, or concerns and communicates effectively despite the sensitivity of the situation

Level 4
Communicates complex messages

- Communicates complex issues clearly and credibly with widely varied audiences
- Handles difficult on-the-spot questions (e.g., from senior executives, public officials, interest groups, or the media)
- Reads nonverbal communications signs and adapts materials and approach as required
- Overcomes resistance and secures support for ideas or initiatives through high-impact communication

Level 5
Communicates strategically

- Scans the environment for key information and messages to form the development of communication strategies
- Communicates strategically to achieve specific objectives (e.g., considers optimal "messaging" and timing of communication)
- Uses varied communication vehicles and opportunities to promote dialogue and develop shared understanding and consensus

Reproduced by permission of the Information and Communications Technology Council (ICTC) of Canada www.ictc-ctic.ca

CHAPTER

6

Building Better IT Leaders from the Bottom Up[1]

For IT to assume full partnership with the business, it will have to take a leadership role on many vital organizational issues.... This leadership role is not the exclusive prerogative of senior executives—it is the duty of all IT employees. Effective leadership has enormous benefits. To realize these benefits, leadership qualities should be explicitly recognized, reinforced, and rewarded at all levels of the IT organization. This only happens when a concerted effort is made to introduce leadership activities into the very fabric of the IT organization. Leadership is everyone's job.

(McKEEN AND SMITH 2003)

This quote, taken from a book we published several years ago, remains as true today as it was then. But a lot has happened in the interim. Chiefly, in the chaotic business conditions of late, IT leadership development got sidetracked. The dot-com boom and bust soured many companies on the top-line potential of IT and refocused most CIOs on developing strong processes to ensure that IT's bottom line was kept under control (Roberts and Mingay 2004). But the wheel has turned yet again, and there is now renewed emphasis on how IT can help the organization achieve competitive differentiation and top-line growth (Korsten 2011).

The many new challenges facing IT organizations today—achieving business growth goals, enterprise transformation, coping with technical and relationship complexity, facilitating innovation and knowledge development, and managing an increasingly mobile and virtual workforce—call for strong IT leadership. Unfortunately, few IT leadership teams are well equipped for the job (Kaminsky 2012; Mingay et al.

---

[1] This chapter is based on the authors' previously published article, Smith, H. A., and J. D. McKeen. "Building Better IT Leaders: From the Bottom Up." *Communications of the Association for Information Systems* 16, article 38 (December 2005): 785–96. Reproduced by permission of the Association for Information Systems.

2004). Traditional hierarchical structures with command-and-control leadership are not only ineffective, but they also can actually become a barrier to the development of a high-performance IT department (Avolio and Kahai 2003). New communications technologies are enabling new ways of leading and empowering even the most junior staff in new ways. These factors are all bringing senior IT managers around to a new appreciation of the need to build strong IT leaders at all levels of their organization.

This chapter looks first at the increasing importance of leadership in IT and how it is changing over time. Next, it examines the qualities that make a good IT leader. Then it looks at how companies are trying to develop better IT leaders at all levels in their organizations. Finally, it outlines the value proposition for investing in IT leadership development.

THE CHANGING ROLE OF THE IT LEADER

The death of the traditional hierarchical organizational structure and top-down command-and-control leader has been predicted for more than two decades (Bennis and Nanus 1985), but it's dying a slow and painful death. Although much lip service is paid to the need for everyone in IT to be a leader, the fact remains that the traditional style of leadership is still very much in evidence, especially in large IT organizations.

There appear to be at least three reasons for this. First, until now, there has been very little pressure to change. As one manager pointed out, "We've been focusing on centralizing our IT organization in the last few years, and centralized decision making is inconsistent with the philosophy of 'Everybody leads.'" Those IT managers struggling with the complexities engendered by nonstandard equipment, nonintegrated systems, and multiple databases full of overlapping but inconsistent data can be forgiven if this philosophy suggests the "Wild West" days of IT, when everyone did their own thing.

Second, the organizations within which IT operates are largely hierarchical as well. Their managers have grown up with traditional structures and chains of command. They are comfortable with them and are uncomfortable when they see parts of their organization (e.g., IT) behaving and being treated differently by their CEO (Feld and Stoddard 2004). Senior management may, therefore, pressure IT to conform to the ways of the rest of the firm. This situation has recently become exacerbated by new compliance regulations (e.g., Sarbanes–Oxley, privacy legislation) that require hierarchical accountability and severely limit flexibility. Third, many senior executives—even within IT—find it difficult to relinquish control to more junior staff because they know they still have accountability for their results. Keeping a hands-on approach to leadership, they believe, is the only way to ensure work gets done right.

However, in spite of the remarkable tenacity of the hierarchical organization, there are signs that traditional leadership modes in IT are now in retreat, and there is a growing recognition that IT organizations must do a better job of inculcating leadership behaviors in all their staff (Bell and Gerrard 2004; Kaminsky 2012). There are some very practical reasons all IT staff are now expected to act as leaders, regardless of their official job titles:

- *Top-line focus.* CEOs are looking for top-line growth from their organizations (Korsten 2011). New technologies and applications largely drive the enterprise differentiation and transformation efforts that will deliver this growth. Strong IT leadership teams are needed to take on this role in different parts of the organization and at different levels. They can do this effectively only by sharing clear goals and direction, understanding business strategy, and having the requisite "soft" skills to influence business leaders (Roberts and Mingay 2004; Weiss and Adams 2011).

- *Credibility.*   No IT leadership initiatives within business will be accepted unless IT is consistently able to deliver results. This aspect of leadership is often called "management" and is considered somewhat less important than transformational aspects of leadership, but IT's credentials in the latter rest solidly on the former (Bouley 2006; Mingay et al. 2004). No business organization will accept IT leadership in other areas unless it has demonstrated the skills and competencies to consistently deliver on what it says it will do. Furthermore, distinguishing between leadership and management leads to a dysfunctional IT organization. "Managers who don't lead are boring [and] dispiriting, [whereas] leaders who don't manage are distant [and] disconnected" (Mintzberg 2004). We have too often forgotten that top-level leaders are developed over time from among the rank and file, and that is where they learn how to lead.
- *Impact.*   There is no question that individuals within IT have more opportunities to affect an organization, both positively and negatively, than others at similar levels in the business. The focus group felt that this fact alone makes it extremely important that IT staff have much stronger organizational perspectives, decision-making skills, entrepreneurialism, and risk-assessment capabilities at lower levels. Today, because even small decisions in IT can have a major impact on an organization, it is essential that a CIO be confident that his or her most junior staff have the judgment and skills to take appropriate actions.
- *Flexibility.*   Increasingly, IT staff and organizations are expected to be responsive to rapidly changing business needs and help the enterprise compete in a highly competitive environment. This situation requires IT staff to have not only the technical skills required to address a variety of needs, but also the ability to act in the best interests of the organization wherever opportunities arise. "We are no longer order takers in IT," stated one manager. "All our staff are expected to do the right things for our firm, even when it means saying 'no' to senior business management." Similarly, doing the right things involves being proactive. These actions take significant amounts of organizational know-how to pull off—leadership skills that rank-and-file IT staff are not noted for at present.
- *Complexity.*   The responsibilities of IT have grown increasingly complex over the past two decades (Smith and McKeen 2012). Not only is IT expected to be a high-performance organization, it is also expected to offer change and innovation leadership, interact with other organizations to deliver low-cost services, chart a path through ever-growing new technology offerings, and offer content leadership. The complexity of the tasks, relationships, knowledge, and integration now needed in IT means that leadership cannot rest in the hands of one person or even a team. Instead, new ways of instilling needed skills and competencies into all IT staff must be found.
- *New technology.*   Smartphones, collaboration tools, instant messaging, and social media are all changing how leaders work—especially in IT. Increasingly, staff are virtual or mobile and their interactions with their managers are mediated

by technology. At the same time, IT staff have much greater access more quickly to the same information as their managers. New technologies change how information is acquired and disseminated, how communication takes place, and how people are influenced and decisions made. Traditional forms of control are, thus, increasingly ineffective (Avolio and Kahai 2003).

All of these factors are driving the need to push leadership skills and competencies further down in the IT organization. Traditional hierarchies will likely remain in place to define authority and accountability, and *leadership* is likely to become increasingly situational—to be exercised as required by tasks and conditions (Bell and Gerrard 2004; Kaminsky 2012). With the demands on IT projected to be ever greater in the next decade, the need for more professional and sophisticated IT leadership is also greater than ever before (Korsten 2011). In fact, many believe that IT leadership will determine "which [IT] organizations disappear into the back office of utility services and which ones build companywide credibility and drive business growth and ability" (Mingay et al. 2004).

WHAT MAKES A GOOD IT LEADER?

In many ways the qualities that make a good IT leader resemble those that make any other good leader. These can be divided into two general categories:

1. *Personal mastery.*   These qualities embody the collection of behaviors that determine how an individual approaches different work and personal situations. They include a variety of "soft" skills, such as self-knowledge, awareness of individual approaches to work, and other personality traits. Most IT organizations include some form of personal mastery assessment and development as part of their management training programs. Understanding how one relates to others, how they respond to you, and how to adapt personal behaviors appropriately to different situations is a fundamental part of good leadership. One company's internal leadership document states, "Leaders must exercise self-awareness, monitor their impact on others, be receptive to feedback, and adjust to that feedback." "The higher up you get in IT, the greater the need for soft skills," claimed one member. Another noted the positive impact of this type of skills development: "It's quite evident who has been on our management development program by their behaviors." An increasingly important component of this quality for IT staff is personal integrity— that is, the willingness to do what you say you are going to do—both within IT and with external parties such as users and vendors.

2. *Leadership skill mastery.*   These qualities include the general leadership skills expected of all leaders in organizations today, such as motivation, team building, collaboration, communication, risk assessment, problem solving, coaching, and mentoring. These are skills that can be both taught and modeled by current leaders and are a necessary, but not sufficient, component of good IT leadership (Bouley 2006).

However, good IT leaders are required to have a further set of skills that could be collectively called "strategic vision" if they are going to provide the direction and deliver the impact that organizations are expecting from IT. Because this is a "soft skill," there is no firm definition of this quality, but several components that help to develop this quality at all levels in IT can be identified, including the following:

- *Business understanding.*   It should go without saying that for an IT leader to have strategic vision, he or she should have a solid understanding of the organization's current operations and future direction. This is well accepted in IT today, although few IT organizations have formal programs to develop this understanding. Most IT staff are expected to pick it up as they go along, mostly at the functional business process level. This may be adequate at junior levels, but being able to apply strategic vision to a task also involves a much broader understanding of the larger competitive environment, financial management, and marketing. "Our customers are now our end users. With our systems now reaching customers and reaching out horizontally in the organization and beyond, IT staff *all* need a broader and deeper appreciation of business than ever before," said one manager.

- *Organizational understanding.*   A key expectation of strategic vision in IT is enterprise transformation (Korsten 2011; Mingay et al. 2004). This involves more than just generating insights into how technology and processes can be utilized to create new products and services or help the organization work more effectively; it also involves the effective execution of the changes involved. IT professionals have long known that technology must work in combination with people and processes to be effective. This is why they are now expected to be experts in change management (Kaminsky 2012). But being able to drive transformation forward involves a number of additional skills, such as political savvy (to overcome resistance and negative influences), organizational problem solving (to address conflicting stakeholder interests), effective use of governance structures (to ensure proper support for change), and governance design (to work with partners and service providers) (Bell and Gerrard 2004; Kim and Maugorgne 2003; Raskino et al. 2013). Because IT people come from a technical background and their thinking is more analytical, they typically do not have strong skills in this area and need to acquire them.

- *Creating a supportive working environment.*   Most IT work is done in teams. Increasingly, these teams are virtual and include businesspeople, staff from vendor companies, and members from different cultures. Motivating and inspiring one's colleagues to do their best, dealing with relationship problems and conflicts, and making decisions that are consistent with the overall goals of the organization and a particular initiative are the job of every IT staff member. Since much leadership in a matrixed organization such as IT is situational, an IT professional could be a leader one day and a follower the next. Thus, that person must know how to create a work environment that is characterized by trust, empowerment, and accountability. This involves clear communication of objectives, setting the rules of engagement, developing strong relationships (sometimes virtually), and providing support to manage risks and resolve issues (Bell and Gerrard 2004; Kaminsky 2012; Light 2013).

- *Effective use of resources.*   A good IT leader knows how to concentrate scarce resources in places where they will have the biggest payoff for the organization. This means not only making use of processes and tools to stretch out limited staff but also understanding where resources should *not* be used (i.e., saying "no"). In the longer term, using resources wisely may mean using job assignments and

Leadership Styles Vary According to the Degree of Involvement of Team Members

- *Commanding.* "Do what I tell you."
- *Pacesetting.* "Do as I do now."
- *Visionary.* "Come with me."
- *Affiliate.* "People come first."
- *Coaching.* "Try this."
- *Democratic.* "What do you think?"

(after Roberts and Mingay 2004)

budgets to enhance people's capabilities, identifying and developing emergent leaders, and using reward and recognition programs to motivate and encourage staff (Anonymous 2004). Unfortunately, IT staff have often been spread too thinly, underappreciated, and not given time for training. Good IT leaders value their people, run interference for them when necessary, and work to build "bench strength" in their teams and organizations.

- *Flexibility of approach.* A good IT leader knows where and how to exercise leadership. "Skill mastery must be complemented with the ability to know when and where particular behaviors/skills are required and…how they should be deployed" (McKeen and Smith 2003). Even though this is true in all parts of the organization, leadership in IT can be a rapidly shifting target for two reasons. First, IT staff are well-educated, well-informed professionals whose opinions are valuable. "Good IT leaders know when to encourage debate and also when to close it down," said a manager. Second, the business's rapid shifts of priority, the changing competitive and technical environment, and the highly politicized nature of much IT work mean that leaders must constantly adjust their style to suit a dynamic topography of issues and priorities. "There is a well-documented continuum of leadership styles.... The most appropriate style depends on the enterprise style and the business and strategic contexts" (Roberts and Mingay 2004).
- *Ability to gain business attention.* A large component of IT leadership is focused not on the internal IT organization but outward toward all parts of the business. One of the biggest challenges for today's IT leaders is the fact that the focus of their work is more on business value than on technology (Korsten 2011). The ability to motivate business executives, often in more senior positions, lead business transformation, and gain and maintain executive attention is central to establishing and maintaining IT credibility in an organization (Kaminsky 2012; McDonald and Bace 2004). A good IT leader knows how to position his or her contribution in tangible, business terms; how to interact with business leaders; and how to guide and educate them about the realities of IT use. "Bringing value to the business is a very important trend in IT leadership," stated one participant.

IT leaders will need more or fewer of these qualities, depending on the scope and type of their work. Obviously, IT staff responsible for sourcing will need a different mix of these skills than will those with an internal IT focus or those with a business focus.

They will also be more important the higher one moves in the management hierarchy. Nevertheless, these are skills that IT organizations should endeavor to grow in all their staff from the most junior levels. Since these skills take time and practice to develop and are in increasing demand, senior IT managers should put concrete plans in place to ensure that they will be present when needed.

HOW TO BUILD BETTER IT LEADERS

Everyone agrees that fostering leadership skills throughout all levels of IT is important to IT's future effectiveness (Bell and Gerrard 2004; Kaminsky 2012; Mingay et al. 2004; Mintzberg 2004). However, the reality is that leadership development is very hit and miss in most IT organizations. Many formal leadership courses have been cut or scaled back substantially because of cost-control initiatives. When offered, most IT leadership programs limit attendance to managers. Few organizations have articulated a comprehensive program of leadership development that includes other initiatives besides training.

Leadership development in IT is not as simple as sending a few handpicked individuals on a training course. In fact, formal training may be one of the *least* effective (and most expensive) aspects of building better IT leaders (Kesner 2003). Any comprehensive leadership development program has three layers (see Figure 6.1). The first, most important, and probably the most difficult one is an environment within which leaders at all levels can flourish. It is often suggested that leaders, like cream, will naturally rise to the top regardless of the conditions in which they work. The reality is that more and better leaders are created when organizations have a supportive process for developing them that is widely understood. What's needed is "a culture that nurtures talented managers, rather than one that leaves them to struggle through a Darwinian survival game" (Griffin 2003). There is general agreement on what constitutes this type of culture:

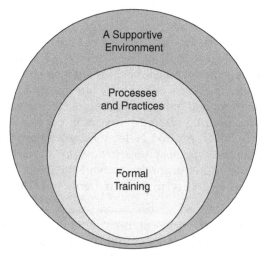

FIGURE 6.1   Effective Leadership Development Involves More then Training

- *Well-articulated and instantiated values.*   Values guide how staff should behave even when their managers aren't around. They provide a basis for sound decision making (IBM 2012; Stewart 2004). "If you're going to push leadership down in the organization, you have to push values down as well," stated one manager. Others noted that senior IT leadership should primarily be about forming and modeling values, not managing tasks. Values are especially important now that staff are more mobile and virtual (Cascio and Shurygailo 2003; IBM 2012). A strong value system is crucial to bringing together and motivating a large, diverse workforce and helping staff act in ways that support the company's brand and values. Unfortunately, although many organizations have values, they are often out of date or not modeled by management (Stewart 2004).

- *A climate of trust.*   Trust that management means what it says about values and leadership development must be established early in any program. Trust is established by setting expectations and delivering results that meet or exceed those expectations. By sending clear messages to staff and exhibiting positive attitudes about staff behavior, senior IT managers will help people feel they can begin to take some risks and initiatives in their work (Cascio and Shurygailo 2003). If people feel their culture is based on fair processes and that they can draw lessons from both good and bad results, they will start to respond with the type of high performance and leadership behaviors that are expected (Kim and Maugorgne 2003). Conversely, senior managers must take steps to weed out counterproductive behaviors, such as poor collaboration, that will undermine this climate (Roberts and Mingay 2004).

- *Empowerment.*   Empowerment thrives in a climate of trust, but leaders need to deliberately encourage it as well. In IT one of the most important ways to do this is to create mechanisms to support staff's making difficult decisions. One company recognized this by explicitly making "We'll support you in doing the right things" a central element in revamping its leadership promise. To make it real and visible, the company established a clear process for junior staff to resolve potential conflicts with users about disagreements on what is "the right thing." Furthermore, they have established committees to help manage the risks involved in IT work, get at the root cause of recurring issues, and protect the promises made to business partners. Such processes, in conjunction with values and trust, create a management system that empowers people and frees them to make appropriate decisions (Stewart 2004). By staying connected with staff as teachers, coaches, champions, and mentors, more senior leaders help more junior staff to take "intelligent risks" and sponsor initiative (Light 2013; Taurel 2000).

- *Clear and frequent communication.*   As with other types of change, one cannot communicate too much about the need to create an environment to foster leadership. "In spite of all we know about communication, it's still one of our biggest leadership gaps," said a participant. Open, two-way communication is the hallmark of modern leadership. Leaders and followers are gradually learning how to effectively use the electronic nervous system that now runs through all organizations (Avolio and Kahai 2003). Use of information technology and multiple channels is now the norm, and redundancy is advisable because of the increased opportunities for miscommunication in the virtual world. Senior executives are using IT to communicate interactively with their most junior staff (Stewart

2004). One company has established an "Ask Phil" e-mail whereby any member of IT can direct questions to the CIO. Leadership is about developing relationships with people. It engages them and helps direct them to a particular goal. Learning to leverage all conduits of communication to build and sustain an array of relationships is, therefore, central to becoming an effective IT leader (Avolio and Kahai 2003).

- *Accountability.* Acceptance of accountability is a key component of leadership. A climate where accountabilities are clear is an important aspect of a leadership development culture (Bell and Gerrard 2004). Natural leaders often first come to senior management's attention because they consistently deliver on what they promise. The concept of accountability is also being extended to include expectations that IT staff will assist the business in achieving its growth goals and that IT will not create technical impediments to implementing business strategies (Mingay et al. 2004). Unfortunately, IT accountability is frequently absent, and this has negatively affected the perceptions of IT leadership in the rest of the organization (Feld and Stoddard 2004). No member of IT should be allowed to abdicate responsibility for delivering results. However, focus group members stressed that in order to create a culture of accountability, IT leaders must also provide the processes, tools, and support to produce successful results.

The second layer of a leadership development program involves building leadership activities into IT's processes and daily work. Well-designed and documented processes for such activities as planning, budgeting, conflict resolution, service delivery, and financial reviews and approvals clearly articulate the individual elements that contribute to leadership in particular situations. They make it easier for more junior staff to carry out these activities and to learn what is expected of them (Bell and Gerrard 2004). They also establish boundaries within which staff can exercise judgment and take risks.

Human resources management practices are a key component of fostering leadership at this level as well. Many companies have begun to document the competencies that they expect staff to exhibit in each job category and level. These typically include leadership as well as technical skills. "It gets harder to do this the higher up the management hierarchy one goes," stated one manager. "At the more senior levels, leadership skills are much more individualized and are more difficult to capture, but we're working on it." Specific training and development strategies work well for each job stream at more junior levels. With more senior positions, development plans should be created for each individual.

Job assignments are one of the most important ways to develop leadership expertise. In fact, some experts suggest that 80 percent of the levers management has at its disposal in this area are related to how a company uses assignments and job postings to influence an individual's experience (Kesner 2003). Job rotations, stretch assignments, and on-the-job coaching and mentoring are all effective ways to build leadership skills. Occasionally, this may entail taking risks and not always appointing the most qualified person for a particular job (Roberts and Mingay 2004). Sometimes, this should involve moving a person out of IT into the business for an assignment. All organizations should have processes in place to identify emergent leaders and take proactive steps to design individualized strategies of coaching and assignments that will fit their unique personalities (Griffin 2003). Succession planning should be a significant part of this process as well. Recruiting leaders from outside is sometimes necessary, but this is a far more risky and expensive way to address succession than growing leaders from within (Roberts and Mingay 2004).

Finally, at the core of any leadership development program is formal training. Commitment to formal leadership training in organizations has been patchy at best. Training can be internally developed or externally purchased. The fastest-growing segment of executive education is customized programs for a particular organization that are specifically tied to business drivers and values (Kesner 2003). In-house programs are best for instilling vision, purpose, values, and priorities. External training is best used for introducing new knowledge, practices, and thinking to leadership.

Because of the time and expense involved, leadership training should be used strategically rather than comprehensively. Often IT resources can be so stretched that finding time for development is the biggest challenge. One company reasserted the importance of training by promising its staff that it would spend its entire annual training budget for the first time! This organization sees training as one tool for helping individuals make their best contributions and achieving success; interestingly, it has found that making it easier to find appropriate courses through the creation of a formal curriculum and streamlining the registration and payment processes has led to a significant uptake in employees' taking advantage of development opportunities.

INVESTING IN LEADERSHIP DEVELOPMENT: ARTICULATING THE VALUE PROPOSITION

Although leadership development is widely espoused, many organizations have reduced their budgets in recent years, and that has hit formal training programs hard. One manager remarked that his staff knew senior management was serious about development when it maintained training budgets while trimming in other areas. However, as mentioned earlier, training is only one facet of a good leadership development program, and doing it right will take executive time and consistent attention, in addition to the costs involved in establishing and following through on necessary communications, procedures, and planning. It is essential to articulate the value proposition for this initiative.

Experts suggest that several elements of value can be achieved by implementing a leadership development program. Using a rubric established by Smith and McKeen (see Chapter 1), these elements include the following:

- *What is the value?* Because different companies and managers have different perceptions of value, it is critical that the value that is to be achieved by a leadership development program be clearly described and agreed on. Some of the value elements that organizations could achieve with leadership development include improved current and future leadership capabilities and bench strength (preventing expensive and risky hires from outside), improved innovation and alignment with business strategy, improved teamwork (both internally and cross-functionally), improved collaboration and knowledge sharing, greater clarity of purpose and appropriate decision making, reduced risk, and a higher-performing IT organization. When these value objectives are understood, it is possible to develop metrics to determine whether or not the program is successful. Having a focus and metrics for a leadership program will ensure that management pays attention to it and that it doesn't get shunted into a corner with the "soft and fuzzy stuff" (Kesner 2003).

- *Who will deliver the value?* Because leadership development is partially HR's responsibility and partially IT's, clarifying which parts of the program should be delivered by which group is important. Similarly, much of the coaching, mentoring, and experiential components will be fulfilled by different managers within IT. It is, therefore, important for senior management to clarify roles and responsibilities for leadership development and ensure they are implemented consistently across the organization. Ideally, senior IT management will retain responsibility for the outer layer of the leadership program—that is, creating a supportive working environment. At one company the senior IT team created several packaged presentations for middle managers to help them articulate their "leadership promises."

- *When will value be realized?* Leadership development should have both long- and short-term benefits. Effective training programs should result in visible behavior changes, as already noted. The initial impacts of a comprehensive leadership initiative should be visible in-house within a year and to business units and vendors within eighteen to twenty-four months (McDonald and Bace 2004). Again, metrics are an essential part of leadership programs because they demonstrate their success and effectiveness. Although there is no causal link between leadership development and improved business results, there should be clear and desirable results achieved (Kesner 2003). Using a "balanced scorecard" approach to track the different types of impacts over time is recommended. This methodology can be used to demonstrate value to IT managers, who may be skeptical, and to HR and senior management. It can also be used to make modifications to the program in areas where it is not working well.

- *How will value be delivered?* This is the question that everyone wants to ask first and that should only be addressed *after* the other questions have been answered. Once it is clear *what* IT wants to accomplish with leadership development, it will be much easier to design an effective program to deliver it.

Conclusion

Leadership development in IT is something that everyone agrees is increasingly important to helping companies achieve their business goals. However, all too often it is a hit-and-miss exercise, depending on management whim and budget availability. It is now clear that senior IT leaders must make leadership development a priority if IT is going to contribute to business strategy and help deliver services in an increasingly competitive environment. To do this, leadership development in IT must start with the most junior IT staff. An effective program involves more than just training. It must include the creation of a supportive work environment and the development of processes that deliver on management's promises. However, no leadership program should be implemented in a vacuum. There should be a clearly articulated proposition outlining its value to the organization and a set of metrics to monitor its effectiveness. Like technology itself, leadership development will be effective only if management takes a comprehensive approach that integrates culture, behavior, processes, *and* training to deliver real business value.

References

Anonymous. "A Guide for Leaders." Presentation to the IT Management Forum, November 2004.

Avolio, B., and S. Kahai. "Adding the 'E' to Leadership: How It May Impact Your Leadership." *Organizational Dynamics* 31, no. 4 (January 2003): 325–38.

Bell, M., and M. Gerrard. "Organizational Chart Is Falling into Irrelevance." Gartner Inc., ID Number: QA-22-2873, July 6, 2004.

Bennis, W. G., and B. Nanus. *Leaders: The Strategies for Taking Charge.* New York: Harper and Row, 1985.

Bouley, J. "Leading versus Managing." *PM Network* 20, no. 2 (2006).

Cascio, W., and S. Shurygailo. "E-leadership and Virtual Teams." *Organizational Dynamics* 31, no. 4 (January 2003): 362–76.

Feld, C., and D. Stoddard. "Getting IT Right." *Harvard Business Review* 82, no. 2 (2004): 72–79.

Griffin, N. "Personalize Your Management Development." *Harvard Business Review* 81, no. 3 (March 2003).

IBM. "CEO Survey 2011: Leading through Connections Executive Summary." Somers, NY: IBM Global Business Services, GBE03486-USEN-00 (May 2012).

Kaminsky, J. "Impact of Non-Technical Leadership Practices on IT Project Success." *Journal of Leadership Studies* 6, no. 1 (May 2012).

Kesner, I. "Leadership Development: Perk or Priority?" *Harvard Business Review* 81, no. 3 (May 2003).

Kim, W., and R. Maugorgne. "Tipping Point Leadership." *Harvard Business Review* 81, no. 4 (April 2003).

Korsten, P. "The Essential CIO." *IBM Institute for Business Value.* Somers, NY: IBM Global Business Services, 2011.

Light, M. "To Discern Potential Mastery, Assess Project Management Leadership and Planning Expertise." Gartner Inc., ID Number: G00258389, November 8, 2013.

McDonald, M., and J. Bace. "Keys to IT Leadership: Credibility, Respect, and Consistency." Gartner Inc., ID Number: TU-22-8013, June 28, 2004.

McKeen, J., and H. Smith. *Making IT Happen: Critical Issues in IT Management.* Chichester, England: John Wiley & Sons, 2003.

Mingay, S., J. Mahoney, M. P. McDonald, and M. Bell. "Redefining the Rules of IT Leadership." Gartner Inc., ID Number: AV-22-9013, July 1, 2004.

Mintzberg, H. "Enough Leadership." *Harvard Business Review* 82, no. 11 (November 2004).

Raskino, M., D. Aron, P. Mecham, and J. Beck. "CEOs and CIOs must Co-Design the C-Suite for Digital Leadership." Gartner Inc., ID Number: G00258536, November 22, 2013.

Roberts, J., and S. Mingay. "Building a More Effective IT Leadership Team." Gartner Inc., ID Number: TU-22-5915, June 28, 2004.

Smith, H. A., and J. D. McKeen. "IT in 2015," Presentation to Center for Information Systems Research (CISR), Massachusetts Institute of Technology, April 2012.

Stewart, T. "Leading Change When Business Is Good: An Interview with Samuel J. Palmisano." *Harvard Business Review* 82, no. 12 (December 2004): 8.

Taurel, S. "On Leadership." Corporate document, Eli Lilly and Co., 2000.

Weiss, J., and S. Adams. "Aspiring and Changing Roles of Technology Leadership: An Exploratory Study." *Engineering Management Journal* 23, no. 3 (September 2011).

MINI CASE

Delivering Business Value with IT at Hefty Hardware[2]

"IT is a pain in the neck," groused Cheryl O'Shea, VP of retail marketing, as she slipped into a seat at the table in the Hefty Hardware executive dining room, next to her colleagues. "It's all technical mumbo-jumbo when they talk to you and I still don't know if they have any idea about what we're trying to accomplish with our Savvy Store program. I keep explaining that we have to improve the customer experience and that we need IT's help to do this, but they keep talking about infrastructure and bandwidth and technical architecture, which is all their internal stuff and doesn't relate to what we're trying to do at all! They have so many processes and reviews that I'm not sure we'll ever get this project off the ground unless we go outside the company."

"You've got that right," agreed Glen Vogel, the COO. "I really like my IT account manager, Jenny Henderson. She sits in on all our strategy meetings and seems to really understand our business, but that's about as far as it goes. By the time we get a project going, my staff are all complaining that the IT people don't even know some of our basic business functions, like how our warehouses operate. It takes so long to deliver any sort of technology to the field, and when it doesn't work the way we want it to, they just shrug and tell us to add it to the list for the next release! Are we really getting value for all of the millions that we pour into IT?"

"Well, I don't think it's as bad as you both seem to believe," added Michelle Wright, the CFO. "My EA sings the praises of the help desk and the new ERP system we put in last year. We can now close the books at month-end in 24 hours. Before that, it took days. And I've seen the benchmarking reports on our computer operations. We are in the top quartile for reliability and cost-effectiveness for all our hardware and systems. I don't think we could get IT any cheaper outside the company."

"You are talking 'apples and oranges' here," said Glen. "On one hand, you're saying that we're getting good, cheap, reliable computer operations and value for the money we're spending here. On the other hand, we don't feel IT is contributing to creating new business value for Hefty. They're really two different things."

"Yes, they are," agreed Cheryl. "I'd even agree with you that they do a pretty good job of keeping our systems functioning and preventing viruses and things. At least we've never lost any data like some of our competitors. But I don't see how they're contributing to executing our business strategy. And surely in this day and age with increased competition, new technologies coming out all over the place, and so many changes in our economy, we should be able to get them to help us be more flexible, not less, and deliver new products and services to our customers quickly!"

---

[2] Smith, H. A., and J. D. McKeen. "Delivering Business Value with IT at Hefty Hardware." #1-L10-1-001, Queen's School of Business, May 2010. Reproduced by permission of Queen's University, School of Business, Kingston, Ontario, Canada.

The conversation moved on then, but Glen was thoughtful as he walked back to his office after lunch. Truthfully, he only ever thought about IT when it affected him and his area. Like his other colleagues, he found most of his communication with the department, Jenny excepted, to be unintelligible, so he delegated it to his subordinates, unless it absolutely couldn't be avoided. But Cheryl was right. IT was becoming increasingly important to how the company did its business. Although Hefty's success was built on its excellent supply chain logistics and the assortment of products in its stores, IT played a huge role in this. And to implement Hefty's new Savvy Store strategy, IT would be critical for ensuring that the products were there when a customer wanted them and that every store associate had the proper information to answer customers' questions.

In Europe, he knew from his travels, IT was front and center in most cutting-edge retail stores. It provided extensive self-service to improve checkout; multichannel access to information inside stores to enable customers to browse an extended product base and better support sales associates assisting customers; and multimedia to engage customers with extended product knowledge. Part of Hefty's new Savvy Store business strategy was to copy some of these initiatives, hoping to become the first retailer in North America to completely integrate multimedia and digital information into each of its 1,000 stores. They'd spent months at the executive committee meetings working out this new strategic thrust—using information and multimedia to improve the customer experience in a variety of ways and to make it consistent in each of their stores. Now, they had to figure out exactly how to execute it, and IT was a key player. The question in Glen's mind now was how could the business and IT work together to deliver on this vision, when IT was essentially operating in its own technical world, which bore very little relationship to the world of business?

Entering his office, with its panoramic view of the downtown core, Glen had an idea. "Hefty's stores operate in a different world than we do at our head office. Wouldn't it be great to take some of our best IT folks out on the road so they could see what it's really like in the field? What seems like a good idea here at corporate doesn't always work out there, and we need to balance our corporate needs with those of our store operations." He remembered going to one of Hefty's smaller stores in Moose River and seeing how its managers had circumvented the company's stringent security protocols by writing their passwords on Post-it notes stuck to the store's only computer terminal.

So, on his next trip to the field he decided he would take Jenny, along with Cheryl and the Marketing IT Relationship Manager, Paul Gutierez, and maybe even invite the CIO, Farzad Mohammed, and a couple of the IT architects. "It would be good for them to see what's actually happening in the stores," he reasoned. "Maybe once they do, it will help them understand what we're trying to accomplish."

A few days later, Glen's e-mailed invitation had Farzad in a quandary. "He wants to take me and some of my top people—including you—on the road two weeks from now," he complained to his chief architect, Sergei Grozny. "Maybe I could spare Jenny to go, since she's Glen's main contact, but we're up to our wazoos in alligators trying to put together our strategic IT architecture so we can support their Savvy Stores initiative and half a dozen more 'top priority' projects. We're supposed to present our IT strategy to the steering committee in three weeks!"

"And I need Paul to work with the architecture team over the next couple of weeks to review our plans and then to work with the master data team to help them outline their information strategy," said Sergei. "If we don't have the infrastructure and integrated information in place there aren't going to be any 'Savvy Stores'! You can't send Paul and my core architects off on some boondoggle for a whole week! They've all seen a Hefty store. It's not like they're going to see anything different."

"You're right," agreed Farzad. "Glen's just going to have to understand that I can't send five of our top people into the field right now. Maybe in six months after we've finished this planning and budget cycle. We've got too much work to do now. I'll send Jenny and maybe that new intern, Joyce Li, who we're thinking of hiring. She could use some exposure to the business, and she's not working on anything critical. I'll e-mail Jenny and get her to set it up with Glen. She's so great with these business guys. I don't know how she does it, but she seems to really get them onside."

Three hours later, Jenny Henderson arrived back from a refreshing noontime workout to find Farzad's request in her priority in-box. "Oh #*!#*@!" she swore. She had a more finely nuanced understanding of the politics involved in this situation, and she was standing on a land mine for sure. Her business contacts had all known about the invitation, and she knew it was more than a simple request. However, Farzad, having been with the company for only eighteen months, might not recognize the olive branch that it represented, nor the problems that it would cause if he turned down the trip or if he sent a very junior staff member in his place. "I have to speak with him about this before I do anything," she concluded, reaching for her jacket.

But just as she swiveled around to go see Farzad, Paul Gutierez appeared in her doorway, looking furious. "Got a moment?" he asked and, not waiting for her answer, plunked himself down in her visitor's chair. Jenny could almost see the steam coming out of his ears, and his face was beet red. Paul was a great colleague, so mentally putting the "pause" button on her own problems, Jenny replied, "Sure, what's up?"

"Well, I just got back from the new technology meeting between marketing and our R&D guys, and it was just terrible!" he moaned. I've been trying to get Cheryl and her group to consider doing some experimentation with cell phone promotions—you know, using that new Japanese bar coding system. There are a million things you can do with mobile these days. So, she asked me to set up a demonstration of the technology and to have the R&D guys explain what it might do. At first, everyone was really excited. They'd read about these things in magazines and wanted to know more. But our guys kept droning on about 3G and 4G technology and different types of connectivity and security and how the data move around and how we have to model and architect everything so it all fits together. They had the business guys so confused we never actually got talking about how the technology might be used for marketing and whether it was a good business idea. After about half an hour, everyone just tuned out. I tried to bring it back to the applications we could develop if we just invested a little in the mobile connectivity infrastructure, but by then we were dead in the water. They wouldn't fund the project because they couldn't see why customers would want to use mobile in our stores when we had perfectly good cash registers and in-store kiosks!"

"I despair!" he said dramatically. "And you know what's going to happen don't you? In a year or so, when everyone else has got mobile apps, they're going to want us to do something for them yesterday, and we're going to have to throw some sort of stopgap technology in place to deal with it, and everyone's going to be complaining that IT isn't helping the business with what it needs!"

Jenny was sympathetic. "Been there, done that, and got the T-shirt," she laughed wryly. "These tech guys are so brilliant, but they can't ever seem to connect what they know to what the business thinks it needs. Sometimes, they're too farsighted and need to just paint the next couple of steps of what could be done, not the 'flying around in jetpacks vision.' And sometimes I think they truly don't understand why the business can't see how these bits and bytes they're talking about translate into something that it can use to make money." She looked at her watch, and Paul got the hint. He stood up. "Thanks for letting me vent," he said. "You're a good listener."

"I hope Farzad is," she thought grimly as she headed down the hall. "Or he's going to be out of here by Thanksgiving." It was a sad truth that CIOs seemed to turn over every two years or so at Hefty. It was almost predictable. A new CEO would come in, and the next thing you knew the CIO would be history. Or the user satisfaction rate would plummet, or there would be a major application crash, or the executives would complain about how much IT cost, or there would be an expensive new system failure. Whatever it was, IT would always get blamed, and the CIO would be gone. "We have some world-class people in IT," she thought, "but everywhere we go in the business, we get a bad rap. And it's not always our fault."

She remembered the recent CIM project to produce a single customer database for all of Hefty's divisions: hardware, clothing, sporting goods, and credit. It had seemed to be a straightforward project with lots of ROI, but the infighting between the client divisions had dragged the project (and the costs) out. No one could agree about whose version of the truth they should use, and the divisions had assigned their most junior people to it and insisted on numerous exceptions, workarounds, and enhancements, all of which had rendered the original business case useless. On top of that, the company had undergone a major restructuring in the middle of it, and a lot of the major players had changed. "It would be a lot easier for us in IT if the business would get its act together about what it wants from IT," she thought. But just as quickly, she recognized that this was probably an unrealistic goal. A more practical one would be to find ways for business and IT to work collaboratively at all levels. "We each hold pieces of the future picture of the business," she mused. "We need to figure out a better way to put them together than simply trying to force them to fit."

Knocking on Farzad's door, she peeked into the window beside it. He seemed lost in thought but smiled when he saw her. "Jenny!" he exclaimed. "I was just thinking about you and the e-mail I sent you. Have you done anything about it yet?" When she shook her head, he gave a sigh of relief. "I was just rethinking my decision about this trip, and I'd like your advice." Jenny gave her own mental sigh and stepped into the office. "I think we have a problem with the business and we need to fix it—fast," she said. "I've got some ideas, and what to do about the trip is just part of them. Can we talk?" Farzad nodded encouragingly and invited her to sit down. "I agree with you, and I'd like to hear what you have to say. We need to do things differently around here, and I think with your help we can. What did you have in mind?"

Discussion Questions

1. Overall, how effective is the partnership between IT and the business at Hefty Hardware? Identify the shortcomings of both IT and the business.
2. Create a plan for how IT and the business can work collaboratively to deliver the Savvy Store program successfully.

MINI CASE

Investing in TUFS[3]

"Why do I keep this around?" Martin Drysdale wondered. "It infuriates me every time I see all that satisfaction over something that is now the bane of my existence."

He looked gloomily at the offending photo, which showed the project team happily "clinking" pop cans and coffee cups in a toast: "Here's to TUFS!" The Technical Underwriting Financial System (TUFS) was the largest single investment in IT ever made by Northern Insurance, and it was going to transform Northern by streamlining the underwriting processes and providing strategic e-business capabilities. The TUFS team had brought the project in on time and on budget, so the party was a thank-you for all of the team's dedicated, hard work. But it was two years ago when the camera captured the happy moment for posterity, and Martin, CIO for Northern, had celebrated with the rest.

"Yeah, right," Martin grimaced as he turned from the photo to the e-mail message on his computer screen, summoning him to a meeting with his boss that morning to discuss TUFS. The system had turned into a nightmare in its first few months of operation. Now his job was on the line. What was supposed to have brought efficiency to the underwriting process and new opportunities for top-line growth had become a major corporate money pit. TUFS was still eating up the vast majority of Northern's IT budget and resources to fix the underwriting errors that kept appearing, and resistance to the system had grown from sniping and grumbling into calls for Martin's head. "No wonder we're not saving any money, though, with senior underwriting managers still insisting on receiving some of their old reports, even though TUFS lets them look up the same information online anytime they want," Martin fumed. The meeting with the CFO was to discuss TUFS and the company's "very significant investment in this system." Feeling like a condemned prisoner on his way to the gallows, Martin grabbed his suit jacket, straightened his tie, and headed up to the seventh-floor executive suite.

An hour later Martin was feeling very well grilled as he was confronted with a long list of the problems with TUFS. The CFO, Melissa Freeman, had done her homework. Before her was a binder full of TUFS documentation, stretching back almost three years from when the project had been first identified. "According to my calculations, Northern has spent almost $4 million on this system, if you include all of the resources dedicated to fixing the problems identified *after* implementation," she noted. "And I have yet to see any cost savings in the underwriting department. Why?"

"It's true that there have been some unanticipated changes to the system that have cost us, but the underwriters have never bought into the system," Martin conceded. "They insist on following their old procedures and then using the system at the last possible moment as a double-check. What can we do if they won't use the system the way it was designed?"

---

[3] Smith, H. A., and J. D. McKeen. "Investing in TUFS." #9-L05-1-003, Queen's School of Business, February 2005. Reproduced by permission of Queen's University, School of Business, Kingston, Ontario, Canada.

"Could there *possibly* be a reason why they don't like the system?" Freeman asked. "It seems to me from looking at these change reports that the system hasn't been meeting our basic underwriting needs."

Martin acknowledged that there had been some problems. "But my guys are technicians, not underwriters. They didn't get much participation from the underwriters in the first place. The underwriting department wouldn't take the time to bring my people up to speed on what they needed and why. As well, we were facing a very tight deadline, which meant that we had to defer some of the functionality we had originally intended to include. That was senior management's decision, and everyone was informed about it when it was made." He added that they were now asking for a TUFS training program and a help desk to handle questions that underwriters might face while using the system!

"A help desk and training program weren't in our original plan," Martin reminded Freeman. "These extras are eating away at the system's benefits." According to the business case prepared by the users, TUFS was supposed to pay for itself over its first two years of operations from savings realized from the underwriting process. The system's problems certainly accounted for some of the extra costs, but the users hadn't made any of the process changes that would help those savings be realized. "They think we can just plug in the system and cost savings will appear like magic. And other parts of the system are going to take time to deliver benefits."

The "other parts" he was referring to were the e-business capabilities that TUFS provided. "If you will recall, this system was approved in the days when we *had* to have e-business or we were going to be dinosaurs. In retrospect, we could have cut back on this functionality more easily and left some of the underwriting functionality in, but who knew?"

"Well, as you know, our financial resources are very limited at present." Freeman leaned forward. "I've been asked to make some recommendations to the executive committee about whether or not we should put more money into this system. TUFS has been our number-one priority for two years now, and quite a few people are saying that enough is enough—that we need to make some major changes around here."

Martin took a deep breath, waiting for the ax to fall. Freeman continued, "What I need to know now from you is this: What went wrong with our TUFS investment, and what can we do to prevent these problems in the future? What do we need to do to realize the benefits that were projected for TUFS? How can we measure these benefits? And how can we best decide how to apportion our IT budget between TUFS and these other projects?"

As he slowly exhaled and felt his pulse resume, Martin nodded. "I've got some ideas. Can I get them to you in writing by the end of the week?"

Discussion Questions

1. What went wrong with the TUFS investment, and what can be done to prevent these problems in the future?
2. What does Northern need to do to realize the benefits that were projected for TUFS?
3. How can Northern measure these benefits?

MINI CASE

IT Planning at ModMeters[4]

Brian Smith, CIO of ModMeters, groaned inwardly as he listened to CEO John Johnson wrapping up his remarks. "So our executive team thinks there are real business opportunities for us in developing these two new strategic thrusts. But before I go to the board for final approval next month, I need to know that our IT, marketing, and sales plans will support us all the way," Johnson concluded.

Brian mentally calculated the impact these new initiatives would have on his organization. He had heard rumors from his boss, the COO, that something big was coming down. He had even been asked his opinion about whether these strategies were technically doable, *theoretically*. But *both* at once? Resources—people, time, and money—were tight, as usual. ModMeters was making a reasonable profit, but the CFO, Stan Abrams, had always kept the lid screwed down tightly on IT spending. Brian had to fight for every dime. How he was going to find the wherewithal to support not one but *two* new strategic initiatives, he didn't know.

The other VPs at this strategy presentation were smiling. Taking ModMeters global from a North American operation seemed to be a logical next step for the company. Its products, metering components of all types, were highly specialized and in great demand from such diverse customers as utility companies, manufacturers, and a host of other industries. Originally founded as Modern Meters, the firm had grown steadily as demand for its metering expertise and components had grown over the past century or so. Today ModMeters was the largest producer of metering components in the world with a full range of both mechanical and, now, digital products. Expanding into meter assembly with plants in Asia and Eastern Europe was a good plan, thought Brian, but he wasn't exactly sure how he was going to get the infrastructure in place to support it. "Many of these countries simply don't have the telecommunications and equipment we are going to need, and the training and new systems we have to put in place are going to be substantial," he said.

But it was the second strategic thrust that was going to give him nightmares, he predicted. How on earth did they expect him to put direct-to-customer sales in place so they could sell "green" electric meters to individual users? His attention was jerked back to the present by a flashy new logo on an easel that the CEO had just unveiled.

"In keeping with our updated strategy, may I present our new name—MM!" Johnson announced portentously.

"Oh, this is just great," thought Brian. "Now I have to go into every single application and every single document this company produces and change our name!"

Because of its age and scientific orientation, ModMeters (as he still preferred to call it) had been in the IT business a long time. Starting back in the early 1960s, the

---

[4] Smith, H. A., and J. D. McKeen. "IT Planning at ModMeters." #1-L05-1-008, Queen's School of Business, September 2005. Reproduced by permission of Queen's University, School of Business, Kingston, Ontario, Canada.

company had gradually automated almost every aspect of its business from finance and accounting to supply chain management. About the only thing it didn't have was a fancy Web site for consumers, although even *that* was about to change. ModMeters currently had systems reflecting just about every era of computers from punch cards to PCs. Unfortunately, the company never seemed to have the resources to invest in reengineering its existing systems. It just layered more systems on top of the others. A diagram of all the interactions among systems looked like a plate of spaghetti. There was *no way* they were going to be able to support two new strategic thrusts with their current budget levels, he thought as he applauded the new design along with the others. "Next week's IT budget meeting is going to be a doozy!"

Sure enough, the following week found them all, except for the CEO, back in the same meeting room, ready to do battle. Holding his fire, Brian waited until all the VPs had presented their essential IT initiatives. In addition to what needed to be done to support the new business strategies, each division had a full laundry list of essentials for maintaining the *current* business of the firm. Even Abrams had gotten into the act this year because of new legislation that gave the firm's outside auditors immense scope to peer into the inner workings of every financial and governance process the organization had.

After listening carefully to each speaker in turn, Brian stood up. "As many of you know, we have always been cautious about how we spend our IT budget. We have been given a budget that is equal to 2 percent of revenues, which seriously limits what we in IT have been able to do for the company. Every year we spend a lot of time paring our project list down to bare bones, and every year we make do with a patchwork of infrastructure investments. We are now at the point where 80 percent of our budget in IT is fixed. Here's how we spend our money." Brian clicked on a PowerPoint presentation showing a multicolored pie chart.

"This large chunk in blue is just about half our budget," he stated. "This is simply the cost of keeping the lights on—running our systems and replacing a bare minimum of equipment. The red chunk is about 30 percent of the pie. This is the stuff we *have* to do—fixing errors, dealing with changes mandated by government and our own industry, and providing essential services like the help desk. How we divide up the remainder of the pie is what this meeting is all about."

Brian clicked to a second slide showing a second pie chart. "As you know, we have typically divided up the remaining IT budget proportionately, according to who has the biggest overall operating budget. This large pink chunk is you, Fred." Brian gestured at Fred Tompkins, head of manufacturing and the most powerful executive in the room. It was his division that made the firm's profit. The pink chunk easily took up more than half of the pie. Tompkins smiled. Brian went on, pointing out the slice that each part of the firm had been allotted in the previous year. "Finally, we come to Harriet and Brenda," he said with a smile. Harriet Simpson and Brenda Barnes were the VPs of human resources and marketing, respectively. Their tiny slivers were barely visible—just a few percent of the total budget.

"This approach to divvying up our IT budget may have served us well over the years"—Brian didn't think it had, but he wasn't going to fight past battles—"however, we all heard what John said last week, and this approach to budgeting doesn't give us *any* room to develop our new strategies *or* cover our new infrastructure or staffing needs. Although we might get a little more money to obtain some new applications and buy some more computers"—Abrams nodded slightly—"it won't get us where we need to go in the future."

A third graph went up on the screen, showing the next five years. "If we don't do something *now* to address our IT challenges, within five years our entire IT budget will be eaten up by just operations and maintenance. In the past we have paid minimal attention to our infrastructure or our information and technology architecture or to reengineering our existing systems and processes." A diagram of the "spaghetti" flashed on. "This is what you're asking me to manage in a cost-effective manner. It isn't pretty. We need a better plan for making our systems more robust and flexible. If we are going to be moving in new directions with this firm, the foundation just isn't there. Stan, you *should* be worried that we won't be able to give our auditors what they ask for. But you should also be worried about our risk exposure if one of these systems fails and about how we are going to integrate two new business ventures into this mess."

Tompkins looked up from his papers. It was clear he wasn't pleased with where this presentation was headed. "Well, I, for one, *need* everything I've asked for on my list," he stated flatly. "You can't expect me to be the cash cow of the organization and not enable me to make the money we need to invest elsewhere."

Brian was conciliatory. "I'm not saying that you don't, Fred. I'm just saying that we've been given a new strategic direction from the top and that some things are going to have to change to enable IT to support the whole enterprise better. For example, until now, we have always prioritized divisional IT projects on the basis of ROI. How should we prioritize these new strategic initiatives? Furthermore, these new ventures will require a *lot* of additional infrastructure, so we need to figure out a way to afford this. And right now our systems don't 'talk' to the ones running in other divisions because they don't use the same terminology. But in the future, if we're going to have systems that won't cost increasing amounts of our budget, we are going to have to simplify and integrate them better."

Tompkins clearly hadn't considered the enterprise's needs at all. He scowled but said nothing. Brian continued, "We are being asked to do some new things in the company. Obviously, John hopes there's going to be a payback, but it may take a while. New strategies don't always bear fruit right away." Now looking at Abrams, he said pointedly, "There's more to IT value than short-term profit. Part of our business strategy is to *make* new markets for our company. That requires investment, not only in equipment and product but also in the underlying processes and information we need to manage and monitor that investment."

Harriet Simpson spoke for the first time. "It's like when we hire someone new in R&D. We hire for quality because we want their ideas and innovation, not just a warm body. I think we need to better understand how we are going to translate our five key corporate objectives into IT projects. Yes, we need to make a profit, but Stan needs to satisfy regulators and Brenda's going to be on the hot seat when we start marketing to individuals. And we haven't even spoken about Ted's needs." As the VP of R&D, Ted Kwok was tasked with keeping one or more steps ahead of the competition. New types of products and customer needs would mean expansion in his area as well.

Abrams cleared his throat. "*All* of you are right. As I see it, we are going to have to keep the cash flowing from Fred's area while we expand. But Brian's got a point. We may be being penny wise and pound foolish if we don't think things through more carefully. We've put a lot of effort into developing this new strategy, and there *will* be some extra money for IT but not enough to do that plus everything all of you want. We need to retrench and regroup *and* move forward at the same time."

There was silence in the room. Abrams had an annoying way of stating the obvious without really helping to move the ball forward. Brian spoke again. "The way I see it, we have to understand two things before we can really make a new budget. First, we need to figure out how each of the IT projects we've got on the table contributes to one of our key corporate objectives. Second, we need to figure out a way to determine the *value* of each to ModMeters so that we can prioritize it. Then I need to incorporate a reasonable amount of IT regeneration so that we can continue to do new projects at all."

Everyone was nodding now. Brian breathed a small sigh of relief. That was step one accomplished. But step two was going to be harder. "We have a month to get back to the board with our assurances that the IT plan can incorporate the new strategies and what we're going to need in terms of extra funds to do this. As I said earlier, this is *not* just a matter of throwing money at the problem. What we need is a *process* for IT planning and budgeting that will serve us well over the next few years. This process will need to accomplish a number of things: It will need to take an *enterprise* perspective on IT. We're all in these new strategies together. It will have to incorporate all types of IT initiatives—our new strategies, the needs of Fred and others for the new IT to operate and improve our existing business, Stan's new auditing needs, and our operations and maintenance needs. In addition, we *must* find some way of allocating some of the budget to fixing the mess we have in IT right now. It must provide a better way to connect new IT work with our corporate objectives. It must help us prioritize projects with different types of value. Finally, it must ensure we have the business *and* IT resources in place to deliver that value."

Looking at each of his colleagues in turn, he asked, "Now how are we going to do this?"

Discussion Question

1. Develop an IT planning process for ModMeters to accomplish the demands as set out above.

IT Governance

Mini Cases

- Building Shared Services at RR Communications
- Enterprise Architecture at Nationstate Insurance
- IT Investment at North American Financial

7

Creating IT Shared Services[1]

A "shared service" is the "provision of a service by one part of an organization where that service had previously been found in more than one part of the organization. Thus the funding and resourcing of the service is shared and the providing department effectively becomes an internal service provider" (Wikipedia 2014). The key idea is "sharing" within an organization. It suggests centralization of resources, uniformity of service, consistent processes for service provisioning, economies of scale, reduced headcount, and enhanced professionalism. As such it has definite appeal for IT organizations, and creating them has been identified as one of the effective habits of successful CIOs (Andriole 2007).

For the business, an IT shared service is also appealing but for a different set of reasons. Although the promise of reducing costs, time, and complexity through reuse and the ability to leverage IT skills and knowledge are attractive, they rank a distant second to the ability to free up resources by transferring responsibility for a noncore activity to another organizational body. Not surprisingly, the successful creation of a shared service is by necessity an exercise in goal alignment (between the business and IT) coupled with a strategy for goal attainment.

A shared services organization constitutes an alternate business model. Therefore, the decision to adopt a shared services model entails a number of critical questions for management, such as What are the key attributes of a good candidate for a shared service? How should a shared service be organized, managed, and governed? What is the relationship between shared services and the parent organization? What can be learned from experience with a shared services model? What theoretical and practical insight is offered by published studies of shared services?

This chapter explores these questions. It begins with a review of the published literature to provide some definitional clarity concerning the shared services model

---

[1] This chapter is based on the authors' previously published article, McKeen, J. D., and H. A. Smith. "Creating IT Shared Services." *Communications of the Association for Information Systems* 29, Article 34 (October 2011): 645–656. Reproduced by permission of the Association for Information Systems.

and to differentiate shared services from other closely related models. The remainder of the chapter focuses on the key management issues surrounding the IT shared services model, including the pros and cons, key organizational factors, and identifying candidate shared services. It concludes with an integrated shared services conceptual model and recommendations for moving toward successful shared services in IT.

IT SHARED SERVICES: AN OVERVIEW

As already noted, the key high-level concepts of a shared service are that a single group within the organization manages the service, the service is offered to any organizational unit in need of the service, and the shared service is a single-source provider. Accenture (2005) similarly defines shared services as "the consolidation of support functions (such as human resources, finance, information technology, and procurement) from several departments into a standalone organizational entity whose only mission is to provide services as efficiently and effectively as possible". While these definitions work in general, they also raise a number of questions. For instance, how does a shared service differ from any other organizational unit that provides service to the organization (e.g., IT or HR)? How does a shared services organization relate to the parent organization? Does a shared service alter customer relationship in significant ways? How is a shared service governed?

Bergeron (2003) offers additional clarity by defining a shared service as a:

> collaborative strategy in which a subset of existing business functions are concentrated into a new, semi-autonomous business unit that has a management structure designed to promote efficiency, value generation, cost savings, and improved service for the internal customers of the parent corporation, like a business competing in the open market.

This definition answers some of the earlier mentioned questions. For instance, it interprets shared services as a "collaborative strategy" that differentiates it from an organizational structure/design exercise. For example, deciding that all customer support functions should report to the COO does not make customer support a shared service.

Bergeron further specifies that the shared service should be a "semiautonomous" business unit with its own management structure, which suggests a different and more "arms-length" relationship with the parent organization—one that allows sufficient management discretion to enable the shared services organization to attain its goals. These goals also differ within this definition with respect to their breadth and scope. Value generation, as a goal, takes the shared services organization well beyond efficiency and cost considerations; the goal of a shared services organization is to "improve the bottom line of the parent corporation, not to create a more efficient, internally streamlined shared business unit *per se*" (Bergeron 2003, p. 5).

Bergeron's definition also differentiates a shared service with respect to its customer orientation. In a shared services model, internal customers are treated as if they were external customers to be won or lost. With this orientation, the shared service competes aggressively for business, places customer satisfaction as a top priority, actively manages customer relationships, collaborates effectively on new business initiatives, markets its services internally, and communicates its performance to the business on the basis of quality, price, and time. This is not the lackadaisical approach to customer service that is typical of organizations that treat their business partners as a captive audience.

Treating internal customers like external customers is a laudable goal but, according to one focus group member, a shared services organization can theoretically go well beyond this. She explained that significant advantages accrue exclusively to an internal provider. For instance, a shared services organization has existing relationships with its internal customers with whom they enjoy unfettered access. Furthermore, they share goals, strategies, and culture. They have common knowledge and are motivated by the same reward systems. Their loyalty is to the same organization and they share financial goals.

External providers, in contrast, lack these advantages but have the benefit of others. Most have credibility beyond internal providers simply because they are competitive in the marketplace. They may also have economies of scale and advanced technology that can be amortized over a broad client base. Moreover, they may have superior skills and knowledge. Her argument was that an effective shared services organization, to the extent that it develops enhanced customer relationships and a competitive market orientation while both facilitating and benefiting from internal customer access, could at least theoretically realize the "best of both worlds". More than just the convergence and streamlining of an organization's functions to ensure that they deliver to the organization the services required of them as effectively and efficiently as possible, the true shared services organization generates value for the parent organization as if (and possibly) competing in the open market.

Shared services are related to, but should not be confused with, more traditional models of delivering IT services (McKeen and Smith 2007). Carefully delineating each of the following points further aids our understanding of shared services.

- A shared service is most easily differentiated from a *decentralized* service delivery model. In the decentralized model, services are provided in various organizational units and managed locally. It is common in highly diversified organizations to find that each business unit has its own IT organization so that the provision of IT services can be tailored to the unique differences existing within each of the strategic business units.

- In contrast, a *centralized* model for IT services brings all resources under a single management structure, adopting virtualization and standardization strategies to increase utilization of key resources and to lower operational costs. There are two primary differences between a centralized model and the shared services model. First, shared services have a customer-centric mind-set (users of the service are viewed as customers, and the shared service is dedicated to providing high-quality, cost-effective, and timely service) and second, shared services are run as an independent business with their own budget and bottom-line accountability. The focus group concluded that a shared service is always centralized but a centralized service is not necessarily a shared service; that is, centralization is a "necessary but insufficient" condition for a shared service.

- The shared services model also differs from *outsourcing* where an external third party is paid to provide a service that was previously internal to the buying organization. While a shared services model is often viewed as a stepping-stone to outsourcing, the focus group suggested that the decision to create a shared service should not be a *de facto* decision to outsource. The relationship between outsourcing and shared services is further explored later.

- A shared services model also differs from a *joint venture* where two or more organizations create a separate, jointly owned, legal, and commercial entity that provides profit to its shareholders/owners. This delivery mechanism is used frequently in various industries such as banking and finance as well as oil and petroleum. As with the outsourcing model, the service is provided by an external agency that owns the profits derived from the provision of the service.

After a lengthy discussion, the focus group reached a consensual understanding of a shared services organization. The members suggested that a true shared service must adhere to the following four principles:

1. Shared services involves more than just centralization or consolidation of similar activities in one location (although this was recognized as an essential part as already noted);
2. Shared services must embrace a customer orientation (i.e., as already mentioned, a shared service cannot behave as a monopolistic provider);
3. Sufficient management discretion and autonomy must exist within the shared services organization to allow freedom to generate the necessary efficiencies to create value for the parent organization; and,
4. Shared services must be run like a business in order to deliver services to internal customers with costs, quality, and timeliness that are competitive with that of external providers.

On this last point, one member of the focus group argued that a shared services provider will never satisfy internal customers unless and until the shared services organization is allowed to offer services to external customers. In his organization, despite spending a considerable amount of money on external consultants to prove that their IT shared services was competitive with that of external providers, the business "just didn't buy it." There seems to be a general unease among business executives about whether or not they are getting real value from their IT investments and this carries over to shared services.

The other major concern for the focus group was the interpretation of "value" as created by the shared services organization. Some members felt that "value" was the demonstration that the shared services unit could provide cost savings to their parent organization. Other members felt that cost savings would be insufficient to justify the creation of a shared services organization, arguing that simply centralizing services would produce similar savings. They felt that a shared services organization should be expected to generate additional value beyond efficiency—offering enhanced quality and/or differentiated services—such that value could be realized in terms of revenue generation. While no resolution emerged, it is clear that the broader interpretation of value aligns better with the group's accepted definition of shared services.

IT SHARED SERVICES: PROS AND CONS

A shared services model for IT has the potential to deliver significant benefits to the organization (Bergeron 2003). From the parent organization's perspective, shared services promise to:

- Reduce costs (due to consolidated operations) and improve service (due to the customer-centric focus)
- Reduce distractions from core competency activities (due to transfer of noncore activities to the shared services organization)
- Potentially create an externally focused profit center (should the shared services decide to offer services beyond the parent organization).

From the perspective of the shared business unit, the shared services model promises:

- Increased efficiencies (due to standardization and uniformity of services)
- Decreased personnel requirements (due to consolidated operations)
- Improved economies of scale (due to the concentration of purchasing, HR, and other specialized functions).

The focus group generally agreed with this list of possible benefits and suggested additional items including:

- Professionalism (due to the adoption of a customer-centric approach in dealing with clients)
- Uniformity of service (due to consistent service provisioning across the enterprise)
- Personnel development (due to focused hiring, training, and skills/knowledge development, all targeted toward service management)
- Control (due to single-sourced service management).

However, there is also a case to be made against shared services (Bergeron 2003). The focus group highlighted the following limitations as being the most relevant for IT shared services:

- Becoming a disruption to the service flow
- Moving work to a central location thereby creating wasteful handoffs, rework, and/or duplication
- Instilling an "us" versus "them" mentality within the provider–consumer relationship
- Lengthening the time it takes to deliver a service.

The focus group also added the following:

- Additional costs associated with management bureaucracy and overhead
- Loss of control experienced by independent business units
- An increased communications burden
- Extraordinary one-time costs at start-up that are reflected within the service offerings.

Thus, while the list of benefits of shared services is long and impressive, the downside risk is equally imposing. The focus group also warned that the list of benefits represents "promised" benefits and that realizing actual benefits is a different matter!

To gain a different perspective of the trade-offs between these pros and cons, members of the focus group were asked to share their actual experiences with IT shared services, highlighting failures as well as successes. Subsequent analysis revealed the following patterns of *failure* (from greatest to least):

- Promised headcount reduction doesn't materialize
- Customer-centric orientation gives way to indifferent service
- Excessive bureaucratization of the service
- Reduced headcount achieved but service levels deteriorate
- Cost efficiencies are realized through "one size fits all" service offerings

The following patterns of *success* were identified (from greatest to least):

- Service improves producing quality, time, and cost advantages
- Service quality and time/cost savings are realized
- Service quality improves but without noticeable savings
- Headcounts are reduced but service levels remain unchanged

The track record of the focus group was equivocal; no organization was celebrating the highest level of success and none was publicly admitting to outright failure. Explaining these differences in outcomes was the next challenge.

IT SHARED SERVICES: KEY ORGANIZATIONAL SUCCESS FACTORS

Interpreting the success of an organizational initiative depends on understanding the goals and objectives of those promoting the initiative. To gain some insight into this aspect of shared services, the focus group was asked what they felt was motivating the current interest in shared services and whether it was being driven primarily from the business or from IT. This allowed us not only to examine the driving factors behind a shared services model but also to highlight any differences between the business and IT perspectives. In the ensuing discussion, a significant gap emerged between the views of the business and the IT organizations with respect to a shared services model—specifically what problems it solved, the benefits it produced, and the unique challenges the adoption of a shared services model presents.

The majority of members felt that the push for shared services was coming from IT and that their IT organizations were sufficiently interested in actively promoting a shared services model. In contrast, two members of the focus group declared that the push within their organizations was definitely coming from the business. One was a large organization whose goal was to become a "globally integrated enterprise" built on shared business services. IT was no exception. Specialized IT services, located globally anywhere that would yield advantage, were offered to all business units within the organization as a shared service. The other organization was undergoing an enterprise-wide initiative to outsource noncore activities and IT had come under the microscope. Here, the focus group member stated that "our management clearly views shared services as a prerequisite for outsourcing."

For organizations where the push for shared services originates within IT, the motivation was clearly cost savings and/or control. According to one manager, "shared services are seen as one way to reduce IT cost and/or complexity and drive IT reuse. This is being driven today out of the IT organization but we understand that our business partners need to be onboard for anything beyond the simplest of IT shared services". Another manager stated that the interest was primarily being driven by her IT organization to achieve the following three key goals:

- To create reusable business functions to enable cost reduction
- To drive agility by means of a set of well-defined horizontal services
- To ultimately create a rationalized and simplified application portfolio.

When asked what problems a shared services model might solve, the focus group cited the following:

- Inconsistent integration patterns that lead to steadily increasing costs for solution maintenance and enhancement
- Building redundant applications using overly specific models because of the lack of a roadmap for sharing functionality
- Lack of integration, which hampers reusability and economies of scale
- Increasing and perhaps unnecessary IT complexity.

The significant gap between how the IT organization approaches shared services as compared to the business is most apparent in the articulation of goals, objectives, and the ultimate justification of a shared services model. This becomes increasingly significant when coupled with the fact that the majority of shared services initiatives are being driven by IT.

In organizations where the driving force for shared services resides within the IT organization, the focus is commonly on that part of a shared service model that addresses IT problems; for example, reducing redundancy, encouraging integration, and rationalizing the application portfolio. Solving these problems, however, only addresses business problems tangentially through reduced costs and streamlined processes and fails outright to attain the goals of customer centricity and enhanced service to the business. The differences between the business vision for shared services and the IT vision, unless aligned, is a recipe for disaster. Based on input from the focus group, we build a conceptual model that bridges this gap by integrating the technical aspects of an IT shared service with the business aspects. But, before we do this, it is necessary to first discuss the key factors that constitute the basis for decision making regarding IT shared services.

IDENTIFYING CANDIDATE SERVICES

An analysis of the existing shared services within the focus group revealed very little in terms of discernible patterns. Some of the shared services were business-oriented services (e.g., payment processing or procurement) while others were IT-oriented (e.g., print management or network services). Some were comprehensive (e.g., application development, disaster recovery) while others were narrowly focused (e.g., credit authorization). Some of the services were deemed "core" while others were "noncore." Other than enterprisewide need, no obvious logical structure emerged from our analysis as a potential decision guideline for nominating shared services.

In general, the focus group felt that the selection criteria of candidate services for the shared services model were best understood by contrasting shared services with outsourcing. They argued that any service being considered for outsourcing could also be a candidate for a shared service subject to three key differences: knowledge reten-tion, control of resources, and value generation. That is, organizations appear to opt for a shared service in preference to outsourcing in order to retain critical knowledge and skills internally, to exercise greater control over these resources, or to capture additional value from the specific service rather than allowing it to accrue to the outsourcing party. The conclusion reached by the focus group was that the processes structured as shared services appear to offer a significant level of either present or future intrinsic value to the parent organization, which makes the organization reluctant to relinquish them to a third party. Services without incremental intrinsic value beyond cost savings are simply outsourced.

AN INTEGRATED MODEL OF IT SHARED SERVICES

One member of the focus group presented his organization's model of a shared service (Figure 7.1). In contrast to the Lacity and Fox (2008) framework, this conceptual model highlights the functional attributes of the business service, the management framework required to monitor and deliver the service, and the common technical infrastructure ser-vices that support it. It suggests that IT shared services is best viewed as interconnected layers of services; that is, business services are built on top of operational processes and common IT infrastructure, each of which deliver "services" but of a different sort. For example, a common business function (e.g., e-forms) is leveraged by multiple busi-ness entities, supported by commonly managed business delivery processes and SLAs,

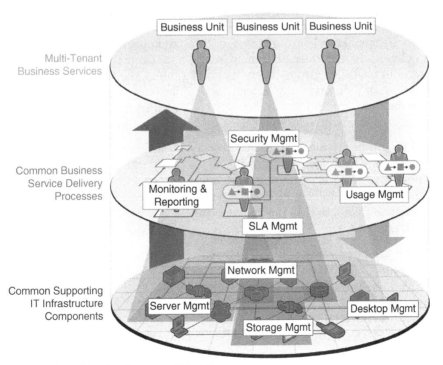

FIGURE 7.1   IT Shared Service Conceptual Model

and runs on common, highly standardized IT infrastructure. This model highlights how successful IT shared services depend on the effective coordination of each of these service layers. Although service delivery processes, such as relationship management and SLA management, are critical for the business, infrastructure processes, such as server and network management, are equally critical for the IT organization. The model also suggests that focusing on a single layer while neglecting key processes existing within other layers is likely to be unsuccessful and lead to the eventual failure of the shared service. In organizations where the shared service is being driven by the IT organization with the goal of reuse, for example, the focus group suggested that the real danger is that attention will be predominantly focused on technical components while neglecting the managerial components (e.g., building effective customer relationships).

RECOMMENDATIONS FOR CREATING EFFECTIVE IT SHARED SERVICES

Based on their experiences, focus group members agreed on four strategies that they believed would contribute to the successful creation of an IT shared services organization.

1. *Create a transparent process for goal alignment.* The group pointed out the importance of establishing a transparent process for articulating common goals. For IT managers, the key attraction of a shared service is typically cost savings and/or reduced complexity. Being able to reduce costs by means of mobilizing reuseable assets standardizing platforms and virtualizing services, and eliminating redundant systems while providing a uniform and consistent level of service is appealing. For business managers, however, the promise of cost savings comes second to the desire for enhanced customer service through improved quality, faster response and delivery, greater financial transparency, and/or improved relationships with IT. Without goal clarity, transparency, and alignment, the shared services organization will champion one set of goals over another, creating animosity between the parent organization and the shared services provider. One manager described the experience in her firm as follows:

> The centralization of the service was soon viewed by the business as a stand-in-line-and-wait for a one-size-fits-all solution...the fact that the business was unable to do an end-run on this delivery process was seen as unresponsive to the urgent and unforeseen demands placed on the business...the elimination of business priorities...no one on the business side wanted to hear about reduced costs of service.

   The focus group suggested that the creation of a shared service need not degrade into a situation of conflicting goals. There is nothing to suggest that improved service and cost reduction cannot be tackled simultaneously. In fact, the centralization process alone should produce sufficient economy of resources to enable enhanced quality of service. The difficulty is typically built in at the outset of the shared service by failing to articulate a set of explicit goals that have acceptance by both the business and IT. Without mutual acceptance and alignment, the shared service can be doomed at inception.

2. *Develop a comprehensive investment model.* Establishing a shared services organization is not a trivial task. In a majority of the cases, the existence of multiple distributed services across the enterprise (perhaps globally) presents formidable barriers to consolidation and coordination. Time differences, cultural differences, and geographical distances all complicate the process. For global enterprises, legal differences also come into play in building an effective shared services organization. The focus group suggested that the larger the organization, the more onerous the task and the longer it takes. But shared services are not just large organization phenomena. As a practical rule, Bergeron (2003) suggests, the "shared services model is a viable option when the savings from reduction in staffing are greater than the added overhead of creating a management structure to run the shared business unit."

Administrative overhead is a significant component of the overall investment in shared services. In addition, there are other substantial one-time costs associated with centralizing operations. These include the relocation of people, consolidation of technology, establishing support roles/activities, developing capabilities/skills, and building communication networks to support centralized operations. Most organizations currently have chargeback mechanisms in place for IT services but, according to the members of the focus group, these are often inadequate for a shared service. For well-defined services (like printing, desktops, or e-forms), the costs are easily identified and associated with the service levels provided. With more complex services (e.g., payroll management, disaster recovery and planning, records management), however, costing of the actual service requires more sophisticated algorithms to apportion costs[2] for services provided. A key component is the ability to establish baselines for existing services. Without these, it is problematic to assess the incremental contribution of a shared service after its implementation.

A shared service investment model needs to account for significant ongoing costs in addition to the start-up costs mentioned earlier. Realistic implementation times range from "at least a year in simple domestic business scenarios involving one or two company locations to five years or more for a major international organization with dozens of locations" (Bergeron 2003). Furthermore, cultural change can present a more formidable challenge than amassing resources (Lacity and Fox 2008). A shared business unit is first and foremost about building relationships between the parent organization and the service unit. Building effective relationships takes time (Smith and McKeen 2010).

The bottom line is that the investment model for the establishment of a shared service requires sophistication, understanding, and a commitment from the business as well as IT to make it work. Depending on the size of the undertaking, even reaching a breakeven point can be protracted. However, to the extent that the investment model is comprehensive and has the backing of senior management, it can withstand the ongoing challenges faced by any significant organizational transformation.

---

[2] Difficulty arises with apportioning actual costs on a service level basis. For instance, actual costs vary over time with usage but business managers prefer to be billed on the basis of standardized rates/costs for specific services.

3. *Redraft the relationship with the business.* The establishment of a shared service necessitates a different type of relationship between the business and the service provider. For instance, with a distributed service, business management has the ability to impose priorities to reflect the demands of the business. These localized priorities, however, rarely survive the transition to a centralized service mechanism. As a result, the business typically experiences feelings of loss of control with the creation of a shared service. The old adage "centralize for control, decentralize for service" applies. Even worse is the potential to develop an "us versus them" mentality, where the business feels a tangible disconnect between the urgent demands of their business and the unresponsiveness of the shared services provider. The risk of this occurring is greatly enhanced in situations lacking goal alignment.

A customer service orientation must therefore be instilled within the shared services organization to guarantee that satisfaction of the client remains the key goal. The need for an effective service orientation, particularly during the early stages of the development, is to counter the risk of the shared service being perceived as a "distant, unresponsive, and overly bureaucratic" provider. Furthermore, this orientation must be conveyed to the parent organization. This involves strengthening internal IT capabilities; changing the mind-set of IT personnel; training and motivation; and commitment from all levels of management (Fonstad and Subramani 2009). To accomplish this, the shared service must build "internal sales and marketing" competencies, which require resources focused on communicating with current and prospective customers (Bergeron 2003).

4. *Make people an integral part of the process.* Lacity and Fox (2008) argue that successful shared services result from effective management of four interrelated change programs: business process redesign (i.e., *what* business processes the shared services organization will perform); sourcing redesign (i.e., *who* performs the business processes); organizational redesign (i.e., *where* business processes will be performed); and technology enablement (i.e., technologies used to implement and coordinate the work). The focus group agreed with the need to manage each of these programs effectively but was particularly enamored with the notion that each of these programs was appropriately viewed as a "change" process. Their experience suggested that the difference between success and failure of an IT shared services initiative was frequently the result of the effectiveness of the change process itself.

The creation of a shared services organization requires significant transformation within the IT organization and directly impacts IT staff. As with outsourcing, dislocations are inevitable. As decentralized staff become centralized, reductions are expected, reporting relationships change, new skills are required, existing skills become redundant, and the overall relationship with the business becomes much more immediate and business-like with the focus on the bottom line. None of this happens automatically. Communications and marketing strategies take on new importance. Customer service is no longer a "take it or leave it" phenomenon. Training is essential. New metrics and key performance indicators become necessary. Service level agreements must be articulated and managed. Together, this represents enormous change for IT. Bergeron (2003) suggests, "The pace of cultural change, not the availability of resources or technology, generally gates the limitation."

The focus group did not provide specific suggestions for organizations to follow but stressed a realization of the enormity and significance of the organizational change that accompanied the adoption of a shared services model and a call to make the "people part" of a shared services implementation the top priority. In short, a customer service orientation is built over time and through the conscious and deliberate attention of all employees. It thus needs to be planned as thoroughly as any other major organizational transformation initiative.

Conclusion

In recent years, the interest in adopting a shared services model for IT has grown substantially. This interest has been driven by the desire of business for a more customer-centric and responsive IT organization and by IT organizations pursuing centralization and standardization strategies. When successful, an IT shared services model can satisfy both goals but key challenges arise during the development and implementation of the shared service. By bringing together a number of senior IT managers with experience in building shared service organizations,

this chapter has clarified what a shared service is and what it is not, identified different forms of success and failure, articulated an integrated conceptual model, and provided a number of suggestions to improve the chances of successful implementation. For those charged with developing IT shared services as well as those investigating this emerging organizational form, this chapter provides insight and understanding for achieving successful shared services and ultimately the goal of improving overall organizational performance.

References

Accenture. "Driving High Performance in Government: Maximizing the Value of Public-Sector Shared Services." http://www.accenture.com/SiteCollectionDocuments/PDF/Accenture_Driving_High_Performance_in_Government_Maximizing_the_Value_of_Public_Sector_Shared_Services.pdf, 2005.

Andriole, S. "The 7 Habits of Highly Effective Technology Leaders." *Communications of the ACM* 50, no. 3 (March 2007): 67–72.

Bergeron, Brian. *Essentials of Shared Services.* Hoboken, NJ: John Wiley & Sons Inc., 2003.

Fonstad, N., and M. Subramani. "Building Enterprise Alignment: A Case Study." *MIS Quarterly Executive* 8, no. 1 (March 2009): 31–41.

Lacity, M., and J. Fox. "Creating Global Shared Services: Lessons from Reuters." *MIS Quarterly Executive* 7, no. 1 (March 2008): 17–32.

McKeen, J. D., and H. A. Smith. "Delivering IT Functions: A Decision Framework." *Communications of the Association of Information Systems* 19, Article 35 (June 2007): 725–39.

Smith, H. A. and J. D. McKeen. "Building a Strong Relationship with the Business." *Communications of the Association of Information Systems* 26, Article 19 (April 2010): 429–40.

Wikipedia. http://en.wikipedia.org/wiki/Shared_services, May 2014.

8 A Management Framework for IT Sourcing[1]

E very five years starting in 1995, the focus group has taken stock of the responsibilities for which IT is held accountable (Smith and McKeen 2006; Smith and McKeen 2012). To no one's surprise, the list of IT responsibilities has grown dramatically. To the standard list of "operations management," "systems development," and "network management" have now been added responsibilities such as business transformation, regulatory compliance, enterprise and security architecture management, information and content management, mobile and social computing, business intelligence and analytics, risk management, innovation, demand management, and business continuity management (Smith and McKeen 2012). Never before has IT management been challenged to assume such diversity of responsibility and to deliver on so many different fronts. As a result, IT managers have begun to critically examine how they source and deliver their various services to the organization.

In the past, organizations met additional demands for IT functionality by simply adding more staff. Today, increasing permanent IT staff is less viable than in the past and this has led IT organizations to explore other options. Fortunately, several sourcing alternatives are at hand for delivering IT functionality. Software can be purchased or rented from the cloud, customized systems can be developed by third parties, whole business processes can be outsourced, technical expertise can be contracted, data center facilities can be managed, networking solutions (e.g., data, voice) are obtainable, data storage is available on demand, and companies will manage your desktop environment as well as all of your support/maintenance functions. Faced with this smorgasbord of sourcing options, organizations are experimenting as never before. As with other forms of experimentation, however, there have been failures as well as successes, and most decisions have been made on a "one-off" basis. What is still lacking is a unified decision framework to guide IT managers through this maze of sourcing options.

---

[1] This chapter is based on the authors' previously published article, McKeen, J. D., and H. A. Smith. "Delivering IT Functions: A Decision Framework." *Communications of the Association for Information Systems* 19, no. 35 (June 2007): 725–39. Reproduced by permission of the Association for Information Systems.

This chapter explores how organizations are choosing to source and deliver IT "functions." The first section defines what we mean by an IT function and proposes a maturity model for IT functions. Following this, we take a conceptual look at IT sourcing options, and then we analyze actual company experiences with four different IT sourcing options—(1) in-house, (2) insource, (3) outsource,[2] and (4) partnership—in order to contrast theory with practice. The penultimate section of the chapter presents a framework for guiding sourcing decisions stemming from the shared experiences and insights of the managers in the focus group. The final section presents strategies for the effective management of IT sourcing.

A MATURITY MODEL FOR IT FUNCTIONS

Smith and McKeen (2012) list the overall responsibilities for which IT is held accountable. IT functions, in contrast, represent the specific activities that are delivered by IT in the fulfillment of its responsibilities. For instance, IT is held *responsible* for delivering process automation, which it may satisfy by providing the following IT *functions* to the organization: project management, architecture planning, business analysis, system development, quality assurance and testing, and infrastructure support. Although an IT department provides myriad functions to its parent organization, a compendium of the key roles was created by amalgamating the lists provided by the members of the focus group (see Table 8.1).[3] This is meant to be representative, not comprehensive, to demonstrate how IT functions can form the basis of a sourcing decision framework.

Participants pointed out that not all IT functions are at the same stage of development and maturity, a fact that has ramifications for how these functions could be sourced. And although some functions are well defined, common to most companies, and commodity-like, others are unique, nonstandardized, and not easily shared. There was general agreement, however, that a maturity model for IT functions has five stages: (1) unique, (2) common, (3) standardized, (4) commoditized, and (5) utility.

1. ***Unique.*** A unique IT function is one that provides strategic (perhaps even proprietary) advantage and benefit. These IT functions seek to differentiate the organization in the marketplace. They are commonly, but not necessarily, delivered by internal IT staff due to the strategic aspect of the function being provided. Alternately, the function may be provided either by "boutique" firms that create special-purpose applications or by firms with in-depth industry experience that cannot be matched by internal IT staff (or even the internal business managers). Examples of unique IT functions might be business analysis, application integration, or knowledge-enabling business processes. Such functions depend on familiarity with the organization's internal systems combined with an in-depth knowledge of the business.

2. ***Common.*** This type of IT function caters to common (i.e., universal) organizational needs. Such a function has little ability to differentiate the business, but it

---

[2] We use the term "outsource" inclusively to reflect specific options such as "off-shoring" and "near-shoring."

[3] We actually prefer the term *service* to *function* but we chose the term *function* to avoid confusion with the usage of *service* as in service-oriented architecture (SOA).

TABLE 8.1	List of IT Functions
IT Function	**Description**
Business analysis	Liaison between IT and the business to align IT planning, match technology to business needs, and forecast future business directions
Systems analysis	Elicits business requirements, designs process flow, outlines document management, and creates design specifications for developers
Strategy and planning	Project prioritization, budgeting, financial planning/accountability, strategy development, policy development, and portfolio analysis
Data management	Transactional data (e.g., invoicing, shipping), customer data (e.g., customer relationship management [CRM]), records management, knowledge management, and business intelligence
Project management	Managing the resources (e.g., money, people, time, and equipment) necessary to bring a project to fruition in compliance with requirements
Architecture	Establishing the interaction of all system components (e.g., hardware, software, and networking), enterprise compliance with specifications and standards
Application development	Designing, writing, documenting, and unit testing required code to enact specific functionality in compliance with a design specification
Quality assurance and testing	Testing all components of an application prior to production to ensure it is functioning correctly and meets regulatory and audit standards
Networking	Managing all networking components (e.g., hubs and routers) to handle all forms of organizational communication (e.g., data, voice, and streaming video)
Operating systems and services	Operating systems for all hardware platforms and other devices (e.g., handhelds), upgrades, maintenance, and enhancements
Application support	Provides enhancements, updates, and maintenance for application systems plus help and assistance for application users
Data center operations	Manages all operations of the production data center and data storage environment, including backup, DRP, security and access, and availability
Application software	Manages all major applications (e.g., purchased or developed) to ensure viability of functionality and upgradability with a special emphasis on legacy systems
Hardware	Data servers, power supplies, desktops, laptops, Blackberries, telephones, and special equipment (e.g., POS, badge readers, and RFID tags)

provides a necessary, perhaps critical, component (e.g., financial systems and HR). Providers capitalize on commonality of function and are motivated to provide functions (e.g., customer relationship management [CRM], quality assurance, and content management) to maximize market applicability. Most print operations are now common functions, for instance. Although they differ from firm to firm, they are required by most firms but are not considered to provide any competitive advantage.

3. *Standardized.*   Standardized IT functions not only provide common tasks/activities but also adhere to a set of standards developed and governed by external agencies. Although multiple, perhaps competing, standards may exist, the attributes of such functions are well articulated, and as a result these functions enjoy wide applicability due to their standardization. Providers of such functionality (e.g., billing/payment functions, check processing, forms management, facilities management, and disaster recovery planning) seek opportunities beyond common functions by promoting (i.e., developing, proposing, and/or adopting) standards to enhance the interoperability of their functional offerings.

4. *Commoditized.*   These functions are considered commodities similar to oil and gas. Once attributes are stipulated, functions are interchangeable and indistinguishable (i.e., any barrel of oil will suffice). Furthermore, there may be many providers of the function. A good example is application service providers (ASPs) who deliver standard applications developed by third-party vendors to client firms without customization. Other commodity functions include network services, server farms, storage capacity, backup services, and universal power supply (UPS). What really distinguishes a commodity is the realization that the "risks imposed by its absence outweigh the burdens of maintaining its availability" (Marquis 2006).

5. *Utility.*   A utility function is a commodity (such as electricity) delivered by a centralized and consolidated source.[4] This source typically consists of an amalgam of suppliers operating within an integrated network capable of generating sufficient resource to fulfill continuous on-demand requests. *Private* utilities operate in competition with other providers, whereas *public* utilities tend to be single providers overseen by regulatory agencies that govern supply, pricing, and size. Examples of utilities include Internet service providers (ISPs) as well as other telecommunication services (e.g., bandwidth on demand, and cloud services).

These stages represent an evolutionary progression (or maturation) in IT functionality. The logic is straightforward: successful, unique functions are copied by other organizations and soon become common; commonality among IT functions paves the way for standardization; standardized functions are easily and effectively transacted as commodities; and finally, commoditized functions can be provided by utilities should an attractive business model exist. The group interpreted this progression as an ongoing process—that is, individual functions would be expected to advance through

---

[4] This concept has generated a significant amount of interest (Hagel and Brown 2001; Rappa 2004; Ross and Westerman 2004). Carr (2005), for example, speculates that not only is the utility computing model inevitable, but it will also dramatically change the nature of the whole computing industry in a fashion similar to electrical generation of the previous century.

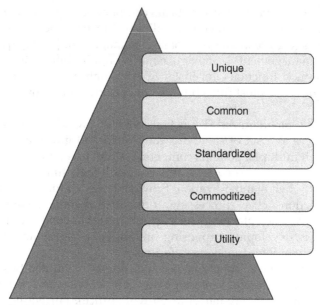

FIGURE 8.1   Maturity Model for IT Function Delivery

the sequence of stages as they matured. Furthermore, the continual discovery of new and unique IT functions, which are required by organizations to differentiate themselves and create strategic advantage in the marketplace, would guarantee the continuation of the whole evolutionary progression as depicted in Figure 8.1.

Using this maturity model, we then classified the IT functions listed in Table 8.1 according to their attained maturity stage. The results are represented in Figure 8.2. The differences among various IT functions are quite remarkable. Hardware (including servers and storage) was considered to reside at the commodity end of the maturity model due to its degree of standardization and interoperability, whereas business analysis remains a relatively unique IT function that differs considerably from organization to organization. Application software is more varied; some application softwares are commodity-like, whereas other applications are highly unique to individual firms. The remaining IT functions vary similarly with respect to the maturity of their development and adoption industrywide.

The impetus for this discussion of function maturity was an implicit assumption that mature functions would be likely candidates for external sourcing, and unique functions would be likely candidates for internal sourcing. For instance, functions such as hardware, networks, common applications, and data center operations would be natural candidates for external provisioning, and IT planning, business and systems analysis, project management, and application development would be more likely provided by internal IT staff. The group agreed that these were indeed *general* trends. What proved to be somewhat of a surprise, though, was the degree that this generalization did not appear to hold as members of the focus group repeatedly shared examples of their specific sourcing activities that ran counter to this generalization; for example, they insourced commoditized functions and outsourced unique functions. We will return to this point later.

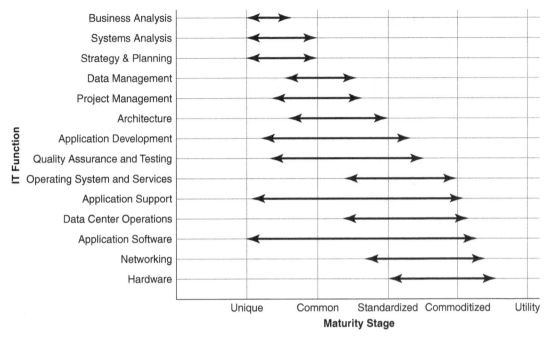

FIGURE 8.2   IT Functions Ranked by Maturity Stage

IT SOURCING OPTIONS: THEORY VERSUS PRACTICE

Building on classifications developed by Lacity and Willcocks (2000), we considered four different sourcing options for IT functions:

1. *In-house.*   Permanent IT staff provide the IT function.
2. *Insource.*   IT personnel are brought into the organization to supplement the existing permanent IT staff to provide the IT function.
3. *Outsource.*   IT functions are provided by an external organization using its own staff and resources.
4. *Partnership.*   A partnership is formed with another organization to provide IT functions. The partnership could take the form of a joint venture or involve the creation of a separate company.

Figure 8.3 depicts the group's assessment of what the relationship between specific IT functions and sourcing options *should be* by superimposing the four IT sourcing options on the maturity grid. From this model it is clear that *in-house* staff should be assigned tasks that are in the unique–common maturity stages. Asking in-house staff to provide commodity-like functions would not be leveraging their unique knowledge of the business; because of their versatility, they can provide any IT function. As a result, their area of application was seen as being on the left of Figure 8.3 from top to bottom. *Insourcing* is basically a strategy of leveraging the in-house IT staff on a temporary basis. As such, contract staff should normally be assigned to work with permanent IT staff on a subset of the full range of tasks provided internally. *Partnerships* tend to exist in the lower part of Figure 8.3 because the truly unique tasks of business/systems analysis,

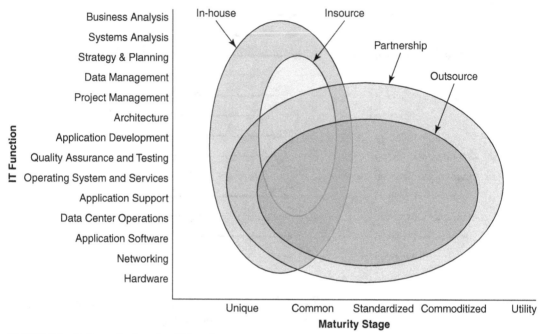

FIGURE 8.3 Delivery Options for IT Functions

planning, data management, and project management tend to be limited to a single organization and its strategy. Instead, partnerships were envisioned to focus on functions such as hardware, applications, software, and networking. Such partnerships could form regardless of maturity stage, which explains the left-to-right positioning of this IT sourcing option in Figure 8.3 Finally, *outsourcing* should comprise a subset of partnerships much the same as insourcing comprises a subset of in-house functions. The reason is due to differences in governance; outsourcing arrangements are well articulated and governed by service-level agreements (SLAs), and partnerships are typically governed by memoranda of understanding (MOU). If an organization is interested in a more flexible, innovative, and open-ended initiative, it would be better advised to seek a joint venture with another firm. Hence, partnerships were seen to have broader potential as a sourcing option for IT functions.

Figure 8.3 represents the focus group's "generally accepted wisdom" regarding IT function sourcing. Unfortunately, due to the extent of the overlap of functions provided by the different sourcing options, Figure 8.3 provides limited guidance for managers tasked with choosing sourcing options for specific IT functions. In order to gain more insight into decision behavior in practice, the group was asked to share recent examples of IT functions they were currently delivering by each of the four sourcing options. In addition, they were asked to describe the justification criteria that their firm used in making these decisions as well as the benefits they felt they had realized.[5] These examples were analyzed and the results used to create Table 8.2.

---

[5] With few exceptions (e.g., Bandula and Hirschheim 2009), relatively little research has focused on understanding the reasons for (and justification of) IT sourcing decisions within organizational settings.

TABLE 8.2	Examples of Usage of the Four Delivery Options		
Delivery Option	Examples	Justification	Realized Benefits
In-house	• Strategic system development • Legacy system support • New system development • Help desk/desktop support • Information/document management • Application support • Intranet development • Technology support • Business systems analysis • Project management • Security services (change control) • Business intelligence and reporting	• Need to have complete control over the intellectual property • Need it *now* • Work is strategic • Skunkworks • Internal consulting to the business	• High-speed delivery • Leverage internal business and system knowledge • Ownership of intellectual property • Security of data • Protection and preservation of critical knowledge • Focus on core systems that are considered key assets
Insource	• Portal development • Specialized system (e.g., POS, CRM) development • Data warehouse development • Database development • Intranet development • Corporate systems development • Contract staff to provide key skills • Both local contractors and offshore company on retainer	• Need to have control over project delivery • Exposing intellectual property not an issue • Recurring program delivery such as ERP and CRM	• Highly flexible (e.g., personnel, engagement, and assignments) • Best of multiple vendors used • No need to expand internal IT staff • Staff easily meshed with existing teams • Semipermanent personnel if desired • Quick access to specific skill sets • Manage people as opposed to contracts • Evens out staffing "hills and valleys"

(continued)

| TABLE 8.2 | Continued |

Delivery Option	Examples	Justification	Realized Benefits
Outsource	• Infrastructure for new product • Business processes (e.g., billing, payroll) • Operations • Help desk • Field service support • Network management • Technology infrastructure (servers, storage, communications) • Web site development and hosting • Technology rollout • New stand-alone project delivery	• The work is not "point of differentiation." • Company does not have the competency in-house. • Deliverable is well understood, and SLAs are articulated to the satisfaction of both parties. • The outsourcer is "world class."	• Speed to market for specific products/ systems • Acquire instant expertise as vendors are experts (often world class) • Business risk transferred to supplier • Outsourcer provides more "levers" for value creation (e.g., size, scope) • Lower cost than in-house
Partnership	• Common service (e.g., statement processing and payment services) • Emergency backup and support • Shared infrastructure • Special application development (e.g., critical knowledge requirement)	• Realize alignment on a benefit-sharing model • Enable collaborating partners to compete with others outside the partnership	• Future business growth and/or opportunities that arose from the partnership • Benefits not limited to a specific product or system deliverable • Decreased learning time and shared learning costs with partners

Perhaps the most surprising result based on the examples in column 2 of Table 8.2 is the lack of evidence of a relationship between IT functions and sourcing options. Such a relationship, were it to exist, would provide a natural basis for a decision framework. However, not only does it not exist, but there is also considerable evidence to the contrary (i.e., the observation that identical IT functions are being delivered by all four sourcing options). As a case in point, various types of systems development as well as application support/maintenance functions are provided by all four sourcing options. Earlier we noted the generally accepted wisdom did not appear to hold up that commodity functions are ready candidates for outsourcing, whereas unique functions are not. The data in Table 8.2 further corroborate this observation. Given this, one wonders what the operative criteria for choosing sourcing options are if not the type (or maturity) of the IT function.

THE "REAL" DECISION CRITERIA

To explore this issue, participants were asked to review a recent business case and to share the *actual* criteria that were used to select the specific IT sourcing option. Column 3 in Table 8.2 illustrates the justifications used for each of the four sourcing options. This paints a much clearer picture of the decision criteria being used by IT managers when selecting sourcing options.[6]

Decision Criterion #1: Flexibility

As a decision criterion, flexibility has two dimensions: *response time* (i.e., how quickly IT functionality can be delivered) and *capability* (i.e., the range of IT functionality). In-house staff rate high on both dimensions. Insourcing, as a complement to permanent IT staff, is also a highly flexible sourcing option. Although outsourcing can *theoretically* provide just about anything, as a sourcing option it exhibits less flexibility because of the need to locate an outsourcer who can provide the specific function, negotiate a contract, and monitor progress. Finally, partnerships enjoy considerable flexibility regarding capability but much less in terms of response time.[7] Within a partnership, the goal is to create value for the members of the partnership beyond what can be created by any single organization. How this value is created is up to the partnership, and as long as the parties agree, virtually anything is possible.

Decision Criterion #2: Control

This decision criterion also has two dimensions: *delivery* (i.e., ensuring that the delivered IT function complies with requirements) and *security* (i.e., protecting intellectual assets). Because they rank high on both dimensions of control, in-house and insourcing options are favored in cases where the work is proprietary, strategic, "below the radar" (i.e., skunkworks), or needed immediately (see Table 8.2). Outsourcing is the preferred delivery option when the function is not considered "a point of differentiation" and the deliverable is well understood and easily governed by means of a service-level agreement. Partnerships are designed to be self-controlling by the membership, and as previously observed, the functions provided by partnerships tend to be more open ended than those provided by other options.

In Table 8.2, column 4 presents the benefits of each sourcing option. For the most part, this list is closely aligned with the list of justifications found in column 3. As such, it reinforces the existence of flexibility and control as key decision criteria. But in addition, a third key factor appears: *knowledge enablement*. Mentioned only tangentially within the list of justifications (e.g., "competence," "internal consulting," and "world class"), it is much more evident within the list of realized benefits (e.g., "leveraging internal business and system knowledge," "preservation of critical knowledge," "quick access to specific skill sets," "decreased learning time," and "sharing the learning costs with

---

[6] This analysis excludes other factors such a political, institutional, or environmental which can sometimes override normal organizational factors in IT sourcing decisions (Mola and Carugati 2012).

[7] Response time within a partnership depends on two interdependent conditions holding: (1) a partnership must already exist, and (2) all partners must be committed to the same delivery timeline.

partners"). Marquis (2006) argues that "what is not easily replicable, and thus is potentially strategic, is an organization's intelligence and capability. By combining skills and resources in unique and enduring ways to grow core competencies, firms may succeed in establishing competitive advantage."

Decision Criterion #3: Knowledge Enhancement

Behind many sourcing decisions is the need to either capture knowledge or retain it. One firm cited the example of developing a new business product. It "normally" would have been outsourced, but it was intentionally developed by in-house staff augmented by key contract personnel. The reason was to transfer knowledge of this new business product to internal IT personnel as well as to business personnel (who were also unfamiliar with this type of business offering). At another firm, the decision was made to insource key expertise "not to *do* the work, but to train internal staff *how* to do the work." The manager stated, "It would have been more logical and far cheaper to outsource the whole project." In another firm the support function for a key application was repatriated because the firm felt that it was losing an important learning opportunity that would keep staff abreast of developments in the market and develop new knowledge concerning a key line of business with growth potential. Furthermore, it is not just knowledge *development* that is the critical factor; knowledge *retention* is equally important. Whether implicitly or explicitly, knowledge enhancement appears to play a key role in most sourcing decisions.

Decision Criterion #4: Business Exigency

Unforeseen business opportunities arise periodically, and firms with the ability to respond do so. Because of the urgency and importance of these business opportunities, they are not governed by the standard planning/budgeting processes and, indeed, most do not appear on the annual IT plan. Instead, a decision is made to seize the opportunity, and normal decision criteria are jettisoned in order to be responsive to the business. In these cases, whichever sourcing option can produce results fastest is selected. The sourcing option could be any of the four but is less likely to be a partnership unless the urgent request can be accommodated within the structure of an existing arrangement. Seen in a resource-planning context, business exigency demands constitute the "peaks" or "spikes." As one manager stated, "We have peaks and valleys, and we outsource the peaks."

The discussion also revealed the existence of two distinct sets of decision criteria: "normal" versus "actual." Manager after manager explained their decisions with the following preface: "*Normally* we would make the decision this way, but in this case we *actually* made the decision differently." When the participants referred to the normal set, they primarily cited issues of flexibility, control, and knowledge enablement. But when they described the actual decision criteria used to select the sourcing option, a fourth factor emerged: "*business exigency.*"

It is difficult to ascertain the full effect of this last decision criterion. Certainly business exigency is a dominant factor. In an urgent situation, the fastest sourcing option will take precedence. However, it is likely that the other three decision criteria play a significant role in the majority of sourcing decisions regarding IT functionality. We are left to conclude that business exigency plays a more dramatic but less frequent role.

A DECISION FRAMEWORK FOR SOURCING IT FUNCTIONS

Finally, the focus group was asked to outline a set of strategies for deciding how to source and deliver IT functions based on their collective experience and insights. The following step-by-step framework emerged.

Identify Your Core IT Functions

The identification of core functions is the first and most critical step in creating a decision framework for selecting sourcing options. One manager captured this as follows:

> *The days of IT being good at all things have long gone.... Today you have to pick your spots.... You have to decide where you need to excel to achieve competitive differentiation.... Being OK at most things is a recipe for failure sooner or later.*

It was argued that the IT organization should approach the exercise of identifying its core functions by taking a page from the business handbook—that is, decide where competitive advantage lies, buttress it with the best resources, and divest all ancillary activities. In the case of IT, "divestiture" translates into seeking external sourcing of functions because the responsibility and accountability for all IT functions will always remain with the IT organization.

Asked what constitutes a core function, the group suggested that it would depend entirely on where and how the IT organization decides it can leverage the business most effectively. Interestingly, what was considered *core* varied dramatically across the sample of organizations represented, spreading across the entire spectrum of IT functions, including legacy system enhancement, business process design, enterprise system implementation, project management, and even data center operations. The only conclusion that resonated with the entire group was that "it matters more that the IT organization has identified core functions than what those functions actually are."

The articulation of core functions has major implications. First, the selection of core functions lays the cornerstone for the decision framework for sourcing options. That is because, ideally, in-house functions reflect the organization's set of core functions. The assignment of permanent IT personnel to core IT functions, by default, assigns noncore activities to the remaining three IT sourcing options (as we will see in the next strategy). Second, the selection of core functions directly impacts the careers of IT personnel. For example, one manager explained that at her organization "project management, business process design, and relationship management are key skills, and we encourage development in these areas." The implications for IT staff currently fulfilling "noncore" roles can be threatening as these areas are key targets for external sourcing.

Create a "Function Sourcing" Profile

One participant introduced the concept of a "function sourcing" profile—a device that had been deployed successfully within his organization. It is reproduced in Table 8.3 and modified to accommodate the list of IT functions found in Table 8.1. This sample profile demonstrates (1) current core functions, (2) future core functions (additions and deletions), and (3) preferred sourcing options for each IT function. What is most important is that this profile is built on an internal assessment of core IT functions. Research

TABLE 8.3	Sample Function Delivery Profile				
Core Function?	**IT Function**	**In-house**	**Insource**	**Outsource**	**Partnership**
Yes	Business analysis	✓			
	Systems analysis		✓		
In Future	Strategy and planning		✓	✓	
In Future	Data management		✓		
Yes	Project management	✓	✓		
Yes	Architecture	✓	✓		
	Application development		✓	✓	✓
	QA and testing		✓		
Now but not in future	Networking	✓			✓
	Operating systems and services		✓		
Yes	Application support	✓			
	Data center operations			✓	
	Application software			✓	✓
	Hardware			✓	

(Bullen et al. 2007) has shown that core functions tend to change over time suggesting that this analysis be conducted perhaps every few years. The justification provided by this particular organization for its specific sourcing profile follows:

- Project management, business analysis, and architecture (both system and enterprise) are primarily provided in-house but may be augmented with insourced resources as required. In-house sourcing is preferred for these functions for two reasons: First, project management and business analysis are recognized strengths within the organization, and second, this gives the organization more control over project direction.
- Because it is not recognized as a core function, development is primarily outsourced or insourced depending on the scope of the project.
- Quality assurance (QA) and testing are largely insourced as these are recognized as highly specialized skills, although not core functions. As a result, an entire division of IT is dedicated to these activities. Resources within this group are primarily contractors from a variety of vendors.

- Application support is a designated core function. Given the depth of business process knowledge needed as well as the in-depth knowledge of key applications required, this function is staffed entirely by internal IT personnel.
- Networking is currently provided by in-house staff augmented by insourced staff but is in transition. A recently formed partnership will eventually make this a noncore activity, and networking will eventually be provided entirely by the partner. This sourcing option allows cost sharing and accommodates future growth. The partnership does not provide competitive advantage; it just makes good business sense.
- The strategy and planning function as well as data management have been designated as future core functions. The firm is insourcing expertise from a top strategy consultancy to transition this skill to internal IT personnel. This explicitly recognizes the emerging importance of IT to the firm. Similarly, data management needs to become a key competitive strength in order to shorten product development cycles and time to market.

The sample profile depicted in Table 8.3 does not represent a "preferred" or even "typical" IT sourcing strategy. Instead, it simply demonstrates how the four sourcing options combine to satisfy the IT needs of a specific organization. Other organizations with a different mix of core functions (or even with the same mix) might well demonstrate a very different profile.

Evolve Full-Time IT Personnel

Because of the alignment between core IT functions and in-house delivery, it is evident that sourcing decisions should be based on leveraging an organization's full-time IT personnel. In fact, the focus group argued that this factor should be used to determine the majority of sourcing decisions. It is based on the realization that permanent IT personnel collectively represent a major investment by the organization and that this investment needs to be maximized (or at least optimized). This reinforces the previous discussion of "knowledge enhancement" as one of the key decision criteria in the selection of IT sourcing mechanisms. One manager said the following:

> We choose a sourcing option based on how it can build strength in one of our designated core competency areas. This may involve insourcing, outsourcing, a partnership, or any combination of these [but] … we have never outsourced a core competency.

The sample profile in Table 8.3 suggests how the three external sourcing options (i.e., insourcing, outsourcing, and partnerships) can be used to supplement permanent IT personnel. Furthermore, the group suggested that a precedence for ordering should exist among the sourcing options. Specifically, in-house and insourcing considerations should be resolved before outsourcing and partnerships are explored. The criteria to be used to decide between outsourcing and partnerships as sourcing options should be flexibility, control, and business exigency (given that knowledge enablement is used to decide between in-house and insourcing). Insourcing, in particular, can be used strategically to bring in expertise to backfill knowledge gaps in core IT functions, address business exigency needs, and take on new (or shed old) core functions. Furthermore, insourcing represents variable costing, so there is usually maximal flexibility, which helps to smooth out resource "peaks and valleys."

The other method suggested to evolve internal IT staff, beyond supplementing them with the three external sourcing options, is to hire strategically.[8] In other words, the range of IT sourcing options permits "strategic" hiring as opposed to "replacement" hiring. In the past, IT organizations felt the need to "cover all the bases" with their hiring, and as individuals departed the organization, replacements were sought. Today, however, there is no such impetus. In fact, attrition in noncore areas is considered advantageous as it permits hiring in designated strategic areas. This approach extends to permanent staff as well—that is, existing staff are strongly encouraged to develop their skills and expertise in alignment with designated core IT functions.

Encourage Exploration of the Whole Range of Sourcing Options

Based on our sample of companies, it can be concluded that we are in the learning phase of IT function sourcing. Some firms are clearly taking advantage of this opportunity and exercising their options in many different, often creative, ways. Others, perhaps more reticent, are sampling less broadly—choosing to stay within their "comfort zone"— and sourcing IT functions predominantly with in-house resources. Most, however, are somewhere in the middle—that is, actively exploring different types of sourcing options mostly for the first time. In all cases, exploration appears to be taking place without any strategy or guidelines; hence, decisions are taken one at a time. As a result, learning has been piecemeal—a phenomenon that may partially explain the lack of established trends in Table 8.2.

Combine Sourcing Options Strategically

One of the key reasons for focusing on IT functions as opposed to another unit of analysis (e.g., projects, applications, or services) became clear by way of an example described by a manager. Satisfying her firm's data storage needs could involve using the provider's equipment, facilities, and staff. Or it could be the organization's hardware and staff in the provider's facilities, or basically any combination of the above. In each of these situations, the organization could justifiably claim that it had "outsourced" its data storage. Such a claim would be highly ambiguous. As a result, decisions need to be focused on the sourcing of *specific* IT functions—that is, a micro- versus a macroview.

Adopting a microview makes it possible to entertain the use of *combinations* of sourcing options for the provision of IT functions. Participants pointed out that multiple sourcing options are often used within a single project. In fact, they suggested that selecting a single sourcing option for a project in its entirety is fast becoming

---

[8] Although organizations continuously search for top IT talent, there appears to be a general aversion to increasing permanent staff among the focus group's companies. The consensus in the focus group was that this hiring aversion is fueling the growth of sourcing options such as insourcing, outsourcing, and partnerships, but the group was reluctant to use this factor to explain IT sourcing behavior. Instead, they claimed that the real driver was the existence of many alternative sourcing options, which have demonstrated the capability of providing superior results.

nonstandard practice. The reality is that multiple providers are necessary to meet today's demands, particularly those of the business-exigency variety. This need for an amalgam of sourcing options is easily understood with functions such as application development. Here requirements and design may be done in-house, coding may be outsourced to a third party, testing and quality assurance may be done by insourced experts, and implementation and rollout might be in partnership. Combining separate sourcing options strategically can result in realizable benefits such as speed to market and quality of product or service. Speed to market results from parallel, synchronized development, and quality results from engaging sourcing options based on demonstrated expertise and best practice.

A MANAGEMENT FRAMEWORK FOR SUCCESSFUL SOURCING

As sourcing takes on a more central part of IT and organizational strategy, we are learning more about what it takes to manage sourcing successfully. Furthermore, these emergent management practices have a reciprocal impact on sourcing decisions. The focus group identified a number of key factors essential to effective management of sourcing options: develop a sourcing strategy, develop a risk mitigation strategy, develop a governance strategy, and understand the cost structures.

Develop a Sourcing Strategy

Whether a company uses sourcing strategically or not, every organization should have an overall sourcing strategy. Using a decision framework (such as that presented in this chapter), organizations need to determine what to source, where to source, and to whom to source. There are many different ways of determining what to source but, in practice, numerous approaches to "right-sourcing" are possible. What is right for one organization is not necessarily right for another. The point is that organizations must go through the exercise of determining for themselves what's core and what's not and this will pave the way for an effective sourcing strategy.

Develop a Risk Mitigation Strategy

"War stories" abound. Every firm can cite examples of activities that had to be resourced to a different vendor, tasks that needed to be reinsourced, or contracts that were renegotiated because of problems. The fact is sourcing introduces new levels of risk to the organization. Loss of control, security and privacy problems, poor-quality work, hidden costs, lack of standards, unmet expectations, and bad publicity are just some of the problems that have been experienced. When moving into new forms of sourcing, it is important to incorporate risk management and mitigation into every aspect of sourcing.

- Detailed planning is essential. Precise definitions of roles, responsibilities, and expectations must be developed. Specialists in outsourcing are now available to provide advice on how to select a vendor and plan the work involved. The specialists can assist—but not replace—the IT sourcing team in understanding how to assess and engage a vendor. This is especially important when considering offshore sourcing because of the additional complexities involved.

- Monitoring and an audit trail must be incorporated into the contract to both encourage self-correction and ensure all parties live up to their commitments.
- All potential risks should be rated as to both the likelihood of occurrence and their impact if they do occur. Appropriate steps should be explicitly taken to reduce and/or manage these risks.
- An exit strategy must be devised. "Any well-designed sourcing strategy must retain alternatives to pull activities back in-house," explained one manager.
- Finally, exercise caution when moving into new avenues of sourcing. The hype in the popular press, often originating from vendors, greatly inflates the benefits that can be achieved while minimizing the risks. It is recommended that managers experiment with a "simple, substantial pilot" before committing the company to a significant new outsourcing initiative.

Develop a Governance Strategy

"With any sourcing option, governance must be super-good," said a manager. Most IT organizations now recognize the importance of relationship management at all levels (i.e., the frontline, middle, and senior management) in delivering value. Nevertheless, it cannot be underestimated. "Layers of governance are critical to successful sourcing relationships," said one manager. Others also suggested retaining strong internal project management and ensuring that vendors also have these skills. "You can't outsource the relationship with the customer," they agreed. Governance problems are exacerbated when offshore sourcing is undertaken because of the difficulties of managing relationships at a distance. This is one reason the larger offshore vendors are setting up local development centers. At minimum, an offshore outsourcer should name an internal manager who will act as the organization's champion and be responsible for quality assurance. Ideally, an outsourcing relationship should be structured to ensure shared risk so both parties are incented to make it work.

Understand the Cost Structures

One of the most important elements of successful sourcing is a complete understanding of the cost structures involved. Previously, vendors have profited from their ability to squeeze value from outsourced activities because they had a better and more detailed appreciation of their costs. Furthermore, they were able to apply disciplines and service-level agreements to their work, which IT organizations were often prohibited from doing. Today this is changing. Companies are applying the same standards to their own work, enabling them to make more appropriate comparisons between the costs of doing an activity internally (i.e., in-house or insource) and outsourcing it. They also have a better understanding of the true costs of outsourcing, including relationship management and contract management, which have frequently been underestimated in the past. "We need to thoroughly understand our economic model," said one manager. "Vendors have the advantage of knowing best practices and economies of scale, but they are at a disadvantage from a profit and knowledge point of view. If we can't compete in-house, we should outsource." Ongoing cost comparisons are effective as they motivate both parties to do their best and most cost-effective work.

Conclusion

Despite a steadily growing industry of third-party providers, IT organizations to date have ventured rather cautiously into this new area of IT sourcing. This chapter attempts to explain why this is so by examining the decision behavior and practices of a number of leading-edge organizations. From this analysis, four key decision criteria were identified: (1) flexibility, (2) control, (3) knowledge enhancement, and (4) business exigency. Today IT managers have an incredible range of available options in terms of how they choose to source and deliver IT functions.

Clearly, the mistake is not to investigate the full range of these options. What has been lacking is greater direction and guidance in selecting IT sourcing options. The concept of a maturity model for IT functions was introduced as was a function-sourcing profile to map sourcing options onto core and noncore IT functions. These elements form the basis of a decision framework to guide the selection of sourcing options. Based on this framework, organizations can develop more strategic, nuanced, and methodological approaches to IT function sourcing and management.

References

Bandula, J., and R. Hirschheim. "Changes in IT Sourcing Arrangements: An Interpretive Field study of Technical and Institutional Influences." *Strategic Outsourcing: An International Journal* 2, no. 2 (2009): 84–122.

Bullen, C., T. Abraham, K. Gallagher, K. Kaiser, and J. Simon. "Changing IT Skills: The Impact of Sourcing Strategies on In-House Capability Requirements." *Journal of Electronic Commerce in Organizations* 5, no. 2 (April–June 2007): 24–37, 39–46.

Carr, N. G. "The End of Corporate Computing." *MIT Sloan Management Review* 46, no. 3 (Spring 2005): 67–73.

Hagel, J., and J. S. Brown. "Your Next IT Strategy." *Harvard Business Review* 79, no. 9 (October 2001): 105–13.

Lacity, M., and L. Willcocks. "An Empirical Investigation of Information Technology Sourcing Practices: Lessons from Experience." *MIS Quarterly* 22, no. 3 (2000): 363–408.

Marquis, H. A. "Finishing Off IT." *MIT Sloan Management Review* 47, no. 4 (Summer 2006): 12–16.

Mola, L., and A. Carugati. "Escaping 'Localisms' in IT sourcing: Tracing Changes in Institutional Logics in an Italian Firm." *European Journal of Information Systems* 21, no. 4 (July 2012): 388–403.

Rappa, M. A. "The Utility Business Model and the Future of Computing Services." *IBM Systems Journal* 43, no. 1 (2004): 32–42.

Ross, J. W., and G. Westerman. "Preparing for Utility Computing: The Role of IT Architecture and Relationship Management." *MIT Sloan Management Review* 43, no. 1 (2004): 5–19.

Smith, H. A., and J. D. McKeen. "IT in 2015." Presentation to Center for Information Systems Research (CISR), Massachusetts Institute of Technology, April 2012.

Smith, H. A., and J. D. McKeen. "IT in 2010: The Next Frontier." *MIS Quarterly Executive* 5, no. 3 (September 2006): 125–36.

9   The IT Budgeting Process

D on't ever try to contact an IT manager in September because you won't get very far. September is budget month for most companies, and *that* means that most managers are hunkered down over a spreadsheet or in all-day meetings trying to "make the numbers work." "Budgeting is a very negative process at our firm," one IT manager told us. "And it takes way too long." Asking many IT managers about budgeting elicits much caustic comment. Apparently, significant difficulties with IT budgeting lead to widespread disenchantment among IT leaders who feel much of the work involved is both artificial and overly time consuming.

Others agree. While there has been little research done on IT budgeting per se (Hu and Quan 2006; Kobelsky et al. 2006), there appears to be broad, general consensus that the budgeting processes of many corporations are broken and need to be fixed (Buytendijk 2004; Hope and Fraser 2003; Jensen 2001). There are many problems. First, budgeting takes too long and consumes too much managerial time. One study found that budgeting is a protracted process taking at least four months and consuming about 30 percent of management's time (Hope and Fraser 2003). Second, most budgeting processes are no longer effective or efficient. They have become disconnected from business objectives, slow, and expensive (Buytendijk 2004). Third, rigid adherence to these annual plans has been found to stifle innovation and discourage frontline staff from taking responsibility for performance (Hope and Fraser 2003; Norton 2006). And fourth, although many researchers have studied how organizations choose among strategic investment opportunities, studies show that the budgeting process frequently undercuts management's strategic intentions, causing significant frustration among managers at all levels (Norton 2006; Steele and Albright 2004).

Finally, the annual planning cycle can cast spending plans "in concrete" at a time when the business needs to be flexible and agile. This is particularly true in IT. "Over time...IT budgeting processes become institutionalized. As a result, IT investments become less about creating competitive advantages for firms [and] more about following organizational routine and creating legitimacy for management as well as organizations" (Hu and Quan 2006). Now that senior business leaders recognize the strategic importance of IT and IT has become many firms' largest capital expenditure (Koch 2006), a hard look at how IT budgets are created is clearly merited.

This chapter first looks at key concepts in IT budgeting to establish what they mean for IT managers and how they can differ among IT organizations. Then it explores why budgets are an important part of the management process. Next the chapter examines the elements of the IT budget cycle. Finally, it identifies some recommended practices for improving IT budgeting.

KEY CONCEPTS IN IT BUDGETING

Before looking at how budgeting is actually practiced in IT organizations, it is important to understand what a budget *is* and *why* an effective IT budgeting process is so important, both within IT and for the enterprise as a whole. Current organizational budgeting practices emerged in the 1920s as a tool for managing costs and cash flows. Present-day annual fixed plans and budgets were established in the 1970s to drive performance improvements (Hope and Fraser 2003). Since then, most organizations have adhered rigidly to the ideals of this process, in spite of much evidence of their negative influence on innovation and flexibility (Hope and Fraser 2003). These problems are clearly illustrated by the impact this larger corporate fiscal management process has on IT budgeting and the problems IT managers experience in trying to make their budget processes work effectively. The concepts and practices of the corporate fiscal world bear little similarity to how IT actually works. As a result, there are clear discontinuities between these two worlds.

These gaps are especially apparent in the differences between the fiscal view of IT and the functional one. *Fiscal IT budgets* (i.e., those prepared for the CFO) are broken down into two major categories: *capital expenditures* and *operating expenses,* although what expenditures go into each is highly variable across firms. In accounting, capital budgets are utilized to spread large expenses (e.g., buying a building) over several years, and operating expenses cover the annual cost of running the business. The distinction between these two concepts gets very fuzzy, however, when it comes to IT.

Generally speaking, all IT organizations want to capitalize as much of their spending as possible because it makes their annual costs look smaller. However, CIOs are limited by both organizational and tax policies when deciding on the types of IT expenditures they can capitalize. It is the CFO who, through corporate financial strategy, establishes what may be capitalized, and this, in turn, determines what IT can capitalize in its fiscal budget and what it must consider as an operating expense. As a result, some firms capitalize project development, infrastructure, consulting fees, and full-time staff, whereas others capitalize only major technology purchases.

How capital budgets are determined and the degree to which they are scrutinized also vary widely. Some firms allocate and prioritize IT capital expenses out of a corporate "pot"; others manage IT capital separately. Typically, capital expenses appear to be more carefully scrutinized than operating expenses, but not always. It is surprising to learn how different types of expenses are handled by different firms and the wide degree of latitude allowed for IT costs under generally accepted accounting principles. In fact, there are few generally accepted accounting principles when it comes to IT spending (Koch 2006). As a result, researchers should use caution in relying on measures of the amount of capital spent on IT in firms or industries.

It is within this rather fuzzy fiscal context that the structure and purpose of *functional IT budgets* (i.e., those used by IT managers as spending plans) must be understood because these accounting concepts do not usually correspond exactly with how IT managers view IT work and how they plan and budget for it. In contrast to how fiscal IT budgets are designed, IT managers plan their spending using two somewhat different categories: *operations costs* and *strategic investments:*

- **Operations costs.**   This category consists of what it costs to "keep the lights on" in IT. These are the expenses involved in running IT like a utility. Operations involves the cost of maintenance, computing and peripheral functions (e.g., storage, network), and support, regardless of how it is delivered (i.e., in-house or outsourced). This category can, therefore, include both operating and capital costs. Between 50 and 90 percent of a firm's IT budget (average 76 percent) is spent in this area, so the spending involved is significant (Gruman 2006). In most firms there is continual pressure on the CIO to reduce operations costs year after year (Smith and McKeen 2006).
- **Strategic investment.**   The balance of the IT budget consists of the "new" spending—that is, spending on initiatives and technology designed to deliver new business value and achieve the enterprise's strategic objectives. Because of the interactive nature of IT and business strategy, this part of the IT budget can include a number of different types of spending, such as business improvement initiatives to streamline processes and cut costs, business-enabling initiatives to extend or transform how a company does business, business opportunity projects to test the viability of new concepts or technologies and scale them up, and sometimes infrastructure (Smith et al. 2007). Because spending in this area can include many different kinds of expenses (e.g., full-time and contract staff, software and hardware), some parts of the strategic investment budget may be considered capital expenses, whereas others are classified as operating expenses.

Another fuzzy fiscal budgeting concept is *cost allocation*—the process of allocating the cost of the services IT provides to others' budgets. The cost of IT can be viewed as a corporate expense, a business unit expense, or a combination of both, and the way in which IT costs are allocated can have a significant impact on what is spent for IT. For example, a majority of companies allocate their operating expenses to their business units' operating budgets—usually using a formula based on factors such as the size and previous year's spending of the business unit. Similarly, strategic expenses are typically allocated on the basis of which business unit will benefit from the investment. In today's IT environment, these approaches are not always effective for a number of reasons.

Many strategic IT investments involve the participation of more than one business unit, but budgeting systems still tend to be designed around the structure of the organization (Norton 2006). This leads to considerable artificiality in allocating development resources to projects, which in turn can lead to dysfunctional behavior, such as lobbying, games, nonsupportive cross-functional work, and the inability to successfully implement strategy (Buytendijk 2004; Norton 2006). "We don't fund corporate projects very well," admitted one manager whose company allocates all costs to individual business units.

Allocations can also lead to operational inefficiencies. "The different allocation models tend to lead to 'gaming' between our business units," said another participant. "Our business unit managers have no control over their percentage of operating costs," explained a third. "This is very frustrating for them and tends to be a real problem for some of our smaller units." Because of these allocations, some business units may not be willing to share in the cost of new hardware, software, or processes that would lead to reduced enterprise costs in the longer term. This is one of the primary reasons so many IT organizations end up supporting several different applications all doing the same thing. Furthermore, sometimes, when senior managers get disgruntled with their IT expenses, this method of allocating operations costs can lead to their cutting their IT operational spending in ways that have little to do with running a cost-effective IT organization. For example, one company cut back on its budget for hardware and software upgrades, which meant that a significant percentage of IT staff then had to be redeployed to testing, modifying, and maintaining new systems so they would run on the old machines. Although IT managers have done some work educating their CEOs and CFOs about what constitutes effective cost cutting (e.g., appropriate outsourcing, adjusting service levels), the fact remains that most business executives still do not understand or appreciate the factors that contribute to the overall cost of IT. As a result, allocations can lead to a great deal of angst for IT managers at budget time as they try to justify each expense while business managers try to "nickel and dime" each expense category (Koch 2006).

As a result of all this fuzziness, modern IT budgeting practices do little to give business leaders confidence that IT spending is both effective and efficient (Gruman 2006). And the challenges IT managers face in making IT spending fit into contemporary corporate budgeting practices are significant.

THE IMPORTANCE OF BUDGETS

Ideally, budgets are a key component of corporate performance management. "If done well, a budget is the operational translation of an enterprise's strategy into costs and planned revenue" (Buytendijk 2004). Budgets are also a subset of good governance processes in that they enable management to understand and communicate what is being spent and where. Ideally, therefore, a budget is more than a math exercise; it is "a blueprint for fiscally sound IT and business success" (Overby 2004). Effective IT budgeting is important for many reasons, but two of the most important are as follows:

1. *Fiscal discipline.*   As overall IT spending has been rising, senior business leaders have been paying much closer attention to what IT costs and how its budgets are spent. In many organizations a great deal of skepticism remains that IT budgets are used wisely, so reducing spending, or at least the operations portion of the budget, is now considered a key way for a CIO to build trust with the executive team (Gruman 2006). Demonstrating an understanding and appreciation of the realities of business finance has become a significant part of IT leadership (Goldberg 2004), and the ability to create and monitor a budget is, therefore, "table stakes" for a CIO (Overby 2004).

It is clear that senior executives are using the budgeting process to enforce tougher rules on how IT dollars are spent. Some organizations have centralized IT budgeting in an effort to better understand what is being spent; others are making the link between reducing operations spending and increasing investment in IT a reason for introducing new operations disciplines (e.g., limiting maintenance, establishing appropriate support levels). Still others have established tighter requirements for business cases and monitoring returns on investment. Organizations also use their IT budgets to manage and limit demand. "Our IT budget is capped by our CEO," stated one manager. "And it's always less than the demand." Using budgets in this way, although likely effective for the enterprise, can cause problems for CIOs in that they must in turn enforce spending disciplines on business unit leaders.

Finally, budgets and performance against budgets are a key way of holding IT management accountable for what it spends, both internally to the leadership of the organization and externally to shareholders and regulatory bodies. Improperly used, budgets can distort reality and encourage inappropriate behavior (Hope and Fraser 2003; Jensen 2001). However, when used responsibly they can be "a basis for clear understanding between organizational levels and can help executives maintain control over divisions and the business" (Hope and Fraser 2003). Research is beginning to show a positive relationship between good IT budgeting practices (i.e., using IT budgets to manage demand, make investment decisions, and govern IT) and overall company performance (Kobelsky et al. 2006; Overby 2004).

2. *Strategy implementation.* Budgets are also the means to implement IT strategy, linking the long-term goals of the organization and short-term goal execution through the allocation of resources to activities. Unfortunately, research shows that the majority of organizations do not link their strategies to their budgets, which is why so many have difficulty making strategic changes (Norton 2006). This is particularly true in IT. As one manager complained, "No one knows what we're doing in the future. Therefore, our goals change regularly and at random." Another noted, "The lines of business pay little attention to IT resources when they're establishing their strategic plans. They just expect IT to make it happen."

Budgets can affect IT strategy implementation in a number of ways. First, *where* IT dollars are spent determines the impact IT can have on corporate performance. Clearly, if 80 percent of IT expenditures are going to operations and maintenance, IT can have less strategic impact than if this percentage is lower. Second, *how* discretionary IT dollars are spent is important. For example, some companies decide to invest in infrastructure, and others do not; some will choose to "bet the company" on a single large IT initiative, and others will choose more focused projects. In short, the outcome of how a company chooses among investment opportunities is reflected in its budgets (Steele and Albright 2004).

Third, the budgeting process itself reflects and reinforces the ability of strategic decision making to have an impact. Norton (2006) states that because budget processes are inherently biased toward the short term, operational needs will systematically preempt strategic ones. In IT the common practice of routinely allocating a fixed percentage of the IT strategic budget to individual business units makes it almost impossible to easily reallocate resources to higher-priority projects at the enterprise level or in other business units. In addition, siloed budgeting processes make it difficult to manage the cross-business costs of strategic IT decisions.

Overall, budgets are a critical element of most managerial decisions and processes and are used to accomplish a number of different purposes in IT: compliance, fiscal accountability, cost reduction, business unit and enterprise strategy implementation, internal customer service, delivering business value, and operational excellence, to name just a few. This, in a nutshell, is the reason IT budgeting is such a complex and challenging process.

THE IT PLANNING AND BUDGET PROCESS

Given that IT budgets are used in so many different ways and serve so many stakeholders, it is no wonder that the whole process of IT budgeting is "painful," "artificial," and in need of some serious improvement. Figure 9.1 illustrates a generic and simplified IT planning and budgeting process. This section outlines the steps involved in putting together an IT budget utilizing some of the key concepts presented earlier.

Corporate Processes

The following three activities set the corporate context within which IT plans and budgets are created.

1. *Establish corporate fiscal policy.*   This process is usually so far removed from the annual budget cycle that IT leaders may not even be aware of its influence or the wide number of options in the choices that are made (particularly around capitalization). Corporate fiscal policies are not created with IT spending in mind but, as already noted, can significantly impact how a fiscal IT budget is created and the

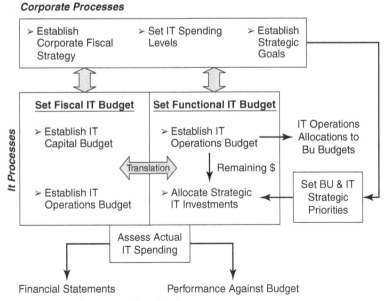

FIGURE 9.1 A Generic IT Planning and Budgeting Process

levels of scrutiny under which certain kinds of expenses are placed. A more direct way that corporate fiscal policies affect IT is in company expectations around the return on investment for IT projects. Most companies now have an explicit expected return rate for all new projects that is closely monitored.

2. *Establish strategic goals.*   Conversely, IT budgeting *is* directly and continuously affected by many corporate strategic goals. The process of establishing IT and business unit strategies occurs within the context of these overall goals. In some organizations there is tight integration between enterprise, business unit, and IT strategic planning; in others these elements are more loosely coupled, informal, and iterative. However, what is truly rare is a provision for enterprise funding for enterprise IT initiatives. Thus, corporate strategic goals are typically broken down into business unit budgets. As one manager explained, "First our executives decide our profits and then the business units decide how to achieve them and then IT develops a plan with the business unit.... We still don't do many corporate projects."

3. *Set IT spending levels.*   Establishing how much to spend on IT is the area that has been most closely studied by researchers. This is a complex process, influenced by many external and internal factors. *Externally,* firms look to others in their industry to determine the level of their spending (Hu and Quan 2006). In particular, companies frequently use benchmarks with similar firms to identify a percentage of revenue to spend on IT (Koch 2006). Unfortunately, this approach can be dangerous for a number of reasons. First, it can be a strong driver in inhibiting competitive advantage and leading to greater similarities among firms in an industry (Hu and Quan 2006). Second, this metric tells management nothing about how well its money is being spent (Koch 2006). Third, it does not address IT's ability to use IT strategically (Kobelsky et al. 2006).

A second and increasingly strong external driver of IT spending is the regulatory environment within which a firm operates. Legislation, standards, and professional practices all affect what IT can and cannot do and how its work is done (Smith and McKeen 2006). These, in turn, affect how much is spent on IT and where it is spent (Hu and Quan 2006). Other external factors that have been shown to affect how much money is spent on IT include the following:

- *Number of competitors.*   More concentration in an industry reduces the amount spent.
- *Uncertainty.*   More uncertainty in a business's external environment leads to larger IT budgets.
- *Diversification of products and services.*   Firms competing in more markets will tend to spend more on IT (Kobelsky et al. 2006).

Internal factors affecting the size of the IT budget include the following:

- *Affordability.*   A firm's overall performance and cash flow will influence how much discretion it has to spend on IT.
- *Growth.*   Growing firms tend to invest more in IT than mature firms.
- *Previous year's spending.*   Firm spending on IT is unlikely to deviate significantly year to year (Hu and Quan 2006; Kobelsky et al. 2006).

IT Processes

These are multilevel and complex and frequently occur in parallel with each other.

*   *Set functional IT budget.*   This budget documents spending as it relates to how IT organizations *work*—that is, what is to be spent on IT operations and how much is available to be spent on strategic investments. As already noted, the operations budget is relatively fixed and contains the lion's share of the dollars. In spite of this, IT managers must go through a number of machinations annually to justify this expenditure. Most IT organizations are still seen as cost centers, so obtaining budget approvals is often a delicate, ongoing exercise of relationship building and education to prevent inappropriate cost cutting (Koch 2006). Once the overall IT operations budget has been established, the challenge of allocating it to the individual business units remains, which, given the complexity of today's shared technical environment, is often a fixed or negotiated percentage of the total. Business units can resent these allocations over which they have no control, and at best, they are viewed as a "necessary evil." In organizations where the IT operations budget is centralized, IT managers have greater opportunity to reduce expenses year by year by introducing standards, streamlining hardware and software, and sharing services. However, in many companies, operations budgets are decentralized into the business units and aggregated up into the overall IT budget. This approach makes it considerably more difficult for IT managers to implement effective cost-reduction measures. However, even in those firms that are highly effective and efficient, the relentless pressure from executives to do more with less makes this part of the annual budgeting process a highly stressful activity.

    Allocating the funds remaining to strategic investments is a completely separate process in which potential new IT projects are prioritized and their costs justified. Companies have many different ways of doing this, and most appear to be in a transition phase between methods of prioritization. Traditionally, IT organizations have been designed to parallel the organization structure, and new development funds have been allocated to business units on the basis of some rule of thumb. For example, each business unit might be allotted a certain number of IT staff and dollars to spend on new development (based on percentage of overall revenue) that would remain relatively stable over time. More recently, however, with greater integration of technology, systems, and data, there has been recognition of the cross-business costs of new development and of the need for more enterprise spending to address these. Increasingly, therefore, organizations are moving to prioritize some or all new development at the enterprise level, thereby removing fixed allocations of new development resources from the business units.

    However it is determined, the strategic portion of the functional IT budget also involves staffing the initiatives. This introduces yet another level of complexity in that, even if the dollars are available, appropriate IT resources must also be available to be assigned to particular projects to address the organization's cost-cutting requirements. Thus, undertaking a new project involves not only cost justification and prioritization but also requires the availability of the right mix of skills and types of staff. Although some firms use fixed percentages of full-time, contract, and offshore staff in their projects, most use a mix of employees and contract staff in their development projects in order to keep overhead costs low. As a result, creating new IT development budgets often involves a complementary exercise in staff planning.

• *Set the fiscal IT budget.*   A second, parallel stream of IT budgeting involves establishing the *fiscal* IT budget, which the CFO uses to implement the company's fiscal strategy and provide financial reports to shareholders and regulatory and tax authorities. This is seen largely by IT managers as a "translation" exercise where the functional IT budget is reconstituted into the operating and capital spending buckets. Nevertheless, it represents an additional "hoop" through which IT managers must jump before their budgets can be approved. In some companies capital funding is difficult to obtain and must be justified against an additional set of financial criteria. Some organizations require IT capital expenditures be prioritized against all other corporate capital expenses (e.g., buildings, trucks), which can be a very challenging exercise. In other firms CFOs are more concerned about increasing operating expenses. In either case this is an area where many IT managers set themselves up for failure by failing to "speak the language of finance" (Girard 2004). Because most IT managers think of their work in terms of operations and strategic investments, they fail to understand some of the larger drivers of fiscal strategy such as investor value and earnings per share. To get more "traction" for their budgets, it is, therefore, important for IT leaders to better translate what IT can do for the company into monetary terms (Girard 2004). To this end, many companies have begun working more closely with their internal finance staff and are seeing greater acceptance of their budgets as a result.

Assess Actual IT Spending

At the other end of the budgeting process is the need to assess actual IT spending and performance. A new focus on financial accountability has meant that results are more rigorously tracked than in the past. In many companies finance staff now monitor business cases for all new IT projects, thus relieving IT of having to prove the business returns on what is delivered. Often the challenge of finding the right resources for a project or unexpected delays means that the entire available development budget may not be spent within a given fiscal year. "We typically tend to spend about 85 percent of our available development budget because of delays or resourcing problems," said one manager. Hitting budget targets *exactly* in the strategic investment budget is, therefore, a challenge, and current IT budgeting practices typically do not allow for much flexibility. On the one hand, such practices can create a "use it or lose it" mentality; if money is not spent in the fiscal year, it will disappear. "This leads to some creative accruals and aggressive forecasting," said the focus group. On the other hand, IT managers who want to ensure there is *enough* money for key expenditures create "placeholders" (i.e., approximations of what they think a project will cost) and "coffee cans" (i.e., unofficial slush funds) in their budgets. The artificial timing of the budget process, combined with the difficulties of planning and estimation and reporting complexity, all mean that accurate reporting of what is spent can get distorted.

IT BUDGETING PRACTICES THAT DELIVER VALUE

Although there is general agreement that current budgeting practices are flawed, there are still no widely accepted alternatives. Within IT itself, companies seem to be experimenting with ways to tweak budgeting to make it both easier and more effective. The following five practices have proven to be useful in this regard:

1. *Appoint an IT finance specialist.*   Many companies now have a finance expert working in IT or on staff with the CFO working *with* IT. "Getting help with finance has really made the job of budgeting easier," said one manager. "Having a good partnership with finance helps us to leverage their expertise," said another. Financial specialists can help IT managers to understand their costs and drivers in new ways. Within operations, they can assist with cost and value analysis of services and infrastructure (Gruman 2006) and also manage the "translation" process between the functional IT budget and the fiscal IT budget. "Finance helps us to understand depreciation and gives us a deeper understanding of our cost components," a focus group member noted. Finance specialists are also being used to build and monitor business cases for new projects, often acting as brokers between IT and the business units. "They've really helped us to better articulate business value. Now they're in charge of ensuring that the business gets the benefits they say they will, not IT." The improving relationship between finance and IT is making it easier to gain acceptance of IT budgets. "Having dedicated IT finance people is great since this is not what IT managers want to do," said a participant.

2. *Use budgeting tools and methodologies.*   About one-half of the members of the focus group felt they had effective budgeting tools for such things as asset tracking, rolling up and breaking down budgets into different levels of granularity, and reporting. "We have a good, integrated suite of tools," said a manager, "and they really help." Because budgets serve so many different stakeholders, tools and methodologies can help "slice and dice" the numbers many ways, dynamically enabling changes in one area to be reflected in all other areas. Those who did not have good or well-integrated tools found that there were gaps in their budgeting processes that were hard to fill. "Our poor tools lead to disconnects all over the place," claimed an IT manager. Good links to the IT planning process are also needed. Ideally, tools should tie budgets directly to corporate strategic planning, resource strategies, and performance metrics, enabling a further translation among the company's accounting categories and hierarchy and its strategic themes and targets (Norton 2006).

3. *Separate operations from innovation.*   Most IT managers mentally separate operations from innovation, but in practical terms maintenance and support are often mixed up with new project development. This happens especially when IT organizations are aligned with and funded by the business units. Once IT funds and resources are allotted to a particular business unit, rather than to a strategic deliverable, it is very difficult to reduce these allocations. Agreement appears to be growing that operations (including maintenance) must be financially separated from new development in order to ensure that the costs of the first are fully scrutinized and kept under control while focus is kept on increasing the proportion of resources devoted to new project development (Dragoon 2005; Girard 2004; Gruman 2006; Norton 2006). Repeatedly, focus group managers told stories of how their current budget processes discourage accuracy. "There are many

disincentives built into our budgeting processes to keep operational costs down," said one manager. Separating operations from innovation in budgets provides a level of visibility in IT spending that has traditionally been absent and that helps business unit leaders better understand the true costs of delivering both new systems and ongoing services.

4. *Adopt enterprise funding models.* It is still rare to find organizations that provide corporate funding for enterprisewide strategic IT initiatives, yet there is broad recognition that this is needed (Norton 2006). The conflict between the need for truly integrated initiatives and traditional siloed budgets frequently stymies innovation, frustrates behavior designed for the common good, and discourages accountability for results (Hope and Fraser 2003; Norton 2006; Steele and Albright 2004). It is, therefore, expected that more organizations will adopt enterprise funding models for at least some IT initiatives over the next few years. Similarly, decentralized budgeting for core IT services is declining due to the cost-saving opportunities available from sharing these. Since costs will likely continue to be charged back to the differing business units, the current best practice is for IT operation budgets to be developed at an enterprise level.

5. *Adopt rolling budget cycles.* IT plans and budgets need attention more frequently than once a year. Although not used by many companies, an eighteen-month rolling plan that is reviewed and updated quarterly appears to be a more effective way of budgeting, especially for new project development (Hope and Fraser 2003; Smith et al. 2007). "It is very difficult to plan new projects a year in advance," said one manager. "Often we are asked for our 'best estimates' in our budgets. The problem is that, once they're in the budget, they are then viewed as reality." The artificial timing of budgets and the difficulty of estimating the costs of new projects are key sources of frustration for IT managers. Rolling budget cycles, when combined with integrated budgeting tools, should better address this problem while still providing the financial snapshots needed by the enterprise on an annual basis.

Conclusion

Although IT budget processes have been largely ignored by researchers, they are a critical linchpin between many different organizational stakeholders: finance and IT, business units and IT, corporate strategy and IT, and different internal IT groups. Not surprisingly, therefore, IT budgeting is much more complex and difficult to navigate than it appears. This chapter has outlined some of the challenges faced by IT managers trying to juggle the realities of dealing with both IT operations and strategic investments while meeting the differing needs of their budget stakeholders. Surprisingly, very few guidelines are available for IT managers in

this area. Each organization appears to have quite different corporate financial policies, which, in turn, drive different IT budgeting practices. Nevertheless, IT managers do face many common challenges in budgeting. Although other IT practices have benefited from focused management attention in recent years (e.g., prioritization, operations rationalization), budgeting has not as yet been targeted in this way. However, as business and IT leaders begin to recognize the key role that budgets play in implementing strategy and controlling costs, it is hoped they will make a serious effort to address the budgeting issues faced by IT.

References

Buytendijk, F. "New Way to Budget Enhances Corporate Performance Measurement." Gartner Inc., ID Number: 423484, January 28, 2004.

Dragoon, A. "Journey to the IT Promised Land." *CIO Magazine*, April 1, 2005.

Girard, K. "What CIOs Need to Know about Money." *CIO Magazine*, Special Money Issue, September 22, 2004.

Goldberg, M. "The Final Frontier for CIOs." *CIO Magazine*, Special Money Issue, September 22, 2004.

Gruman, G. "Trimming for Dollars." *CIO Magazine*, July 1, 2006.

Hope, J., and R. Fraser. "Who Needs Budgets?" *Harvard Business Review* 81, no. 2 (February 2003): 2–8.

Hu, Q., and J. Quan. "The Institutionalization of IT Budgeting: Empirical Evidence from the Financial Sector." *Information Resources Management Journal* 19, no. 1 (January–March 2006): 84–97.

Jensen, M. "Corporate Budgeting Is Broken—Let's Fix It." *Harvard Business Review* 79, no. 11 (November 2001): 95–101.

Kobelsky, K., V. Richardson, R. Smith, and R. Zmud. "Determinants and Consequences of Firm Information Technology Budgets." Draft paper provided by the authors, May 2006.

Koch, C. "The Metrics Trap … and How to Avoid It." *CIO Magazine*, April 1, 2006.

Norton, D. "Linking Strategy and Planning to Budgets." *Balanced Scorecard Report*. Cambridge, MA: Harvard Business School Publishing, May–June 2006.

Overby, S. "Tips from the Budget Masters." *CIO Magazine*, Special Money Issue, September 22, 2004.

Smith, H. A., and J. D. McKeen. "IT in 2010." *MIS Quarterly Executive* 5, no. 3 (September 2006): 125–36.

Smith, H. A., J. D. McKeen, and S. Singh. "Developing IT Strategy for Business Value." *Journal of Information Technology Management* XVIII, no. 1 (June 2007): 49–58.

Steele, R., and C. Albright. "Games Managers Play at Budget Time." *MIT Sloan Management Review* 45, no. 3 (Spring 2004): 81–84.

10 Managing IT-Based Risk[1]

Not so long ago, IT-based risk was a fairly low-key activity focused on whether IT could deliver projects successfully and keep its applications up and running (McKeen and Smith 2003). But with the opening up of the organization's boundaries to external partners and service providers, external electronic communications, and online services, managing IT-based risk has morphed into a "bet the company" proposition. Not only is the scope of the job bigger, but also the stakes are much higher. As companies have become more dependent on IT for everything they do, the costs of service disruption have escalated exponentially. Now, when a system goes down, the company effectively stops working and customers cannot be served. And criminals routinely seek ways to wreak havoc with company data, applications, and Web sites. New regulations to protect privacy and increase accountability have also made executives much more sensitive to the consequences of inadequate IT security practices—either internally or from service providers. In addition, the risk of losing or compromising company information has risen steeply. No longer are a company's files locked down and accessible only by company staff. Today, company information can be exposed to the public in literally hundreds of ways. Our increasing mobility, the portability of storage devices, and the growing sophistication of cyber threats are just a few of the more noteworthy means.

Therefore, the job of managing IT-based risk has become much broader and more complex, and it is now widely recognized as an integral part of any technology-based work—no matter how minor. As a result, many IT organizations have been given the responsibility of not only managing risk in their own activities (i.e., project development, operations, and delivering business strategy) but also of managing IT-based risk in all company activities (e.g., mobile computing, file sharing, and online access to information and software). Whereas in the past companies have sought to achieve security

---

[1] This chapter is based on the authors' previously published article, Smith, H. A., and J. D. McKeen. "A Holistic Approach to Managing IT-Based Risk." *Communications of the Association for Information Systems* 25, no. 41 (December 2009): 519–30. Reproduced by permission of the Association for Information Systems.

through physical or technological means (e.g., locked rooms, virus scanners), under-standing is now growing that managing IT-based risk must be a strategic and holistic activity that is not just the responsibility of a small group of IT specialists but also part of the mind-set that extends from partners and suppliers to employees and customers.

This chapter explores how organizations are addressing and coping with increas-ing IT-based risk. It first looks at the challenges facing IT managers in the arena of risk management and proposes a holistic view of risk. Next it examines some of the charac-teristics and components needed to develop an effective risk management framework and presents a generic framework for integrating the growing number of elements involved in it. Finally, it describes some successful practices organizations could use for improving their risk management capabilities.

A HOLISTIC VIEW OF IT-BASED RISK

With the explosion in the past decade of new IT-based risks, it is increasingly recog-nized that risk means more than simply "the possibility of a loss or exposure to loss" (Mogul 2004) or even a hazard, uncertainty, or opportunity (McKeen and Smith 2003). Today, *risk* is a multilayered concept that implies much more is at stake.

> "IT risk has changed. IT risk incidents harm constituencies within and outside companies. They damage corporate reputations and expose weaknesses in com-panies' management teams. Most importantly, IT risk dampens an organization's ability to compete." (Hunter and Westerman 2007)

As a result, companies are now focused on "enterprise risk management" as a more comprehensive and integrated approach to dealing with risk (Slywotzky and Drzik 2005). Although, not every risk affecting an enterprise will be an IT-based risk, the fact remains that an increasing number of the risks affecting the enterprise have an IT-based component. For example, one firm's IT risk management policy notes that the goal of risk management is to ensure that technology failures or data integrity do not compromise the company's strategic objectives, the company's reputation and stake-holders, or its success and reputation.

But, in spite of the increasing number and complexity of IT-based threats facing organizations and evidence that links risk management with IT project success (Didraga 2013), it remains difficult to get senior executives to devote their attention (and commit the necessary resources) to effectively manage these risks. A recent global survey noted, "while the security community recognizes that information security is part of effective business management, managing information security risk is still overwhelmingly seen as an IT responsibility worldwide" (Berinato 2007). Another study of several organizations found that none had a good view of all key risks and 75 percent had major gaps in their approach to IT-based risk management (Coles and Moulton 2003). In short, while IT has become increasingly central to business success, many enterprises have not yet adjusted their processes to incorporate IT-based risk management (Hunter and Westerman 2007).

Knowing what's at stake, risk management is perennially in the top ten priorities for CIOs (Hunter et al. 2005) and efforts are being made to put effective capabilities and processes in place in IT organizations. However, only 5 percent of firms are at a high level of maturity in this area, and most (80 percent) are still in the initial stages of this work (Proctor 2007). Addressing risk in a more professional, accountable, and transparent fashion is an evolution from traditional IT security work. At a Gartner symposium the following was pointed out:

> "[T]raditionally, [IT] security has been reactive, ad hoc, and technically-focused.... The shift to risk management requires an acceptance that you can't protect yourself from everything, so you need to measure risk and make good decisions about how far you go in protecting the organization." (Proctor 2007)

Companies in the group largely reflected this transitional state. "Information security is a primary focus of our risk management strategy," said one manager. "It's very, very visible but our business has yet to commit to addressing risk issues." Another stated, "We have a risk management group focused on IT risk, but lots of other groups focus on it too.... As a result, there are many different and overlapping views, and we are missing integration of these views." "We are constantly trying to identify gaps in our risk management practices and to close them," said a third.

There is, however, no hesitation about identifying the sources of risk. Every company in the group had its own checklist of risk items, and experts have developed several different frameworks and categorizations that aim to be comprehensive (see Appendix A for some of these). What everyone agrees on is that any approach to dealing with IT-based risk must be holistic—even though it is an "onerous" job to package it as a whole. "Every category of risk has a different vocabulary," explained one focus group manager. "Financial, pandemic, software, information security, disaster recovery planning, governance and legal—each view makes sense, but pulling them together is very hard." Risk is often managed in silos in organizations, resulting in uncoordinated approaches to its management and to decision-making incorporating risk. This is why many organizations, including several in the focus group, are attempting to integrate the wide variety of issues involved into one holistic enterprise risk management strategy that uses a common language to communicate.

The connection among all of the different risk perspectives is the enterprise. Any IT problem that occurs—whether with an application, a network, a new system, a vendor, or a hacker (to name just a few)—has the increasing potential to put the enterprise at risk. Thus, a holistic view of IT-based risk must put the enterprise front and center in any framework or policy. A risk to the enterprise includes anything (either internal or external) that affects its brand, reputation, competitiveness, financial value, or end state (i.e., its overall effectiveness, efficiency, and success).

Figure 10.1 offers an integrated, holistic view of risk from an enterprise perspective. A wide variety of both internal and external IT-based risks can affect the enterprise. Externally, risks can come from the following:

- Third parties, such as partners, software vendors, service providers, suppliers, or customers
- Hazards, such as disasters, pandemics, geopolitical upheavals, or environmental considerations
- Legal and regulatory issues, such as failure to adhere to the laws and regulations affecting the company, including privacy, financial reporting, environmental reporting, and e-discovery

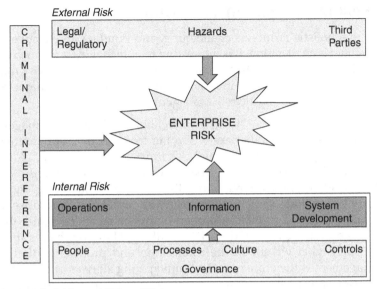

FIGURE 10.1 A Holistic View of IT-Based Risk

Internally, some risks are well known, such as those traditionally associated with IT operations (availability, accessibility) and systems development (not meeting schedules or budgets, or delivering value). Others are newer and, although they must be managed from within the organization, they may include both internal and external components. These include the following:

- Information risks, such as those affecting privacy, quality, accuracy, and protection
- People risks, such as those caused by mistakes or lack of adherence to security protocols
- Process risks, such as problems caused by poorly designed business processes or by failure to adapt business processes to IT-based changes
- Cultural risks, such as risk aversion and lack of risk awareness
- Controls, such as ineffective or inadequate controls to prevent or mitigate risk incidents
- Governance, such as ineffective or inadequate structure, roles, or accountabilities to make appropriate risk-based decisions

Finally, there is the risk of criminal interference, either from inside or outside the organization. Unlike other types of risk, which are typically inadvertent, criminal actions are deliberate attacks on the enterprise, its information, or sometimes its employees or customers. Such threats are certainly not new. Everyone is familiar with viruses and hackers. What is new, however, is that many more groups and individuals are targeting organizations and people. These include other national governments, organized crime, industrial spies, and terrorists. "These people are not trying to bring systems down, like in the past," explained a group member. "They are trying to get information."

HOLISTIC RISK MANAGEMENT: A PORTRAIT

Tackling risk in a holistic fashion is challenging, and building an effective framework for its management is challenging. It is interesting to note that there is much more agreement from the focus group and other researchers about what effective risk management *looks like* than *how* to do it. With this in mind, we outline some of the characteristics and components of an effective, holistic risk management program:

1. *Focus on what's important.* "Risks are inevitable," admitted a manager. "The first question we must ask is 'What are we trying to protect?'" said another. "There's no perfect package, and some residual risk must always be taken." A third added "Risks are inevitable, but it's how they're managed—our response, contingency plans, team readiness, and adaptability—that makes the difference." In short, risk is uncertainty that matters, something that can hurt or delay an enterprise from reaching its objectives (Hillson 2008). Although many managers recognize that it's time to take a more strategic view of risk, "[W]e still don't have our hands around what's important and what we should be monitoring and protecting" (Berinato 2007). Risk management is therefore not about anticipating all risks but about attempting to reduce significant risks to a manageable level and knowing how to assess and respond to it (Slywotzky and Drzik 2005). Yet, more than protecting the enterprise, risk management should also enable IT to take more risk in the safest possible way (Caldwell and Mogul 2006). Thus, the focus of effective risk management should not be about saying "no" to a risk, but how to say "yes," thereby building a more agile enterprise (Caldwell and Mogul 2006).

2. *Expect changes over time.* Few companies have a good grasp of risk management because IT is a discipline that is evolving rapidly (Proctor 2007). As a result, it would be a mistake to codify risk practices and standards too rapidly, according to the focus group. Efforts to do this have typically resulted in "paperwork without context," said one manager. Within a particular risk category, risk management actions should be "continuous, iterative, and structured," group members agreed. In recognition of this reality, most participant organizations have a mandatory risk assessment at key stages in the system development process to capture the risk picture involved with a particular project at several points in time and many have regular, ongoing reviews of required operational controls on an annual or biannual basis to do the same thing. In addition, when incidents occur, there should always be a process for evaluating what happened, assessing its impact, and determining if controls or other management processes need to be adapted (Coles and Moulton 2003). Finally, organizations should also be continually attempting to simplify and streamline controls wherever possible to minimize their burden. This is a process that is often missed, admitted one manager.

    However, despite the fact that each of these steps is useful, it is also essential to stand back from these initiatives and see how the holistic risk image is developing. It is this more strategic and holistic view that is often missing in organizations and that firms often fail to communicate to their staff. One of the greatest risks to organizations comes from employees themselves, not necessarily through their intentional actions, but because they don't recognize the risks involved in their actions (Berinato 2007). Therefore, many believe it is time to recognize that risk cannot be managed solely through controls, procedures, and technology but that all employees must understand the concepts and goals of risk management because the enterprise will always need to rely on their judgment to some extent (Symantec Corporation 2007). In the same vein, many managers frequently do not comprehend the size and nature of the risks involved and thus resource their management inappropriately (Coles and Moulton 2003). As a result they tend to delegate many aspects of risk management to lower levels in the organization, thus preventing the development of any longer-term, overall vision (Proctor 2008; Witty 2008).

3. *View risk from multiple levels and perspectives.*   Instead of dealing with security "incidents" in a one-at-a-time manner, it is important to do root cause analysis in order to understand risks in a more multifaceted way. To date, risk management has tended to focus largely on the operational and tactical levels and not viewed in a strategic way. One manager explained, "We need to assess risk trends and develop strategies for dealing with them. Tactics for dealing with future threats will then be more effective and easier to put in place." Another noted, "We must aim for redundancy of protection—that is, multiple layers, to ensure that if one layer fails, others will catch any problems."

Furthermore, risk, security, and compliance are often intermixed in people's minds. Each of these is a valid and unique lens through which to view risk and should not be seen as being the same. For example, one expert noted that 70 percent of a typical "security" budget is spent on compliance matters, not on protecting and defending the organization (Society for Information Management 2008), and this imbalance means that overall spending in many firms is skewed. One firm uses the "prudent man" rule to deal with risk, which recommends a diversity of approaches—being proactive, prevention, due diligence, credibility, and promoting awareness—to ensure that it is adequately covered and that all stakeholders are properly protected. Monitoring and adapting to new international standards and laws, completing overall health checks, and analysis of potential risks are other new dimensions of risk that should be incorporated into a firm's overall approach to risk management.

DEVELOPING A RISK MANAGEMENT FRAMEWORK

With a holistic picture in mind, organizations can begin to develop a framework for filling in the details. The objective of a risk management framework (RMF) is to create a common understanding of risk, to ensure the right risks are being addressed at the right levels, and to involve the right people in making risk decisions. An RMF also serves to guide the development of risk policies and integrate appropriate risk standards and processes into existing practices (e.g., the SDLC). No company in the focus group had yet developed a comprehensive framework for addressing IT-based risk, although many had significant pieces in place or in development. In this section, we attempt to piece these together to sketch out what an RMF might contain.

An RMF should serve as a high-level overview of how risk is to be managed in an enterprise and can also act as a structure for reporting on risk at various levels of detail. Currently, many companies have created risk management policies and require all staff to read and sign them. Unfortunately, such policies are typically so long and complex as to be overwhelming and ineffective. "Our security policy alone is two hundred pages. How enforceable is it?" complained a manger. Another noted that the language in his company's policy was highly technical. As a result, user noncompliance in following the recommended best practices was considerable. Furthermore, a plethora of committees, review boards, councils, and control centers are often designed to deal with one or more aspects of risk management, but they actually contribute to the general complexity of managing IT-based risk in an organization.

It should not be surprising that this situation exists, given the rapidity with which technologies, interfaces, external relationships, and dependencies have developed within the past decade. Organizations have struggled to simply keep up with the waves of legislation, regulation, globalization, standards, and transformation that seem to continually threaten to engulf them. An RMF is thus a starting point for providing an integrated, top-down view of risk, defining it, identifying those responsible for making key decisions about it, and mapping which policies and standards apply to each area. Fortunately, current technology makes it easy to offer multiple views and multiple levels of this information, enabling different groups or individuals to understand their responsibilities and specific policies in detail and see links to specific tools, practices, and templates, while facilitating different types of reporting to different stakeholders at different levels. By mapping existing groups, policies, and guidelines into an RMF, it is easier to see where gaps exist and where complexities in processes should be streamlined.

A basic RMF includes the following:

- *Risk category.* The general area of enterprise risk involved (e.g., criminal, operations, third party).
- *Policies and standards.* These state, at a high level, the general principles for guiding risk decisions, and they identify any formal corporate, industry, national, or international standards that should apply to each risk category.[2] For example, one company's policy regarding people states the following, in part:

> Protecting the integrity and security of client and corporate information is the responsibility of every employee. Timely and effective reporting of actual and suspected privacy incidents is a key component of meeting this responsibility. Management relies on the collective experience and judgment of its employees.

Another company policy regarding culture states, "We need to embed a risk management focus and awareness into all processes, functions, jobs, and individuals."

- *Risk type.* Each type of risk associated with each category (e.g., loss of information, failure to comply with specific laws, inability to work due to system outages) needs to be identified. Each type should have a generic name and definition, ideally linked to a business impact. Identifying all risk types will take

---

[2] Some international standards include Committee of Sponsoring Organizations (COSO) of the Treadway Commission, www.coso.org; SAI Global, www.saiglobal.com; and the Office of Government Commerce's Management of Risk (M_o_r) (www.ogc.gov.uk/guidance_management_of_risk.asp).

time and probably require much iteration as "there are an incredible variety of specific risks" (Mogul 2004). However, developing lists and definitions is a good first step (Baccarini et al. 2004; Hillson 2008; McKeen and Smith 2003) and is already a common practice among the focus group companies, at least for certain categories of risk.

- *Risk ownership.* Each type of risk should have an owner, either in IT or in the business. As well, there will likely be several stakeholders who will be affected by risk-based decisions. For example, the principal business sponsor could be the owner of risk decisions associated with the development or purchase of a new IT system, but IT operations and architecture as well as the project manager will clearly be key stakeholders. In addition to specialized IT functions, such as IT security, audit and privacy functions in the business will likely be involved in many IT risk-based decisions. Owners and stakeholders should have clear responsibilities and accountabilities. In the focus group, some major risk types were owned by committees, such as an enterprise risk committee, or the internal audit, social responsibility and risk governance committee, or the project risk review council on which stakeholder groups were represented.

- *Risk mitigation.* As an RMF is developed, each type of risk should be associated with controls, practices, and tools for addressing it effectively. These fall into one of two categories: compulsory and optional. Group members stressed that overemphasis on mitigation can lead to organizational paralysis or hyper-risk sensitivity. Instead participants stressed the role of judgment in right sizing mitigation activities wherever possible. "Our technology development framework does not tell you what you have to do, but it does give you things to consider in each phase," said one manager. "We look first at the overall enterprise risk presented by a project," said another, "and develop controls based on our evaluation of the level and types of risk involved." The goal, everyone agreed, is to provide a means by which risks can be managed consistently, effectively, and appropriately.[3]

- *Risk reporting and monitoring.* This was a rather controversial topic in the focus group. Although everyone agreed it is important to make risk and its management more visible in the organization, tracking and reporting on risk have a tendency to make management highly risk averse. One manager said:

> We spent a year trying to quantify risks and developing a roll-up report, but we threw it away because audit didn't understand it and saw only one big risk. This led to endless discussion and no confidence that IT was handling risk well. Now we use a very simple reporting framework presenting risk as high, medium, or low. This is language we all understand.

There are definitely pressures to improve risk measurement (Proctor 2007), but clearly care must be taken in how these metrics are reported. For example, one company

---

[3] "Risk Management Guide for Information Technology Systems" (csrc.nist.gov/publications/nistpubs/800-30/sp800-30.pdf), the National Institute of Standards and Technology's Special Publication 800-30, provides guidance on specific risk mitigation strategies.

uses a variety of self-assessments to ensure that risks have been properly identified and appropriate controls put in place. However, as risk management procedures become better understood and more codified, risk reporting can also become more formalized. This is particularly the case at present with operational process controls and fundamental IT security, such as virus or intrusion detection.

However, risk monitoring is an ongoing process because levels and types of risk are changing continually. Thus, an RMF should be a dynamic document as new types of risk are identified, business impacts are better understood, and mitigation practices evolve. "We need to continually monitor all categories of risk and ask our executives if the levels of risk are still the same," said a focus group member. It is clear that failure to understand how risks are changing is a significant risk in itself (Proctor 2007). It is therefore especially important to have a process in place to analyze what happens when an unforeseen risk occurs. Unless efforts are made to understand the root causes of a problem, it is unlikely that effective mitigation practices can be put in place.

IMPROVING RISK MANAGEMENT CAPABILITIES

Risk management in most areas does not yet have well-documented best practices or standards in place. However, the focus group identified several actions that could lead to the development of effective risk management capabilities:

- *Look beyond technical risk.*   One of the biggest inhibitors of effective risk management is too tight a focus on technical risk, rather than on business risk (Coles and Moulton 2003). A traditional security approach, for example, tends to focus only on technical threats or specific systems or platforms.
- *Develop a common language of risk.*   A clearer understanding of business risk requires all stakeholders—IT, audit, privacy, legal, business managers—to speak the same language and use comparable metrics—at least at the highest levels of analysis where the different types of risk need to be integrated.
- *Simplify the presentation.*   Having a common approach to discussing or describing risk is very effective, said several focus group members. While the work that is behind a simple presentation may be complex, presenting too much complexity can be counterproductive. The most effective approaches are simple: a narrative, a dashboard, a "stoplight" report, or another graphic style of report.
- *Right size.*   Risk management should be appropriate for the level of risk involved. More effective practices allow for the adaptation of controls while ensuring that the decisions made are visible and the rationale is communicated.
- *Standardize the technology base.*   This is one of the most effective ways to reduce risk, according to the research, but it is also one of the most expensive (Hunter et al. 2005).
- *Rehearse.*   Many firms now have an emergency response team in place to rapidly deal with key hazards. However, it is less common that this team actually rehearses its disaster recovery, business continuity, or other types of risk mitigation plans.

One manager noted that live rehearsals are essential to reveal gaps in plans and unexpected risk factors.

- *Clarify roles and responsibilities.* With so many groups in the organization now involved in managing risk in some way, it is critical that roles and responsibilities be documented and communicated. Ideally, this should be in the context of an RMF. However, even if an RMF is not in place, efforts should be made to document which groups in the organization are responsible for which types of enterprise risk.

- *Automate where appropriate.* As risk management practices become standardized and streamlined, automated controls begin to make sense. Some tools can be very effective, noted the focus group, provided they are applied in ways that facilitate risk management, rather than becoming an obstacle to productivity.

- *Educate and communicate.* Each organization has its own culture, and most need to work with staff, business managers, and executives to make them more aware of risks and the need to invest in appropriate management. However, some organizations, like one insurance company in the focus group, are so risk-phobic that they need education to enable them to take on more risk. Such companies could benefit from better understanding their "risk portfolio" of projects (Day 2007). Such an approach can often help encourage companies to undertake more risky innovation initiatives with more confidence.

Conclusion

Organizations are more sensitized to risk than ever before. The economy, regulatory, and legal environment; business complexity; the increasing openness of business relationships; and rapidly changing technology have all combined to drive managers to seek a more comprehensive understanding of risk and its management. Whereas in the past, risk was managed in isolated pockets by such functions as IT security, internal audit, and legal, today recognition is growing that these arenas intersect and affect each other. And IT risk is clearly involved in many types of business risk these days. Criminal activity, legal responsibilities, privacy, innovation, and operational productivity, to name just a few, all have IT risk implications. As a result, organizations need a new approach to risk—one that is more holistic in nature and that provides an integrative framework for understanding risk and making decisions associated with it. Accomplishing this is no simple task, so developing such a framework will likely be an ongoing activity, as experts in IT and others begin to grapple with how to approach such a complex and multidimensional activity. This chapter has therefore not tried to present a definitive approach to risk management. There is general agreement that organizations are not ready for this. Instead, it has tried to sketch an impression of how to approach risk management and what an effective risk management program might look like. IT managers and others have been left to fill in the details and complete the portrait in their own organizations.

References

Baccarini, D., G. Salm, and P. Love. "Management of Risks in Information Technology Projects." *Industrial Management + Data Systems* 104, no. 3–4 (2004): 286–95.

Berinato, S. "The Fifth Annual Global State of Information Security." *CIO Magazine,* August 28, 2007.

Caldwell, F., and R. Mogul. "Risk Management and Business Performance Are Compatible." Gartner Inc., ID Number: G00140802, October 18, 2006.

Coles, R., and R. Moulton. "Operationalizing IT Risk Management." *Computers and Security* 22, no. 6 (2003): 487–92.

Day, G. "Is It Real? Can We Win? Is It Worth Doing? Managing Risk and Reward in an Innovation Portfolio." *Harvard Business Review,* December 2007.

Didraga, O. "The Role and the Effects of Risk Management in IT Projects Success." *Informatica Economica* 17, no. 1 (2013): 86–98.

Hillson, D. "Danger Ahead." *PM Network,* March 2008.

Hunter, R., and G. Westerman. *IT Risk: Turning Business Threats into Competitive Advantage.* Boston: Harvard Business School Press, 2007.

Hunter, R., G. Westerman, and D. Aron. "IT Risk Management: A Little Bit More Is a Whole Lot Better." *Gartner EXPCIO Signature Report,* February 2005.

McKeen, J., and H. Smith. *Making IT Happen: Critical Issues in IT Management.* Chichester, England: John Wiley & Sons, 2003.

Mogul, R. "Gartner's Simple Enterprise Risk Management Framework." Gartner Inc., ID Number: G00125380, December 10, 2004.

Proctor, P. IT "Risk Management for the Inexperienced: A CIO's Travel Guide to IT 'Securistan.'" Presentation to Gartner Symposium ITxpo 2007 Emerging Trends, San Francisco, CA, April 22–26, 2007.

Proctor, P. "Key Issues for the Risk and Security Roles, 2008." Gartner Inc., ID Number: G00155764, March 27, 2008.

Rasmussen, M. "Identifying and Selecting the Right Risk Consultant." Forrester Research Teleconference, July 12, 2007.

Slywotzky, A., and J. Drzik. "Countering the Biggest Risk of All." *Harvard Business Review,* April 2005.

Society for Information Management. "Executive IT security." Private presentation to the SIM Advanced Practices Council, May 2008.

Symantec Corporation. "Trends for July–December 2006." *Symantec Internet Security Threat Report* XI (March 2007).

Witty, R. "Findings: IT Disaster Recovery Can Upsell Business Continuity Management." Gartner Inc., ID Number: G00155402, February 19, 2008.

APPENDIX A

A Selection of Risk Classification Schemes

MCKEEN AND SMITH (2003)

- Financial risk
- Technology risk
- Security
- Information and people
- Business process
- Management
- External
- Risk of success

BACCARINI, SALM, AND LOVE (2004)

- Commercial risk
- Economic circumstances
- Human behavior
- Political circumstances
- Technology and technical issues
- Management activities and controls
- Individual activities

JORDAN AND SILCOCKS (2005)

- Project risk
- IT services
- Information assets
- IT service providers and vendors
- Applications
- Infrastructure
- Strategic
- Emergent

RASMUSSEN (2007)

- Information security risk
- Policy and compliance
- Information asset management
- Business continuity and disaster recovery
- Incident and threat management
- Physical and environment
- Systems development and operations management

COMBINED FOCUS GROUP CATEGORIES

- Project
- Operations
- Strategic
- Enterprise
- Disaster recovery
- Information
- External
- Reputation
- Competitive
- Compliance and regulatory
- Forensic
- Opportunity
- Ethical
- Physical
- Business continuity
- Business process

11 Information Management: The Nexus of Business and IT[1]

M ore than ever before, we are living in an information age. Yet until very recently, information and its sibling, knowledge, were given very little attention in IT organizations. Data ruled. And information proliferated quietly in various corners of the business—file cabinets, PCs, databases, microfiche, e-mail, and libraries. Then along came the Internet and social media, and the business began to understand the power and the potential of information. For the past few years, businesses have been clamoring for IT to deliver more and better information to them (IBM 2012; Smith and McKeen 2005c). As a result, information delivery has become an important part of IT's job.

Now that businesses recognize the value of improved information, IT is facing huge challenges delivering it:

> Not only does effective information delivery require IT to implement new technologies, it also means that IT must develop new internal nontechnical and analytic capabilities. Information delivery makes IT work much more visible in the organization. Developing standard data models, integrating information into work processes, and forcing (encouraging) business managers to put the customer/employee/supplier first in their decision making involves IT practitioners in organizational and political conflicts that most would likely prefer to avoid. Unfortunately, the days of hiding in the "glass house" are now completely over and IT managers are front and center of an information revolution that will completely transform how organizations operate. (Smith and McKeen 2005a)

This points out a truth that is only just beginning to sink into the organization's collective consciousness. That is, although information *delivery* may be the responsibility

---

[1] This chapter is based on the authors' previously published article, Smith, H. A., and J. D. McKeen. "Information Management: The Nexus of Business and IT." *Communications of the Association for Information Systems* 19, no. 3 (January 2007): 34–46. Reproduced by permission of the Association for Information Systems.

of IT, information *management* (IM) requires a true partnership between IT and the business. IT is *involved* with almost every aspect of IM, but information is the heart and soul of the business, and its management cannot be delegated or abdicated to IT. Thus, IM represents the true nexus of the business and IT. Because of this, IM has all the hallmarks of an emerging discipline—the offspring of a committed, long-term relationship between the business and IT. It requires new skills and competencies, new frames of reference, and new processes. As is often the case, IT workers are further advanced in their understanding of this new discipline, but many business leaders are also recognizing their responsibilities in this field. In some organizations, notably government, IM is now a separate organizational entity, distinct from IT.

This chapter explores the nature and dimensions of IM and its implications for IT, looking at IM from the enterprise point of view. Information delivery can be viewed from a purely IT perspective, whereas information management addresses the business *and* IT issues and challenges in managing information effectively. The first section examines the scope and nature of IM and how it is being conceptualized in organizations. The next presents a framework for the comprehensive management of information. Then the key issues currently facing organizations in implementing an effective IM program are addressed. Finally, the chapter presents some recommendations for getting started in IM.

INFORMATION MANAGEMENT: HOW DOES IT FIT?

Information management is an idea whose time has come for a number of reasons. One focus group member explained it in this way:

> *In today's business environment, it is a given that we must know who our customer is and ensure our organization's information enables us to make the right business decisions. As well, emerging regulations are starting to shape the IM requirements of all companies. These include privacy and security safeguards on customer information, long-term storage of historical records, and stronger auditability. We are now being held legally accountable for our information.*

Thus, IM has three distinct but related drivers: (1) compliance, (2) operational effectiveness and efficiency, and (3) strategy.

Information, as we are now recognizing, is a key organizational resource, along with human and financial capital. Captured and used in the right way, many believe information is a different form of capital, known as *structural capital* (Stewart 1999). However, unlike human and financial capital, information is not finite. It cannot be used up, nor can it walk out the door. Furthermore, information capabilities—that is, the ability to capture, organize, use, and maintain information—have been shown to contribute to IT effectiveness, individual effectiveness, and overall business performance (Kettinger and Marchand 2005; Marchand et al. 2000; Perez-Lopez and Alegre 2012). Therefore, many companies now believe that creating useful structural capital is a strategic priority (IBM 2012; Kettinger and Marchand 2005).

Unlike information technology, which provides the technology, tools, and processes with which to *capture, store, and manipulate data,* or knowledge management

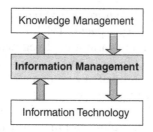

FIGURE 11.1   IM is Fundamental to Organizational Success—Both IT Effectiveness and Individual Performance

(KM), which focuses on how best to leverage the know-how and *intangible experience* of the organization's human capital, IM provides the mechanisms for managing enterprise information itself. IM represents the "meat" in the data–information–knowledge continuum and provides a foundation that can be used by both IT and KM to create business value (see Figure 11.1).

As noted earlier, organizations today are beset with demands for more and better information and more controls over it. IM is the means to get above the fray and clarify how the enterprise will manage information as an integrated resource. In theory, it covers all forms of information needed and produced by the business, both structured and unstructured, including the following:

- Customer information
- Financial information
- Operational information
- Product information
- HR information
- Documents
- E-mail and instant messages
- Customer feedback
- Images and multimedia materials
- Business intelligence
- Relationship information (e.g., suppliers, partners)
- Information about physical objects (i.e., the internet of things)
- Externally generated information (e.g., government records, weather information)
- Geolocation information

In practice, some of these forms will be more thoroughly managed than others, depending on the organization involved.

The "IM function" is also responsible for the complete information life cycle: acquisition or creation, organization, navigation, access, security, administration, storage, and retention. Because IM falls into the gray area between the business and IT and is not yet a separate organizational entity, many organizations are finding it is essential to develop an enterprisewide framework that clarifies the policies, principles, roles, responsibilities and accountabilities, and practices for IM in both groups.

A FRAMEWORK FOR IM

Because much information use crosses traditional functional boundaries, organizations must take an enterprise perspective on IM for it to be effective. A framework for implementing IM involves several stages that move from general principles to specific applications. Although these are presented as distinct activities, in practice they will likely evolve iteratively as the organization and its management learn by doing. For example, one company developed and implemented its privacy policy first then recognized the need for an information security policy. As this was being implemented, it created a more generic IM policy that incorporated the other two in its principles.

Stage One: Develop an IM Policy

A policy outlines the terms of reference for making decisions about information. It provides the basis for corporate directives and for developing the processes, standards, and guidelines needed to manage information assets well throughout the enterprise. Because information is a corporate asset, an IM policy needs to be established at a very senior management level and approved by the board of directors. This policy should provide guidance for more detailed directives on accountabilities, quality, security, privacy, risk tolerances, and prioritization of effort.

Because of the number of business functions affected by information, a draft policy should be developed by a multidisciplinary team. At minimum, IT, the privacy office, legal, HR, corporate audit, and key lines of business should be involved. "We had lots of support for this from our audit people," said one manager. "They recognize that an IM policy will help improve the traceability of information and its transformations, and this makes their jobs easier." Another recommended reviewing the draft policy with many executives and ensuring that all business partners are identified. "Ideally, the policy should also link to existing IM processes such as security classifications," stated another. "It's less threatening if people are familiar with what it implies, and this also helps identify gaps in practices that need to be addressed."

Stage Two: Articulate the Operational Components

The operational components describe what needs to be in place in order to put the corporate IM policy into practice across the organization (see Figure 11.2). In turn, each component will have several "elements." These could vary according to what different organizations deem important. For example, the strategy component at one company has six elements: (1) interacting with the external environment, (2) strategic planning, (3) information life cycle, (4) general planning, (5) program integration, and (6) performance monitoring (for a description of the elements identified by this firm, see Appendix A). Together, the operational components act as a context to describe current IM practices in the organization and reference existing best practices in each area. "This is a living document, and you should expect it to be continually refined," noted a focus group member.

The IM framework's operational components and individual elements act as a discussion document to position IM in the business and to illustrate its breadth and scope. "There's a danger of IM being perceived as a 'technology thing,'" stated a manager.

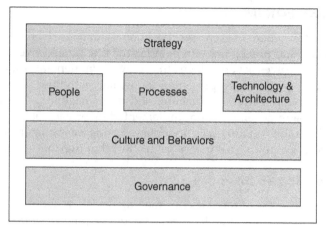

FIGURE 11.2 Operational Components of an IM Framework

Although it is often IT groups that spearhead the IM effort, they recognize that it shouldn't necessarily be located in IT permanently. "Ideally, we need a corporate information office that cuts across lines of business and corporate groups, just like IT," said another manager.

Stage Three: Establish Information Stewardship

Many roles and responsibilities associated with IM need to be clearly articulated. These are especially important to clarify because of the boundary-spanning nature of information. Both political and practical issues arise when certain questions are asked: Who is responsible for the quality of our customer data? Whose version of name and address do we use? Who must sign off on the accuracy of our financial information? Ideally, most organizations would like to have a single version of each of their key information subjects (e.g., customer, product, employees) that all lines of business and systems would use. This would enable proper protections and controls to be put in place. And this is clearly a long-term IM goal for most. However, legacy environments, politics, and tight budgets mean that the reality is somewhat less perfect with duplicate versions of the same information and several variants being used by parts of the business.

Information stewards are businesspeople. They should be responsible for determining the meaning of information "chunks" (e.g., customer name and address) and their business rules and contextual use. They should be responsible for the accuracy, timeliness, consistency, validity, completeness, and redundancy of information. Stewards also determine who may access information according to privacy and security policies and provide guidance for the retention and deletion of information in accordance with regulatory and legal requirements. In addition, stewards make the information's characteristics available to a broad audience through the organization's metadata.

Stewardship, like IM, is an evolving role that few understand fully. Ideally, there should be one steward for each key information subject, but this is nowhere near the reality in most organizations. One organization has established a working group for each of its major subjects, with representatives from all affected stakeholder groups as well as IT. The working groups' goals are to reduce duplicate records, correct information, simplify processes, and close "back doors." In the longer term, these groups hope to develop standard definitions and a formal stewardship process and ultimately use these to retool IT's data infrastructure.

"We are struggling with this concept," admitted a manager. "This is not a simple task, and no one in our business wants to take accountability as yet." Stewardship also takes time, and many business units are not yet prepared to allocate resources to it. "At present, we are hitching our wagons to other projects and hoping to make some progress in this way," said another manager. "Every area is taking some steps, but they're all at different levels of maturity. This can be frustrating because progress is so slow." All agreed that the role of information steward needs to be better defined and incorporated into organizational and HR models. New performance metrics also need to be established to monitor progress against these goals in ways that link IM activities to key business objectives.

Stage Four: Build Information Standards

Standards help ensure that quality, accuracy, and control goals can be met. When all parts of an organization follow the same standards, it is relatively easy to simplify the processes and technology that use a piece of information, said the focus group. Conversely, different information standards used by different business groups will inhibit effective IM. *Setting* information standards can be challenging, and it's even harder to actually *implement* them, participants noted. The latter is partly due to the large number of legacy applications in most organizations and also because it is difficult to get funding for this work.

Not all information needs to be standardized, however—only that which is used by more than one business unit. When information *is* used more broadly, a standard needs to be established. A metadata repository is useful for this. This repository stores information definitions; standards for use and change; and provides cross-references for all models, processes, and programs using a particular piece of information. A metadata repository can be jointly used by the business, when beginning a new project, and IT, when developing or modifying applications. It can be invaluable to both groups (and the enterprise) in helping them to understand how their work will affect others, thus preventing potential problems.

Typically, cross-functional working groups composed of business and IT staff establish standards. "Metadata is really where the rubber meets the road," said one manager. "It can be a very powerful tool to prevent the duplication of data in the organization." However, it is a huge undertaking and takes time to show value. "You need strong IT executive support for this," he said. "It is not something that those outside of IT initially understand." The focus group recommended starting with what exists currently (e.g., a data warehouse), then growing from there. One firm initially established a procedure that any changes to production systems had to update the metadata repository first. "We weren't prepared for the demand this created," stated the manager involved. "It's much better to incorporate this step in front-end analysis than at the end of development."

Finally, education and awareness play an essential role at this stage. "We always underestimate the importance of awareness," said a participant. "We must make sure that no project starts in the organization that doesn't use standards. The only way to

---

Standards require . . .

- A unique name and definition
- Data elements, examples, and character length (e.g., name prefix)
- Relationship rules
- Implementation requirements
- Spacing and order

---

do this is to keep this issue continually in front of our business executives." The other group members agreed. "Standards are the cornerstone of IM," said one. "If they are followed, they will ensure we don't add further layers of complexity and new steps."

ISSUES IN IM

As with anything new, those involved with IM in their organizations face a host of challenges and opportunities as they try to implement more effective processes and practices around information. Some of these can be mixed blessings in that they are both drivers of IM and complications (e.g., legislation). Others are simply new ways of looking at information and new perspectives on the way organizations work. Still others are genuinely new problems that must be addressed. When combined with the fact that IM "belongs" exclusively to neither IT nor the business, these add up to a huge organizational headache, especially for IT. "Sometimes the businesspeople are not ready for the disciplines associated with IM," said one manager. "If they're not ready, we move on to an area that is." Another said, "Sometimes it's more trouble than it's worth to involve the business, and we just do the work ourselves."

Culture and Behavior

In the longer term, however, the focus group agreed that IM is something that all parts of the organization will have to better understand and participate in. One of the most comprehensive challenges is changing the culture and behavior surrounding information. Marchand et al. (2000) suggest that six interdependent beliefs and behaviors are needed by all staff to support a positive "information orientation." These have been strongly correlated to organizational performance when they are present with strong IT and IM practices:

1. *Integrity.* Integrity "defines both the boundaries beyond which people in an organization should not go in using information and the 'space' in which people can trust their colleagues to do with information what they would do themselves" (Marchand et al. 2000). Where integrity exists, people will have confidence that information will not be used inappropriately.

2. *Formality.* Formality is the ability to trust formal sources of information (as opposed to informal ones). Formality enables an organization to provide accurate and consistent information about the business and establish formal processes and information flows that can be used to improve performance and provide services to customers.

3. *Control.*   Once formal information is trusted, it can be used to develop integrated performance criteria and measures for all levels of the company. In time, these will enable monitoring and performance improvement at the individual and work unit levels and can be linked to compensation and rewards.
4. *Transparency.*   Transparency describes a level of trust among members of an organization that enables them to speak about errors or failures "in an open and constructive manner without fear of unfair repercussions" (Marchand et al. 2000). Transparency is necessary to identify and respond effectively to problems and for learning to take place.
5. *Sharing.*   At this level, both sensitive and nonsensitive information is freely shared among individuals and across functional boundaries. Information exchanges are both initiated by employees and formally promoted through programs and forums.[2]
6. *Proactiveness.*   Ultimately, every member of an organization should be proactive about acquiring new information about business conditions and testing new concepts.

Information Risk Management

The increasing breadth and scope of IT, combined with greater use of outsourcing and mobility, has made information more vulnerable to both internal and external fraud and has raised the level of risk associated with it. Management must, therefore, take proactive measures to determine an appropriate risk/return trade-off for information security. Costs are associated with information security mechanisms, and the business must be educated about them. In some cases these mechanisms are "table stakes"—that is, they must be taken if the company wants to "be in the game." Other risks in information security include internal and external interdependencies, implications for corporate governance, and impact on the value proposition. Risk exposures can also change over time and with outsourcing, mobile applications, and cloud computing.

The focus group agreed that security is essential in the new world of IM. Today most organizations have basic information protection, such as virus scanners, firewalls, and virtual private networks. Many are also working on the next level of security, which includes real-time response, intrusion detection and monitoring, and vulnerability analysis. Soon, however, information security will need to include role-based identity and access management. An effective information-security strategy includes several components:

- An information protection center, which classifies data, analyzes vulnerabilities, and issues alerts
- Risk management
- Identity management, including access management, digital rights management, and encryption technology
- Education and awareness
- Establishment of priorities, standards, and resource requirements
- Compliance reviews and audits

---

[2] Privacy laws in many countries inhibit the sharing of personal information for any purpose other than that for which it was collected. Customer information can, therefore, be shared only with consent.

Many of the decisions involved must be made by the lines of business, not IT, as only the business can determine access rules for content and the other controls that will facilitate identity and access management.

Information Value

At present, the economics of information have not yet been established in most organizations. It is, therefore, often hard to make the case for IM investments not only because the benefits are difficult to quantify but also because of the large number of variables involved. A value proposition for IM should address its strategic, tactical, and operational value and how it will lower risk and develop new capabilities. Furthermore, an effort should be made to quantify the value of the organization's existing information assets and to recognize their importance to its products and services.

Determining "value" is a highly subjective assessment. Thus, different companies and even different executives will define it differently. Most businesses define *value* broadly and loosely, not simply as a financial concept (Ginzberg 2001). However, because there is no single, agreed-on measure of information value, misunderstandings about its definition can easily arise (Beath et al. 2012). Therefore, it is essential that everyone involved in IM activities agree on what value they are trying to deliver and how they will recognize it. Furthermore, value has a time dimension. It takes time for an IM investment to pay off and become apparent. This also must be recognized by all concerned.

Privacy

Concern for the privacy of personal information has been raised to new levels, thanks to legislation being enacted around the world. All companies need enterprisewide privacy policies that address the highest privacy standards required in their working environments. For example, if they operate globally, policies and practices should satisfy all legislation worldwide. Privacy clearly should be both part of any long-term IM initiatives, and also what an organization is doing *currently*. As such, it is both an IM issue and an initiative in its own right. Both existing processes and staff behavior will be affected by privacy considerations. "Privacy is about respect for personal information and fair and ethical information practices. Training should start with all new employees and then be extended to all employees," said a manager. Many countries now require organizations to have a chief privacy officer. If so, this person should be a key stakeholder in ensuring that the organization's IM practices for data quality and accuracy, retention, information stewardship, and security are also in keeping with all privacy standards and legislation.

As with other IM initiatives, it is important that senior management understand and support the changes needed to improve privacy practices over time. "Good practices take time to surface," said a manager. "It takes time and resources to ensure all our frontline staff and our information collection and management processes are compliant." Accountabilities should be clearly defined as well. Ideally, IM policy and stewards set the standards in this area with privacy specialists and operational staff (in both IT and the business) responsible for implementing them. With the increase in outsourcing, particularly to offshore companies, all contracts and subcontracting arrangements must be reviewed for compliance in this area. "Our company is still liable for privacy breaches if they occur in one of our vendor firms," noted a group member.

Knowledge Management

Although many organizations have been soured on knowledge management (KM) because of its "soft and fuzzy" nature (Smith and McKeen 2004), the fact remains that IM provides a solid foundation that will enable the organization to do more with what it knows (see Figure 11.1). Even firms that do not have a separate KM function recognize that better IM will help them build valuable structural capital. There are many levels at which IM can be improved. At the most elementary, data warehouses can be built and the information in them can be analyzed for trends and patterns. One company is working on identifying its "single points of knowledge" (i.e., those staff members who have specialized knowledge in an important area) and capturing this knowledge in a formal way (e.g., in business processes or metadata). Many firms are making customer information management a priority so they can use this information to both serve their customers better and to learn more about them.[3] This clearly cannot be done unless information is integrated across processes and accessible in a usable format (Beath et al. 2012; Smith and McKeen 2005b). Finally, information can be aggregated and synthesized to create new and useful knowledge. For example, Wal-Mart takes transaction-level information from its sales process and aggregates and analyzes it to make it useful both to the sales process and to other areas of the business. It identifies trends and opportunities based on this analysis and enables information to be viewed in different ways, leading to new insights.

The Knowing–Doing Gap

Most organizations assume that better information will lead to better decisions and actions, but research shows that this is not always (or even often) the case. All too often companies do not utilize the information they have. One problem is that we really understand very little about how organizations and groups actually use information in their work (Beath et al. 2012; Pfeffer and Sutton 2000). Some organizations do not make clear links between desired actions and the acquisition and packaging of specific information. Although this may seem like common sense, the focus group agreed that the complex connections between decisions and actions are not always well understood. Effective technology, strong IM practices, and appropriate behaviors and values are *all* necessary to ensure the information–action connection is made (Smith et al. 2006).

GETTING STARTED IN IM

Although IM is not IT, the fact remains that IT is still largely driving IM in most organizations. Whether this will be the case in the longer term remains to be seen. Most members would like to see the situation reversed, with the business driving the effort to

---

[3] Customer information is particularly sensitive and may be analyzed only with a customer's consent in many countries. The need to monitor consents adds a further layer of complexity to this already challenging activity.

establish appropriate IM policies, procedures, stewardship, and standards and IT supporting IM with software, data custodianship, security and access controls, information applications and administration, and integrated systems. In the shorter term, however, IT is working hard to get IM the attention it deserves in the business.

Focus group participants had several recommendations for others wishing to get started in IM:

- *Start with what you have.*   "Doing IM is like trying to solve world hunger," said one manager. "It just gets bigger and bigger the longer you look at it." Even just listing all of the information types and locations in the organization can be a daunting task, and the job will probably never be fully complete. The group, therefore, recommended doing an inventory of what practices, processes, standards, groups, and repositories already exist in the organization and trying to grow IM from there. It is most important to get the key information needed to achieve business objectives under control first. For many companies, this may be customer information; for others, it may be product or financial information. "It's really important to prioritize in IM," said a manager. "We need to focus on the right information that's going to have the biggest return." It may help to try to quantify the value of company information in some way. Despite the fact that there is no accepted accounting method for doing so as yet, some firms are adapting the value assessment methodologies used for other assets. "When you really look at the value of information, it's worth a staggering amount of money. This really gets senior management attention and support," noted a focus group member.

  A top-down approach is ideal, yet it may not always be practical. "It took us over a year to get an information policy in place," said a participant. "In the meantime, there are significant savings that can be realized by taking a bottom-up approach and cleaning up some of the worst problems." Harnessing existing compliance efforts around privacy, security, and the other types of regulation is also effective. At minimum, these will affect information architecture, access to data, document retention, and data administration for financial and personal information (Smith and McKeen 2006). "We can take either an opportunity or a fear mindset toward regulation," said a manager. Companies that see compliance from a purely tactical perspective will likely not see the value of increased controls. If, however, they see regulation as a chance to streamline and revamp business processes and the information they use, their compliance investments will likely pay off. Those interested in IM can also take advantage of the dramatically elevated attention levels of the board and executives to compliance matters.

- *Ensure cross-functional coordination among all stakeholders.*   Business involvement in IT initiatives is always desirable, and it is impossible to do IM without it. "No IM effort should go ahead without fully identifying all areas that are affected," stated one manager. Typically, legal, audit, and the privacy office will have a keen interest in this area. Equally typical, many of the business units affected will not be interested in it. For operational groups, IM is often seen as bureaucratic overhead and extra cost, which is why education and communication about IM are essential. "You have to allow time for these groups to get on board with this concept and come around to the necessity of taking the time to do IM right," said a participant. He noted that this effort has to be repeated at each level of the organization. "Senior management may be supportive, but members of the working groups may not really understand what we're trying to accomplish."

- *Get the incentives right.*   Even with IM "socialization" (i.e., education and communication), politics is likely to become a major hurdle to the success of any IM efforts. Both giving up control and taking accountability for key pieces of information can be hard for many business managers. Therefore, it is important to ensure incentives are in place that will motivate collaboration. Metrics are an important way to make progress (or the lack of it) highly visible in the organization. One firm developed a team scorecard for its customer information working group that reported two key measures to executives: the percentage of remaining duplicate records and the percentage of "perfect" customer records. Each of these was broken down into a number of leading indicators that helped focus the group's behavior on the overall effort rather than on individual territories. Another firm linked its process and information simplification efforts to budgets. The savings generated from eliminating duplicate or redundant information (and its associated storage and processing) were returned to the business units involved to be reinvested as they saw fit. This proved to be a huge motivator of enterprise-oriented behavior.

- *Establish and model sound information values.*   Because frontline workers, who make many decisions about information and procedures, ultimately cannot cover all eventualities, all staff need to understand the fundamental reasons for key company information policies and directives. Corporate values around information guide how staff should behave even when their managers aren't around. And they provide a basis for sound decision making about information (IBM 2012; Stewart 2004). Others have noted that senior IT leadership should primarily be about forming and modeling values, not managing tasks, and this is especially true for IM, said the focus group. Values are particularly important, they noted, now that staff are more mobile and virtual and, thus, more empowered. If such values are effectively articulated and modeled by leaders, they will drive the development of the appropriate culture and behaviors around information.

Conclusion

Information management is gaining increasing attention in both IT and the business. Driven by compliance and privacy legislation, the increasing vulnerability of corporate information, and the desire for greater integration of systems, IM is beginning to look like an emerging discipline in its own right. However, the challenges facing organizations in implementing effective IM practices are many and daunting. Not least is the need to try to conceptualize the scope and complexity of work to be done. Tackling IM is likely to be a long-term task. IT managers have a huge communications job ahead in trying to educate business leaders about their responsibilities in information stewardship, developing sound IM practices, and inculcating the culture and behaviors needed to achieve the desired results. Developing a plan for tackling the large and ever-increasing amount of information involved is only the first step. The more difficult effort will be involving every member of the organization—from the board to frontline workers—in seeing that it is carried out effectively. Although IT can lead this effort initially and provide substantial support for IM, ultimately its success or failure will be due to how well the business does its part.

References

Beath, C., I. Bercerra-Fernandez, J. Ross, and J. Short. "Finding Value in the Information Explosion." *MIT Sloan Management Review* 53, no. 4 (Summer 2012).

Ginzberg, M. "Achieving Business Value Through Information Technology: The Nature of High Business Value IT Organizations." Report commissioned by the Society for Information Management Advanced Practices Council, November 2001.

IBM. *CEO Survey 2011: Leading through Connections Executive Summary.* Somers, NY: IBM Global Business Services, May 2012, GBE03486-USEN-00.

Kettinger, W., and D. Marchand. "Driving Value from IT: Investigating Senior Executives' Perspectives." Report commissioned by the Society for Information Management, Advanced Practices Council, May 2005.

Marchand, D., W. Kettinger, and J. Rollins. "Information Orientation: People, Technology and the Bottom Line." *MIT Sloan Management Review* 4, no. 41 (Summer 2000): 69–80.

Perez-Lopez, S., and J. Alegre. "Information Technology Competency, Knowledge Processes and Firm Performance." *Industrial Management and Data Systems* 112, no. 4 (2012): 644–62.

Pfeffer, J., and R. Sutton. *The Knowing-Doing Gap.* Boston: Harvard Business School Press, 2000.

Smith, H. A., and J. D. McKeen. "Marketing KM to the Business." *Communications of the Association for Information Systems* 14, article 23 (November 2004): 513–25.

Smith, H. A., and J. D. McKeen. "Information Delivery: IT's Evolving Role." *Communications of the Association for Information Systems* 15, no. 11 (February 2005a): 197–210.

Smith, H. A., and J. D. McKeen. "A Framework for KM Evaluation." *Communications of the Association for Information Systems* 16, no. 9 (May 2005b): 233–46.

Smith, H. A., and J. D. McKeen. "Customer Knowledge Management: Adding Value for Our Customers." *Communications of the Association for Information Systems* 16, no. 36 (November 2005c): 744–55.

Smith, H. A., and J. D. McKeen. "IT in the New World of Corporate Governance Reforms." *Communications of the Association for Information Systems* 17, no. 32 (May 2006): 714–27.

Smith, H. A., J. D. McKeen, and S. Singh. "Making Knowledge Work: Five Principles for Action-Oriented Knowledge Management." *Knowledge Management Research and Practice* 4, no. 2 (2006): 116–24.

Stewart, T. *Intellectual Capital: The New Wealth of Organizations.* New York: Doubleday, 1999.

Stewart, T. "Leading Change When Business Is Good: An Interview with Samuel J. Palmisano." *Harvard Business Review* 82, no. 12 (December 2004).

APPENDIX A

Elements of IM Operations

A. STRATEGY

- External environment
- Strategic planning
- Information life cycle
- Planning
- Program integration
- Performance monitoring

B. PEOPLE

- Roles and responsibilities
- Training and support
- Subject-matter experts
- Relationship management

C. PROCESSES

- Project management
- Change management
- Risk management
- Business continuity
- Information life cycle:
  - Collect, create, and capture
  - Use and dissemination
  - Maintenance, protection, and preservation
  - Retention and disposition

D. TECHNOLOGY AND ARCHITECTURE

- IM tools
- Technology integration
- Information life cycle: organization
- Data standards

E. CULTURE AND BEHAVIORS

- Leadership
- IM awareness
- Incentives
- IM competencies
- Communities of interest

F. GOVERNANCE

- Principles, policies, and standards
- Compliance
- IM program evaluation
- Quality of information
- Security of information
- Privacy of information

MINI CASE

Building Shared Services at RR Communications[4]

Vince Patton had been waiting years for this day. He pulled the papers together in front of him and scanned the small conference room. "You're fired," he said to the four divisional CIOs sitting at the table. They looked nervously at him, grinning weakly. Vince wasn't known to make practical jokes, but this had been a pretty good meeting, at least relative to some they'd had over the past five years. "You're kidding," said Matt Dawes, one of the more outspoken members of the divisional CIO team. "Nope," said Vince. "I've got the boss's OK on this. We don't need any of you anymore. I'm creating one enterprise IT organization, and there's no room for any of you. The HR people are waiting outside." With that, he picked up his papers and headed to the door, leaving the four of them in shock.

"That felt good," he admitted as he strode back to his office. A big man, not known to tolerate fools gladly (or corporate politics), he was not a cruel one. But those guys had been thorns in his side ever since he had taken the new executive VP of IT job at the faltering RR Communications five years ago. The company's stock had been in the dumpster, and with the dramatically increased competition in the telecommunications industry as a result of deregulation, his friends and family had all thought he was nuts. But Ross Roman, RR's eccentric but brilliant founder, had made him an offer he couldn't refuse. "We need you to transform IT so that we can introduce new products more quickly," he'd said. "You'll have my full backing for whatever you want to do."

Typically for an entrepreneur, Roman had sketched the vision swiftly, leaving someone else to actually implement it. "We've got to have a more flexible and responsive IT organization. Every time I want to do something, they tell me 'the systems won't allow it.' I'm tired of having customers complaining about getting multiple bills for each of our products. It's not acceptable that RR can't create one simple little bill for each customer." Roman punctuated his remarks by stabbing with his finger at a file full of letters to the president, which he insisted on reading personally each week. "You've got a reputation as a 'can do' kind of guy; I checked. Don't bother me with details; just get the job done."

Vince knew he was a good, proactive IT leader, but he hadn't been prepared for the mess he inherited—or the politics. There was no central IT, just separate divisional units for the four key lines of business—Internet, mobile, landline, and cable TV service—each doing its own thing. Every business unit had bought its own hardware and software, so introducing the common systems that would be needed to accomplish Roman's vision would be hugely difficult—that is, assuming they wanted them, which they didn't. There were multiple sales systems, databases, and customer service centers, all of which led to customer and business frustration. The company was in trouble not only with its customers but also with the telecommunications regulators and with its

[4] Smith, H. A., and J. D. McKeen. "Shared Services at RR Communications." #1-L07-1-002, Queen's School of Business, September 2007. Reproduced by permission of Queen's University, School of Business, Kingston, Ontario, Canada.

software vendors, who each wanted information about the company's activities, which they were legally entitled to have but which the company couldn't provide.

Where should he start to untangle this mess? Clearly, it wasn't going to be possible to provide bundled billing, responsiveness, unified customer care, and rapid time to market all at once, let alone keep up with the new products and services that were flooding into the telecommunications arena. And he hadn't exactly been welcomed with open arms by the divisional CIOs (DIOs), who were suspicious of him in the extreme. "Getting IT to operate as a single enterprise unit, regardless of the product involved, is going to be tough," he admitted to himself. "This corporate culture is not going to take easily to centralized direction."

And so it was. The DIOs had fought him tooth and nail, resisting any form of integration of their systems. So had the business unit leaders, themselves presidents, who were rewarded on the basis of the performance of their divisions and, therefore, didn't give a hoot about "the enterprise" or about anything other than their quarterly results. To them, centralized IT meant increased bureaucracy and much less freedom to pick up the phone and call their buddy Matt or Larry or Helen, or Dave and get that person to drop everything to deal with their latest money-making initiative. The fact that it cost the enterprise more and more every time they did this didn't concern them—they didn't care that costs racked up: testing to make sure changes didn't affect anything else that was operational; creation of duplicate data and files, which often perpetuated bad data; and loss of integrated information with which to run the enterprise. And the fact that the company needed an army of "data cleansers" to prepare the reports needed for the government to meet its regulatory and Sarbanes–Oxley requirements wasn't their concern. Everyone believed his or her needs were unique.

Unfortunately, although he had Roman's backing in theory, in practice Vince's position was a bit unusual because he himself didn't have an enterprise IT organization as yet and the DIOs' first allegiance was clearly to their division presidents, despite having a "dotted line" reporting relationship to Vince. The result was that he had to choose his battles very, very carefully in order to lay the foundation for the future. First up was redesigning the company's internal computer infrastructure to use one set of standard technologies. Simplification and standardization involved a radical reduction of the number of suppliers and centralized procurement. The politics were fierce and painful with the various suppliers the company was using, simultaneously courting the DIOs and business unit leaders while trying to sell Vince on the merits of their brand of technology for the whole company. Matt Dawes had done everything he could to undermine this vision, making sure that the users caused the maximum fuss right up to Roman's office.

Finally, they'd had a showdown with Roman. "As far as I'm concerned, moving to standardized hardware and software is nondiscussable," Vince stated bluntly. "We can't even begin to tackle the issues facing this company without it. And furthermore, we are in serious noncompliance with our software licensing agreements. We can't even tell how many users we have!" This was a potentially serious legal issue that had to be dealt with. "I promised our suppliers that we would get this problem under control within eighteen months, and they've agreed to give us time to improve. We won't have this opportunity again."

Roman nodded, effectively shutting down the argument. "I don't really understand how more standardization is going to improve our business flexibility," he'd growled, "but if you say so, let's do it!" From that point on, Vince had moved steadily to consolidate his position, centralizing the purchasing budget; creating an enterprise architecture; establishing a standardized desktop and infrastructure; and putting tools, metrics, and policies in place to manage them and ensure the plan was respected by the divisions.

Dawes and Larry Hughes, another DIO, had tried to sabotage him on this matter yet again by adopting another manufacturer's customer relationship management (CRM) system (and yet another database), hoping that it could be up and running before Vince noticed. But Vince had moved swiftly to pull the plug on that one by refusing the project access to company hardware and giving the divisional structure yet another black mark.

That episode had highlighted the need for a steering committee, one with teeth to make sure that no other rogue projects got implemented with "back door funding." But the company's entrepreneurial culture wasn't ready for it, so again foundational work had to be done. "I'd have had a riot on my hands if I'd tried to do this in my first few years here," Vince reflected as he walked back to his office, stopping to chat with some of the other executives on his way. Vince now knew everyone and was widely respected at this level because he understood their concerns and interests. Mainly, these were financial—delivering more IT for less cost. But as Vince moved around the organization, he stressed that IT decisions were first and foremost business decisions. He spoke to his colleagues in business terms. "The company wants one consistent brand for its organization so it can cross-sell services. So why do we need different customer service organizations or back-end systems?" he would ask them. One by one he had brought the "C"-level executives around to at least thinking about the need for an enterprise IT organization.

Vince had also taken advantage of his weekly meetings with Roman to demonstrate the critical linkage between IT and Roman's vision for the enterprise. Vince's motto was "IT must be very visible in this organization." When he felt the political climate was right, he called all the "Cs" to a meeting. With Roman in the room for psychological support, he made his pitch. "We need to make all major IT decisions together as a business," he said. "If we met monthly, we could determine what projects we need to launch in order to support the business and then allocate resources and budgets accordingly."

Phil Cooper, president of Internet Services, spoke up. "But what about our specific projects? Won't they get lost when they're all mixed up with everyone else's? How do we get funding for what we need to do?"

Vince had a ready answer. "With a steering committee, we will do what's best for the organization as a whole, not for one division at the expense of the others. The first thing we're going to do is undertake a visioning exercise for what you all want our business to look like in three years, and then we'll build the systems and IT infrastructure to support that vision."

Talking the language of business had been the right approach because no one wanted to get bogged down in techno-jargon. And this meeting had effectively turned the tide from a divisional focus to an enterprise one—at least as far as establishing a steering committee went. Slowly, Vince had built up his enterprise IT organization, putting those senior IT managers reporting to him into each of the business divisions. "Your job is to participate in all business decisions, not just IT ones," he stated. "There is nothing that happens in this company that doesn't affect IT." He and his staff had also "walked the talk" over the past two years, working with the business to identify opportunities for short-term improvements that really mattered a lot to the divisions. These types of quick wins demonstrated that he and his organization really cared about the business and made IT's value much more visible. He also stressed accountability. "Centralized units are always seen to be overhead by the business," he explained to his staff. "That's why we must be accountable for everything we spend and our costs must be transparent. We also need to give the business some choices in what they spend. Although I won't compromise on legal, safety, or health issues, we need to let them know where they can save money if they want. For example, even though they can't choose not to back up their files, they can choose the amount of time it will take them to recover them."

But the problem of the DIOs had remained. Used to being kings of their own kingdoms, everything they did appeared to be in direct opposition to Vince's vision. And it was apparent that Roman was preaching "one company" but IT itself was not unified. Things had come to a head last year when Vince had started looking at outsourcing. Again the DIOs had resisted, seeing the move as one designed to take yet more power away from them. Vince had offered Helen a position as sourcing director, but she'd turned it down, seeing it as a demotion rather than a lateral move. The more the DIOs stonewalled Vince, the more determined he became to deal with them once and for all. "They're undermining my credibility with the business and with our suppliers," Vince had complained to himself. "There's still so much more to do, and this divisional structure isn't working for us." That's when he'd realized he had to act or RR wouldn't be able to move ahead on its next project: a single customer service center shared by the four divisions instead of the multiple divisional and regional ones they had now.

So Vince had called a meeting, ostensibly to sort out what would be outsourced and what wouldn't. Then he'd dropped the bombshell. "They'll get a good package," he reassured himself. "And they'll be happier somewhere else than always fighting with me." The new IT organizational charts, creating a central IT function, had been drawn up, and the memo appointing his management team had been signed. Vince sighed. That had been a piece of cake compared to what he was going to be facing now. Was he ready for the next round in the "IT wars"? He was going to have to go head to head with the business, and it wouldn't be pretty. Roman had supported him in getting the IT house in order, but would he be there for the next step?

Vince looked gloomily at the reports the DIOs had prepared for their final meeting. They documented a complete data mess—even within the divisions. The next goal was to implement the single customer service center for all divisions, so a customer could call one place and get service for all RR products. This would be a major step forward in enabling the company to implement new products and services. If he could pull it off, all of the company's support systems would, for the first time, talk to each other and share data. "We can't have shared services without common data, and we can't have good business intelligence either," he muttered. Everything he needed to do next relied on this, but the business had seen it differently when he'd last tried to broach the subject with them. "These are our data, and these are our customers," they'd said. "Don't mess with them." And he hadn't.... but that was then. Now it was essential to get their information in order. But what would he have to do to convince them and to make it happen?

Discussion Questions

1. List the advantages of a single customer service center for RR Communications.
2. Devise an implementation strategy that would guarantee the support of the divisional presidents for the shared customer service center.
3. Is it possible to achieve an enterprise vision with a decentralized IT function?
4. What business and IT problems can be caused by lack of common information and an enterprise IM strategy?
5. What governance mechanisms need to be put in place to ensure common customer data and a shared customer service center? What metrics might be useful?

MINI CASE

Enterprise Architecture at Nationstate Insurance[5]

Jane Denton looked around at her assembled senior IT leadership team waiting to hear what she was going to say. Most were leaning forward eagerly, though some appeared more cautious. They were a good team, she knew, and she wanted to lead them well. A seasoned CIO, with a whole career behind her in IT, Jane was the newly appointed global CIO of Nationstate Insurance. This would be her last job before retirement in three years and she wanted to find a way to make a lasting difference in this company. Nationstate was an excellent company—Jane had done her homework. It was one of the largest in the United States, with a worldwide presence in personal and commercial insurance, and had recently been voted one of Forbes' "Best Big Companies." It had good systems, good user–IT relationships, and good people. But the company aspired to be great and Jane wanted to help them by taking IT to the next level. She knew that the world was changing—largely as a result of technology—and she knew that IT and its traditional approach to systems development was also going to have to change. "Our IT function needs to become more cutting edge in adopting emerging technologies," she had told the CEO shortly after she was hired, "and we need to become more flexible and agile in our approach to development work." Now she had this time and this team to accomplish her goals.

However, it was much easier said than done. Like almost every large organization, Nationstate had a hodgepodge of different systems, data, and processes—most serving just one of its six business units (BUs). Nationstate's decentralized structure had served it well in the past by enabling individual BUs to respond quickly to changing market needs but a couple of years before Jane's arrival, recognizing the need for some enterprise thinking, the CEO had created a federated structure with some centralized functions, including parts of IT. So some of IT was now centralized and shared by all the BUs (e.g., operations) and reported directly to Jane, while the rest (e.g., system development) was decentralized. Each BU had its own CIO and IT staff who reported jointly to the BU's president and to Jane.

This potentially unwieldy structure was made more palatable by the fact that the business unit CIOs had great business knowledge and were well trusted by their presidents. In fact, it was central IT that was often seen as the roadblock by the BUs. She had never led an IT organization like it, she reflected, and in her first few months, she had made a considerable effort to understand the strengths and weaknesses of this model and how responsibilities had been divided between centralized enterprise services and the decentralized IT groups (each quite large themselves) in the business units.

---

[5] Smith, H. A., and J. D. McKeen. "Enterprise Architecture at Nationstate Insurance." #1-L11-1-001, Queen's School of Business, September 2007. Reproduced by permission of Queen's University, School of Business, Kingston, Ontario, Canada.

Now she thought she had a good enough handle on these that she could begin work with her senior leadership team (the BU CIOs) to develop a plan to transform IT into the kind of technology function Nationstate would need in the years to come.

"I know you are both enthusiastic and apprehensive about transformation," she said. "We have a great organization and no one wants to lose that. We need to be responsive to our business needs but we also need to incorporate new development techniques into our work, do a better job with emerging technologies, and begin to rationalize our application and technology portfolios. We have duplicate systems, data and software all over the place. Our CEO and the BU Presidents want to see us use our technology resources more efficiently, but more than that, they want our leadership in using technology *effectively* for the organization as a whole. We can't do this if we're all working in separate silos."

Heads began nodding around the room as she continued. "At present, every business unit has its own IT architecture and architects and each of you believe you are making the 'right' technology decisions *but* you are all doing it differently." The head nodding stopped and a mood of wariness took over. "No one in our organization has the big picture of what we have and where we need to go. We have to learn what makes sense for us to do at an enterprise level and what's best left in the business units. Architecting our technology, information, business and applications properly is the key to doing it right."

"What exactly are you proposing?" asked Owen Merton, CIO of the Casualty Division. "I think you're right that we need an enterprise architecture, but I don't want to lose the good work we've done at the BU level."

"Well, I really want to centralize all architecture," said Jane. "I think that's what works best in other organizations and that's going to be the most effective way to make it work here. BUT..." she added, "I'd like to speak with each of you individually and with your senior architects before I do. I'm open to your ideas as long as they address the needs that I've just outlined."

Over the next two weeks, Jane listened carefully to what the divisional CIOs had to say. They all agreed with Merton that the relationships with the BUs were extremely important and centralizing architecture had to be done carefully. All of them had heard horror stories about the "architecture police" in other companies—hard-line techies who set standards and created blueprints and insisted on them being followed in spite of the difficulties their policies caused for the business.

"Architecture can't live in an ivory tower," explained Vic Toregas, CIO of Claims. "It has to be rooted in the reality of our business and it can't be seen to slow things down." Jane agreed. "We must make sure that our architecture function is designed and managed to ensure rapid delivery to the business."

On the other hand, Nick Vargo, CIO of Group Health, was concerned that without a strong enforcement mechanism, standards wouldn't be followed. "What's the point of having standards if we don't enforce them?" he asked.

Jane's head whirled. It wasn't going to be easy to strike the right balance between developing a good, sustainable process that would provide a blueprint for where the company needed to go and enable the company to build the common capabilities it would need for the future, while delivering solutions quickly and flexibly for the BUs. "What we don't need is a 'Winchester Mystery House'," she reflected, recalling the famous local house whose owners kept adding to it over many years with no overall plan.

She became more worried when she began to speak with the BU architects, with an eye to appointing one of them as her chief enterprise architect. They seemed to be technically competent but were not what she would call "relationship people" or business strategists. The job, as she envisioned it, would combine strong leadership skills, a good understanding of the business, and excellent communication skills to translate *why* the business should care about architecture, with strong technical skills. Her day became a bit brighter when she began her final interview with Seamus O'Malley, the senior architecture manager of the commercial BU.

As they spoke, Jane was impressed with his vision and pragmatism, as well as his strong communication skills. By the end of the hour she knew she had found her new chief enterprise architect. "I'd like you to take this new job," she told him. "I think you are the right person to ensure we have the standards, tools and practices in place to develop a common architecture for Nationstate." Seamus thought for a moment before replying. It was a great offer but he had his doubts that Jane's plan would work and this situation had to be carefully handled.

"Thank you for your faith in me," he began diplomatically, "but I would like to suggest a slight modification to your plan. You see, I've been an architect in centralized organizations and there has always been an 'us versus them' mentality between the architecture group and both the rest of IT and the business units." Jane recalled the horror stories of the "architecture police." "So what I'd like to propose is a compromise. I would become Chief Enterprise Architect but I would also remain Senior Architecture for Commercial and involve the other BU Senior Architects in creating a strong enterprise architecture that works for us all. That way, no one will see me as just 'the enterprise guy' and whatever standards we set and decisions we make centrally will affect me in Commercial, just like they'll affect all the other BUs. When the other business units see that I'm willing to eat my own dog food, I think they'll be more ready to accept the standards and changes we'll be introducing."

While not sure the compromise would work, Jane agreed to try it for a year and Seamus set out to build a centralized architecture function from scratch. With the authority given to him by Jane, all of the BU senior architects now had a dual reporting relationship—to their CIO and to him as the chief architect.

At their first weekly meeting with the BU senior architects, Seamus outlined his role and agenda. "As you know, each of us has been individually responsible for developing an effective IT architecture for our business units but we haven't done any coordination between them. That is no longer good enough for our business needs and I, with your help, have been given the job of establishing an *enterprise* architecture that will create an enterprise technology blueprint for Nationstate, which we will all have to follow in the business units. I want to work collaboratively with you so that we come up with a plan and processes that will work for each of us in the business units, as well as for the enterprise as a whole. We will need to build our enterprise architecture slowly but steadily so that people will trust us, and that means having good governance, good processes and a collaborative approach to this work," he stated. "Our first priority is building strong relationships with both Jane and the other CIOs and our BU Presidents. Enterprise Architecture sits in the middle between these groups, so good relationships are essential." "However," he continued. "We are going to need a way to establish and enforce standards—enterprise ones, not the ones you have now—and this is going to be difficult to explain."

"I'll say," remarked Sarah Jensen, the senior architecture manager from Personal Insurance. "What do we say when the business asks why they can't do something that's important to them because our 'standards' won't let them?"

"That's a good question Sarah," said Seamus. "And it gets right to the heart of why architecture is important. We need to present architecture in ways that are easy for the business to understand, without scaring or threatening them. For example, we need an application reduction strategy designed to eliminate duplication, reduce complexity and save money. The business already understands the pain of having to jump from system to system and knows that owning two cars is more expensive than one. If we explain it to them in this way, they will understand the advantages of having a single system and a single workflow."

"But isn't good architecture about *more* than cost savings?" asked Michael Lee, senior architecture manager from Claims. "We need to develop a foundation of common information, tools and processes so that we're not reinventing the wheel going into the future. And someone needs to decide what new technologies we're going to need and where we're going to use them. There are so many new applications and devices coming out every day now, we're going to be in a real mess if we don't do this properly."

"You're exactly right," said Seamus. "These things do have to be managed for the good of the enterprise—both to make it more effective *and* more efficient. But it's *how* we manage them that's important. If we put lots of bureaucracy in place and don't add value, no one is going to support us and they'll find ways to undermine what we are trying to do. We can't take a 'field of dreams' approach to architecture. We need to attach our work to real business value and real projects. Once our leaders understand this, we'll get their support."

"So here's our challenge," Seamus told his assembled team a few minutes later. "We need to design an Enterprise Architecture function that does all these things. It's got to be a process that comes up with the standards and guidelines that each of you can live with and support in the BUs. And, as you know, I myself will have to live with them in Commercial as well."

"Here's what I believe we need to accomplish as soon as possible," he stated, flashing a PowerPoint slide on the screen:

1. An enterprise governance process to set architecture strategy, policies and standards for technology, applications, and information that reflects the federated structure in the organization.
2. A means of monitoring that all new projects comply with the agreed-upon architecture while ensuring that this process doesn't present an obstacle to getting IT projects completed quickly.
3. A process for allowing "variances" to the current standards, if necessary, and a way to manage them back to the agreed-on standards.
4. A means of identifying important new IT capabilities and services that should be shared by the enterprise.
5. A means of evaluating emerging new technologies and setting standards for them.
6. Identifying roles and responsibilities for the enterprise architecture function and the LOB architecture functions.
7. Developing a means of incorporating feedback and continuous improvement into our work.

"I want to blend and weave our work into the architecture teams we already have in the business units as much as possible," Seamus concluded. "This will keep us close to business needs and enable us to get enterprise value from the teams we have in place. And I don't want to add any more process than we need to at an enterprise level. For example, if the Claims group needs a new technology, their architecture group could do the preliminary evaluation and make recommendations for what we should do. *But* we need to ensure that the resulting decision is a good one for the entire enterprise."

"I've got to report back to Jane in a month, so I'd like you to think about what might and might not work for your division and for us as an enterprise. I've scheduled a couple of working sessions for us over the next two weeks so we can hash this out. We have an exciting opportunity to take IT to the next level at Nationstate if we do this right, so let's not mess this up."

Discussion Questions

1. List and describe all of the potential benefits (and costs) that Nationstate would realize from the establishment of an enterprisewide architecture as envisioned by Jane Denton?
2. Build a business case for Seamus O'Malley to present to the senior management team at Nationstate in order to get their buy-in. In addition to benefits and costs, the business case must answer the "what's in it for me" question that the BU 3presidents all have.
3. Seamus O'Malley is rightfully worried about governance (i.e., making sure that the enterprise architectural standards are adopted by all BUs). Both he and Jane are wary of forced compliance because such measures lead to "architecture police." What governance procedures could they put in place that would win "hearts and minds"; that is, BU architects would comply with the enterprise architecture standards because *they believe in them*—not because they are *forced to comply with them*?

MINI CASE

IT Investment at North American Financial[6]

Caroline Weese checked her makeup and then glanced at her watch for the tenth time. Almost 10:45. Showtime. As North American Financial's (NAF) first female CIO, she knew she had to be better than good when she met with the company's senior executives for the first time to justify her IT budget. They had shown their faith in her three months ago by giving her this position, when NAF's long-serving senior vice president of IT had had to retire early due to ill health. But women were just beginning to crack the "glass ceiling" at the bank, and she knew there was a lot more riding on this presentation than just this budget.

That said, the budget situation wasn't great. As she well knew from her earlier experience in more subordinate roles, the CIO had the unenviable task of justifying the company's $500 M budget to a group of executives who only saw the expense of IT, not its value. This was especially frustrating because NAF's IT management was excellent, when looked at by any standard. NAF's IT group consisted of almost 7,000 professionals who followed all the recommended standards such as CMM, CMMI, ISO9001, and ITIL to ensure that its IT processes were efficient, cost effective, and on par with, if not higher than, industry standards. It had been certified at a minimum Level 3 CMMI and was an industry leader in delivering projects on time, on budget, and in scope. But in the past few years, NAF executives had implemented rigorous cost containment measures for IT, leaving the CIO to struggle to be all things to all people.

"They want innovation, they need reliability and stability, and we're required by law to meet ever-more stringent government regulations, but they're still nickel-and-diming us!" Caroline thought indignantly. She envied the bank's business units that could clearly show profit-and-loss statements, and their ability to make strategic decisions about what to do with the excess capital they often had. In her world, business strategies changed regularly and, thus, IT's goals had to as well. But strategies were not linked to budgets, which were typically set six to nine months in advance. As a result, IT was always struggling to keep up and find the resources to be flexible.

She squared her shoulders, took a deep breath, pasted a smile on her face, and pushed open the door to the executive conference room to face her colleagues and her future. The room was full of "suits"—a few females here and there, but mostly tough, middle-age males who expected answers and action. Following a few pleasantries about how she was adjusting to her new role, they got down to business. "The thing we're most concerned about, Caroline," said Bill Harris, NAF's CEO, "is we simply don't see where we're getting value from our IT investments. There's no proof in the bottom line." The CFO added, "Every year we approve hundreds of millions of dollars

---

[6] Smith, H. A., and J. D. McKeen. "IT Investment at North American Financial." #1-L09-1-001, Queen's School of Business, October 2009. Reproduced by permission of Queen's University, School of Business, Kingston, Ontario, Canada.

for IT projects, which are supposedly based on sound cost–benefit analyses, but the benefits never materialize." Heads around the room began nodding.

Caroline's mind was whirling. What did they really want from her? Pulling her thoughts together quickly, she responded. "If you're looking for IT to tell you which projects will deliver the most business value, or if you want me to monitor the business units after the projects they asked for are implemented to see if they are delivering value, you're asking me to do something that's well beyond IT's scope of expertise. We're not the experts in your business case, and it shouldn't be up to us to monitor how you use the technology we give you. I'll take full responsibility for the quality of our work, its timely delivery, and its cost, but we really have to work together to ensure we're investing in the right projects and delivering benefits."

"What do you recommend then?" asked Sam Patel, head of Retail Banking. "I think we need an IT Investment Committee that I would co-lead jointly with you, Matt," Caroline said while looking pointedly at the CFO. "We need a strong partnership to explore what can be done and who should be responsible for doing it. Finance is the only place where all the money comes together in this organization. Although I have to pull together an IT budget every year, it's really contingent on what each business unit wants to spend. We don't really have an enterprise IT budgeting process that looks across our business silos to see if what we're spending is good for NAF as a whole." Matt Harper looked thoughtful. "You could be on to something here, Caroline. Let's see if we can figure this out together."

The rest of the meeting passed in a blur, and before Caroline knew it, she and Matt were trying to identify who they should assign to help them look at their IT investment challenges. These were significant. First, there was inconsistent alignment of the total IT development budget with enterprise strategies. "We have enterprise strategies but no way of linking them to enterprise spending," Caroline pointed out. IT budgets were allocated according to the size of the business unit. Smaller lines of business had smaller IT budgets than larger ones. "For some small business units like ours, government mandatory projects eat up our entire IT budget," complained Cathy Benson, senior vice president of Business Banking Product Management. This made it extremely difficult to allocate IT resources strategically—say, for example, to grow a smaller business unit into a larger one.

Second, project approvals were made by business units without addressing cross-unit synergies. Looking at the projects IT had underway revealed that the company had eighteen separate projects in different parts of the business to comply with anti–money laundering regulations. "We've got to be reinventing the wheel with some of these," complained Ian Ha, senior director of NAF's Risk and Compliance department.

Third, although business cases were required for all major projects, their formats were inconsistent, and the data provided to justify the costs lacked rigor. "There seems to be a lot of gaming going on here," observed Michael Cranston, director of Financial Strategy. "A lot of these numbers don't make sense. How come we've never asked the business sponsors of these projects to take ownership for the business benefits they claim when they ask for the money in the first place?"

Fourth, once a project was approved, everyone focused on on-time, on-budget delivery. No one ever asked whether a project was still necessary or was still on track to deliver the benefits anticipated. "Do we ever stop projects once they've started or review the business case 'in-flight'?" mused Matt. Finally, no one appeared to be accountable for delivering these benefits once an IT project was developed and implemented; rather, everyone just heaved a great sigh of relief and moved on to the next project.

Because the total IT budget for new development work was allocated by business unit, the result was a prioritization process that worked reasonably well at the business unit level but not for NAF as a whole. Enterprise executives created enterprise strategies, but they didn't get involved in implementing them in the business units, which left the business unit heads to prioritize initiatives within their own silo. In prioritization meetings, leaders would argue passionately for their own particular cause and focusing on their own needs, not on NAF's overall strategies. "We really need to align this process with our enterprise priorities," said Caroline. Matt agreed. "There's got to be a process to bring all our investment decisions for new projects together so we can compare them across business units and adjust our resourcing accordingly."

Looking deeper into these matters revealed that there was more to IT spending than simply prioritizing projects, however. Almost 60 percent of the bank's IT budget was spent not on strategic new development projects but on maintaining existing systems, interfaces, and data. And another 20 percent was work that had to be done to meet the demands of government legislation or the bank's regulators. "How is this possible?" asked Sam. "No wonder we're not getting much 'bang for our buck'!" Caroline exclaimed. "Every time we develop or acquire a new system without getting rid of something else, we add to our 'application clutter.' When we continually add new systems while holding IT budgets and head counts relatively flat, more and more of our resources have to be devoted to supporting these systems." New systems meant new interfaces between and among existing systems, additional data and dependencies, and increasing risk that something could go wrong. "We've tried to get the business units interested in sponsoring an initiative to reduce duplication and simplify our applications portfolio, but they're not interested in what they call 'IT housekeeping.' They don't see how dealing with this will help them in the long run. I guess we haven't explained it to them very well."

Brenda Liu, senior director of IT Infrastructure, added, "We also have to keep our IT environment up to date. Vendors are continually making upgrades to software, and there are also license fees to consider. And, as you know, we have to build in extra reliability and redundancy for our critical systems and data, as well as privacy protection for our banking customers. It's an expensive process." "I get all this," said Benson, "but why can't you explain it to us properly? How can you just expect us to accept that 80 percent of your budget is a 'black box' that doesn't need justification? Although every dime you spend may be critical to this company, the fact remains that IT's lack of transparency is damaging its internal credibility with the business."

Round and round the issues they went. Over the next two months, Caroline, Matt, and their team hammered away at them. Eventually, they came up with a set of five principles on which their new IT investment process would be based:

1. Alignment of the IT development portfolio with enterprise strategies
2. Rigor and common standards around IT planning and business casing
3. Accountability in both business and IT for delivering value
4. Transparency at all levels and stages of development
5. Collaboration and cross-group synergies in all IT work

In their team update to the bank's executive committee, Caroline and Matt wrote, "Our vision is for a holistic view of our IT spending that will allow us to direct our resources where they will have the greatest impact. We propose to increase rigor and discipline in business casing and benefits tracking so NAF can invest with confidence in IT. The result will be strategic partnerships between IT and business units based on trust, leading us to surprise and delight our customers and employees and amaze our competitors."

With the executive committee's blessing, the IT Investment Office was created to design and implement a detailed investment optimization process that could be implemented throughout the bank in time for the next budget cycle. Cathy Benson was named its new director, reporting to Matt. Speaking to her staff after the announcement, Caroline stated, "I really believe that getting this work out of IT and into the business will be critical for this process. We need to make the decision-making process clearer and more collaborative. This will help us learn how to jointly make better decisions for the enterprise."

With the hand-off from IT officially in place, Cathy and Matt knew they had to move quickly. "We've got three months before the next budget cycle begins," said Matt. "You've got to make it real by then. I'll back you all the way, but you're going to have to find some way to deal with the business unit heads. They're not going to like having their autonomy for decision making taken away from them. And you have to remember they need some flexibility to do work that's important to them." Cathy nodded. She had already heard some of the negative rumors about the process and knew she was going to have to be tough if it was going to be successful and not torpedoed during its implementation.

Calling her project team together for its first meeting, she summarized their challenge. "We have to design and implement three interrelated practices: a thorough and rigorous method of project categorization and prioritization, comprehensive and holistic governance of IT spending and benefits delivery at all levels, and an annual IT planning process that provides transparency and accountability for all types of IT spending and which creates an integrated and strategically aligned development portfolio. Then we have to roll it out across the organization. And the change management is going to be massive. Now, who has any ideas about what to do next?"

Discussion Questions

Cathy Benson, the director of the newly created IT Investment Office, is tasked with the "design and implementation of a detailed investment optimization process to be implemented throughout the bank in time for the next budget cycle." She has three months to do this and it must be in accordance with the five established principles to guide the bank's IT investment process. Your task is to design and implement the following:

1. A thorough and rigorous method of project categorization and prioritization.
2. A comprehensive and holistic governance of IT spending and benefits delivery at all levels.
3. An annual IT planning process that provides transparency and accountability for all types of IT spending and that creates an integrated and strategically aligned development portfolio.

SECTION III

IT-Enabled Innovation

Mini Cases

- Innovation at International Foods
- Consumerization of Technology at IFG
- CRM at Minitrex
- Customer Service at Datatronics

12 Innovation with IT[1]

I t is well known that innovation with IT enables new business models (e.g., Amazon, iTunes), new products and services (e.g., tablets, mobile banking), new or improved processes (e.g., ERP, supply chain), and cost savings (e.g., self-service, offshore sourcing). Yet, such innovation is still very much a hit-or-miss proposition. For as many successful innovations as there are with technology, there are an equal or greater number of failures. Furthermore, although it is possible to do many innovative things with technology, it is much more difficult to find the ones that will deliver real and sustainable value to an organization.

IT organizations have always been expected to *improve* what is currently being done but it is much more difficult to undertake something that is *different* from what has traditionally been done. When innovating with technology, not only must the market be ready for the innovation (i.e., timing), but also network effects and complementary products and services must be available for it to succeed (e.g., one telephone is not very useful; mobile banking failed before the introduction of smart phones). Finally, many innovations fail because an organization's culture cannot sustain or exploit them (e.g., Kodak with digital imaging). In short, successful innovation is still a bit of a mystery and many IT leaders are trying to explore how best to operationalize it to deliver real business value.

This chapter explores innovation—an organization's need to reinvent its products and services and occasionally itself—with a focus on IT-enabled innovation. We begin by examining why innovation is critical, and how/why IT is driving most innovation today. Following this, we examine various types of innovation. Then we present a typical innovation life cycle and examine some of the challenges encountered by organizations when attempting to achieve innovation. In the final section of this chapter, we offer advice for managing IT-enabled innovation.

---

[1] This chapter is based on the authors' previously published article, McKeen, J. D., and H. A. Smith. "Strategic Experimentation with IT." *Communications of the Association for Information Systems* 19, article 8 (January 2007): 132–41. Reproduced by permission of the Association for Information Systems.

THE NEED FOR INNOVATION: AN HISTORICAL PERSPECTIVE

It is well-established that the need to innovate is necessary for long-term organizational survival (Christensen and Raynor 2003; Hamel and Välikangas 2003). According to Christensen (1997), there are two types of innovation: sustaining and disruptive. *Sustaining* innovation improves an existing product or enhances an existing service for an existing customer. In contrast, *disruptive* innovation targets noncustomers and delivers a product or service that fundamentally differs from the current product portfolio. Sustaining innovation leaves organizations in their comfort zone of established markets, known customers, and realizable business models. Disruptive technologies enjoy none of these benefits. To be successful for the initiating organization, the disruptive innovation must meet two basic requirements: it must create value as perceived by customers, and it must enact mechanisms to appropriate or capture a fair share of this new value (Henderson et al. 2003). For other organizations and particularly dominant players, disruptive innovation can be devastating. Christensen (1997) refers to this as "the innovator's dilemma." For an excellent discussion of disruptive technologies and a review of six leading theories of innovation, see Denning (2005).

Innovation comes about through organizational change, and here, too, we see two dominant forms: continuous change versus punctuated equilibrium. Brown and Eisenhardt (1997) describe *continuous change* as "frequent, relentless, and perhaps endemic to the firm," whereas the *punctuated equilibrium* model of change "assumes that long periods of small, incremental change are interrupted by brief periods of discontinuous, radical change." In this latter case, change is primarily seen as "rare, risky, and episodic." Although it is tempting to equate sustaining innovation with continuous change and disruptive innovation with punctuated equilibrium, it is not so simple. In fact, Brown and Eisenhardt (1997) cite examples of firms that have successfully reinvented themselves through continuous change as opposed to abrupt, punctuated change. These authors suggest "in firms undergoing continuous change, innovation is intimately related to broader organization change."

THE NEED FOR INNOVATION NOW

Today, there is an increased sense of urgency about innovation with technology. "Our business partners now 'get' the importance of IT," said one manager. "But they're looking for IT to tell them what's possible." Another added, "They're telling us 'We don't know what we don't know' and they expect IT to make new things possible." What this means is that IT leaders are being challenged by business leaders to spearhead innovation in their organizations. This is a new mandate for IT.

Different industries are feeling different levels of pressure about innovation. At *level one*, experienced by virtually every industry, new forms of technology are driving up the expectations of both business and consumers for more mobility, more usability, more customer-friendliness, and more cost-effectiveness. "There's a marketplace shift happening towards the customer," said a manager. "We are moving from being product and process-centric to being customer-centric." This shift is driving more horizontal views in the organization and demand for end-to-end processing, as opposed to the deeply vertical, siloed perspectives of the past.

Within *level two* industries, there is a belief that IT can be a strategic differentiator for an organization and that technology is a fundamental component of business strategy. "Our business sees technology as the key to new growth," said a manager. Unfortunately, this pressure plus the greater availability of technology in the cloud is leading some in the business world to "take technology decisions into their own hands" and "do an end-run" on the IT department thinking that they don't need IT. In response, IT is feeling new pressure to get ahead of business needs and demonstrate its innovative capabilities.

Level three industries experience a deep sense of unease that the fundamental assumptions upon which their business is based are changing. "We can no longer be complacent," said a manager. In these industries, there is growing uncertainty and fear that an upstart company could steal away huge chunks of business value by using technology to provide their products or services more cheaply or effectively. At this level, innovation is about survival and making sure that an organization is able to quickly adapt to new business models and withstand strategic challenges. Companies in these industries have seen that threats today can come from non-traditional competitors and they recognize that innovation with technology is the only way to ensure they will continue to stay viable.

UNDERSTANDING INNOVATION

Innovation with technology is a complex concept. One participant defined it as, "Fresh ideas that create value." It can include a variety of new things that are created by or enabled with technology, such as new markets, new products, new demand, new processes, new capabilities, and new practices. "It's all about *value*," he stressed. "I, like many others, am guilty of sometimes getting distracted by shiny, new gadgets rather than focusing on the value that innovation brings." Typically, innovation is not the *invention* of something completely new, but its use in a new way, bringing something new to an industry for the first time, or combining it with another service to provide new value. In short, innovation in an organization lies at the intersection of the answer to three significant questions that create the strategic environment within which innovation with technology can deliver value (see Figure 12.1):

*   What is viable in the marketplace?
*   What is desirable to the business?
*   What is possible with technology?

Ideally, innovation also refers to the *process* whereby a company creates new things that deliver value. There is no generally accepted methodology for innovation but we have learned that effective, successful innovation has at least five stages. The first stage is *ideation*—generating innovative ideas. There are many ways of doing this—ranging from focused executive meetings to the modern online version of the suggestion box. This stage must address two questions: How do we get people to share their ideas? How do we respond to their ideas? In most cases, there are lots of ideas out there. In fact, managers noted that attempts to stimulate innovation in their organizations led to them being initially deluged with new ideas. However, lacking the ability to screen and prioritize or act on them, the ideas soon dried up. Research shows that the biggest reason why people do not share their ideas is that past experience has shown them that management doesn't respond to or act on them (DeSouza 2011).

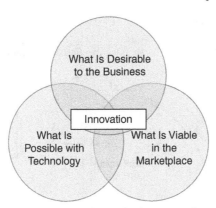

FIGURE 12.1 The Organization's Strategic Environment for Innovation with Technology

Thus, the second stage is *advocacy*. Good ideas need a sponsor who firms up promising innovative suggestions, seeks funding for them, and acts as a mentor to take them to the next level. One company has an advocacy process that seeks advocates from a business unit other than the one where an idea is generated, thereby encouraging broader organizational support for good ideas.

Stage three is *proof of concept*. This can consist of laboratory testing over a period of a few weeks to explore the viability of key technologies or ideas that are central to the success of an innovation. This part of the process is very agile and adaptive and highly dependent on business–IT collaboration. Teams are kept small and focused.

A successful proof of concept can lead to a fuller *trial* or *pilot* in stage four where the innovation is exposed to the market in a limited and measured way. A market segment is defined, and certain customers (who may be employees) are offered the chance to experiment with the new product or service. Measurements are taken to understand results, which may include marketing/branding issues, financial price points, and operational impacts. Typical pilots take about four to twelve weeks, but may be extended.

The fifth and final stage is *transition* or "go to market," where the innovation enters into the mainstream IT production process to ensure the idea is "industrial strength." Many shortcuts, which served well enough for the pilot, must now be engineered to meet production standards. For example, in one proof of concept, a financial organization developed a mobile application without privacy or security protections. These were then added in at this final stage.

Unlike other types of IT projects, the goals of innovation projects can be fuzzy. Focus group participants stressed that innovation projects should not have to meet the same ROI or defined benefits as other IT projects. "Enforcing traditional stage gate criteria too early in our innovation process killed off a lot of good ideas," said one manager whose company has now changed this practice. Furthermore, the full value of some innovations may not be immediately apparent. "We are innovating to develop a platform for direct customer interaction," said a manager, "but we are not telling our sales staff this right now." The results of this process can be both "'big I' innovation that refers to substantial and significant changes and 'little i' innovation that refers to smaller ongoing improvements," explained one participant.

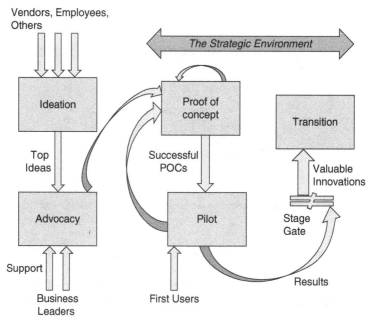

FIGURE 12.2   The Technology Innovation Process

A major difference between innovation projects and more traditional IT projects is that failure at any stage is anticipated for many ideas and should be expected.
Participants stressed that the learning gained from unsuccessful ideas is an asset that
is valuable. "We need to document our failures so that we can learn from them in the
future," said one. "Innovation is not a binary process," said another. "We need to recognize that we can leverage many elements in different ways over time to build successful
innovations." Thus, feedback from all participants and at all stages of innovation is an
especially crucial component of the innovation process (see Figure 12.2).

THE VALUE OF INNOVATION

Increased business value is the goal of innovation, but sometimes it is not always
clear what that value is. Many innovations do not deliver results in terms of ROI or
other measureable metrics. "You can't use traditional metrics, like revenue generation,
when it comes to innovation," said a manager. "Value can't always be quantified," said
another. Yet, it is important to understand where and how value is delivered by innovation or this effort will soon lose out to more measurable initiatives that have a clearer
short-term value.

Communication of value is therefore essential to ensuring innovation is sustainable in the organization over the long term. From this perspective, value has two
components:

1. *Is it desirable?* "Our business users and customers can't always articulate a
   clear value proposition," said a manager "but they can tell you if they want it
   and like it." Therefore, customer testimonials and social media comments can be

good mechanisms for companies to tell if they are on the right track with innovation and user perceptions of value should be carefully monitored. "Even a simple change can go viral if users perceive its value," said a manager. "And customers also know when the value is *not* there," added another.

2. *Does it build our innovative capabilities?*   Innovations in many industries rapidly become table stakes. "The real value of innovation is the ability to innovate continuously and consistently," said a manager. The capability to rapidly scan the environment, incorporate new ideas and technologies into an evolving business strategy, make the associated organizational and technological adaptations, and execute quickly, is the real prize. "Innovation isn't a one-time project, but the ability to deliver over and over again," said a manager.

INNOVATION ESSENTIALS: MOTIVATION, SUPPORT, AND DIRECTION

Three conditions are necessary for innovation to be successful: (1) motivation, (2) support, and (3) direction. As one manager stated, "Without motivation, little will happen; without support, little can happen; and without direction, anything can happen." The focus group's recommendations to others seeking to improve their innovation practices include the following:

1. *Motivate: Establish rewards for innovation.*   Although many individuals are naturally drawn to innovation, the demands of everyday work often drive this interest and inclination into remission. Furthermore, innovation is risky, and not all people are willing to jeopardize their reputations. As a result, innovation does not flourish without intervention. According to focus group members, the way to create an innovation-enabled organization is twofold: provide incentives and rewards to support innovation and risk taking, and make it everyone's job. Good ideas are good ideas, and experience shows that they are as apt to originate at the customer interface as they are within the laboratory or the executive ranks.

   Taking this a step further, one company has made innovation a component of everyone's annual performance assessment. This organization offers specific types of formal rewards for different types of innovation that range from patentable ideas to emerging business opportunities. Not all rewards need be formal though. One firm uses a system of frequent informal rewards (e.g., books, tickets, cards, recognition days, and executive citations) to recognize innovative ideas and encourage and reward innovation with IT. Another company discovered that the best reward for IT personnel is simply the opportunity to work and play with new technology! In this company, enterprising IT personnel win the right to experiment with new technology without the need for champions or sponsors. According to the manager involved, this activity is funded by "skunkworks" and "beg and grovel."

2. *Support: Create infrastructure to sustain innovation.*   Offering rewards for innovation sends employees the signal that innovation is encouraged and will be recognized and valued. This provides the motivation for individuals to experiment, but organizations need to provide support for such experimentation if they want it to happen. Over time, the combination of recognition and support builds a culture of innovation.

Many firms believe it is also necessary to build some infrastructure around IT innovation. One company, for instance, created the position of "chief scientist" and provided that office with a budget and resources. This was the organization's "way to signal to everyone that the lifeblood of the organization is discovery...not just innovation," said the manager involved. At this company, "innovation is a given" and expected in all parts of the business. "Discovery," however, conveys a sense of urgency as well as the notion that the company needs to continually reinvent itself to survive in the marketplace.

Many companies have formal centers (or laboratories) to support innovation. Depending on the firm, the roles of these centers vary from "new product introduction" to "new technology introduction" to "business venturing" to "incubation centers." Where IT is considered a key business driver, they usually focus almost exclusively on strategic IT innovation. The critical aspect of their creation is the provision of support and infrastructure to enable idea review and experimentation. Most centers are formally entrenched within the organization with ongoing funding, permanent staffing, and well-developed procedures and processes to encourage, guide, and support innovation. According to one manager, the key element is "to link sponsorship to innovation," reflecting the fact that "good ideas don't make it on their own."

Companies in the group reached consensus on the mandate for innovation centers, but they disagreed about their governance. Two distinct strategies surfaced:

- *Insulate.* This strategy creates innovation centers as places where "all lines of business can come together to address common problems." According to proponents, the key benefit of this approach is the ability to foster synergies across the business in the belief that innovation is best "nurtured away from the mainstream business."
- *Incubate.* Those following this strategy place their innovation centers within specific lines of business (LOBs). Proponents suggested that forcing innovation to be housed within a single LOB focuses innovation on "real" problems and opportunities with committed local ownership.

The innovation infrastructure that was common to virtually all organizations in the group was the maintenance of an intranet for launching ideas. These sites are considered to be effective for soliciting, vetting, and sharing ideas and/or opportunities. According to one manager, an intranet's chief value is that "anyone can input and everyone gets access" to build on ideas. In firms with innovation centers, intranets are effective "feeder" systems. In organizations lacking the formal support of an innovation center, ideas identified on the intranet require a sponsor to marshal support to turn them into realizable products and/or services.

A common form of financial support is the establishment of internal venture funds. In about half of the participating organizations, funding mechanisms had been set up to support IT innovation. Typically, such funds are made available on a competitive basis with an oversight committee in place to award resources and to monitor progress and completion.

3. *Direct: Manage innovation strategically.* One manager pointed out that "experimentation never fails as long as there has been learning." Strictly speaking, the focus group agreed *but* felt that "any such learning would have to be strategically important for the organization" for it to be considered successful. According to the group, learning for the sake of learning was "an activity enjoyed by academics"—much to our chagrin! They suggested that providing motivation and support for individuals to experiment freely would be a recipe for disaster. Organizations must provide *direction* for these activities. Strategic IT innovation does not occur by happenstance. Some participant suggestions for directing IT innovation in order to ensure that it was strategically relevant include the following:

   a. *Link innovation to customer value.* A simple yet effective way to accomplish this is to focus on emerging pain points. At one company, all new ideas had to articulate the specific customer pain point (CPP) that would be addressed. This requirement, in and of itself, produced results. As the manager involved related, "The identification and surfacing of CPPs stimulated considerable and sometimes heated discussion. Many people were surprised to learn of CPPs, and many potential solutions emerged. It was a case of 'if only I had known.'" Unfortunately, failure to articulate business value to the customer is a common phenomenon.

   b. *Link experimentation to core business processes.* The opposite approach focuses IT experimentation internally on core business functions. One participant, whose organization is "currently reluctant to experiment in the market," focuses all its experiments on core business activities. "Our belief is that innovation is strategic only if it produces significant efficiencies for internal operations in a way that can be captured on the bottom line," she said.

   c. *Use venture funds to guide strategic initiatives.* Although establishing venture funding for innovation is a form of support (as already noted), the governance of such funds can be instrumental in achieving strategic alignment. Venture funds are typically given for initiatives that do the following:

      • Make greater use of innovation resources
      • Focus on new business models
      • Explore new/disruptive technologies
      • Focus on penetrating new markets
      • Leverage cross-organizational capabilities
      • Streamline decision making
      • Focus on opportunities that can be scaled.

CHALLENGES FOR IT LEADERS

Although all of the managers in the focus group felt strongly that innovation is essential both to the future of their organizations and IT, they expressed a number of caveats and concerns about how innovation and an innovation process would be implemented in their organizations. These fell into four major themes:

1. *Strike the correct balance.*   IT managers are acutely aware that they have the responsibility to ensure that their organization's data and systems are kept safe, secure, and private. Furthermore, many of the so-called "bureaucratic IT processes" were put in place for good reason, such as to ensure quality, interoperability, and cost-efficacy. "We don't want to go back to the days when cowboys ran IT," said one manager. "There's a risk to throwing out all our rules for the sake of rapid innovation." In fact, in many highly regulated industries, such as finance and health care, laws and risk-aversion prohibit much innovation. "We need to balance urgency and quality, and not forget architecture and integration," said another manager. "These 'innovations' can turn into a legacy nightmare very quickly." Nevertheless, they recognize that there is a need to reconcile these competing priorities and rethink IT processes to facilitate innovation, although at present, there is no accepted way of doing this.

2. *Create a sustainable process.*   One focus group company was on its third innovation process. During the first one, they had lots of input from employees but a lack of interest from executives in taking action on their ideas. The second process, designed to rectify this problem, gave funding to the CIO to implement innovative ideas, but executives flooded the pipeline with ideas to get the "free" IT funding. Now, in its third iteration, the process is focused on innovation in business intelligence and how this will improve the way work gets done. "Whatever process is put in place, it must be collaborative and include a process for fleshing out ideas," said the manager involved. "There are too many half-baked ideas out there." In addition, there must be recognition from executives that innovation requires risk. Thus, the innovation process must enable rapid proof of concept and trial development, and link into traditional development procedures during the transition stage.

3. *Provide adequate resources.*   IT staff often become too busy "fixing messes" and doing other types of IT work to undertake innovation. In fact, many companies have had to address this resource gap by carving out specific resources or time periods dedicated for innovation. This is not ideal and most managers would rather see innovation integrated into everyone's job. Similarly, many executives are simply "too busy" to focus on work with such a vague return. As a result, "there is no real alignment in either IT or our organization about how to undertake and resource innovation," said a manager. Thus, many IT functions are waiting for senior management to say "go" before implementing a serious innovation process.

4. *Reassess IT processes and practices.*   The IT function needs to be characterized by disciplined thinking, rapid action, agile development, and supported by new technologies that facilitate this. We need to transition from "IT control" to "IT coordination," explained a manager. "Our structures need to be changed to enable us to get us 80% of the way in a project and then to pivot and change direction, if necessary," said another. A third noted that IT and organizational rewards need to be restructured to motivate more innovation. Finally, existing structures and governance mechanisms need to be changed to accommodate innovative practices. For example, as already noted, traditional stage gates are not appropriate for early-stage innovation projects. As well, roles such as relationship manager, which serve as gatekeepers into the business, may prevent the learning and collaboration that is needed to promote innovation.

FACILITATING INNOVATION

In spite of these challenges and reservations, the focus group agreed that IT's goal should be to develop an organization with the capability to change and adapt in order to deliver value with technology. Focus group organizations were trying a variety of practices to facilitate innovation. From these, a number of guiding principles for effective innovation may be inferred:

- *Focus on achievable targets.* Innovation should be manageable and targeted but, at the same time, built so they can scale up easily. According to one manager, "It is far easier to ramp up a proven venture than to plan, build, and deliver a winner." At one company an innovation involved a "proof of concept" for a new technology involving six sites. Management then rapidly decided to expand the innovation to three hundred sites! This action literally ended experimentation, and the task immediately became large-scale implementation.

- *Don't rush to market.* Positive results from an experiment should be viewed as justification for further experimentation, not as a "license to launch." At one company, a decision to go to market based on very favorable pilot results quickly ran into difficulty. The customers involved in the initial innovation turned out to be unrepresentative of the overall customer base, and the uptake in the market plummeted as the rollout broadened its base.

- *Be careful with "cool" technology.* Because innovation deals with technology, it is sometimes easy to be misled by cool technology. The buying public may not understand what the technology does (e.g., it's a browser pen), may have no need for the things that the technology does (e.g., it tracks unvisited sites), and/or may not find the technology appealing (e.g., it's a mouse with arms and hands). On the other hand, this same technology may become the item that every teenager on the planet must have!

- *Learn by design.* The goal of innovation is to learn. The group provided several examples of innovation attempts where nothing was learned. In these cases insufficient controls were designed into the process to enable the organization to ascertain after the fact what had actually happened. Was failure due to product features and/or functioning? A lack of effective marketing? The price point? Thus, the first step with innovation should be to identify the critical questions that need to be answered, then to design these into the process.

- *Link innovation to business strategy.* It has already been noted, but bears repeating, that valuable innovation is closely linked to an organization's strategy and long-term vision. This must be the first level of screening for all new ideas. A close second is business sponsorship to ensure that the idea will be funded and protected during its early stages of development.

- *Incubate innovation.* Until innovation is fully incorporated into daily work, it is important to provide a safe time/place/manner to promote it. Focus group companies were doing this in different ways. Some have appointed an innovation team; others host focused innovation meetings; still others use innovation labs and "safe" environments. Each of these enables rapid idea generation and screening and places a spotlight on innovation outside of normal practices.

- *Collaborate with vendors.* "It's important for IT to get out of its bubble and expand its boundaries," said one manager. The focus group agreed that IT must now proactively move out of its comfort zone to enable innovation and innovative processes. Working with vendors who can bring a broader perspective into the organization was the most common way of doing this. In some cases, organizations are inviting vendors to present to both IT and the business community in planned "innovation summits," where new possibilities can be brainstormed and screened for potential value in a very short period of time.

- *Integrate business and IT.*   This is table stakes for effective innovation. "IT must be plugged into the business, able to speak business language, and articulate potential benefits," said a manager. One good way of doing this is for IT to participate in regular "huddles" with the business to better understand their pain points and what their interests and challenges are.
- *Send clear messages.*   If an organization really wants innovation, it must send clear messages about its importance from the top down. This means that leaders must promote it, resource it, reward it, and most important of all, agree to take on the risks involved. Failure is a given in innovation, but unless management explicitly acknowledges and accepts this, it is unlikely that an organization's culture will change to become innovative.
- *Manage the process.*   Innovation will not just happen without attention. It requires active and intentional management to design and monitor a process and determine what works and what doesn't in a particular organizational culture. Innovation initiatives can sometimes have unforeseen side effects, such as demotivation of noninnovation staff, disappointment and cynicism when management doesn't respond to ideas, resistance to poorly communicated changes, and confusion over the process itself. In addition, existing budgets, structures, processes, and governance can work against innovation, unless there is proper attention to these factors.
- *Promote learning agility.*   Because innovation is still not a factory-like process and is continuing to evolve, IT leaders must cultivate capabilities that promote innovation, rather than specific skills. Chief among these, said the focus group, is learning agility or the ability to be flexible to learn new things and new ways of doing things. Whether it's business language, agile development, a new technology, or working with new partners, the best IT staff will be able to take on new challenges, learn, and thrive.

Conclusion

Organizations are just beginning to grasp the scope of the new world of continuous change that is being ushered in by technology, and to grapple with how it will affect their traditional processes of implementing technology for value. This new world is faster paced, with change taking place in smaller, more frequent increments that create and enable flexibility for the organization. Today, we are just at the cusp of this transition, which will result in a transformation of how both organizations and IT functions operate. Although business as usual can continue for the short term, IT leaders are well aware that their current structures and processes must adapt rapidly to this new world of change. "Innovation" is thus merely the vanguard of what is to come; but addressing it thoughtfully and intentionally is the best way to ensure that an organization is prepared for the future.

References

Brown, S. L., and K. M. Eisenhardt. "The Art of Continuous Change: Linking Complexity Theory and Time-Paced Evolution in Relentlessly Shifting Organizations." *Administrative Science Quarterly* 42, no. 1 (March 1997): 1–34.

Christensen, C. *The Innovator's Dilemma: When New Technologies Cause Great Firms to Fail.* Boston: Harvard Business School Press, 1997.

Christensen, C., and M. Raynor. *The Innovator's Solution: Creating and Sustaining Successful Growth.* Boston: Harvard Business School Press, 2003.

Denning, S. "Why the Best and Brightest Approaches Don't Solve the Innovation Dilemma." *Strategy & Leadership* 33, no. 1 (2005): 4–11.

DeSouza, Kevin. *Intrapreneurship.* Toronto, Canada: University of Toronto Press, 2011.

Hamel, G., and L. Välikangas. "The Quest for Resilience." *Harvard Business Review* (September 2003).

Henderson, J. C., N. Kulatilaka, N. Venkatraman, and J. Freedman. "Riding the Wave of Emerging Technologies: Opportunities and Challenges for the CIO." Working paper, Boston University, School of Management, 2003.

13 Big Data and Social Computing

I t's a time of significant change for organizations *and* for IT. Tools for implementing social business (i.e., social media) are being rapidly adopted by the population as a whole and, at a slower pace, by businesses (Kiron et al. 2013; Maoz et al. 2013). At the same time, tools associated with huge amounts of data they generate are facilitating new ways of understanding business through insights, analytics, and predictions (Davenport et al. 2012). These tools enable organizations to engage customers, suppliers, partners, and potential customers in real time and in a multitude of different ways. And they make it possible to incorporate a wide variety of data into organizational processes, enable decision making, and offer new products, services, and delivery channels.

It's a substantial extension of the trend to move computing to new parts and levels of the organization and beyond traditional corporate boundaries. Whereas big data and social media have been seen as separate organizational challenges in the past, these two fields are now converging in numerous ways, depending on the industry and a company's needs. Social media is becoming the organization's front line data collection point, while big data tools use it to drive information and analytics insights that in turn will guide business strategy development. And this is just the beginning. Underlying all of these initiatives are more improved data, whether from customers, applications, or myriad external data sources. In turn, organizations must focus these data on real business problems to gain real business insights, drive real business actions, and deliver real business value (see Figure 13.1).

The challenges for organizations are huge. And IT is at the center of it all, architecting the new platforms, selecting the tools, enabling them, participating in content analysis and design, integrating results with more traditional data and processes, and most importantly, working with the business to innovate, redesign and reimagine all aspects of corporate work. Today, organizations of all types are feeling increasing pressure to take action in these areas but most are still in the earliest stages of maturity, typically experimenting with the data generated from social media (Beath et al. 2012).

This chapter explores how IT leaders are trying to conceptualize the integration of big data and social media concepts to deliver value. It begins by discussing the

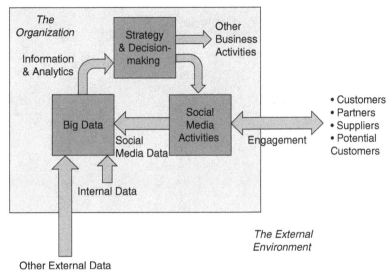

FIGURE 13.1 The Relationship Between Big Data and Social Media

opportunities presented by these technologies and what value organizations could expect from them. Next, it examines the different components that must be addressed in order to deliver value successfully. Then, it looks at some longer-term opportunities for deriving value through innovation with big data. Finally, it examines some of the challenges IT leaders face as they try to adapt their work to the significant changes these tools require and presents some actions for IT managers to consider when beginning to implement big data and social media tools and applications.

THE SOCIAL MEDIA/BIG DATA OPPORTUNITY

Today's organizations process over 1,000 times more data than they did a decade ago and the volume of data is growing by 30–50 percent annually (Beath et al. 2012). Social media is the largest component of online data and therefore a major source of data for organizations. In 2013, Facebook had 1.15 billion users with Twitter and LinkedIn following close behind (Maoz et al. 2013). Although over 77 percent of Fortune 500 companies are now using social media to build relationships with their brands, there is still a significant gap between social media usage and how companies are using the data generated by these tools (Fitzgerald et al. 2014). This underscores the fact that social media data are *not* valuable in and of themselves, but must be analyzed and presented in ways that derive insights into key business questions. Thus, a major question companies should be asking before embarking on any social media initiative is, *how can we use insights from the data we collect to improve our interactions with customers, suppliers or employees?* (LaValle et al. 2011). "There's a wide gamut of opportunities out there," one manager noted. "The quick wins are probably internal with customer and product information. However, companies must keep an open mind and look at everything because sometimes, relevant data can come from unlikely places" (see box).

Some Types of Social Media Data

- Wikis
- Blogs
- Videos
- 3D user interface/visualization
- Presence awareness
- Instant messaging, Twitter
- Social networking communities (e.g., Facebook, LinkedIn)
- Reputation systems
- Collective intelligence systems
- Authoring
- RSS feeds
- Podcasts
- Gamified data

In the past, disparate, siloed internal data in systems made data consolidation challenging because massive data "plumbing" was required before analysis could begin and data definitions had to be created before data could be stored or consolidated. Today, big data management technologies enable all types of data from multiple sources to be available in one place in native form, thereby providing greatly increased flexibility of analysis. More granular data then allow for finer classifications and segmentations to be made so that a business can tailor information or services for a single person or situation, if necessary (Davenport et al. 2012).

A large part of the value of the current business value of social media comes from the people, processes, and technologies that turn the data they generate into *insights* that drive business decisions and actions (McKeen and Smith 2012). Appropriately applied, companies can then use these data to

- Respond more quickly to the market by making faster decisions.
- Make patterns more evident, such as problems with a new product.
- Facilitate innovation in products and services, based on customer and other types of feedback.
- Improve reputation and brand awareness.

The value delivered through social media and other forms of big data management increases as tools and methods become more mature and integrated across the entire value chain (Davenport et al. 2012). While early analytics were based on historic, siloed internal data and rudimentary techniques, more mature approaches use frequently refreshed internal and external data and more complex analytical techniques that enable rapid decisions based on robust insights.

And this is just the beginning. Emerging approaches will be based on a deep understanding of real-time data sets from a variety of internal and external sources (Davenport 2013). They will enable real-time decisions supported by multilayered insights from multiple business functions. Companies are just now beginning to combine improved sensing capabilities of physical things (i.e., the Internet of things) with other internal and external data sets (Davenport 2013; Laney and White 2014; Smith and

Konsynski 2007). Future business opportunities will incorporate real-time information in a variety of new ways, such as:

- *Sensing*—detecting the current state of a given entity, such as the location of a plane, the speed of a car, or the mood of an individual.
- *Mass Visibility*—the combination of real-time sensing of multiple entities contextualized by their relationships. It can be used to identify such issues as traffic route congestion or how gas prices vary across the country.
- *Experimentation*—the integration of real-time sensing with the ability to generate and gather reliable data quickly. It can be used to monitor the impact of such things as new Web site layouts or to undertake rapid analytics on new brands.
- *Coordination*—combining the current state of other entities with the ability to adjust behavior based on fast-cycle feedback, for example, locating people and coordinating their behavior in real time.

To date, most CIOs and business leaders still haven't identified the value propositions associated with these new types of data or fully understood their organizational implications (McAfee and Brynjolfsson 2012). They are still trying to determine how and where to effectively use social media data.

DELIVERING BUSINESS VALUE WITH BIG DATA

Delivering business value with the big data derived from social media and other data sources requires developing new organizational capabilities in a variety of areas, especially in data and information management. And although it is a truism today that organizational change requires improved governance, sponsorship, processes, and controls, in addition to new skills and technology, these are all essential components of delivering on the opportunities presented by social media and ultimately, big data (Beath et al. 2012; LaValle et al. 2011). This section explores the key components of developing an organizational capability that can deliver business value from big data and adapt to the rapidly evolving world it represents (see Figure 13.2).

Governance

One of the most important questions for companies to ask with respect to social media is, *who's responsible for social media in your organization?* Some companies see marketing or corporate communications as having primary responsibility for this function; others have created an internal social marketing organization, or a committee. Delivering social media today is still fragmented in most organizations, said the IT managers in the group. However, they agreed that because social media also represents an information asset, ultimately it is IT's responsibility because, once inside the organization, social media data become part of the organization's data repository—or big data. Therefore, with the huge amounts of data flooding into organizations, someone needs to be making decisions about it if it is to deliver business value (Ross 2012).

There are a number of issues that IT leaders need to consider when addressing social media/big data governance, such as the control, legal, security, access, staffing, and logistical implications of its management (Laney and White 2014). As just one

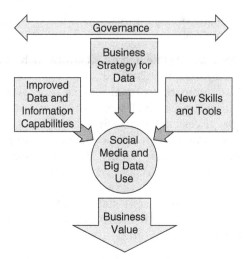

FIGURE 13.2   Components of a New Organizational Capability for Big Data

example, governance will need to determine which data can be exposed to the public, and this decision in turn will affect all other aspects of governance. In addition, companies need to understand their tolerances for risk and experimentation and develop appropriate governance mechanisms to determine whether the risks involved in any social media/big data initiative are appropriate for their organization.

A Business Strategy for Data

Increasingly, companies are demanding more and better information to meet their needs (Redman 2013). To obtain it however, companies must first recognize that new big data/social media technologies have the capacity to significantly redefine business models and they will therefore need a business strategy for how to manage what is done with them (Fitzgerald et al. 2014). "These could be dis-intermediating technologies," said one manager. "We're at a critical juncture as companies are beginning to build strong relationships with their customers." Although many executives fear learning what their customers are saying about their company and their products and services, taking this step *can* be a strategic differentiator for an organization. Similarly, improved insights gleaned from other types of data can also radically transform how a business operates (Davenport 2013). Companies should start strategizing by asking relevant business questions that address key value levers, such as *what are the biggest drivers of our profits?* Or, *how can we increase customer loyalty?* Then, indicators can be developed and key data collected. For example, one focus group firm is developing a consolidated view of its customers using structured and unstructured data from both internal and external sources because it felt that knowing more about its customers would help it target products and services more effectively to them.

Data can also be used to drive the development of strategy *after* it has been collected. However, this can only occur if useful information is developed that is *used* by the organization (Marchand et al. 2000; Marchand and Peppard 2013). Although social media is a marketing tool, it is also extremely important for a business to have the capability to *use* the data that are generated from it to inform decision making and strategy development over time. Companies should therefore ask, *do we have information that is easy to use?* and *is it useful?* This means working with IT to embed insights into business processes and make them more understandable and actionable through a variety of methods such as dashboards, visualization, trend analysis and simulations, and traditional reports, and then validating their usefulness with the business (LaValle et al. 2011).

Better Data Capabilities

Data have four dimensions (Marchand et al. 2000):

- *Unstructured*, such as that gained through social media.
- *Structured*, such as that found in databases.
- *Internal* data, information, and knowledge that are found within an organization.
- *External* sources of data or information from outside the company, such as customer comments, external databases, or sensor data.

Improving big data capabilities involves collecting more data from different data sources to gain a more complete view of customers, supply chains, or other strategic situations. Determining what data to collect and how to get it is an organization's first challenge. Here, the goal is to transition from siloed data, supporting siloed processes and decisions acting on a partial awareness, to integrated data (both internal and from social media) that will provide a 360° understanding of an entity or a situation (Austin et al. 2006; Davenport et al. 2012).

A second challenge is how best to organize data and capture context and meaning in order to get to the most useful insights. Although big data tools increase the volume and velocity of data available and reduce the costs involved, companies must still decide how to dissect it to turn data into insights (Beath et al. 2012). "Simply making data available is no guarantee of value. Organizations need data context, centers of excellence, and governance to manage it properly," said one manager.

Furthermore, most companies still have much room for improvement in structuring their data and analytics capabilities, said the focus group. For example, it is still often unclear where in the organization these activities are best performed. In some firms, IT has this responsibility; in others it is an enterprise service or divided among the business units. Such pockets of data capability in different places can detract from what an organization is able to do with data.

Research shows there are three levels of analytics maturity in organizations (Kiron and Shockley 2011; LaValle et al. 2011):

1. *Aspirational.*   At this level, analytics are siloed and largely based on structured data and the use of spreadsheets. Typically, these support targeted activities such as finance and supply chain management.
2. *Experienced.*   More mature companies also use visualization, advanced modeling, and data integration to support more holistic strategy development and marketing and operations activities.
3. *Transformational.*   At this level, firms use a broad portfolio of tools to analyze integrated structured and unstructured data to support day-to-day strategy and operations in a planned and coordinated fashion.

Most companies today are between the first two levels, but the field is moving rapidly (Kiron and Shockley 2011). Much of what is "emerging" today will be mainstream in a very few years, so it's important for companies to be ready for this by ensuring they learn how to think about data, develop more discipline about collecting data, experiment with analytics models, and change corporate culture to enable some risk as business models evolve.

New Skills and Tools

Although tools are a necessary component of building new data capabilities in an organization, improving skills is largely an organizational challenge (Austin et al. 2006; Kiron and Shockley 2011). Internally, IT's data skills are often separated into three different organizational groups that have operated as silos, the focus group explained. Operations have been responsible for speed of delivery, back-up and recovery, 24×7 support, uptime, security and compliance, and process. Decision support has been responsible for number crunching, visualization, metrics, ad hoc requirements, sandboxes, and subject matter expertise. And knowledge and content management has been responsible for tagging, taxonomy, search, incentives, work routines, and knowledge. Today, these three skill sets are converging and ensuring they intersect appropriately is essential to leveraging an organization's existing tools.

However, companies will likely also need to hire and develop IT people who can create value with data and existing IT skills will have to change as well (LaValle et al. 2011). Initially, technical skills will be needed to architect, select, and implement the most appropriate new technologies. Following this phase, data sources need to be identified, collected, and prepared before analytics and other types of information delivery activities can be developed. In this step, it is critical to have people with a combination of business, analytics, and data skills, who are not isolated from the business. Although hiring more data scientists is part of the solution, "the bigger problem is that we lack the managers and analysts who can ensure that big data can be effectively consumed and used by organizations," said one manager. "These people need a very broad skill set, ranging from communication to business knowledge to technical and data knowledge."

The effective use of social media data and analytics to deliver value also requires a tighter integration of business unit and IT functions (Maoz et al. 2013). Business units will also need specialized staff who work closely with IT to develop applications and learn, tightly cycling through the iterative development and implementation of new products as services, as insights are gained. These specialized business unit staff should have considerable technical and analytic skills but should not be viewed as a "shadow IT group," but rather a new type of business professional who delivers important data and ideas to business and IT leaders. Therefore, increasingly there will be a growing gradation in staff skills between business and IT with the people in the middle skilled in both technology and business, said the focus group.

Overall, companies should have three specific sets of competencies for dealing with big data (Laney and White 2014; McAfee and Brynjolfsson 2012):

1. *Information management expertise.* This includes data governance, good data management practices, and the ability to deliver the right data to the right people.
2. *Business analytic expertise.* This is the analytic talent, tools, and technology needed to deliver insights from data.

3. *An analytic-oriented culture.*   This is a broad organizational belief that data and analytics are a strategic asset. It includes analytics champions, a mandate, and us of insights for both strategic and tactical decisions.

INNOVATING WITH BIG DATA

In addition to these fundamental components of delivering business value with data, leaders are also looking for IT to help them innovate with data (Fitzgerald et al. 2014; Kruschwitz 2011). We are just beginning to recognize that there are data external to the organization, in addition to social media data, that can be used to generate new and entirely different sources of value for companies (Piccoli and Pigni 2012). In strategizing about how to take full advantage of the internal and social media data they already have, business and IT should also be exploring how best to leverage these external data sets. This process begins by asking five questions:

1. Do we know what data people have socialized around our business and our product?
2. Do we have an inventory of the data streams in our ecosystem and those surrounding us?
3. Have we thought about the data streams we produce? Could they be valuable outside our organization?
4. How many of our organizational systems could be architected easily to provide data in real time?
5. Are we keeping an eye on the changing value of our digital assets?

The answers to these questions can then be used to develop new strategic opportunities for organizations with external data (Piccoli and Pigni 2012). These include the following:

1. *Data generation.*   Many firms generate data that can be used by others to create new products or services. For example, TripIt taps into a variety of travel data streams, such as reservations made with airlines, hotel and car rental agencies, and integrates confirmations into a master itinerary for a traveler or a group of travelers. The company is seeking to be the home base for all of a consumer's travel information.
2. *Aggregation.*   Here, a firm identifies and harvests a variety of data streams, which are then repurposed and made available to potential users, thereby creating a data platform. For example, Socrata is a platform for government agencies and provides access to public, real-time data in a one-stop shop.
3. *Service.*   Here, a firm uses data to create new services for consumers or to improve service quality. For example, Mycityway is a real-time app designed to help users navigate an urban environment. Integrating over 100 real-time feeds, it helps one find a type of restaurant, a wireless hotspot, buy tickets, connect with other users, or check live traffic feeds.
4. *Efficiency.*   A firm can also use data streams to optimize internal operations, such as waste reduction. For example, Trafikanten in Norway uses real-time feeds to locate buses and optimize traffic lights, as well as inform customers when their bus will arrive. It has generated 15 percent more bus efficiency as a result, while providing a new customer service.

5. *Analytics.* Companies are using a variety of data to develop superior insight or knowledge. For example, Mint brings a person's financial accounts together from a variety of sources and automatically categorizes transactions, and helps set budgets and develop savings goals.

Once in place, companies can leverage several of these approaches at the same time or shift between them as their understanding matures.

PULLING IN TWO DIFFERENT DIRECTIONS: THE CHALLENGE FOR IT MANAGERS

As is so often the case with new technologies, IT managers feel torn between their everyday reality and the glamorous and dynamic vision of the future as painted by the proponents of big data and social computing (Spanbauer 2006). Focus group participants were concerned about how demands for new information and ways of working would mesh with their ongoing responsibilities of managing an efficient and effective IT organization. "Social computing is a challenge in our locked down environment," said one. Another noted, "Our information security principles conflict with it. There are some things we don't want hitting the 6 o'clock news." Similarly, big data use requires opening up established and structured organizational processes to a wide variety of data sources, collaborating more extensively with business and enabling flexible and transient applications and information (Davenport 2013; Smith and McKeen 2007).

"We're being pulled in two directions by these trends. We need to change," said one manager, "but we also need to protect our corporate assets. We really need to develop policies for how to do these things properly." They saw their biggest challenge for social computing and accessing external data streams as security and protecting the reliability of the infrastructure they have built up. "If the security issue was addressed, we'd see some of these things as much more acceptable," said another manager. With big data, the challenges involve rethinking how data management is done, speeding up IT analysis work, and redesigning business processes to be more data-driven, rather than process-driven. Table 13.1 summarizes the vision of social computing and big data and contrasts it with the challenges it poses to IT management.

Some of their other challenges include the following:

- *Short business horizons.* As has often been the case in the past, business leaders have a much shorter time horizon in their thinking than IT and are often not prepared to anticipate or explore new technologies and their implications that *might* be important in the future. *Then,* when the technology hits public awareness, they want it *yesterday!* "We have no active support for social computing or big data," said one manager. "It's very hard for the business to see its value as yet." Yet, in some cases, business users see IT as holding them back because of security and regulatory considerations. "We need to work together with the business to identify the risks associated with these new ways of working and protect our operational processes," said another. "And we need to make sure the decision-makers understand what's involved in becoming more open and information-oriented."
- *Resources.* Social computing is touted as an effective collaboration and innovation tool but using it for this purpose requires support and facilitation. "Our staff

TABLE 13.1	The Challenges of Big Data and Social Computing from an IT Manager's Perspective	
The Vision	**The IT Manager's Challenge**	
Blurred process and organizational boundaries	Firewalls and structured processes	
Collaboration and sharing both internally and externally	Intellectual property and privacy protection; formalized external engagement	
Situational applications	Maintaining transactional applications and operational integrity	
Mass participation and accessibility	Authentication and authorization	
Data orientation	Process orientation	
Transient information (i.e., systems of engagement)	Creating a permanent record (i.e., systems of record)	
Support for social behavior	Support for business behavior	
Innovation and creativity	Efficient use of resources	
Viral	Secure	
Dynamic	Backup	
Situational roles	Regulatory accountabilities	
Date governance and etiquette	Project governance and policy	
Collective intelligence; bottom up innovation; empowerment with data	Top down business strategy	
Emergent value	Defined business value based on a business case	
Data discovery and exploration	Managed data environments	
Anywhere, anytime connectivity	Controlled communication	
Ad hoc applications and inquiries	Scalable applications	

is maxed out at present," said a manager. "If we go down this road, we need to commit resources to doing it properly." Similarly there must be business support for incorporating new ways to utilize big data. This involves more than just adding a few data scientists but, as noted earlier, requires top-down attention to thinking about, using, and making decisions with data. Even in those companies that are actively promoting these changes, getting the right resources in both business and IT is a challenge. "And when we're stressed, we revert to our old behaviors," explained a participant.

- *Changing the culture.* IT managers recognize that organizational behavior must change if the value of these tools is to be realized. However, changing embedded cultural practices is often extremely difficult. Even where there is a strong emphasis on making information and people more accessible, champions are needed to make sure "we don't slip back into our comfortable ways of behaving," agreed the focus group. For example, some organizations have tried experiments with more social ways of working with and sharing information but have found that while the adoption rate is initially high, the drop off in participation is equally steep. This is consistent with the challenges KM managers faced in the past, which effectively killed this function in most organizations. The question for many (and which remains unanswered) is whether these tools will be able to drive the behavioral and cultural changes needed to make the technology effective (Spanbauer 2006; Smith and McKeen 2007).

FIRST STEPS FOR IT LEADERS

Established mental models, business models, and systems can be serious inhibitors to the new ways of working implied by social media and big data. Discontinuous change requires thinking about needs differently and envisioning what is possible. As Henry Ford once said, "If I had asked people what they wanted, they could have said 'faster horses'." At that time, few would have imagined the automobile and its industry and infrastructure as it is today. Getting the mindset and model right involves much change, such as obtaining data from multiple sources, making sense of huge amounts of data, developing complex analytics algorithms, and dealing with cultural objections to standardized data. IT leaders should begin the change process by asking themselves a number of questions including the following:

- How can we attract, grow, and retain employees with the skills we will need?
- What data do we need and what is the optimal way to collect and manage the massive amounts of structured and unstructured data involved?
- How can we best support varied and dynamic business needs for information more rapidly?

The focus group believed it is not necessary to spend large amounts of money to demonstrate the value of these new approaches. "Expensive analytics projects are not required to get started with big data," said one manager. "Companies should start small and focus on proving value at each step." He noted that it is possible to begin inexpensively with open systems, which are scalable and require no licenses. "While you wouldn't want to run an entire enterprise this way, you can start small and then add variables and improve your models," he said.

Big data technologies can coexist with existing data warehouses and so can be introduced slowly, replacing specific storage and computing scenarios over time. "Start with the basics to build competencies, reduce processing, and take care of the mundane, and *then* grow," recommended one manager. As a company gets some quick wins, it will be more willing to develop pilot use cases for enterprise value realization. "As you move up the maturity curve, you will be able to figure out value optimization with big data," he added.

There are still many immediate big data and social media issues that need to be considered. These include immature technologies, legal and regulatory considerations, ownership of data quality, expectation management, establishing an effective organization structure, and optimal utilization of specialized resources. Privacy and data quality are also critical issues that must be properly managed if these initiatives are going to succeed. The IT managers groups collectively had the following recommendations for IT leaders:

1. *Focus.* Identify specific problems and then use data and/or social media to solve them. "If we just look at generic opportunities, the scope can be overwhelming," said one manager. Leaders should look for the biggest play they can get, either on the top or bottom line. "Start tactically and use success stories to illustrate how social media/big data can fit into your organizational strategy," they recommended.

2. *Develop business-savvy IT staff* and encourage development practices such as shadowing and colocation. Tap into your own expertise, promote business–IT rotation programs, and hire power users into IT. Colocating business intelligence delivery groups from IT in the business units and developing a business-led governance structure for data and social media prioritization projects are best practices. These steps will enable IT to focus on foundational components such as, standards, metadata, and data models, while business can focus on delivering intelligence.

3. *Become a "data factory"* with supportive methodologies and practices and an optimized ecosystem of advanced and traditional data technologies. Work to improve data quality, usability, and integration. Clarify responsibilities for data and manage the conflicts between security, privacy, and compliance requirements and information delivery. Finally, CIOs should consider reorganizing to facilitate the convergence of operational with decision support data, and unstructured with structured data.

4. *Listening and engaging.* Ensure your company is listening to its customers and others to find out their concerns and interests. Build deliverables that will engage customers with the company and provide superior customer service. Identify "killer apps" and highlight their value and relevance to customers.

5. *Consider hiring a graphic designer.* This will support IT in developing intuitive and easy interface designs and efforts to move to mobile devices.

6. *Support actions that improve use.* Communicate the link between use and value to keep teams focused on usefulness and ease of use in social media/big data applications.

Conclusion

Today, many organizations are thinking about how to use social technologies and new forms of data to change the products and services we use daily. Over the next few years, they will create new information platforms on which ideas that we never dreamed of will surface. Social media and the data they generate are still immature as are other new types of data and companies should therefore adopt them in an evolutionary fashion rather than in a "big bang." However, they cannot be ignored because they are going to be a part of every business. The question is, *how big?* The key to success is learning how to manage and think about data in an evolutionary way. If companies don't begin, they won't know what they can leverage and risk being disintermediated by those that are willing to try.

References

Austin, T., D. Cearley, J. Mann, G. Phifer, D. Sholler, K. Harris, T. Bell, R. Knox, M. Cain, and M. Silver. "Predicts 2007: Big Changes Ahead in the High Performance Workplace." Gartner Research Inc., ID Number: G00144476, December 5, 2006.

Beath, C., I. Bercerra-Fernandez, J. Ross, and J. Short. "Finding Value in the Information Explosion." *MIT Sloan Management Review* 53, no. 4 (Summer 2012): 18–20.

Davenport, T. "Analytics 3.0." *Harvard Business Review,* Reprint No. R1312C (December 2013).

Davenport, T., P. Barth, and R. Bean. "How Big Data is Different." *MIT Sloan Management Review* 54, no. 1 (Fall 2012): 43–46.

Fitzgerald, M., N. Kruschwitz, D. Bonnet, and M. Welch. "Embracing Digital Technology: A New Strategic Imperative." *MIT Sloan Management Review* 55, no. 2 (Winter 2014): 1–12.

Kiron, D., and R. Shockley. "Creating Business Value with Analytics." *MIT Sloan Management Review* 53, no. 1, Reprint No. 53112 (Fall 2011).

Kiron, D., D. Palmer, A. N. Phillips, and R. Berkman. "The Executive's Role in Social Business." *MIT Sloan Management Review* 54, no. 4 (Summer 2013): 83–89.

Kruschwitz, N. "The Second Annual New Intelligent Enterprise Survey." *MIT Sloan Management Review* 54, no. 4 (Summer 2011): 87–89.

Laney, D., and A. White. "Agenda Overview for Information Innovation and Governance 2014." Gartner Research Inc., ID Number: G0025982, January 10, 2014.

LaValle, S., E. Lesser, R. Shockley, M. Hopkins, and N. Kruschwitz. "Big Data, Analytics and the Path from Insights for Value." *MIT Sloan Management Review* 52, no. 2, Reprint No. 52205 (Winter 2011).

Maoz, M., J. Davies, J. Sussin, and O. Huang. "Predicts 2014: Customer Support and the Engaged Enterprise." Gartner Research Inc., ID Number: G00257816, November 15, 2013.

Marchand, D., W. Kettinger, and J. Rollins. "Information Orientation: People, Technology and the Bottom Line." *MIT Sloan Management Review* (Summer 2000).

Marchand, D., and A. Peppard. "Why IT Fumbles Analytics." *Harvard Business Review* 91, nos. 1, 2 (January/February 2013): 104–12.

McAfee, A., and E. Brynjolfsson. "Big Data: The Management Revolution." *Harvard Business Review* 90, no. 10 (October 2012): 61–68.

McKeen, J., and H. Smith. *IT Strategy: Issues and Practices,* 2nd ed. Upper Saddle River, NJ: Pearson, 2012.

Piccoli, G., and F. Pigni. "Harvesting External Data: The Potential of Digital Data Systems." SIM Advanced Practices Report, August 5, 2012.

Redman, T. "Data's Credibility Problem." *Harvard Business Review* 91, no. 12 (December 2013): 84–88.

Ross, J. "Do You Need a Data Dictator?" *MIT Sloan Management Review,* Reprint No. 54123 (August 2012).

Smith, H., and B. Konsynski. "Grid Computing." *MIT-Sloan Management Review* 46, no. 1 (2004).

Smith, H., and J. McKeen. "Social Networks: KM's 'Killer App?'" *Communications of the Association of Information Systems,* 19, no. 27 (2007): 611–21.

Spanbauer, S. "Knowledge Management 2.0." *CIO* 20, no. 5 (December 1, 2006).

14 Improving the Customer Experience: An IT Perspective

It used to be so simple. Customers "experienced" a company through its products or services. Brand managers handled the products and customer service handled any problems with services. Products were bought in only one or two ways and services were developed accordingly. Thus, a store was the sole channel for retail products, while the agent was the sole channel for insurance products and so on. Today, of course, we live in a very different world of multichannel access, thanks to a plethora of new Web-based computing devices. Now, we can find products and services anywhere in the world, undertake transactions 24×7 from almost anywhere with our mobile devices, and compare and contrast our perceptions, feelings, and quality of interactions with others through new forms of social media. As a result, an increasing number of businesses are looking to differentiate themselves not just on products or services but also on a superior customer experience (Thompson 2011).

However, recognizing the need and delivering an outstanding customer experience are two different matters. While all organizations give their customers an "experience"—either positive or negative—few as yet have committed the time and resources to analyze, manage, and improve it on an ongoing and holistic basis (Davies and Thompson 2009). So where does IT fit into this mix? As with so much else, information technology is essential to the solution but not the whole answer. There are many stakeholders, technologies, and even strategies involved and no one "silver bullet" (Thompson 2011). And yet "it is clear now that technology will be playing an increasingly important role in delivering positive customer experiences and, when implemented poorly, can destroy them" (Thompson 2011). A key challenge is delivering a consistent experience across all channels, but technology is also important for improving both front office and online knowledge management, and listening and responding to customers after interactions are completed. As well, in order to address these matters, there is considerable foundational work that needs to be undertaken by IT, such as integrating all information about a customer, analyzing the different processes involved in dealing with customers, and even coming up with a clear definition of what the customer experience *is*[1] (Thompson and Herschel 2009).

This chapter explores the IT function's role in creating and improving an organization's customer experiences. It first examines the nature of "customer experience"—both its business value and its many dimensions. Then it describes the role technology plays in creating experiences for customers and helping companies understand their customers' experiences. Finally, it looks at the foundational elements an IT organization must put in place in order to be able to support and deliver enterprise–customer experience initiatives and describes some of the advice our focus group managers had for others trying to improve their customers' experience with IT.

CUSTOMER EXPERIENCE AND BUSINESS VALUE

Improving their customers' experience was the top strategic priority for many members of the focus group and an extremely high priority for all the others. One global study of CEOs found that 88 percent of all CEOs selected "getting closer to the customer" as the most important dimension of realizing their business strategy over the next five years. It noted that

> Customers encountering new products, services and experiences…are growing less loyal to their brands…Reputations can be built and burned by opinions shared online, "texted" or "tweeted" by friends, bloggers and advocacy groups. CEOs told us they need to re-ignite customer interest and loyalty or risk losing ground to competitors. (Korsten 2011)

There are many good business reasons for this strong interest in creating a positive customer experience. First and foremost, studies show that a consistent and excellent customer experience positively impacts an organization's bottom line. One found that strong returns on investment of up to 50 percent are related to initiatives designed to improve customer experience (Dardan et al. 2007). Profit and growth are primarily stimulated by customer loyalty, which in turn is stimulated by customer satisfaction, which is driven by positive customer experiences with an organization and its brands and services (Thompson and Herschel 2009).

Conversely, today's customers are more willing to complain, switch brands, and tell others about it (Thompson and Davies 2011). "In our competitive world, customer acquisition is expensive, so we want to retain them once we get them," said a focus group manager. For example, 59 percent of customers will stop doing business with a brand after just one bad experience in just one channel (Gagnon et al. 2005). On the other hand, 82 percent of consumers will recommend a brand to friends and family if they have a satisfying experience with it (Kioa and Zapf 2002).

Second, customer experience can also be a strong company differentiator—both positive and negative—thereby directly affecting sales. For example, Apple's consistent ability to delight its customers and make their experience with its products enjoyable

---

[1] Voice of the Customer, Customer Relationship Management, Master Data Management, Customer Experience Management and multichannel distribution are all interrelated aspects of this concept.

illustrates that *how* a product or service is provided is as important as *what* is provided (Meyer and Schwager 2007). In fact, an excellent customer experience is one of the most sustainable forms of business differentiation (Thompson 2011). In contrast, poor quality experiences can humiliate an organization and damage its credibility and stock prices, and lead to customer determination to do business elsewhere (Meyer and Schwager 2007).

Efforts to improve customers' experience can also result in a number of other less well-known benefits to an organization, such as improved customer data quality, reduced operations and service costs, more effective brand launches, and better segmentation and marketing (Sarner and Davies 2011). While customer experience projects typically look at customer-facing applications, there are other less obvious impacts on customers from back-end processes, such as billing and logistics (Thompson and Davies 2011). One focus group manager found that her company's invoicing practices not only had the largest impact on customer experience but also a very strong potential to dissatisfy. Poor customer service at the end of the sales cycle in particular can have a strong negative impact on customer experience as anyone who has been trapped in "voice mail hell" or stuck on hold can attest (Alcock and Millard 2007). And good customer service that enables customers to solve their problems with a minimum amount of time and interaction can both save the company money and dramatically improve customer satisfaction (Hopkins 2010; Jacobs 2011).

In short, today's customers have growing expectations of the organizations they deal with. They don't want to waste time; want better options; and want their relationship with an organization to be recognized and respected (Hopkins 2010). The gap between their expectations and their experience spells the difference between an organization's ability to delight them or to repel them and will directly affect a firm's competitive advantage. Unfortunately, this gap is only too apparent in most modern organizations. While 8 percent of customers described their experiences with organizations as superior, 80 percent of companies believe that they provide superior service (Meyer and Schwager 2007). Focus group members agreed that their companies had not focused on creating a good customer experience in the past. "We are gradually changing our behaviour to ask what we can do to become more customer-centric," said one manager. "We are recognizing that while our vision for the *type* of customer relationships we want is strong, we need to do a much better job in *delivering* on projects that will build them," said another.

MANY DIMENSIONS OF CUSTOMER EXPERIENCE

"Customer experience" is a multidimensional concept that is often misunderstood or poorly defined by organizations (Thompson and Herschel 2009). For example, many organizations do not distinguish between surveys that measure satisfaction with a particular experience or at a point in time and customer experience, which is a more comprehensive, holistic, and continuous accumulation of a variety of experiences with all aspects of an organization (Meyer and Schwager 2007). As a focus group manager explained, "We are beginning to recognize that we must understand *all* our customers' needs and experiences across *many* dimensions such as price, personal interaction, promotions, products, processes, and place."

Customer experience is thus not just customer service or customer relationship management, although these are key components of it. Nor is it derived from a single interaction or channel. It also varies according to the type of customer involved because experiences are both rational and emotional (Davies and Thompson 2009). Altogether, it encompasses customer touch points from every part of an organization, across multiple channels and departments, and the full sales cycle from marketing to order processing to billing to post-sales service.

As well, it incorporates *both* positive and negative experiences. One focus group company assesses its touch points along two dimensions: their potential to delight or dissatisfy, and the size of the impact if they succeed or fail. "All our departments must recognize that they have a role to play in creating a positive (or negative) customer experience," said a manager. "We need to better understand customer perceptions of our entire organization," said another "and to recognize that different customers may have different experiences." Customer experience is also influenced by whether or not a company is perceived to be actively working to address its problems (Markey et al. 2009). In short, customer experience is an enterprise challenge that reaches across all parts of an organization, touch points, and channels (Dougherty and Murthy 2009).

Some additional dimensions customer experiences include the following:

- *Consistency and reliability.* Customer experience is shaped by expectations and these, in turn, are positively influenced by products and services that deliver consistently across channels, over time, and as promised (Thompson 2011).
- *Knowledge and data.* The ability of an organization to assist, support, and educate its customers is based on how well knowledge about products, services, and customer preferences, is either built into its customer-facing applications or made available to its staff (Jacobs 2011). In addition, organizations need to know *about* their customers' experiences in order to better understand and act to improve them (Dougherty and Murthy 2009).
- *Timeliness.* Clearly, the best time to positively influence a customer's experience is while the customer is interacting with the organization. The longer it takes to accomplish an interaction, the less likely a customer will be satisfied. This is particularly true if an experience is mediated by technology. Members cited studies that showed that 65 percent of customers abandon online shopping carts if frustrated (Kioa and Zapf 2002). They also stated that their firms lose millions of dollars if their Web sites are down even for a few minutes.
- *Innovation.* Since it is now a strategic differentiator for organizations, innovation is an increasingly important dimension of the customer experience. While many think first about innovative usability, some suggest there are whole new layers of customer experience that can be improved through the innovative use of technology (Korsten 2011; Martin 2011). For example, one company that manufactured medical scanning equipment used IT to create a personalized environment with pictures and sound, which helped reduce anxiety in patients—something that had never previously been thought of as a role for technology (Verganti 2011).

Finally, the focus group managers and researchers both stressed that it is important for companies to hear what their customers are saying about their experiences and to take action to improve problems. "We are now undertaking a wide variety of feedback initiatives," said a manager, "because we need a more nuanced understanding of how customers are experiencing our company." Unfortunately, too many organizations fear what data will reveal about their organizations and don't stress this dimension (Meyer and

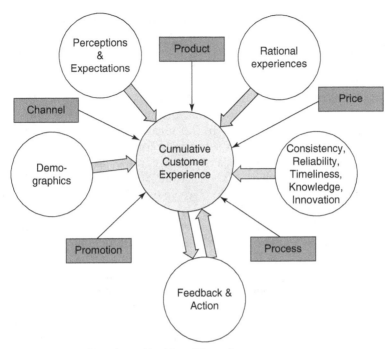

FIGURE 14.1 A Customer's Experience Has Many Dimensions

Schwager 2007). Getting real-time customer feedback is especially important so that problems can be quickly identified. In today's connected world, rapid action to correct problems is the best way to deal with specific issues that arise. "We are implementing technology to get near real time feedback so we can take corrective actions at once," said one manager.

Figure 14.1 combines all these dimensions into one holistic view of customer experience.

THE ROLE OF TECHNOLOGY IN CUSTOMER EXPERIENCE

Organizations today rely on technology for nearly every facet of customer interaction, making IT a significant component of the customer experience (Violino 2005). Studies show that companies are investing considerably in technologies that will affect customer experiences. Ninety-one percent have automated some aspects of the customer experience and 61 percent say that they are investing in IT in order to improve it (Violino 2005). And there are literally hundreds of vendors selling many different technologies to "help" (Davies et al. 2011). A focus group manager described the scope of IT's influence in her organization as follows: "Technology and IT play a big role in a variety of customer experiences. We're using in-store kiosks for self-service; providing better information for our staff; better analysing our customer data; improving our website; training our staff better; simplifying our returns process, integrating products and services across all our lines of business and offering the same consumer campaigns across all channels."

There are several broad categories of technology that are typically thought of in relation to customer experience management. These include technologies that are customer-facing such as, customer relationship management (CRM), interactive voice recognition (IVR), and online and mobile self-service applications. However, as we have noted, there are many other customer touch points in organizations where IT is used, such as billing, complaints and dispute resolution, and incorporating technology into innovative products and services that will also affect the customer experience. Finally, there are the underpinning technologies, such as master data management, knowledge management, infrastructure management, and metrics and analytics that will in the longer term make a huge difference in how a customer experiences an organization.

However, the use of technology by no means guarantees a positive customer experience. All too often technology is substituted for people in an effort to slash costs, resulting in a *less* satisfying or negative experience, rather than using it to create more meaningful and positive experiences (Davies et al. 2011; Verganti 2011). Members of the focus group agreed with this assessment. "We've used IT for cost reduction, seeing our customer services as a factory model," said a manager. Bad technology unfortunately leads to a bad or mediocre customer experience. For example, one study found that some companies hide behind their Web sites so that customers have no way to communicate with a human being (Weill 2008).

Effective architecture underpins a consistent and holistic approach to addressing an organization's customer experience needs. "We have typically proceeded to implement customer-oriented technology without the end architecture in mind and this has been a mistake," said a manager. "As a result, we've made assumptions in key decisions based on superficial analysis." Architecture is essential for delivering a consistent, cross-channel customer experience and for ensuring that all touch points are well integrated, explained another manager.

There is broad agreement that the most positive (and cost-effective) customer experiences come from the right combination of investment in a combination of technology, improved processes, and knowledgeable and empowered employees (Davies and Thompson 2009; Jacobs 2011; Verganti 2011). Ideally, the channel used to interact with a company should be the choice of the customer. Customers will then self-select an appropriate channel depending on the nature of the transaction, customer perceptions, time of day, and concerns about privacy and security (Alcock and Millard 2007). Thus, an effective use of technology doesn't degrade one channel (e.g., the telephone) in order to promote another (e.g., a Web site). Often this approach is not deemed to be cost-effective. However, although enforced self-service can result in substantial cost savings for an organization, it can also translate into no service and become a brand destroyer (Alcock and Millard 2007). In contrast, where technology is adopted taking direct customer input into consideration, experiences tend to be viewed more positively (Sarner and Davies 2011).

CUSTOMER EXPERIENCE ESSENTIALS FOR IT

There is no shortage of advice about what IT needs to do in order to facilitate a positive customer experience. However, the group agreed that there are five essential capabilities that IT needs to develop, which will serve as foundational elements for whatever customer initiatives a company decides to focus on:

1. *Visioning.* The ability to creatively envision how to create a more positive experience for customers came up over and over in the group. "We need to stop seeing IT as a back office function," said one manager, "and develop better skills

in researching emerging technologies and doing experiments." Another added, "We need to work more closely with the business and ask the right questions so we can do creative problem solving." Research stresses that innovation is critical to delighting customers and that organizations can boost their capacity for innovation by making more of an effort to understand them (Martin 2011). As Apple's success has shown, "we must stop thinking that copying others will yield uniquely attractive results" (Martin 2011). Instead, IT needs to envision what technology can make possible and broaden its horizons about what can be done to make services more meaningful (Verganti 2011). Many of these will only be discovered through experimentation and trying out new ideas in the field, said the focus group. Still others will come from "thinking like a customer" and leveraging current capabilities. From these dreams, business and IT then need to develop the strategies and capabilities that will deliver differentiated interactions with customers (Feig 2007).

2. *Customer Focus.*   Group members concurred that improving customers' experience involves their companies and IT functions becoming more customercentric and that doing this properly will involve redefining large parts of business processes and systems. "The first thing we are doing is identifying specific touch points where customers come into contact with our organization and analyzing their journeys through the processes involved," said one manager. Many experts in the field also stress the need to analyze actual customer experience, rather than the generic experience (Alcock and Millard 2007). In order to become more customer-focused, IT staff must understand and internalize the customers' point of view. Finding ways to make the customer experience real for IT staff will build customer empathy and improve IT's ability to design appropriate technology. This can be done by sharing customer stories and letters, and engaging front line staff to share their experiences with customers. In addition, having selected IT staff meet with customers has been shown to have a demonstrable impact on the quality of a design from a user's point of view and to be a significant source of inspiration for innovation (Grant 2011; Heller 2011).

3. *Designing for utilization.*   Because most IT projects now have an impact on customer experience, designing for a positive experience has become a key IT capability (Shih 2012; Thompson and Davies 2011). There are several components to effective design from a user point of view. First, it must be useful. Second it must be useable. Third, it must be used. The real test of a good design is therefore not its features but its utility (Alcock and Millard 2007). One focus group manager cited a study that showed that 65 percent of customers abandon online shopping carts due to usability barriers at a potential loss of $25 billion (Kioa and Zapf 2002). "We should not be rewarding [IT] for 'bloatware,'" said one researcher, "but for stuff that people use and are happy to use and are willing to pay to use.... It's customer use that really matters now" (Hopkins 2010).

Other important elements of customer-centered design include the ability of a customer to personalize how he/she interacts with a company through offering different channels and combinations of human and technical interaction (Alcock and Millard 2007). For example, it's not good design to force customers to use a Web site or IVR when they have complex needs or prefer to speak with a human being. Properly designed technology will encourage customer use but incorporate options for them. Similarly, business processes should also be designed to prevent customers being handed off or made to wait (Feig 2007). The goal of good customer experience design is to make it easy for people to interact with a company and to minimize frustration across all touch points (Hopkins 2010). Finally, focus group managers emphasized that an outstanding customer experience extends to the design of the full range of customer interactions. "We should be designing an end-to-end experience that addresses both upstream and downstream needs, as well as purchases," said one.

4. *Data management.* The delivery of complete, current, and accurate data is central to the ability to provide high-quality customer service with technology (Feig 2007; Jacobs 2011). This is one reason why many of the focus group's companies are undertaking master data management initiatives[2] (Davies et al. 2011). Good information is not only important for customer service representatives who interact with customers, but it is also essential for the managers and executives who are working to understand how best to address customer needs (Davies et al. 2011). Focus group members pointed out that data should enable mangers to understand the customer experience from a variety of perspectives across an organization, help resolve problems at first contact (a well-known satisfier), and identify problems that should be addressed.

However, going forward, even more data and better data classification systems will be needed in order to personalize company services and offerings to its customers (Davenport et al. 2011). "We want to create personalized, memorable experiences," said one focus group manager "and that means having good data for customers and about them so that we can measure and fine tune the customer experience." The growing availability of social, mobile, and location data is creating new data sets that can be mined to better serve and delight customers. However, since this is a huge field, it is also important to be selective about the data that will be used to meet corporate strategies (Hopkins 2010).

5. *Delivery.* Execution is where it all comes together. Well-designed customer experiences can easily fall apart if they are not executed well and this is too often the case, according to the focus group. The number one order of business, they said, is to deliver existing products and services reliably and consistently across channels and products. Several focus group members acknowledged that their companies had different customer service experiences for different products or different locations. They also spoke about having multiple customer experience initiatives in different business units, which didn't integrate or weren't consistent. "Ideally, the customer experience should be seamless across all channels," said a manager. Others underlined the importance of having *both* good technology *and* knowledgeable and caring staff, who are themselves supported and empowered by good technology. The key to effective execution of a customer experience therefore is to deliver technology that enables the right balance of human "touch" and technical convenience for a particular customer in a particular situation (Alcock and Millard 2007).

---

[2] For a more complete discussion of this topic see "Master Data Management" at Pearson's Web site.

FIRST STEPS TO IMPROVING CUSTOMER EXPERIENCE

"Improving customer experience is a journey, not a project," said a focus group manager. Addressing it will take multiple small improvements that together add up to create an overall positive impact (Thompson 2011). However, members of the focus group had some advice and recommendations for those beginning this journey.

First, it's important to take a holistic approach to it and doing this requires central management. "We want to have 'one company and one customer,'" said a manager. "In the past, each business unit had their own unique approaches to improving customer experiences. Now, we want to make it part of everything we do, so we've created an EVP of Customer Experience." Another company has also created a senior vice president position to address all dimensions of customer experience. "This is giving us a single, shared view of the customer across the entire value chain," said the manager. Studies show that 75 percent of companies still have fragmented customer processes that are disconnected or disorganized. Appointing a single senior executive with responsibility to improve customer experience thus provides the executive sponsorship that many enterprisewide initiatives often lack (Thompson 2011).

Second, companies need to think clearly about the kind of value they want to create with their customer experience strategy (Hopkins 2010). Unfortunately, this critical discussion is often ignored as companies leap directly to what technology can do for them. However, if value is not addressed, it is doubtful that IT will be able to deliver what is expected (see Chapter 1). Thus, a company should first ask, "What kind of world am I trying to create?" before determining what technology they need to deliver it (Hopkins 2010). Focus group managers agreed strongly. "In the past, we've traded off customer ease of use for cost containment and we've lost customers," said one. "We've realized that acquiring new customers is expensive and retaining them is important." Another cited research showing that having a clear customer relationship management strategy and value proposition is a strong contributor to profitable growth (Korsten 2011).

Third, it follows that an *integrated* business and IT strategy is needed to develop a roadmap for improving the customer experience and to design the initiatives that will operationalize it. A manager explained, "We believe that establishing a cross-functional team, mapping key journeys from a customer point of view, and assessing gaps in our corporate capabilities are critical to developing an effective strategy to improve customer experience." Another stated: "We have decided to have one view of the customer and one common set of business rules. This is giving us common ground for cohesive business-IT strategy development because we are all hearing the same message."

Fourth, IT needs to identify and develop new capabilities to deal with customers, not just business users. "We need people who keep the big picture in mind and who can connect the dots," said a manager. Another added, "we need people with a blend of business and IT skills—who can think like a customer, communicate in business language, and ask 'so what?' questions." Skills with designing experiments, learning about new and emerging technologies, usability design and testing, and working with customers are all currently in short supply. "We must meet our customers on their own turf," said a manager. "While not all IT people can speak with customers, we must be able to collaborate with our business colleagues and particularly with front line staff to test new ideas." One company is doing this by creating and engaging its various customer "communities" to learn about how to improve its customer experiences with different demographic groups.

Finally, the focus group stressed that IT must keep working away at the basics—common data, integration across applications and channels, and reliability. "We need to develop a single source of truth," said a manager. "This is the best way to ensure that we all have the same understanding and are working towards the same ends." Customers want and value simplicity and common data and integration ensures that interactions are easy and convenient (Hopkins 2010). And these three basics are essential to delivering a *consistent* experience that will develop a positive perception of a company and its products, which in turn will lead to customer satisfaction, loyalty, and ultimately profitability (Thompson and Herschel 2009).

Conclusion

Until relatively recently, customers' experience with a company was simply a by-product of whatever business strategy an organization selected. Outsourcing, IVR, online "self-service," and complex processes apparently designed to confound the customer and save the company money were the order of the day. Consequently, when a company did appear to care about its customers' experience, it was a breath of fresh air. Apple's huge success is based largely on its "obsess[ion] about [customers'] experience and being dedicated to creating unique improvements to delight them...cobbled together in the most magical ways with the [customer] rather than the scientist at the center of the picture" (Martin 2011).

Today, customer experience is recognized by most organizations as being essential to their current and future success and, as a result, it has become a top priority for most executives. IT plays an integral part in almost all customer experience initiatives and this fact is putting new pressures on the IT function to become more customercentric and think differently about how technology is delivered to the organization. As the members of this focus group made clear, everything a company does—and especially its technology—must now be designed with the customer in mind. This is a significant shift of mind-set for IT staff in particular, but it is an essential one if technology is going to be able to deliver on its potential to delight and differentiate. For companies, the stakes are high: change to meet rising customer expectations or lose out against the competition and risk losing customer loyalty and corporate reputation.

References

Alcock, T., and N. Millard. "Self-service—But Is It Good to Talk?" *BT Technology Journal* 25, nos. 3 & 4 (July/October 2007): 313–20.

Dardan, S., R. Kumar, and A. Stylianou. "The Impact of Customer-related IT Investments on Customer Satisfaction and Shareholder Returns." *The Journal of Computer Information Systems* 47, no. 2 (Winter 2007): 100.

Davenport, T., L. Mule, and J. Lucker. "Know What Your Customers Want Before They Do."

Harvard Business Review 89, no. 12 (December 2011): 84–89.

Davies, J., J. Jacobs, and M. Maoz. "Balance Customer Experience with Customer Service Productivity in Customer Service Automation Initiatives." Gartner Inc., ID Number: G00216492, September 2011.

Davies, J., and E. Thompson. "Manage the Customer Experience to Improve Business Performance." Gartner Inc., ID Number: G00169030, June 30, 2009.

Dougherty, D., and A. Murthy. "What Service Customers Really Want." *Harvard Business Review* 87, no. 9, Reprint No. 00178012 (2009).

Feig, N. "BPM: Beyond Workflow—Banks Are Using Business Process Management to Improve the Customer Experience." *Bank Systems and Technology* 44, no. 7 (July 2007).

Gagnon, J., H. Kleinberger, and G. Morrison. *The Customer-Centric Store: Delivering the Total Experience.* IBM Institute for Business Value (2005). http://www-935.ibm.com/services/us/imc/pdf/g510-4027-the-customer-centric-store.pdf.

Grant, A. "How Customers Can Rally Your Troops." *Harvard Business Review* 89, no. 6 (June 2011).

Heller, M. "The Customer Will See You Now; CIOs and Their Teams Must Spend More Quality Time With End Customers." *CIO* 24, no. 7 (February 1, 2011).

Hopkins, M. "Value Creation, Experiments and Why IT Does Matter." *MIT Sloan Management Review* 51, no. 3 (Spring 2010).

Jacobs, J. "Case Study: Exploiting Agent Knowledge to Enhance Customer Experience." Gartner Inc., ID Number: G00213917, July 6, 2011.

Kioa, K., and M. Zapf. *ISM/Forrester Research Report on e-Business.* October 2002. http://www.ism.ws/ISMReport/content.cfm?ItemNumber=14177.

Korsten, P. "The Essential CIO." *IBM Institute for Business Value.* Somers, NY: IBM Global Business Services, 2011.

Markey, R., F. Reichheld, and A. Dullweber. "Closing the Customer Feedback Loop." *Harvard Business Review* 87, no. 12 (December 2009).

Martin, R. "Canada, Like Steve Jobs, Should Zero in on Innovation." *The Globe and Mail,* November 21, 2011.

Meyer, C., and A. Schwager. "Understanding Customer Experience." *Harvard Business Review,* 85, no. 2 (February 2007).

Sarner, A., and J. Davies. "Balance Customer Experience with Marketing Productivity in Marketing Automation Initiatives." Gartner Inc., ID Number: G00216115, September 2, 2011.

Shih, G. *In Silicon Valley Designers Emerge as Rock Stars.* April 16, 2012. http://uk.reuters.com/article/2012/04/16/oukin-uk-designers-startup-idUKBRE83F1BD20120416.

Thompson, E. "Key Issues for Customer Experience Management 2011." Gartner Inc., ID Number: G00213321, June 8, 2011.

Thompson, E., and J. Davies. "Ranking Technology Projects by Improved Customer Experience." Gartner Inc., ID Number: G00227323, November 9, 2011.

Thompson, E., and G. Herschel. "The Definition of Customer Experience Management." Gartner Inc., ID Number: G00169354, August 7, 2009.

Verganti, R. "Designing Breakthrough Products." *Harvard Business Review* 89, no. 10 (October 2011).

Violino, B. "Focus on Customer Experience." *Information Week,* no. 1054 (September 5, 2005).

Weill, N. "Five Things I've Learned; Actors Know a Thing or Two about Serving the Customer." *CIO* 21, no. 9 (February 15, 2008).

CHAPTER

15 Building Business Intelligence

It goes without saying that every business *wants* to be intelligent in its strategies and actions and every business manager *wants* to make intelligent decisions. The question is therefore, *how* does a business or a manager become "more intelligent"? Clearly, smart people, with lots of graduate degrees, good instincts, talents, and a little bit of luck are going to be well on their way as individuals and their decisions should benefit the organization, but is there a way to make *everyone* more intelligent? Are there practices, methods, techniques, or processes that could raise the level of decision-making performance of the whole organization such that it becomes *more* than the sum of its parts?

While *in principle* IT has long been considered a key way to achieve business intelligence (BI)—remember group support systems, decision support systems, expert systems or knowledge management systems—*in practice*, few companies have significant business intelligence capability in their IT organizations, nor do they have plans to develop one (Bitterer 2010; Davenport 2007). Many reasons for this exist including a lack of data standards and definitions, inadequate processing and analytic power, poor data governance, and low priority among business executives. Today, however, the situation is beginning to change. First, the business world has become more complex and competitive and managers are looking for better ways to understand their changing marketplace. Second, the Internet and the enhanced connectivity it enables through Web sites, mobile computing, and social networking, is generating huge amounts of data that have the potential to inform the organization about its products, services and customers, and identify new and lucrative business opportunities. Third, technology is finally catching up with the need. Data storage has become cheaper; new analytic tools are available; and extra processing power is available as needed through the cloud. Thus, many IT organizations are concluding that it is time to look more seriously at business intelligence and how IT can effectively enable it.

This chapter explores how IT can help make business intelligence a reality. It first examines the nature of business intelligence, where it fits with other internal and external forms of data, information and knowledge, and how it is evolving in organizations.

Next, it explores the demand for BI in organizations, what is driving it, and the value organizations are seeking from it. Some of the obstacles to effective BI are then described, as well as the role of IT in delivering BI. Finally, it concludes with ways managers can improve BI in their organizations.

UNDERSTANDING BUSINESS INTELLIGENCE

The first challenge when writing about BI is clarifying what is meant by this term. For some, it appears to be another level in the data–information–knowledge–intelligence continuum, whereby data are collected, organized, connected with other data, analyzed, and presented in a format that can be used to make decisions (Chowdhury 2011). For others, it is characterized by the use of analytics to make better decisions, optimize a distinctive capability or external relationship, or to provide customers with a new or augmented product or service (Davenport 2013; Davenport and Harris 2007). Still others see BI as *different* from analytics, focusing on integrating data from multiple internal and external sources to provide historical, current, and predictive views of business operations (Shen 2011). Finally, BI has been portrayed as a set of information manipulation practices, such as query, mining, reporting, and interactivity that is linked to but separate from information management practices (including master data management, information architecture, data quality, data administration, and data integration) (Bitterer 2010).

The members of the focus group did not spend time discussing an exact definition of BI. Instead, they saw the term as referring to "an evolving ecosystem around our data vision" or "an electronic nervous system." They viewed BI as an organizational *capability* that could be used to bring the right data, information, knowledge, and intelligence to bear on a business problem, opportunity, or decision. This capability builds on a strong foundation of good quality internal data, effective information management practices, and a comprehensive and holistic knowledge of the business and marries these to a variety of new and older types of internal and external data and new practices for understanding, manipulating, and presenting data. Focus group members stressed that it is the *combination* of data, practices, and knowledge that creates good BI.

Their organizations all recognize that the nature of the data they use is changing and becoming more complex. While traditionally their BI functions have focused on historical reporting, BI is now morphing to enable more real time and predictive views of business operations. The consensus of the group could be summarized as follows:

Our BI activities should help us develop the capability to

- **Anticipate** *the future instead of reacting to the past;*
- **Empower** *employees' memory, insight, and reach and give them the authority to decide and act;*
- **Sense** what is happening in the organization's environment through gathering and using both internal and external structured and unstructured information;
- **Connect** internal and external functions and resources across geographies to accomplish desired business outcomes;
- **Question** the status quo and create new opportunities;
- **Focus** on only the most relevant information to support timely decisions/actions closer to the point of impact and consequence.

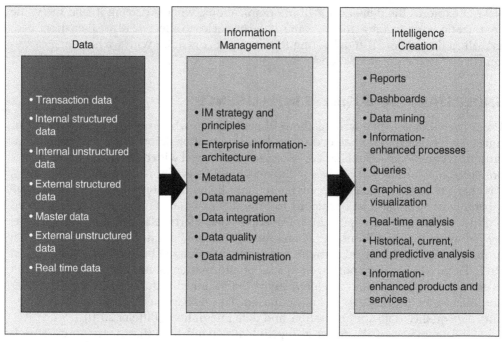

FIGURE 15.1   The BI Ecosystem

The focus group concluded that effective BI initiatives start with a cultural "information orientation" that percolates through all organizational activities to develop mechanisms to support processes and decisions with information; capabilities to discover new patterns, associations, and relationships among data; a flexible technical infrastructure that incorporates new types of data and their governance into work for added value; tools to exploit data more effectively; and the knowledge and skills to do so at all levels of the organization. Figure 15.1 illustrates the many components of this BI ecosystem.

THE NEED FOR BUSINESS INTELLIGENCE

The need for good intelligence about a business, its customers, and its operations is not new. In the 1990s, many companies jumped on the knowledge management bandwagon seeking to build a knowledge-creating company and to use knowledge for strategic advantage (Davenport and Prusak 1998; Hatten and Rosenthal 2001; Stewart 1997). Similarly, the need for improved information to support decision making is something that has been revisited about every six or seven years over the past three decades, using slightly different names, such as decision support systems, executive support systems, online analytical processing (OLAP), and competitive analytics (Davenport 2013; Davenport and Harris 2007).

What is new is the recognition within IT, if not the rest of the organization, that BI is a top priority for new IT development (Davenport and Harris 2007; Hostmann et al. 2009). For CIOs, there are two major reasons for this new interest:

1. *The explosion of data.*   It is well documented that both the amount and type of data are increasing exponentially and this is creating both headaches and opportunities for the IT function (Hopkins et al. 2010; Shen 2011). Combined with lower storage costs and increased processing power, companies are now able to capture, store, and analyze a much wider variety of data than in the past. Chief among these are a wide variety of unstructured data such as e-mails, reports, presentations, voice mail, photographs, videos, instant messages, blogs, tweets, and Facebook postings (Mann 2010; Robb 2004). Estimates show that about 85 percent of data are now unstructured and this amount is doubling every year (Mann 2010). Furthermore, it is coming from a much broader range of devices and channels, such as mobile phones, social media apps, and tablets. And the focus group is already anticipating the need to be able to capture and exploit information from the physical value chain through RFID tags and other devices. IT managers in the group feel it is important for them to be able use IT tools and skills to capture, manage, and exploit these new forms of information for their businesses.

2. *Changing information needs.*   The focus group also felt strong pressure from the business side of the organization to do a better job of delivering just-in-time information. "Our executives are screaming for data," said one. "But we really don't know what they need in order to run the business." Increasingly, information needs to be presented in different and more holistic views, rather than in traditional reports. For example, the shift toward enterprise thinking is driving the demand for enterprise information. Executives want the "big picture" on their products and customers. "We need to have a 360° view of our customer," said one manager. There is also a need to be able to explore data differently— to uncover new patterns and trends and to do different kinds of analysis on it (Chowdhury 2011). "Our business is pressing to have data served differently," said a manager, noting the proliferation of "data marts" in his organization, each with a different subset of the same data. Furthermore, the enormous amounts of data available are simply too difficult to comprehend without better analysis and presentation. Without this, technological support managers' ability to use data effectively for decision making and innovation is impaired (Hemp 2009; Shen 2011).

Finally, there is a growing recognition among business executives that organizations that are "sophisticated exploiters of data and analytics" are three times more likely to be top performers than others (Hopkins et al. 2010). While not mentioned expressly by the focus group, research is consistently showing that more effective use of information affects both company performance and customer satisfaction (Davenport and Harris 2007; Marchand et al. 2001).

THE CHALLENGE OF BUSINESS INTELLIGENCE

Although there was little disagreement about what effective BI looks like and its value, the focus group and researchers also recognize that this vision is extremely difficult to attain. "Few executives receive the information they say they could use," one study noted (McGee 2004). Another found that while 9/10 companies *say* BI is strategic to them, virtually none (2 percent) have a BI strategy (Bitterer 2010). A third compared how well companies believe they are doing with BI (4.5/10) with how well experts feel they are doing (2.2/10) (Hopkins et al. 2010).

Focus group members cited a number of obstacles they face in helping their companies improve BI. These include the following:

- *Perspective.*   One of the biggest challenges said the group is changing organizational mind-sets and culture regarding data. "We've never looked at data this way and so we don't know what we want to be," said a manager. "Our managers still stress intuition, not facts and their focus is local, not enterprise," said another. A third manager cited disagreements between business units seeking to better understand the company's customers. "Instead of working together to come up with a common definition of 'customer,' they are all fighting about who 'owns' the customer," he said. BI experts concur that business perspectives need to change. "There is a huge chasm between leveraging information as an enterprise asset and predicting future outcomes through deep data analysis...and reviewing reports and making reactive decisions" (Mohanty 2011).

- *Lack of business knowledge.*   Group members stressed the need to truly understand business data and the context in which it is generated. "We need to get at the real questions and develop the right questions," said one manager. Another explained "we are struggling to understand the real meaning of pieces of data. For example, we have many different meanings of the term 'in-stock' in our business, so we need to figure out what this means before we can provide good information on whether or not items are in-stock." Both business and IT leaders tend to lack knowledge and skills about how best to use BI to improve the business (Hopkins et al. 2010). "We don't know what we don't know and it's difficult to be perceptive about BI without a full range of knowledge," said a manager.

- *Lack of sponsorship and accountability.*   In spite of the demand for better information, businesses have been slow to invest in BI. "It's still not a priority at senior levels," a manager explained. Without funding and sponsorship, IT is finding it difficult to develop effective data governance mechanisms. "BI is a significant cost and it's an uphill battle to sell a structured approach," explained a group member. "We have no executive accountable for BI and no common governance or data definitions so data can't be reconciled. This leads to everyone doing their own thing." "We have the 'wild west' out there!'," said another.

- *Silo thinking.*   Traditional silo thinking has been exacerbated by the lack of governance and enterprise perspective and has resulted in fragmentation and duplication of data. "We have spreadsheets everywhere!" said one manager. "Everyone's going for local optimization." Group members explained that many business partners are frustrated with the inflexibility of standard data warehouses. As a result, they build their own "data marts" containing the information they alone need and these have limited utility and availability across business functions. "Control versus flexibility with data is an ongoing issue," said one member.

- *Lack of BI skills.*   BI sits squarely between the IT function and business and requires both business and technical skills, a combination that is hard to find. Focus group members explained that a BI skillset requires competencies in data management, analytics, BI tools, statistics, thought leadership, and interpretation of data. This is consistent with studies that have shown that companies lack analytics and interpretive skills to use BI strategically or competitively (Hopkins et al. 2010). "We need to revalidate our interpretations to understand which data are best and we need a model for interpreting patterns and trends that is consistent across the business," said a manager. "We must feel comfortable with our models and interpretations and then integrate context."

THE ROLE OF IT IN BUSINESS INTELLIGENCE

As with so much else in IT in recent years (e.g., e-business, social media, and strategic applications), the focus group stressed that successful BI requires active business involvement at all levels. The experts have surprisingly little to say about IT responsibilities for BI; many simply assume that the right technology with the right data will be there for the business to work with. Ideally, there is broad consensus that IT provides the "heavy lifting" of BI work, while the business provides the knowledge of what is needed and ability to manipulate and interpret data to provide intelligence (Hostmann et al. 2009). However, the reality in many companies is that "the business has abdicated thought leadership on BI to IT," a manager stated. Typically, in the focus group, IT is taking the initiative on BI just to get it started. "We are working on building the foundations for BI," said one manager.

There is a clear gap between the disciplined approaches IT feels are needed to "bring it all together for the common good" and the "get it done now" demands for particular information made by business leaders (Meehan and Roberts 2010). Thus, while IT staff try to view the BI picture holistically, with strategies, architectures, models, data definitions, taxonomies, and governance, the business partnerships, vision, and interpretive skills also needed are often lacking (Mohanty 2011). In business, "data is [still] too often seen as a technology issue, rather than a business asset" (Mann 2010).

BI cannot be implemented on any scale without technology and IT organizations are still coming to terms with the scope and complexity of the issues involved in creating common data, managing it effectively, and delivering it to multiple functions and layers in the organization. It is impossible to cover these topics in depth here, so this section simply provides a high-level overview of the major IT activities that contribute to successful BI. All too often, these are either not visible to others in the organization or the effort involved in accomplishing them is not well understood.

The focus group identified four sets of IT activities that together form the foundation of IT's role in BI:

1. *BI strategy and planning.*   Although focus group members understood the general vision for BI, most didn't have a clear strategy or roadmap for how to achieve it in their organizations. A BI strategy is broader and more business focused than an information strategy and architecture. Since its stakeholders are almost everyone in the organization, BI plans and strategies need to be inclusive at the high level, recognizing the widely diverse types of BI and their value, and incorporating governance to focus resources on enterprise priorities. Both IT and business need to be part of this process because BI must integrate both with other business strategies and with the technology and information architectures used by IT to guide its work (Bitterer 2010). Focus group members believed that at this point

in its evolution, BI strategy and planning is more likely to be an exploratory and iterative process that helps focus the organization in this area, rather than a formal process that is prescriptive in nature.

2. *Data acquisition and management.*   There is still much to be done in simply understanding and improving the data that already exist in most organizations, said the focus group. Duplicate data, multiple data marts, and inflexible data warehouses that cannot incorporate new forms of data, are the norm for many. "Much useful data lies in spreadsheets that are all over our organization," said a manager. "People don't trust our data warehouse," said another. The "holy grail" of IT is to have a single authoritative source for all data. Thus, most have master data management and data definition initiatives to work on their core structured data. Beyond this, focus group members are streamlining their applications to reduce duplicate data stores and revisiting their data warehouse strategy and technologies to make them more useful. Data architectures are being developed to minimize redundancy and incorporate new types of data. And increasingly, external data—both structured and unstructured—will need to be part of data architectures and plans, as will real-time data. Focus group managers recognized that they will not be able to control all data but they felt strongly that core company data need to be better managed. "Our goal is to have a governed space that is managed tightly," said a manager, "and a user-defined space that allows the business to play with data in any way they want."

3. *Information management.*   This involves improving the value that can be obtained from data by developing a framework within which information can be developed from it. It includes information architecture, data integration, aggregation, context (metadata), quality, governance, security, and privacy activities. Building trust in information is a key driver of this work (Bitterer 2010). "If we are going to make business decisions based on information, we need to trust that it's accurate," explained a manager. Usefulness is also essential and better understanding of business needs is necessary before this can be developed. Information is typically provided in reports, dashboards, and subject area infomarts. Unfortunately, much information in organizations is not used and there is still no clear understanding of what makes it useful (Davenport and Snabe 2011). As we have noted elsewhere, high quality information management must be a collaborative effort between business and IT, incorporating attention to information behaviors (e.g., sharing), risks, value, and roles and accountabilities (e.g., data stewardship) (see Chapter 11).

4. *Intelligence delivery.*   IT has long been responsible for the basics of information delivery, that is, reports and dashboards, and for providing the data warehouses against which queries can be run and historical analysis done. More recently, the knowledge management movement sought to enhance organizational processes and services with useful knowledge that would make them easier to perform, provide decision support, or add value (Smith et al. 2006). However, most organizations have not yet been able to take the next step to use information strategically or do real-time or predictive analysis (Bitterer 2010; Chowdhury 2011). New tools are therefore needed to help them model, interpret, and present information so it can be used to solve business problems and make business decisions (i.e., to create intelligence). Intelligence delivery cannot be done in a structured way, agreed the focus group, because the business environment is simply too dynamic. This is the

core of the challenge of BI, they believe, because while IT can provide the data, the tools to manipulate it, and the mechanisms to present it effectively, they are still not asking the right questions or doing the right analysis to understand how intelligence can best be delivered and to whom (Davenport and Snabe 2011; Hostmann et al. 2009). Until this happens, intelligence delivery will likely be plagued by the "knowing–doing" gap, in which clear links are not made between information and desired actions (Pfeffer and Sutton 2000).

IMPROVING BUSINESS INTELLIGENCE

Although there are pockets of BI excellence in many organizations and some companies that are actually competing on it, for most, improving BI remains an iterative, evolutionary process rather than a straight line journey (Bitterer 2010; Davenport and Harris 2007). Unfortunately, a company's information maturity may not equate to a strong BI capability (Finneran and Russell 2011). Although the first is foundational, culture, perspective, skills, and decision processes all need to be addressed to be able to use information intelligently for business decisions and competitive advantage (Mohanty 2011). Although there are no textbook answers about how to improve BI, the focus group and research are beginning to discover practices that can help move companies in the right direction:

1. *Learn from the past.* If the failure of knowledge management has taught us anything, it is that it is not easy to influence how people use information for decision making or to change what they do:

   > One of the main reasons that knowledge management efforts are often divorced from day to day activities is that the [people] who design and build the systems for collecting, storing and retrieving knowledge have limited, often inaccurate views of how people actually use knowledge in their jobs. (Pfeffer and Sutton 2000)

   All too often, incorrect assumptions are made about what information is wanted or needed in a given activity (McGee 2004). Therefore, learning about how people utilize knowledge for action and then using this as the basis for improving an organization's intelligence is critically important for successful BI. The key to delivering useful knowledge for action is developing the links between a direct action in a specific setting and the information that can drive or facilitate it (Dixon 2000). The most effective way to do this is to build linkages *backward* from a specific desired action in a core capability *toward* the acquisition and packaging of targeted intelligence for a specific group in ways that it finds useful. Though this may seem like common sense, "it is interesting how uncommon, common sense is in its implementation" (Pfeffer and Sutton 1999).

2. *Have a strategy for continuous improvement.* Organizations need a strategy for making sure that intelligence continues to be useful and used. Companies are typically littered with databases that no one uses because they are out of date or not complete. Successful BI initiatives consistently anticipate the need to maintain and improve the quality and type of information provided as their users learn more about what is possible, useful, and practical to do (Smith et al. 2006). For example, as one organization learned what information people would like to know about

others in the organization, it made an increasing number of connections to new sources of information (e.g., availability, skills). Ultimately, this BI application has now become a key tool in the globalization of the firm's work. Ideally therefore, BI should evolve as methods of gaining insights improve (Ball 2010). As a focus group manager noted, "you must stay flexible and be willing to change the tool to fit working with people."

3. *Focus.* "Implementing BI can be like trying to boil the ocean," said one manager. "It's impossible." Clear focus on targeted pain points where BI can make a difference is therefore essential, agreed the focus group. Successful initiatives take "a relentless focus on a very limited set of burning business questions to guide users to BI-enabled decisions with maximum impact" (Roberts and Meehan 2010). Within this targeted area, it's best to bring multiple points of view to bear on the issue at hand. For example, Proctor and Gamble did a large statistical survey to understand its customers' needs but also sent employees out to live with families to learn about them first hand and in context (Kanter 2011). By focusing on a goal, it is also easier to target the specific data that are needed and how these might be changing over time (Ball 2010). Finally, focus helps to bring executive attention to bear on the value being delivered by BI, which can result in improved sponsorship and resources (Hemp 2009).

4. *Cross-functional governance.* It should not be surprising to learn that cross-functional governance is needed for BI initiatives, which tend to have broad organizational scopes. Most members of the focus group mentioned developing effective governance processes as being central to BI success. What is important to note is that such processes are required at several different levels and also need to be integrated with one another. For example, data governance is needed to develop data definitions and come to a "single version of the truth" for core company data. Strong governance is also needed for information management practices, such as determining acceptable levels of risk, privacy and security, how to deal with regulatory matters, and determining what is core and noncore data. Finally, BI governance is needed to focus BI and develop a plan for its evolution. With the increasing use of external sources of data in BI processes, decisions also need to be made about whether or not to trust a source and how use of this data could have strategic implications for an organization (e.g., if it is no longer produced or if the company producing it decides to charge for it).

5. *Acquire new IT and analytics skills.* More than any other aspect of IT work, BI requires the integration of technology and business knowledge to be successful, said the focus group. "We will need a collaborative BI team in IT at all times," one manager stated, "because we need to understand business data deeply." Furthermore, if IT is to lead and facilitate BI, at least initially, as many believe, IT staff will need the skills to bridge the gap between traditional business and technical areas of expertise (Hostmann et al. 2009; Schlegel 2010). And while good BI requires the right people asking the right questions, it also needs the right information and tools to do the job successfully (Gassman et al. 2010). Other skills that will need to be acquired under the "BI umbrella" whether in the business or within IT, include improved analytics skills to test hypotheses, predict future trends, and discover new patterns in data; improved visualization and simulation skills to present information effectively; and the ability to utilize these insights

in decisions, new products, services, and strategies. People with these capabilities are hard to find and BI skills will need to be developed internally as well as acquired if BI is to be used proactively rather than reactively.

6. *Take process views.* Both decision making and innovation can be viewed as processes that connect the organization horizontally (Ball 2010; Roberts and Meehan 2010). Ideally, the more BI can be embedded in processes, the more likely it is to be effective (Shen 2011). As already noted, such processes are complex blends of insight, information, and behavior that a BI team is more likely to get wrong before it gets right (Kanter 2011). The key to success is to focus on a process that really matters to the business and to design the analytic capabilities needed to enhance it. Agile development processes are ideal because these let a BI capability evolve as new insights emerge (Ball 2010). Some aspects of a process that could benefit from BI include reducing event-to-decision latency, automating common analysis tasks, ensuring consistent analysis, and capturing and reusing expert knowledge (Davenport and Snabe 2011; Mohanty 2011).

7. *Move from the inside out.* BI is likely to be more successful if it grows organically rather than as a one-time comprehensive initiative (Mohanty 2011). Many focus group organizations are already doing BI in smaller ways at a business unit level and are looking for ways to incorporate enterprise and external data to make what they are doing more useful. This is an effective strategy, given most organizations' lack of sophistication in this area (Hopkins et al. 2010). Managers need to recognize that BI is still maturing and take an experimental approach to its use in business, while at the same time working on the foundational data and information that will be needed to make it successful (Gassman et al. 2010; Mann 2010).

8. *Tell stories to articulate value.* The value of BI is still unclear, said the focus group and it is hard to document it with quantitative benefits. "The best way to capture the value of BI is through stories told by the business," said one manager. This conclusion is very much in keeping with the conclusions of knowledge management experts (e.g., Denning 2005; Nonaka and Takeuchi 2011), who believe that the complex benefits of higher order knowledge are best articulated qualitatively rather than quantitatively.

9. *Watch out for implementation.* Too often, managers become dependent on the explicit aspects of BI and forget their context, leading them to invalid conclusions and inappropriate decisions (Nonaka and Takeuchi 2011). There are many ways that BI can be implemented badly. For example, one manager found that "there's a fine line between customer loyalty and stalking the customer" in her BI work. Immaturity about BI can also lead to bias and "group think" rather than better decision making (Gassman et al. 2010). Novel situations can be dismissed as insignificant and hardened preferences get in the way of good decisions (Kanter 2011). Training in how to use intelligence appropriately is therefore essential. For example, some European banks used analytics to identify their most profitable customers and then discarded their least profitable ones. Scandal ensued and governments had to pass legislation to force the banks to accept clients who receive disability and other social support payments (Davenport and Harris 2007). In short, access to intelligence is simply not enough; managers need "practical wisdom" to make prudent judgments. This can be summarized as, "know why; know how; and know what should be done" (Nonaka and Takeuchi 2011).

Conclusion

BI is not a new idea but it is one to which organizations keep returning on a regular basis. This time, the technologies, the data, and the perspective have changed and become broader and more complex, while at the same time enabling an infinite number of new possibilities for supporting organizations with analysis and intelligence. This chapter has clarified some of the similarities and differences between the current pressures for BI and those of the past and outlined a holistic view of BI that incorporates both the IT foundations of data and information management and the uses to which these can be put to derive value for the organization. It is clear that organizations will need to do a better job at all three levels if BI is going to realize its promise. While there is much theoretical value to be gained from BI, the fact remains that there are many complex organizational and behavioral challenges to be addressed before it can be realized. IT has the opportunity to take a leadership role in BI but its ability to do so is limited by how much it understands about the business and its ability to integrate technical and business knowledge to deliver intelligence. Its success in the future will depend on how well it can develop these new capabilities.

References

Ball, M. "Five Simple Steps to Better Decisions: Your Business Processes Can Lead You to Targeted Variables for Improvement." *Information Management* 20, no. 5 (September 1, 2010).

Bitterer, A. "The BI(G) Discrepancy: Theory and Practice of Business Intelligence." Gartner Inc., ID Number: G00176038, August 2, 2010.

Chowdhury, S. "A Soft Computing Environment for Data Mining." *The Business Review, Cambridge* 18, no. 1 (Summer 2011).

Davenport, T. "Analytics 3.0." *Harvard Business Review* 91, no. 12 (December 2013).

Davenport, T., and J. Harris. *Competing on Analytics: The New Science of Winning.* Boston, MA: Harvard Business School Publishing, 2007.

Davenport, T., and L. Prusak. *Working Knowledge: How Organizations Manage What They Know.* New York: Boston, Harvard Business School Press, 1998.

Davenport, T., and J. Snabe. "How Fast and Flexible Do You Want Your Information, Really?" *MIT Sloan Management Review* 52, no. 3 (Spring 2011).

Denning, S. *The Leader's Guide to Storytelling: Mastering the Art and Discipline of Business Narrative.* San Francisco: Jossey-Bass, 2005.

Dixon, N. *Common Knowledge.* Boston, MA: Harvard Business School Press, 2000.

Finneran, T., and B. Russell. "Balanced Business Intelligence: Each Level of BI is a Stepping Stone that Adds Capability to Meet Growing User Needs." *Information Management* 21, no. 1 (January 1, 2011).

Gassman, B., R. Sallam, A. Bitterer, J. Hagerty, and N. Chandler. "Predicts 2011: New Relationships will Change BI and Analytics." Gartner Inc., ID Number: G00209225, November 25, 2010.

Hatten, K., and S. Rosenthal. *Reaching for the Knowledge Edge.* New York: Amacom, 2001.

Hemp, P. "Death by Information Overload." *Harvard Business Review* 87, no. 9 (September 2009).

Hopkins, M., S. LaValle, F. Balboni, R. Shockley, and N. Kruschwitz. "Ten Insights: What Survey Reveals about Competing on Information and Ten Data Points: Information and Analytics at Work." *MIT Sloan Management Review* 52, no. 1 (Fall 2010).

Hostmann, B., N. Rayner, and G. Herschel. "Gartner's Business Intelligence, Analytics and Performance Management Framework." Gartner Inc., ID Number: G00166512, October 19, 2009.

Kanter, R. "Zoom In, Zoom Out." *Harvard Business Review* 89, no. 3 (March 2011).

Mann, J. "Highlights for the Business Intelligence and Information Management Track at Gartner European Symposium/ITxpo 2010." Gartner Inc., ID Number: G00209468, December 6, 2010.

Marchand, D., W. Kettinger, and J. Rollins. *Making the Invisible Visible*. Chichester, England: John Wiley & Sons, 2001.

McGee, K. "Give Me that Real-Time Information." *Harvard Business Review* 82, no. 4 (April 2004).

Meehan, P., and J. Roberts. "Executive Summary: Business Intelligence and Decision Impact." Gartner Inc., ID Number: G00200706, May 1, 2010.

Mohanty, S. "Having Analytics May Not Be Enough: Organizations Need to Improve Business Intelligence and Decision-Making through Guided, Predictive Analytics." *Information Management* 21, no. 1 (January 1, 2011).

Nonaka, I., and H. Takeuchi. "The Wise Leader." *Harvard Business Review* 89, no. 5 (May 2011).

Pfeffer, J., and R. Sutton. "Knowing 'What' to Do Is Not Enough: Turning Knowledge into Action." *California Management Review* 42, no. 1 (Fall 1999).

Pfeffer, J., and R. Sutton. *The Knowing-Doing Gap*. Boston, MA: Harvard Business School Press, 2000.

Robb, D. "Getting the Bigger Picture: Dealing with Unstructured Data." *Datatmation* (September 13, 2004).

Roberts, J., and P. Meehan. "From Business Intelligence to Intelligent Business," Gartner Inc., ID Number: G00208713, November 11, 2010.

Schlegel, K. "Prepare for Customer-Facing Business Intelligence." Gartner Inc., ID Number: G0020630, October 15, 2010.

Shen, G. "Unplugged: The Disconnect of Intelligence and Analytics." *Information Management* 21, no. 1 (January 1, 2011).

Smith, H. A., J. D. McKeen, and S. Singh. "Making Knowledge Work: Five Principles for Action-Oriented Knowledge Management." *Knowledge Management Research and Practice* 4, no. 2 (2006).

Stewart, T. *Intellectual Capital: The New Wealth of Organizations*. New York: Doubleday, 1997.

16 Enabling Collaboration with IT[1]

Our increasing connectedness is driving new ways of working together to deliver business value. Globalizing organizations, outsourcing, mobile work, innovation, interorganizational teams, innovation, and reaching out to suppliers and customers are driving today's need to improve collaboration within firms. And, of course, IT is at the center of these trends. A study on what makes widely dispersed virtual teams effective found that, contrary to expectations, technology was a significant factor in facilitating their success (Majchrzak et al. 2004). However, literally hundreds of software packages are being promoted for improving collaboration. These technologies, such as virtual worlds, Web 2.0 applications, social networking, content management, and new ways of communicating (e.g., blogs, wikis, instant messages, tweets) appear almost daily and are being adopted and adapted rapidly in the wider society. They are challenging many of the traditional conventions of how work is done and the role of IT functions themselves.

As the menu of available technologies widens, becomes virtually free, and employees clamor to use them anywhere, anyplace, and anytime, IT managers are asking many questions including the following:

- What is the business value of these technologies?
- What is the best way to assess them and make decisions about their use?
- How can these technologies best be managed and adapted for organizational purposes?

Furthermore, as new technologies appear, businesses are experimenting with different types of collaboration, such as those already listed, and IT functions are often expected to make collaboration happen through the implementation of technology, even though technologies are only one piece of any collaboration initiative. Certainly,

---

[1] This chapter is based on the authors' previously published article, Smith, H. A., and J. D. McKeen. "Enabling Collaboration with IT." *Communications of the Association for Information Systems* 28, no. 16 (March 2011): 243–54. Reproduced by permission of the Association for Information Systems.

IT functions provide the "heavy lifting," such as connectivity and information integrity, without which most collaboration efforts would not be effective, and a well-designed IT architecture is a key enabler of collaboration (Johansen 2007). And, at the most basic level, IT also protects the privacy and security of information and users. But how new applications are implemented is often as important as the technology itself in delivering business value. As one IT manager stated, "We sometimes jump directly to the tool without thinking through the strategy and tactics involved." As a result, IT managers can sometimes feel that the deployment of collaboration is less than optimal.

This chapter explores IT's role in enabling collaboration in organizations, and at the same time what IT's role should not be (i.e., what responsibilities and accountabilities should properly be the function of the business). It accomplishes this by identifying the principal forms of collaboration used and the primary business drivers involved in them, how business value is measured, and the roles of IT and the business in enabling collaboration. The chapter first looks at some of the reasons why collaboration is becoming so important in organizations and the business value it enables. Next it examines some of the different characteristics of collaboration in various organizations. Focus then switches to the key components of a collaboration program, how these influence its effectiveness, and IT's role in promoting collaboration. The chapter concludes with a series of recommendations for IT managers to use as a guide for how they can best facilitate collaboration in their organizations.

WHY COLLABORATE?

There is no doubt that information and communications technologies are enabling different ways of working—within organizations and between them. Who could imagine life without texting? Without Google? Without cell phones? These technologies and others have changed forever how we interact with others both personally and professionally, how we share information, and where work gets done. Thus, it should be no surprise that there's strong interest in collaboration among business practitioners and academics alike. A simple Internet search on this topic yields literally thousands of articles. And it is no secret that what we are seeing now is just the tip of the technology iceberg. Whether we do or do not yet actually use the next generation of collaboration or social networking technologies in our work, everyone has heard about them, including instant messaging, Twitter, Facebook, webcams, and others, and no one is a stranger to speculation about how these technologies are going to change the face of organizations yet again.

Almost any business or IT journal these days contains speculative "think pieces" or case studies about how essential it will be to collaborate (in various ways) in the future and how failing to do this will result in the organization becoming a dinosaur (Amabile and Khaire 2008; Lynch 2007; Romano et al. 2007). And it is certainly without question that hundreds of new technologies—including hardware, software, applications, and services—are currently being promoted to businesses as enabling collaboration and all of the benefits it will bring. Yet business and IT managers are struggling to cut through the hype to get at the real value collaboration will bring. They have seen this before in both the "Internet bubble" and the knowledge management fad and know from bitter experience with previous generations of groupware, knowledge management, and collaboration investments that achieving positive results is not as easy as plugging in a piece of technology (Iandoli 2009a). Many have a long history of deploying collaboration technology and seeing it gather dust (McAfee 2006).

It is therefore no surprise that the focus group reported a great deal of conflicting feelings in their organizations about collaboration, from wildly enthusiastic to highly skeptical. One company has invested substantial amounts of time and money in collaboration technologies and in adapting its organizational culture and behaviors accordingly and believes that they have become more productive, effective, and successful as a result. On the other hand, another manager reported his company's senior executives were grumbling that no one has yet given them a real business need for collaboration. Some members reported that there's a lack of business push for collaboration in their organization, and others stated that their business units were "coming around in some areas because they feel they need to be where their customers are." Most agreed that virtual interaction is becoming increasingly commonplace and that the percentage of time employees work virtually (and therefore need collaboration technology) is increasing (Drakos et al. 2009; Romano et al. 2007). One study found that spending on collaborative software represents one-fifth of most organizations' technology budgets, but business leaders are still uncertain if these investments are improving either collaboration or the quality of work (Cross et al. 2005). This sentiment was reflected by most of the focus group participants. "We're still experimenting with collaboration," explained one. "We don't have a business project, but we're developing a collaboration strategy."

Because collaboration is evolving so rapidly, it's difficult to definitively articulate the business drivers and benefits involved. However, there appear to be five main categories of potential business value:

1. *Top-line value.* A great deal has been written about the importance of collaboration in improving and/or increasing creativity and innovation in organizations. One study found that collaboration technologies play a critical role in improving knowledge creating and sharing practices and in developing new processes, products, and services (Fink 2007). Another noted that "great ideas can come from anywhere and IT has dramatically reduced the cost of accessing them" (Pisano and Verganti 2008). The expectation is that collaboration both across an organization and with customers, suppliers, and other third parties, will strengthen an organization's ability to identify new business opportunities and formulate creative solutions (Fink 2007). The goal is "real time, rich, location independent collaboration" by creative teams that can rapidly process and assimilate knowledge from many different sources and apply it in practical ways (Gordon et al. 2008). This type of value is especially important in highly dynamic and competitive industries where the generation of a large number of new, good ideas is critical to competitive advantage. Within the focus group, most organizations were just beginning to recognize how technology, collaboration, and innovation could be harnessed to change their business models, products, and services. "We're beginning to see our executives more open to these concepts and how changing how we work together and with our customers can make a difference," said one. One firm has included collaboration and innovation in its performance review criteria.

Nevertheless, these appear to be the exceptions, and focus group managers mainly commented that their business leaders were not yet really thinking about how technology could help them in this area.

2. *Cost savings.*   In a number of focus group companies, collaboration is seen as having real cost savings potential in such ways as reducing travel costs through virtual meetings, improving communications, and enabling remote access to documents. Participants noted that collaborative technology facilitates the work of global and virtual teams by compressing work flow, reducing development costs, increasing communication, minimizing misunderstandings, improving coordination between groups, and enabling linkages with vendors, suppliers, and customers that speed up the supply chain and other work processes.

3. *Effectiveness.*   There is wide recognition that collaboration technology, used properly, can make group work more effective. This is particularly true for virtual teams. For example, one focus group company uses social networking technologies (behind its firewall) to enable team members from around the world to learn about each other, have fun events, and understand each others' customs and culture. "This has been really useful for us in building strong global teams," said the manager involved. Collaboration technology, particularly unified communications, is especially useful in integrating remote and mobile workers seamlessly into team or project activities. It enables them to "touch down" in an office and plug into the applications and information they need, wherever they are in the world. Increasingly, too, for many professionals, whose work consists of participation in a number of ad hoc projects, collaboration technology enables them to more effectively juggle a variety of commitments. One firm uses it extensively for its multidisciplinary projects, such as pandemic planning. Finally, online education is a big application of this technology, allowing employees to participate from a variety of locations, have virtual and real-time discussions, and incorporate learning into the demands of their workday.

4. *Accessibility of people.*   A key feature of collaboration and its associated technology is that it provides a company with access to a much broader range of skills, capabilities, resources, and services than have been traditionally available. Collaboration technology significantly expands the number of potential partners and expertise available to a company (Pisano and Verganti 2008), and in recent years different types of interorganizational alliances—from supply chain integration to design coordination to innovative partnerships—have become commonplace (Attaran 2007). However, it is the ability to access internal expertise that is currently of most interest to the focus group companies. Only one firm had successfully implemented a comprehensive enterprise directory, including phone book, expertise location anywhere in the organization, reporting structures, and connection with social networking information. Yet even this firm recognized how difficult building such a capability can be. "Over the years, it has been a huge stumbling block for us," one focus group member said. Other members were envious. "We're trying to build this facility," said one, "because right now it's really hard for us to find people in our organization." Ideally, this type of accessibility also enables the development of communities of interest within the organization—either work focused or built around personal interests. In our virtual, networked

world that is rapidly losing the "human touch" and is characterized by "ephemeral relationships," these communities can help build staff morale and create a sense of belonging (Tebbutt 2009; Thomas and Bostrom 2008).

5. *Accessibility of information.*   One of the biggest benefits of collaboration and its associated technology is that it makes information much more accessible than in the past. Information repositories, such as the intranet, enable the management and sharing of digital content on an as needed basis (Chin et al. 2008). Other technologies, such as wikis, support the creation of new content and its publication. These tools enable information and knowledge sharing across time and space in ways that were unheard of a mere decade ago (Fink 2007). Many focus group members believe that portal and content management applications will be the biggest value of collaboration. But they also feel it will take a lot of work to get there. "Our intranet is just a garbage scow of information," sighed one manager. "The same document can exist in literally hundreds of places." Another noted, "While our corporate level content is well managed, it gets messier and messier the lower down in the organization you go. We need much more information management and filtering to make our Intranet really useful." Finally, although everyone agrees that collaboration will only be successful if more information is made more widely available, there is still a great deal of fear that "someone will do something bad with it," which explains why in many organizations the default position is not to share.

6. *Flexibility.*   The world is becoming increasingly volatile, uncertain, complex, and ambiguous and this is creating a highly dynamic business environment for many companies (Johansen 2007). Flatter, more networked, and collaborative structures create the right work and leadership environment, facilitating fluid workforces and speedy decision making and providing transparency of information and capabilities while retaining clarity around the organization's beliefs, values, and responsibilities (Reeves et al. 2008). A networked organization, with situational leadership, less structure, and the ability to create new capabilities through its networks, will be much more able to cope with these challenges. Flexibility will involve space, technology, and protocols for working in networks and will exist at the intersection of real estate, HR, and IT (Johansen 2007). Flexibility underlies many of the reasons why focus group members are interested in collaboration. Although most are still seeing this as a need within a more traditional, hierarchical organizational structure, some recognize that their structure and governance practices will have to change substantially.

CHARACTERISTICS OF COLLABORATION

Although there is much talk about the benefits of collaboration and the need for more of it in organizations, clarity is significantly lacking about what collaboration actually is. As one focus group member put it, "If you asked a hundred people to describe collaboration, you would get a hundred different answers. There's a huge disparity in understanding about this topic." There is also significant confusion about collaboration, which is a human activity, and collaboration technology, which is the hardware, software, and applications that enable the work of collaboration (Camarinha-Matos et al. 2009). Finally, the group noted that collaboration is often used interchangeably with such terms as networking, social networking, and cooperation. It is therefore important

Who Is Collaborating?	What Are They Collaborating on?	Where Are They Collaborating?	How Are They Collaborating?

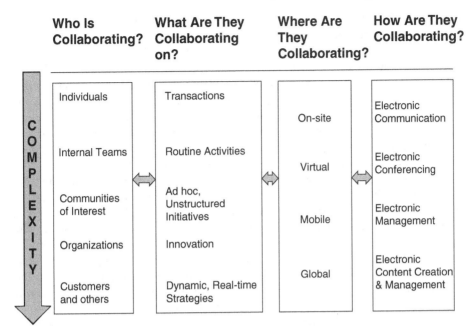

FIGURE 16.1 The Range and Scope of Collaboration

to be clear about the range and scope of collaboration in organizations these days, including who is involved in collaboration, what type of work is being done, and where it is being done, since these have a direct bearing on how the IT function can best support collaboration with technology (see Figure 16.1).

- *Who is collaborating?*   At its simplest, *collaboration* describes work that is done jointly with others (Wikipedia 2011). In modern organizations, this covers a lot of territory. Sometimes, collaboration can be as basic as two people working together to achieve a goal, but it also refers to a wide spectrum of different types of collaborative participants. In organizations, there can be collaboration within teams (both formal and ad hoc), between business units, and within communities of interest. Collaboration can also occur beyond a firm's boundaries, including between an organization and its customers, between one or more organizations (as in a supply chain or an innovative partnership), and, as we are beginning to see, with the world at large (also known as "mass collaboration"). As organizations have become more comfortable with collaborative work, they are extending it in new ways and to more and more types of participants. Most focus group organizations still focus on internal collaboration, yet there was general agreement that the trend is toward opening up collaboration beyond organizational boundaries. At present, most organizations are fairly "locked down" but have practices in place to enable key suppliers and trusted third parties to access internal company data and to work collaboratively with internal participants.
- *What are they collaborating on?*   Collaboration can take many forms. The early wins in organizations, according to the focus group, were simple transactions. These included e-mails, conferencing, extranets with partners, and basic

workflow. Next came collaboration around routine activities, such as access to information and its reuse, ease of information creation and publishing; coordination of experts to solve common problems and to reduce the work involved in mundane tasks, such as coordination and planning (Cross et al. 2005; Edmonston 2008; Fedorowicz et al. 2008). Most organizations in the focus group have substantial initiatives in this area, although they believe there's more work to be done, especially in such matters as improving content management and creating enterprise directories. A third type of collaboration is more unstructured in nature and includes the development of communities for various purposes, creating collaborative work environments where innovation can occur, and collaboration for issue and information management. Most focus group members had only just begun to understand how best to leverage this type of collaboration, and their efforts in this area are still mainly experimental. However, one firm has created a new technology adoption environment, where any technology innovation can be shared and where others can use and provide feedback about its utility and effectiveness. The most challenging form of collaboration is probably best epitomized at present by the online gaming community. Here, various participants work together in real time to achieve structured goals under rapidly changing conditions. Dynamic collaboration is characterized by speed of decision making with incomplete information, the ability to modify decisions in response to changing conditions, trial and error, the continual need to address and deal with risk, hyper-transparency of information, and situational leadership (Reeves et al. 2008). None of the organizations in the focus group had achieved this type of collaboration, but all recognized that this is increasingly the way members of the younger generation expect to work and also felt that as business challenges become more complex, organizations will have to find better ways of collaborating in this way.

- *Where are they collaborating?*   Increasingly, collaboration needs to take place on an anywhere, anytime basis. Inside organizations, members noted the need for more meeting spaces and meeting rooms as well as "touch down" areas where contractors and outside staff can temporarily set up office. Almost all focus group organizations already support virtual and mobile work, at least to some extent. Several members of the focus group also routinely utilize international or global teams where collaboration takes place across time zones, national boundaries, cultures, and language groups. Some were also beginning to experiment with different forms of collaboration with individuals and enterprises beyond their organizational boundaries, which requires dealing with different organizational cultures, practices, processes, systems, and data.

- *How are they collaborating?*   Collaborative technology comprises the tools that are used to facilitate the work of collaboration. These fall into four main categories: electronic communication (such as e-mail, instant messaging, blogs), electronic conferencing (e.g., video conferencing, meeting software), electronic management (e.g., file sharing, activity assignment, task management), and electronic content creation and management (e.g., publishing tools, enterprise directories). However, newer collaborative technologies, such as social networking applications, tend to fall into multiple categories depending on how they are used (e.g., for communication or information creation). As a result, the boundaries between the categories are blurring with the rapid evolution of this technology.

COMPONENTS OF SUCCESSFUL COLLABORATION

Understanding what collaboration and its potential benefits are is important to achieving an awareness of how collaboration can be effectively used in an organization, but the high failure of collaboration projects suggests that successful collaboration requires mastering how to implement and manage it (Schuh et al. 2008). The key challenges for managers (both business and IT) are to create a supportive working environment and motivational conditions and to develop the skills and organizational arrangements within which collaboration can flourish (Fedorwicz et al. 2008; Thomas et al. 2007). Four components of collaboration must work together to ensure successful collaboration of any type (MacCormack and Forbath 2008):

1. *People.* Collaborative work requires different skills than more traditional forms of work. In particular, strong communication skills are essential. This is especially true the more work is mediated through technology, virtual, and across organizational and cultural boundaries (Romano et al. 2007). Cultural differences around social expectations, the need for more openness, flexibility, and interdependence in work assignments; the need to develop trust in an "opaque" environment (i.e., one that lacks many traditional social cues); and differences in organizational practices all add up to a requirement for managers to rethink how people will work together in this new world of work (Evans and Wolf 2005; Fiore et al. 2008). Inexperienced teams, lack of management attention, and different expectations of partners are some of the major reasons why collaboration initiatives can fail (Schuh et al. 2008). Thus, when implementing collaboration, managers should be aware that it is not "business as usual" and should pay more attention to the social and behavioral changes that will be necessary (Edmonston 2008; Thomas and Bostrom 2008). One focus group manager noted, "You cannot overemphasize the importance of culture. It will make or break you." Finally, as the complexity of the tasks involving coordination increases, so does the need for management attention to coordination (Schuh et al. 2008). In short, creating the working environment within which collaboration occurs becomes the primary role of the manager, rather than monitoring individual productivity or performance. Signs that these efforts have been successful are engaged, satisfied, and committed staff who fully participate in collaborative processes (Nohria et al. 2008). Conversely, managers who cultivate a fear of failure or who do not protect their staff from what is often a larger, hostile corporate environment, are likely to see collaborative initiatives fail (Amabile and Khaire 2008).

2. *Program.* Collaboration needs to be part of a coherent program to create and capture value, not a series of stand-alone efforts (Schuh et al. 2008). It is highly unlikely that collaboration initiatives will achieve an organization's goals unless they are managed holistically (MacCormack and Forbath 2008). Furthermore, it is essential that managers understand the strategic trade-offs involved in collaboration and make conscious decisions about how to structure and govern it. This is especially true when external partners are involved (Pisano and Verganti 2008). Most important, organizations need to understand comprehensively how to use their knowledge and information assets. Focus group members stressed that well-organized, searchable information is the foundation for any type of

collaboration, and this resource requires a significant investment to develop and maintain. As a result, many companies are working primarily on content management strategies. In addition, high-level decisions need to be made about how to develop new collaboration capabilities, determine what types of collaboration the organization seeks to engage in, what policies are needed, and how to create an environment where the desired collaboration can thrive. Two key principles of any collaboration program are emergence (i.e., the recognition that we don't always know who will make the greatest contribution to a problem in advance) and planned serendipity (i.e., designing a working environment where underexplored relationships between people, data, and applications can become visible) (Majchrzak 2009).

3. *Processes.* Within a strategic and holistic approach to collaboration, it is important to develop processes that support or help manage this type of work. Since collaboration is a moving target in the modern enterprise, managers need ways to rapidly learn what is working and what isn't and to make changes as the work unfolds (Edmonston 2008). Managers also need a process to take advantage of successful innovations and a way of recognizing failures and killing them off quickly (Amabile and Khaire 2008). Effective processes are also required to support collaborative teams and partnerships, to help them know what they know and coordinate their thinking (Johansen 2007). Specific processes that the focus group identified as being supportive of collaboration include administrative practices that recognize the convergence of many different types of communication (the management of which is often separated), content management processes, the ability to identify a "single source of truth" (i.e., the official documents pertaining to any topic), and the creation of parameters to help staff understand how and under what conditions they can collaborate. Conversely, a siloed focus and an emphasis on process efficiency above all else will likely stifle collaboration (Kleinbaum and Tushman 2008).

4. *Platforms.* These are the tools, technologies, and standards that enable people to share data and to work together seamlessly from a variety of locations. The advent of cheap connectivity has been the driving force behind many new ways of collaborating in recent years, yet efforts to promote collaboration have focused largely on connectivity with little recognition of the other factors that make it effective (Cross et al. 2005). Technology is a key resource in enabling collaboration, but it must be designed to achieve the organization's goals and fit with its culture and practices. As with the other components of collaboration, the objective of a platform is to create an environment within which collaboration can take place, rather than the traditional systems approach of hardwiring specific information and work processes (Iandoli 2009b). An effective technology platform should support plug-and-play communications, provide access to information, and enable the transformation of information into knowledge. It should also provide tools for the rapid creation of communities, teams, and networks; be based on open standards; and be flexible and adaptive (Camarinha-Matos et al. 2009; Iandoli 2009b). However, most focus group organizations are nowhere near creating such a platform. Most are still questioning whether they should invest in collaborative technologies rather than look for ways to coherently manage a set of business tools for collaborative work (Drakos et al. 2009).

THE ROLE OF IT IN COLLABORATION

Clearly, the IT function alone cannot make collaboration happen, even if it provides robust collaboration technology. The business plays a critical role in determining its strategy and creating processes and a working environment that make it possible to collaborate for business value. That said, there is still no answer to where an organization's collaboration strategy "belongs." In most, IT still owns it and, as a result, the whole field of collaboration is an opportunity for IT managers to demonstrate real business leadership (Lynch 2007; Mann 2008). CIOs can work with business executives to identify and orchestrate collaborative capabilities, coordinate enterprise services, and educate leaders about opportunities and possibilities.

In addition, IT leaders have some very specific technology responsibilities that must be put in place to enable collaborative work to occur. At present, four major technology areas must be addressed iteratively and concurrently. These are merely the fundamentals, however. Because this field is evolving rapidly, IT leaders must be prepared to continually reassess all aspects of collaboration technology, its governance, and policies and to rebalance these as necessary (Smith et al. 2007).

1. *Communication.*   A significant and growing area of collaborative technology is enabling a wide spectrum of communications options, from voice mail to video and everything in between. "Users increasingly see communications and collaboration not as separate activities but as a smooth continuum of modalities where the difference between talking on the phone and posting on a wiki becomes a matter of choice and preference" (Mann and Elliot 2007). As such unified communications become a technological reality, IT leaders will need to develop an architecture that supports them as a single technology spectrum rather than as separate components. Gartner Group predicts that phone directories, e-mail, voicemail, instant messaging, presence awareness, computer telephony, and conferencing technologies will increasingly converge over the next five years, leading to serious organizational challenges in how these services are managed (Mann and Elliot 2007). However, other types of communication and collaboration software, such as voice, call centers, mobile, team workspaces, and social software will not be part of this convergence and will have to be appropriately managed as they too evolve. Ultimately, communications technology will be embedded in all business applications and will need to be ubiquitous, reliable, secure, and integrated (Andriole 2006).

2. *Information access and management.* Developing an improved information processing capability, including accurate and visible information, manipulability, exchangeability, and ease of information transfer is a primary goal for all IT functions in supporting collaboration. One focus group member explained his mandate as follows: "We want to make it easy for anyone to share information via the intranet, to support collaboration with information, and to link people to documents and vice versa." To accomplish this goal, it is important for organizations to reduce the number of databases and data management platforms they maintain and to develop the intranet into a robust information-sharing platform. Typically, organizations also need a document management system with proper versioning and access controls, although these systems are notoriously difficult to integrate with other information management tools. "We're finding it really hard to upload

and share documents," said one manager. "It's a big headache for us." Content management, particularly at the business unit and team levels, is also challenging as the use of many separate tools tends to replicate information in a relatively unmanaged fashion. At present in most companies, attention needs to be paid to integrating fragmented information resources, improving information visibility, filtering and navigation, and establishing principles for information access (Cain 2008; Thomas et al. 2007).

Several focus group companies commented that the perception is still widespread in their organizations that if information is made more widely available "bad things will happen." "We instinctively don't want to share," said one manager. Managing the tension between the need for information availability to facilitate collaboration and protecting the organization from the associated risks is an area where IT managers should be working proactively to ensure they deliver the optimal value (Gordon et al. 2008; Smith et al. 2007).

3. *Security and risk.*   It is a primary responsibility of the IT function to protect the integrity of its systems and data. This is becoming increasingly more challenging as both internal and external organizational boundaries break down and new forms of collaboration are introduced (Smith et al. 2007). IT managers recognize that removing the traditional layers of separation between departments and enterprises makes the organization more vulnerable and their job more difficult. Therefore, IT departments can often be viewed as obstacles to collaboration (Gordon et al. 2008). There is no easy answer to this dilemma. Companies need safe and secure communications, but it is no longer possible to use "stovepipe" security to ensure this. Instead, IT functions must improve security architectures and infrastructures and continually assess the balance between the openness required by collaboration and the risks involved. Focus group members noted that security must become more granular and principles based. "We are beginning to develop a policy for how we as a company use social networking tools," said one manager. "The broader the team, the greater the risks involved." Another added, "We need better authentication tools, and we must be clearer about the types of information that can be shared." Others noted that security must be commensurate with the risks involved. "We must use the most appropriate tools for the particular task at hand." Finally, they pointed out that this task is about to get much more difficult as companies begin to open themselves up to collaboration with their end customers. "This is a huge challenge that we have not yet faced up to," said one.

4. *Technology integration.*   The more IT can achieve integration of data, applications, hardware, and software, the easier it will be to provide the information and tools needed to facilitate collaboration. Thus, focus group members recommended the massive simplification and rationalization of applications, databases, and software as a precursor to any significant collaboration initiative. The drive to collaboration is also behind the increasing interest in industry-neutral and global IT standards of all types (Chituc et al. 2009). "Technology should be a facilitator of collaboration, not an obstacle," said one manager. "Our users want to plug and play in this area, and we can only achieve this through standardization." Some organizations in the focus group provide "canned" collaboration tools, such as blogs, personal Web sites, team sites, and wikis that allow the rapid formation of

ad hoc teams and ease of social networking. These can then be tailored to particular needs requiring just enough information so they can be effectively managed and decommissioned in the longer term.

In addition, centralized and integrated structures within IT for developing enterprisewide communications and collaboration capabilities can facilitate synergistic interactions between these tools and create useful cross-technology opportunities that might not previously have been obvious (Sanders 2007). Focus group organizations varied widely in this area. Some assigned IT a leading role in delivering collaboration technology, and others are implementing it on a more piecemeal basis. All agreed, however, that without centralized support for this technology, it is unlikely to deliver enterprise-level value.

These four collaborative technology building blocks are the most critical elements to which IT should pay attention at present. However, new technologies are already on the horizon, and these will require continual assessment from IT managers as to their usefulness and how they can be integrated into the existing organizational infrastructure and collaboration architecture. Some of these technologies include dynamic modeling tools, simulation engines, visualization tools, data reduction and summarization applications, and intelligence gathering tools. In short, IT managers are going to have to remain aware in this very rapidly changing market and be willing to adapt quickly to changing conditions. Paying attention to these four fundamental building blocks now will enable them to do this more easily and effectively in the future.

FIRST STEPS FOR FACILITATING EFFECTIVE COLLABORATION

Given the multifaceted nature of collaboration and its many potential but as yet unproven benefits, IT managers could understandably adopt a wait-and see approach. In fact, this is what many members of the focus group are doing: talking about strategy and planning small pilots to test the waters. However, amid all the confusion, they also had some practical ideas for ways that organizations could begin to approach this complex and dynamic new way of working and using technology.

1. *Develop a coherent vision.* Effective collaboration requires a multidisciplinary approach and a shared business–IT vision (Lynch 2007). It is essential that such a vision begin with understanding the organization's values, legal requirements, and core intellectual property. From this, a strategic perspective can be developed about what the business wants to accomplish with collaboration and what types of technology would best support it. Focus group members suggested that developing a vision for collaboration must be carefully approached because "the judgment line is shifting rapidly" and our static paradigms of work are rapidly becoming much more dynamic. These factors will change business models and strategies and affect how companies will need to manage the complex business environment of the near future. Ideally, a vision for collaboration should include a unified strategy and business models, tools, and experiments to help the organization gain further insights. The vision's ultimate goal should be to nurture an internal working environment (and in the longer term a broader business ecosystem) that will enable productive collaboration to emerge. At this

early stage, both business and IT leaders should play a key role in articulating a collaboration vision and connecting it to the right people who can make it happen.

2. *Plan for adaptation.*   If there's one aspect of collaboration about which everyone agrees, it's that collaboration is evolving and complex and will require significant and ongoing management attention (Schuh et al. 2008). Organizations, and particularly IT functions, therefore need to develop the "flexing skills" needed to cope with the rapid development of collaboration and its associated technologies (Iandoli 2009b). Focus group members noted that their organizations are already becoming flatter and more complex as collaboration and networks emerge. "Business is speeding up, and we will need new skills for coping and adapting rapidly," said one. It is therefore essential that organizations develop processes for learning what is working with collaboration and what isn't and mechanisms for sharing these lessons. Above all, the management of collaboration needs to be multidisciplinary and responsive to change.

3. *Start with specific fundamentals.*   Facilitating effective collaboration will take time—both to build a strategy and to get the technology fundamentals in place. Many organizations have specific "pain points" that could be worthwhile places to start putting energy into collaboration. In the focus group, these were clearly around information management and access. "Our Intranet is unmanaged and not relevant," complained one manager. Another noted that it was very hard finding people in his organization. "We'd love to have a 'blue pages' to enable us to start internal social networking," he said, referring to one firm's internal company directory. In addition, several participants noted that their office space doesn't support collaboration. "We need to have many more collaborative workspaces," one participant noted. A simple assessment of these gaps and some management attention to them could lead to a great improvement in how people are able to collaborate.

4. *Establish principles of behavior.*   As already noted, much of the governance of collaboration is based on principles, rather than rules. The most basic principle is transparency, not only of information but also of behavior (Majchrzak 2009). Some focus group companies have already established a code of conduct to govern electronic communication and collaboration, and others are working on one. A big fear is that providing improved communication will enable employees and customers to post negative comments about the organization. One important way of allaying these fears is to eliminate online anonymity. "Anonymity results in bad behavior," said one manager. "With a clear online identity, negativity is quickly found out and is usually self-policed by others in the community." Another noted, "In a business environment where all posts are traceable, abuse is unlikely." As social networking takes hold in our culture, and organizations explore ways they can use it to connect with their customers, they are realizing that establishing rules of etiquette for how to do this is important. "We have a hard and fast rule that if you are using social networking to do business, you must state your company affiliation," said a manager.

Cultural and behavioral practices are changing as a result of collaboration, and agreement is widespread that these will require serious management attention. For example, as staff become empowered to innovate and make real-time decisions, organizations will need to foster increased psychological safety so people don't fear being penalized if they make a mistake (Edmonston 2008). Similarly, work will need to be done to align work management and human resources practices, as well as incentives, if collaboration is to really make a difference (Cross et al. 2005). Finally, as connectivity becomes more pervasive and global, companies will have to develop policies and practices that enable staff to achieve an effective work–life balance. For example, one global firm has developed a small scheduling application to determine the least invasive time to have a meeting across different time zones. Tools can also be used to assist staff with controlling their accessibility and protecting their privacy (Mann 2008).

5. *Gradually move beyond the firewall.*   None of the focus group companies was comfortable as yet extending collaboration beyond their firewalls, unless in very tightly controlled circumstances (e.g., with vendors or third-party service providers). Major concerns about risk, privacy, and corporate liability remain. These issues need to be discussed and managed so that the power of collaboration can be realized. For example, one firm's privacy officer is now involved in determining what information can and cannot be shared. Some initial external target groups will include retirees, clients, and business partners. "We are gradually working through our concerns because of the unbelievable power of these tools," one manager said.

Conclusion

Collaboration is a complex concept with uncertain benefits and requires major organizational change. The drive to adopt collaboration is being accelerated by the possibilities enabled by information technology, which support real-time, global communication and anytime, anywhere access to information. In addition, companies are feeling considerable pressure to adopt collaboration technology because of their increasingly widespread use among individuals, many of whom are becoming their employees. There is no question that collaboration will play a major role in how we work and live in the future. However, as we move into this new era, companies are taking their time to determine how best to take advantage of what collaborative technology has to offer. This chapter has identified the major ways companies might want to collaborate and the benefits that are anticipated from each. It has also explored some of the major characteristics

and components of collaboration in order to clarify concepts and to distinguish between the work of collaboration, which is a human activity, and collaboration technology, which facilitates it. It has shown that effective collaboration will not result from simply implementing more collaboration software. Instead, it will require a proactive and holistic strategy that integrates business goals and technology potential. At present, all aspects of collaboration and collaboration technology are in their infancy, so it is understandable that many companies are proceeding cautiously into this new world. Nevertheless, the speed with which both technology and practice are moving suggests strongly that it is time for managers to put some collaborative fundamentals in place. Furthermore, IT managers have an opportunity to provide business leadership around collaboration if they can clearly articulate its business potential and benefits, rather than focusing on the technology itself.

References

Amabile, T., and M. Khaire. "Creativity and the Role of the Leader." *Harvard Business Review* 86, no. 10 (October 2008).

Andriole, S. "The Collaborate/Integrate Business Technology Strategy." *Communications of the ACM* 49, no. 5 (May 2006).

Attaran, M. "Collaborative Computing: A New Management Strategy for Increasing Productivity and Building a Better Business." *Business Strategy Series* 8, no. 6 (2007): 387–93.

Cain, M. "Key Issues for Unified Communications and Collaboration, 2008." Gartner Inc., ID Number: G0015672, April 10, 2008.

Camarinha-Matos, L., H. Afsarmanesh, N. Galeano, and A. Molina. "Collaborative Networked Organizations—Concepts and Practice in Manufacturing Enterprises." *Computers and Industrial Engineering* 57, no. 1 (2009): 46–60.

Chin, K., D. Gootzit, and J. Mann. "Key Issues for Portals, Content Management and Collaboration Best Practices Projects." Gartner Inc., ID Number: G00155820, April 24, 2008.

Chituc, C., A. Azevedo, and C. Toscano. "A Framework Proposal for Seamless Interoperability in a Collaborative Networked Environment." *Computers in Industry* 60, no. 5 (June 2009): 317–38.

Cross, R., J. Liedtka, and L. Weiss. "A Practical Guide to Social Networks." *Harvard Business Review* 83, no. 3 (March 2005).

Drakos, N., C. Rozwell, M. Cain, and J. Mann. "Key Issues for Social Software and Collaboration Initiatives, 2009." Gartner Inc., ID Number: G00164866, January 30, 2009.

Edmonston, A. "The Competitive Imperative of Learning." *Harvard Business Review* 86, nos. 7/8 (July–August 2008).

Evans, P., and B. Wolf. "Collaboration Rules." *Harvard Business Review* 83, nos. 7/8 (July–August 2005).

Fedorowicz, J., I. Laso-Ballesteros, and A. Padill-Melendez. "Creativity, Innovation and e-Collaboration." *International Journal of e-Collaboration* 4, no. 4 (2008): 1–10.

Fink, L. "Coordination, Learning and Innovation: The Organizational Roles of e-Collaboration and Their Impacts." *International Journal of e-Collaboration* 3, no. 3 (2007).

Fiore, S., R. McDaniel, and F. Jentsch. "Narrative-Based Collaboration Systems for Distributed Teams: Nine Research Questions for Information Managers." *Information Systems Management* 26, no. 1 (Winter 2009): 28.

Gordon, S., M. Tarafdar, R. Cook, R. Maksimoski, and B. Rogowitz. "Improving the Front End of Innovation with Information Technology." *Research-Technology Management* 51, no. 3 (May/June 2008): 50–58.

Iandoli, L. "JITCAR Special Issue—IT Collaboration in Organizations." *Journal of Information Technology Case and Application Research* 11, no. 1 (2009a).

Iandoli, L. "Leveraging the Power of Collective Intelligence Through IT-Enabled Global Collaboration." *Journal of Global Information Technology Management* 12, no. 3 (2009b).

Johansen, B. *Get There Early: Sensing the Future to Compete in the Present.* San Francisco: Berrett-Koehler, 2007.

Kleinbaum, A., and M. Tushman. "Managing Corporate Social Networks." *Harvard Business Review* 86, no. 7–8 (July–August 2008).

Lynch, C. "Five Things Wikipedia's Founder Has Learned About Online Collaboration." *CIO Magazine,* June 28, 2007. www.cio.com/article/121711/Five_Things_Wikipedia_s_Founder_Has_Learned_About_Online_Collaboration (accessed March 9, 2011).

MacCormack, A., and T. Forbath. "Learning the Fine Art of Global Collaboration." *Harvard Business Review* 86, no. 1 (January 2008).

Majchrzak, A. "Social Networking and Collaboration." Presentation to the Society for Information Management's Advanced Practices Council, Atlanta, Georgia, January 21–22, 2009.

Majchrzak, A., A. Malhotra, J. Stamps, and J. Lipnack. "Can Absence Make a Team Grow Stronger?" *Harvard Business Review* 82, no. 5 (May 2004): 131–37.

Mann, J. "Q&A: Answers to Practical Questions about Collaboration Tools." Gartner Inc., ID Number: G00154888, February 1, 2008.

Mann, J., and B. Elliot. "The New Market for Unified Communications and Collaboration." Gartner Inc., ID Number: G00153236, November 23, 2007.

McAfee, A. "Enterprise 2.0: The Dawn of Emergent Collaboration." *MIT Sloan Management Review* 47, no. 3 (Spring 2006): 20–28.

Nohria, N., B. Groysberg, and L. Lee. "Employee Motivation: A Powerful New Model." *Harvard Business Review* 86, nos. 7/8 (July–August 2008).

Pisano, G., and R. Verganti. "Which Kind of Collaboration Is Right for You?" *Harvard Business Review* 86, no. 12 (December 2008).

Reeves, B., T. Malone, and T. O'Driscoll. "Leadership's Online Labs." *Harvard Business Review* 86, no. 5 (May 2008).

Romano, N., J. Pick, and N. Roxtocki. "Editorial Introduction to the Special Issue on Collaboration Issues in Cross-Organizational and Cross-Border IS/IT." *Journal of Information Technology Theory and Application* 8, no. 4 (2007).

Sanders, N. "An Empirical Study of the Impact of e-Business Technologies on Organizational Collaboration and Performance." *Information Systems and Operations Management* 25, no. 6 (2007): 1332–47.

Schuh, G., A. Sauer, and S. Doering. "Managing Complexity in Industrial Collaborations."

International Journal of Production Research 46, no. 9 (May 2008): 2485–98.

Smith, G., K. Watson, W. Baker, and J. Pokorski. "A Critical Balance: Collaboration and Security in the IT-Enabled Supply Chain." *International Journal of Production Research* 45, no. 11 (June 2007).

Tebbutt, D. "The Business Value of Collaboration Software." *CIO Magazine,* February 17, 2009. www.cio.com/article/481329/The_Business_Value_of_Collaboration_Software (accessed March 9, 2011).

Thomas, D., and R. Bostrom. "Building Trust and Cooperation Through Technology Adaptation in Virtual Teams: Empirical Field Evidence." *Information Systems Management* 25, no. 1 (2008): 45–56.

Thomas, D., R. Bostrom, and M. Gouge. "Making Knowledge Work in Virtual Teams." *Communications of the ACM* 50, no. 11 (November 2007).

Wikipedia. "Collaboration." en.wikipedia.org/wiki/Collaboration (accessed March 9, 2011).

MINI CASE

Innovation at International Foods[2]

Josh Novak gazed up at the gleaming glass-and-chrome skyscraper as he stepped out of the cab. "Wow!" he thought to himself. "I've hit the big time now." The International Foods Group (IFG) Tower was a Chicago landmark as well as part of the company's logo, which appeared on the packages of almost every type of food one could imagine—breakfast cereals, soft drinks, frozen pizza, cheese, and snack foods, to name just a few. Walking into the tower's marble lobby, Josh could see displays of the company's packaging from its earliest days, when its dairy products were delivered by horse and wagon, right up to the modern global entity it had become.

After signing in with security, Josh was whisked away to the 37th floor by an efficient attendant who walked him down a long hall of cubicles to a corner office overlooking Lake Michigan. On the way, Josh passed display photos of the company's founder, old Jonas Wilton looking patriarchal, and several of the family scions, who had grown the company into a major national brand before the IPO in the 1980s had made IFG a public company. Josh, having "Googled" the company's history last night in response to this summons, knew that IFG was now the largest purveyor of food products the world had ever known. While many decried the globalization of the food business, IFG kept right on growing, gobbling up dozens of companies each year—some because IFG wanted to stomp on its competition and others because it wanted their good ideas.

Josh's own small company, Glow-Foods, a relative newcomer in the business, was fortunately one of the latter, but Josh was a little puzzled about this command performance. After all, he himself wasn't anyone important. The owners of the company all received multiple millions and were sticking around—as per contract—during the transition. The next level, including Josh's boss, had mostly jumped ship as soon as the "merger" was announced. "This isn't my thing," drawled Nate Greenly over beer one night at the local pub. "Corporate America isn't going to let us stay as we are, no matter what they say. Get out while you can," he advised. But Josh, with a freshly minted MBA in his pocket, thought differently. And so here he was, walking into the CIO's office hundreds of miles away from the cramped loft in Toronto where Glow-Foods was headquartered.

As the office door swung open, two people dressed in "power suits" turned to meet him. "Uh oh, I'm not in Kansas anymore," thought Josh as he mentally reviewed his outfit of neatly pressed khakis and golf shirt, which was a big step up from his usual attire of jeans and a T-shirt. A tall man with silver hair stepped forward with his hand held out. "You must be Josh," he boomed. "Welcome. I'm John Ahern, and this is my associate, Tonya James, manager of IT marketing. Thanks for coming today. Please, have a seat." Josh complied, slinging his backpack over the corner of the leather chair

[2] Smith, H. A., and J. D. McKeen. "Innovation at International Foods." #1-L09-1-002, Queen's School of Business, December 2009. Reproduced by permission of Queen's University, School of Business, Kingston, Ontario.

while taking in the rich furnishings of the office and the panoramic view. After a bit of chitchat about the weather and the prospects of their respective baseball teams, John pulled out a black leather folder.

"Well, we won't keep you in suspense anymore, Josh. As you know, when we took over Glow-Foods we decided to completely align our processes, including IT. It doesn't make any economic sense to run separate data centers and applications, so we already have a team in place to transfer all your hardware and software to our centralized corporate systems over the next month. We'll be replacing your Macs with PCs, and everyone will get training on our ERP system. We're going to keep a small team to deal with the specifically Canadian issues, but other than that we see no need for an IT function in Toronto any more." Josh nodded glumly, thinking about his friends who would be losing their jobs and all the fun they'd had during those all-nighters brainstorming new ways to help Glow-Foods products go "viral." *Nate was right,* he thought glumly. *They don't really get us at all.*

"That said," John continued. "We are very impressed with the work you and your team have done in using social networking, mashups, and multimedia to support your marketing strategy. Your ability to reach the under-thirty demographic with technology is impressive." He turned to Tonya, who added. "Here at IFG, we have traditionally marketed our products to women with children. We have a functional Web site—a place where customers can find out about our products and where to buy them. More recently, we've added their nutritional content, some recipes, and a place where customers can contact us directly with questions, but it's really unidirectional and pretty dry."

Josh nodded in agreement with this assessment. The difference in the two companies' approaches was night and day. Although not everything they had tried at Glow-Foods had worked, enough of it had succeeded that demand for the company's products had skyrocketed. Young adults and teens had responded en masse to the opportunity to post pictures of themselves drinking their Green Tea Shakes in unusual places on the Glow-Foods Web site and to send a coupon for their favorite Glow-Foods product to a friend. Serialized company mini-dramas popped up on YouTube and viewers were asked to go online to help shape what happened to the characters—all of them using Glow-Foods products extensively. Contests, mass collaboration in package design, and a huge network of young part-time sales reps linked through Facebook all contributed to making the brand hip and exciting—and drove sales through the roof.

John adjusted his French cuffs. "We want to tap into the youth and young adult market with IT, and we think you're the one who can help us do this. We're going to give you a team and whatever resources you need right here in Chicago. With our global reach and much larger budgets, you could do great things for our company." John went on to outline a job offer to Josh that sent tingles down his spine. "I really have hit the big time," he thought as he signed the documents making him a team manager at IFG at a salary that was almost double what he was earning now. "I can't wait to get started."

Six weeks later he was being walked down the same hall by Tonya, now his immediate boss, and into her office, a smaller version of his with a window looking onto another high-rise. "What's next?" he asked. "I've booked a meeting room for you to meet your new team at ten-thirty," Tonya explained. "But before that, I want to go over a few things with you first. As the manager of IT Marketing, I am personally thrilled that we're going to be experimenting with new technologies and, as your coach and mentor at IFG, I'm going to make it my job to see that you have the resources and support that you need. However, you may find that not everyone else at this company will be as encouraging. We're going to have some serious obstacles to overcome, both within IT and with the larger company. It will be my responsibility to help you deal with them over the next few months as you put your ideas together. But you need to know that IFG may have different expectations of you than Glow-Foods. And you may find you will get a better reception to your ideas if you look a bit more professional." Josh winced and nodded. He'd already ramped up the wardrobe for his first day with a sports jacket, but clearly he needed to do more. "Finally, I'd like you to come up here every Friday afternoon at four o'clock to go over your progress and your plans. My schedule is usually fully booked, but if you have any questions you can always send me an e-mail. I'm pretty good at getting back to people within twenty-four hours. Now let's go meet your new team. I think you'll be happy with them."

An hour later Josh and his new team were busy taking notes as Tonya outlined their mandate. "You have a dual role here," she explained. "First, I want you to work with Ben here to develop some exciting new ideas for online marketing. We're looking for whatever creative ideas you have." Ben Nokony was the team's marketing liaison. Any ideas would be vetted through him, and all proposals to the individual product teams would be arranged by him. "Second, I need you to keep your eyes open and your ears to the ground for any innovative technologies you think might work here at IFG. These are our future, and you're our vanguard." Josh glanced around at his team, an eclectic group. They seemed eager and enthusiastic, and he knew they were talented, having had a say in choosing them. With the exception of Ben, all were new to IFG, experienced in using a variety of new media, and under thirty years old. They were going to do great things together, he could see.

The next couple of weeks were taken up with orientation. Ben introduced each of the major product divisions to the team, and everybody had come back from each meeting full of new possibilities. Tonya had also arranged for the team to meet with the chief technology officer, Rick Visser, who was in charge of architecture, privacy and security, risk management, and the technology roadmap. Rick had been pleasant but cool. "Please remember that we have a process for incorporating new technology into our architecture," he explained as he handed over a thick manual of procedures. "In a company our size we can't operate without formal processes. Anything else would be chaos." The team had returned from that meeting full of gloom that their ideas would all be shot down before they were even tried. Finally, they had met with the IT finance officer. "I'm your liaison with corporate finance," Sheema Singh stated. "You need to work with me to develop your business cases. Nothing gets funded unless it has a business case and is approved through our office."

Finally, having dragged some chairs into Josh's eighteenth-floor and marginally larger cubicle and desk, the team got down to work. "This is ridiculous," fumed Mandy Sawh, shuffling her papers on her lap. "I can't believe you need to book a conference room two weeks in advance around here. Who knows when you need to get together?" "Okay, team, let's settle down and take a look at what you've got," said Josh. One by one, they outlined their preliminary ideas—some workable and some not—and together they identified three strong possibilities for their first initiatives and two new technologies they wanted to explore. "Great work, team," said Josh. "We're on our way."

The problems began to surface slowly. First, it was a polite email from Rick Visser reminding them that access to instant messaging and Facebook required prior approval from his group. "They want to know why we need it," groused Veejay Mitra. "They don't seem to understand that this is how people work these days." Then Ben got a bit snippy about talking directly to the product teams. "You're supposed to go through me," he told Josh's team. "I'm the contact person, and I am supposed to be present at all meetings." "But these weren't 'meetings,'" Candis Chung objected. "We just wanted to bounce some ideas around with them." Next, it was a request from Sheema to outline their proposed work, with costs and benefits, for the next fiscal year—beginning six months from now. "Can't we just make up a bunch of numbers?" asked Tom Webster. "We don't know how this stuff is going to play out. It could be great and we'll need lots of resources to scale up, or it could bomb and we won't need anything." Everywhere the team went, they seemed to run into issues with the larger corporate environment. Tonya was helpful when Josh complained about it at their Friday afternoon meetings, smoothing things over with Rick, helping Josh to navigate corporate procedures, and even dropping by to tell the team they were doing a great job.

Nevertheless, Josh could sense his own and everyone else's frustration as they pre-pared for their first big project review presentation. "They want us to be innovative, but they keep putting us in a straight-jacket with their 'procedures' and their 'proper way to go about things,'" he sighed to himself. Thank goodness, the presentation was coming together nicely. Although it was only to the more junior executives and, of course, John and Rick, he had high hopes for the vision his team was developing to get IFG out and interacting with its customers.

"And in conclusion, we believe that we can use technology to help IFG reach its customers in three new ways," Josh summarized after all of his team members had presented their ideas. "First, we want the company to connect directly with customers about new product development ideas through an interactive Web site with real-time response from internal staff. Second, we want to reach out to different communities and gain insights into their needs and interests, which in turn will guide our future marketing plans. And third, we want to implement these and other ideas on the 'cloud,' which will enable us to scale up or down rapidly as we need to while linking with com-pany databases. Any questions?"

There was a moment of stunned silence, and then the barrage began. "What's the business value of these initiatives?" asked Sheema. "I can't take them upstairs to our finance committee meeting without a clear commitment on what the benefits are going to be." Ben looked nonplussed. "We don't really know," he said. "We've never really done this before, but we like the ideas." "I'm concerned that we don't bite off more than we can chew," said John thoughtfully. "What if these customers don't like the company or its products and say bad things about us? Do we have any procedures for handling these types of situations?" "There's definitely a serious risk to our reputation here," said Rick, "but I'm more concerned about this 'cloud' thing. We haven't even got cloud in our architecture yet, and this plan could make company intellectual property available to everyone in cyberspace!" Sheema spoke again. "I hate to mention this, but didn't we do something like this community project about ten years ago? We called it knowledge management, and it flopped. No one knew what to do with it or how to handle the information it generated." On and on they went, picking holes in every part of every idea as the team slumped lower in their seats.

Finally, Tonya stood up. "I'd like to thank you all for raising some legitimate and important concerns," she said. "And I'd like to thank Josh and his team for some fine work and some excellent ideas. Marketing was looking for creativity, and we have delivered on that part of our mandate. But now we have a more important job. And that is innovation. Innovation is about more than good ideas; it's about delivering the best ones to the marketplace. We're in a new world of technology, and IT can't be the ones to be saying 'no' all the time to the business. Yes, we need to protect ourselves, and we don't want to throw money at every half-baked idea, but we've got to find a way to be open to new ideas at the same time. We know there's value in these new ideas—we saw it work at Glow-Foods. That's why Josh is here. He has a proven track record. We just have to find a way to identify it without taking too much risk."

The room sat in stunned silence as Tonya looked from one to the other. At last, John cleared his throat. "You're right, Tonya. We want creativity and innovation, and we need a better way to get it than we have now. I think what we need is a process for creativity and innovation that will help us overcome some of the roadblocks we put in place." As Josh mentally rolled his eyes at the thought of yet another process, Tonya replied. "I think you're partially right, John. Processes do have their place, but we also need some space to play with new ideas before we cast them in concrete. What I'd like to do over the next two weeks is speak with Josh and his team and each of you and then develop a plan as to how we can, as an IT department, better support innovation at IFG."

Discussion Questions

1. In discussion with Josh, Tonya foreshadows "some serious obstacles to overcome." Describe these obstacles in detail.
2. How can Josh win support for his team's three-point plan to use technology to help IFG reach its customers?

MINI CASE

Consumerization of Technology at IFG[3]

"There's good news and bad news," Josh Novak reported to the assembled IT management team at their monthly status meeting. "The good news is that our social media traffic is up 3000% in the past two years. Our new interactive website, Facebook presence, and our U-Tube and couponing promotions have been highly successful in driving awareness of our 'Nature's Glow' brand and are very popular with our target demographic—the under-30s. Unfortunately, the bad news is that our competitors at GPL are eating our lunch with the new mobile apps they've developed."

Everyone frowned at the mention of Grocers' Products Limited, their fiercest competitor, which had the largest chain of integrated food and retail stores in the country and whose Premier Choice products were showcased on their shelves, making it increasingly harder for IFG to get prime space for their top brands.

"Our web and social media presence has helped us to begin to develop a relationship with our customers," Josh continued, "but our Marketing folks are very worried that we're going to be falling behind, isn't that so Tonya?"

Tonya James, manager of IT Marketing, nodded her head. As the IT person working directly with marketing, it had been under her watch that IFG had transformed its dowdy online presence into something that was hip and trendy. Together, she and Josh, now manager of IT Innovation, had begun experimenting with new media, creating an innovation process that took a large number of new technologies and ideas for products and services and created a protected "sand box" that enabled trial implementations for employees only. Feedback and experience at this level then helped Josh and his business colleagues select the best ones for development in full "heavy-duty" production mode for the public, complete with privacy and security protection and following all architectural standards. Only then would the chief technology officer, Rick Visser, who was charged with protecting company data and systems, allow new technologies to be fully integrated into IFG's internal technical environment.

Mark Szabo, the newly appointed head of IFG's Business Intelligence (BI) team reported next. "As you all know, our executives are all screaming for more and more information to help them but it's not going to be easy. What we have here at IFG is a data mess and it's only going to get worse from what I can see." The picture wasn't pretty he warned. IFG had thousands of traditional systems all of which produced data and reports. The problem was that each used somewhat different definitions of important company concepts, like "in stock."

---

[3] Smith, H. A., and J. D. McKeen. "Consumerization of Technology at IFG." #1-L11-1-002, Queen's School of Business, December 2009. Reproduced by permission of Queen's University, School of Business, Kingston, Ontario.

"If our goal is to improve the stocks of our products on the shelves, we'll have to go back to rewrite many of these systems. Some of them believe that a product is 'in stock' when it's on the shelves; others when it's in our back room waiting to be put on the shelves; still others when we have received the order from the supplier or when it's arrived at our regional distribution centers." He went on to describe similar problems with varying understandings of such core company data as "customer," "supplier," "employee," and others. "It's hard to tell our executives how 'sales' are going when we don't have a single definition of what 'sales' are!" he said with frustration. "Right now, I've got two people working full time on spreadsheets trying to reconcile data to answer the questions we continually get from the 37th floor," he concluded referring to the executive suite. "We can't tell them we don't have the information but we need a better way to get it, that's for sure."

The meeting droned on with the CIO, John Ahern, calling on all his managers one at a time. As far as most of them were concerned, it was "business as usual" in IT. Josh didn't say anything else in the meeting but he cornered Mark as it broke up. "Have you got time for a coffee? I think we need to talk."

"Sure, what's up?," Mark asked as they headed toward the company cafeteria.

"I liked what you had to say in the meeting about BI," said Josh. "You seem to be one of the few managers here who understands that what we do in IT is going to have to change dramatically over the next few years. And that a lot of our work is going to focus on information—getting it; analyzing it; and delivering it in packages that people can use for their work. I believe that there's a data tsunami rapidly heading our way and we haven't got a clue how to deal with it."

Mark grimaced as he filled his cup with what the cafeteria called "coffee." "I know, I know," he agreed. "I've only been in BI a couple of months but all those articles and books out there about competing on analytics and analyzing unstructured data, like emails and tweets and blogs, are making my head spin. If we can't agree on what a 'customer' is, how are we *ever* going to manage the rest?"

Josh made a sympathetic face. "You've got that right, but I'm afraid it's even worse than you think." Over the next thirty minutes he described what he was seeing out in the field as he looked for innovative new technologies and applications that could help IFG.

"You think we have problems with our existing systems, but there are guys out there in our business units buying full-scale applications from the cloud with company credit cards!" He went on to tell Mark about the pressure he was getting from the sales guys to buy everyone iPads so they could write up orders on the road. "We've already been forced by our C-team to buy them and the board iPads and so far, we've kept them locked down tightly, but that's going to change very soon."

Users were also creating local "data marts," which included copies of core company data as well as external data feeds, and then building complex spreadsheets with information derived from these.

"Our business units don't use the centralized company reports anymore," he stated. "They create their own. We've got the 'wild west' out there!"

Mark looked shocked. "What about our company data warehouse? Isn't that what they're supposed to use?" He had spent a few years building the warehouse a while back and the team had put a lot of thought into making it the best they could.

Josh was aware of this but ploughed on. He and Mark needed to be on the same page about this if these issues were ever going to be resolved. "The world has changed," he said gently. "Our business guys are online all the time now; software vendors are targeting them directly and because of the low costs involved they can afford to make an end run around IT; there are literally thousands of free data sets out there; and computing power and storage cost aren't an issue any more with the cloud. Our data warehouse is seen as a dinosaur. It's inflexible because we insist on reviewing all the data that goes in there for quality and provenance and it takes forever (i.e., 30 seconds) to get a response."

Mark looked down at the table and sighed. "So what you're saying is that all my work in BI is too little, too late?"

Josh thought for a moment before replying. "That's not exactly what I've been saying, Mark. What I meant to point out is that we in IT are caught in the middle between two opposing trends. The first is the trend to analytics and business intelligence that you're working on. That's important. The execs want to get at more information to run the company and it has to be based on good, trustworthy data. There are whole businesses out there that are winning because they've found a way to do this.

But the *other,* opposite trend is what I'm seeing. And it's important too. Everyone working in our business is also a consumer of technology and when the devices and applications they can use in their personal lives are more powerful and flexible than those in their business lives, they naturally want to work around the clunky technology we provide them with and use their own. And, since we're now trying to build relationships with our customers, we are going to have to start thinking and working like they do."

"In some ways, this is just like the 'old days' in IT," Mark smiled. "I'm a lot older than you and I remember when those new-fangled PCs came in and everyone in IT was worrying about how we were going to handle people working on their own computers at home. And then when the web first hit business, we had people running around saying 'the sky is falling' and developing their own personal and localized websites. We don't handle new stuff well around here, do we?"

Josh grinned. He was notoriously frustrated with the IT "powers that be" that always wanted to lock everything down and wrap it in layers of privacy and security before allowing it out there. "Well, let's just say that we've got some way to go before I believe we can be as innovative as I'd like us to be. We've got to be aware of these trends and how they're going to hit us. Or our business model could change and we'll be out in the cold. Where are all the book stores, video stores and music stores these days? What happened to those companies?"

"You're right of course," said Mark "but we have to get more people involved in figuring out what we need to do here. This is a HUGE issue and we can't 'boil the ocean'! Somehow we need to get our arms around the most important things to do so we can make some sort of progress. Otherwise, we're spinning our wheels and the situation's just going to grow more and more out of control."

"I'll tell you what," said Josh. "Let me speak with Tonya. She's terrific at stick-handling these situations. I'll get back to you with a plan." And with that, they began to talk about the upcoming company softball game as they cleared the table and headed back to their respective cubicles.

Josh laid the situation out for Tonya at the first opportunity he could find in her busy schedule. "So you see," he concluded. "We need the discipline and rigor of BI and all of the good things we in IT can do for our executives and employees if we get them better and more trustworthy information. But we also need to keep moving ahead in the mobile and social space for consumers without putting handcuffs on us. And we need to recognize that the business is likely already doing their own thing on the cloud without IT and using their own personal devices, because it's so cheap and easy to do and we don't help them! If we don't somehow figure out how all this stuff fits together—especially the data—we'll never be able to use what we know either operationally or strategically."

"You've done a good job articulating the challenges we're facing," Tonya said. "I know that the Marketing people are putting lots of pressure on me to help them with better information and tools. In my experience, when business is in turmoil they want everything right away and they'll do whatever it takes to get it *now*. What would you say our biggest need is right now?"

Josh fiddled with his pen for a moment. He had hoped Tonya would tell *him*. "Well...," he said slowly. "We need to be seen to be doing *more* in this space. It's okay to work on the big systems and core data. In fact, that's our main job. But we also need to help the business help itself. With my tiny innovation team, I can't possibly deal with all of the ideas and technologies that are out there. And the business guys are seeing many more opportunities than I can deal with. It's really hard to tell what's going to work and what isn't until they play with things. I can provide some of this in my 'innovation sandbox' but I don't think that's going to be enough. And...," he said as another idea popped into his head, "we don't have the right people to do some of this work. We need information analysts, mobile developers, visualization specialists and lots of business people to work with us and teach us about the business. I don't have all the answers here but we can't stick our heads in the sand and let the world change around us. Are we going to be reactionary or visionary?"

Tonya smiled. "There's never a dull moment around here is there? You've got an important point of view here but I think Rick Visser does too. Just in IT alone, we've got a number of groups that need to have some input on this, in addition to my area. We have to get ahead of this 'tsunami' of yours and be proactive in a way we've never been before. This doesn't mean that we throw all our tried and true practices out the window but it also means that we should do *some* things differently around here and that means John has to be involved. We need a plan to manage all these new trends and he's in the best position to help us because there are going to be a lot of cultural, organizational and structural changes involved, not just for IT but for the whole business. But we can't dump this in his lap. We need to do our homework first. I'll talk with him and tell him what we're doing and try to identify the stakeholders involved. Can you come up with some key issues and preliminary recommendations about what you think we should be doing and how we should do it? Sit down with Mark and get his ideas too. Then we'll see if we can get everyone in a room together to 'talk turkey' and hammer out a more proactive IT strategy for handling this mess."

Discussion Questions

1. Describe the problem at IFG as succinctly as you can. Use this description to identify the main stakeholders.
2. IFG can't afford the resources to identify, define, cleanse, and validate all of its data. On the other hand, building yet another data mart to address a specific problem worsens the data situation. Propose a solution that will enable IFG to leverage a key business problem/opportunity using their BI tools that does not aggravate their existing data predicament.

MINI CASE
CRM at Minitrex[4]

Georges Degas, Director of Sales at Minitrex, looked at his salesman with concern and sympathy as the man described another sales call where he had been made to look unprofessional! It was bad enough that he didn't know that the company he'd just phoned was already a Minitrex customer, but being told that he was the third caller this week from Minitrex was horrible. "I'd be better off with a Rolodex and handwritten notes than this system," he grumbled.

To keep track of customer information, salespeople use the Customer Contacts system, the brainchild of Degas's boss, Jon Bettman, VP of marketing. Bettman's position was created eighteen months ago in an effort to centralize sales and marketing activities at Minitrex. The sales and marketing team is responsible for promoting and selling an array of products to its customers. There are two distinct product lines, each developed by a separate division (insurance and financing) that also provides after-sale customer service. The idea behind having a department dedicated to sales and marketing was to create opportunities for cross-selling and up-selling that didn't exist when salespeople were tied to just one of the company's product categories.

The insurance division, led by Harold Blumfen, VP of insurance, is a major profit maker for Minitrex. Blumfen's group is divided into industry-specific teams whose goals are to develop deep industry knowledge and design short-term insurance products to meet clients' needs. Irascible and brilliant, Blumfen believes that computers are good for billing and other accounting functions but cannot replace people for customer knowledge and support. His division uses a credit administration system (developed more than twenty years ago) to track customer billings and payments and a general management system to keep track of which products a customer has bought and what services the customer is entitled to. Both are fundamentally back-end systems. The industry teams keep front-end customer knowledge in their own documentation and in their heads.

The mission of the financing division is to provide business sectors with financing services that are competitive with those of the big banks. As with the insurance division, its products and customer service are designed and delivered through its own industry-specific teams. However, unlike Blumfen, the VP of financing, Mariella Hopkins, is an IT enthusiast. Hopkins joined Minitrex about four years ago after a successful banking career. Her mandate, which she has undertaken with alacrity, was to "combine big banking services with small company flexibility." To do this, her division funded the development of a management business center application, which acts as an online customer self-service system. Customers can obtain statements and financing

[4] Smith, H. A., and J. D. McKeen. "CRM at Minitrex." #9-L05-1-002, Queen's School of Business, January 2005. Reproduced by permission of Queen's University, School of Business, Kingston, Ontario.

online and often can get credit approved instantly. Customer-service representatives use the same basic system, with additional functionality, to track customer transactions and to provide customer support as needed.

"The company is always promising better systems, 'thought Degas,' but when it comes down to it, no one can agree on what to do. Being customercentric seems to depend on whose view of the customer is being used. Meanwhile, salespeople can't do their jobs properly. Just imagine what our customers think!"

Bettman has been trying to get the company to see the importance of having timely, accurate, and integrated customer information without much success. To give his sales force a better way to keep track of sales prospects, he developed his Customer Contacts system, which schedules sales calls on a periodic basis and provides mechanisms for generating and tracking new leads; it also forms the basis on which the marketing department pays the salespeople's commissions. Real-time information on sales by product, salesperson, and region gives Bettman and his team excellent feedback on how well their centralized marketing strategies are performing. For purposes of invoicing and servicing the accounts, the Customer Contacts system also feeds data into the insurance and financing divisions' systems after sales are made.

"I'll see what I can do about this," Degas had promised his frustrated salesman, knowing that it would take a miracle to improve the situation. "I'll speak with the director of IT today and get back to you."

Degas put in a call to Denny Khan, Minitrex's long-suffering director of IT. Khan, who reported to the CFO, was outranked by Bettman, Blumfen, and Hopkins. To his surprise, Khan answered the phone right away. "I was just leaving for lunch," he explained. "What can I do for you?"

As soon as Degas began to explain what had happened that morning, Khan cut him off. "I know, I know. But the VPs would say, 'Our systems work fine for our needs, so why change them? We have a lot more urgent IT needs to spend our money on.' Blumfen doesn't want to spend a nickel on IT and doesn't want to have to work with Hopkins. Hopkins is open to collaboration, but she doesn't want to compromise her existing system, which is working well. And Bettman can't do anything without their cooperation. Furthermore, none of them will assign dedicated business staff to help us put together a business case and requirements. Their line is 'We don't have the budgets for this. Of course, we'll answer IT's questions, but it's their job to give us the systems we need.'"

"I see the same attitude in our business activities," agreed Degas. "Our sales force often doesn't know what services the business teams are providing to the customers. I don't see how management can expect to make informed decisions when they're not sharing basic information. Isn't there some way we could at least get common customer data—even if we use the data in different ways? And surely, with each unit identifying, prioritizing, and paying for IT opportunities, the duplication of support services must cost an arm and a leg."

"Sure," Khan agreed, "but each unit developed its own terminology and specialized data items over time, so these only work for *their* systems. Sharing is impossible unless everyone agrees on what information everyone needs about our customers. I'd like to see something done about this, but when I take it to the IT prioritization committee, it always seems to get bumped off the list. To the best of my knowledge, there has never been an effective business case to improve CRM. And anyway, I don't own this issue!"

"You're probably right, but I'm not sure how to go about this," said Degas. "Let me think about it and get back to you."

Discussion Questions

1. Explain how it is possible for someone at Minitrex to call a customer and not know (a) that this is a customer and (b) that this is the third time this week that they had been called.
2. Outline the steps that Bettman must take in order to implement CRM at Minitrex. In your plan be sure to include people, processes, and technology.

MINI CASE

Customer Service at Datatronics[5]

Matt Rubenzahl winced as the all-too-familiar, soothing machine voice crooned in his ear: "All our operators are busy. Your call is important to us. Please stay on the line as our calls are being answered in priority sequence...." He glanced at his watch. Only fifteen minutes left of his lunch break before the big meeting, and he had to resolve this problem with the bank. "Why do they call this the 'Customer Help line'?" he grumbled. "It seems like it's there to help them, not us!"

As the Muzak droned on in the background, punctuated briefly by a hopeful click and then the machine voice again, Matt's mind wandered to the upcoming meeting. As the development manager of E-Z RP, an end-to-end, fully integrated CRM/ERP/ service management suite for small- and medium-size enterprises (SMEs), he'd had his dream job. Leading a small team of developers and working actively with both the sales and service group, E-Z RP had made quite a name for itself, carving out a profitable business in the SME niche that the bigger players hadn't (until now) wanted to touch. E-Z RP was everything they weren't—user friendly, integrated, flexible, and intuitive. A service-based product, E-Z RP modules were accessed over the Web and hosted at the E-Z RP data center. Online training and friendly service completed the package, making E-Z RP one of the fastest growing service-based products on the market.

That was the good news, but it was also the bad news because E-Z RP's success had attracted the corporate vultures, and the company had been taken over a few weeks ago by Datatronics. Of course, the party line had been "business as usual," but today they were going to find out what the takeover would really mean for the people who worked there. Matt worried about his little development team. The seven of them had been together for a while now, and they liked and respected each other's skills. More important, they knew their product and understood how it helped their customers, thanks to Bill Blatherwick, their CEO. Bill had taken over E-Z RP as a start-up from its innovative founder, Todd Wylie, and had grown it into the successful enterprise it was today. It had been Bill who had made sure that Matt and his team went out on sales calls, sat in with the customer service reps (CSRs), and got to know the needs of the businesses firsthand.

Matt's reverie was interrupted by a cheery voice, "This is Tanya. How may I help you today?" Matt glanced at his watch—ten minutes of waiting for him, zero for the bank. Quickly he explained that the electronic transfer of funds from his checking account into his money market account had gone the other way, and now he had twice as much money in his checking account. He had the confirmation number right here in front of him. How could this happen? "Oh, I can explain that, sir," chirped Tanya. "You see, when you transfer funds, the request gets printed out here at the bank and then rekeyed into the money market system the next day. One of the keyers must have made

---

[5] Smith, H. A., and J. D. McKeen. "Customer Service at Datatronics." #1-L08-1-001, Queen's School of Business, September 2008. Reproduced by permission of Queen's University, School of Business, Kingston, Ontario.

a mistake. I can correct that." Matt rolled his eyes—some "electronic" banking—just a slick-looking front end and the same transaction-based system in the back office.

"I know this isn't your fault," he said. "But the bank should know the problems this is causing. Can you please file a report about this?"

"They don't really listen to us, but you could write a letter. I could give you our ombudsperson's address," said Tanya.

"Thanks, but I don't have time," Matt said, with more courtesy than he felt, and hung up, grabbing his jacket and tightening his tie as he dashed off to the main conference room.

It was standing-room only as everyone in the company crowded in to see the broadcast message of Brent Hinchcliffe, CEO and chief vulture of Datatronics. The company was noted for growing through acquisitions, and Hinchcliffe had a reputation as having a good eye for value but leaving the rest of his staff to sort out the messy details of the actual integration. As the booming voice welcomed them all to the "Datatronics family—the best technology for companies in the world," Matt tuned out Hinchcliffe's platitudes. He'd been through these things before. That was how he'd ended up at E-Z RP: His former company had been taken over, and six weeks later he'd been out of a job. The last few years here had been great, though, and he didn't relish the thought of having to change again. He was in management now, and jobs were tougher to find and his family was settled here. Matt sighed as Jennifer Merkley, the head Datatronics honcho in the room, clicked off the video and connected her PowerPoint presentation.

Merkley started by making an effort to be highly complementary about the E-Z RP organization and to assure everyone that they had a place on the "Datatronics team." It soon became clear, however, that E-Z RP was going to exist as a product only. Behind the scenes, there was going to be a whole new organizational structure. As Matt had expected, Blatherwick was moving on "to other opportunities," while Matt's group and the customer service group were going to be integrated with the other teams, leaving only sales as a separate unit. One box in the org chart was labeled "E-Z RP Development," and several others were marked with the other Datatronics products, including Data-Pro, Bus-I, Web-Spider, and Delphi-Plus. The latter was Datatronics's main offering, an ERP for larger businesses, and it was an inflexible piece of software that reflected the company's Teutonic roots. For Delphi-Plus users it was "My way or the highway," and E-Z RP had been picking off some of its lower-end and more frustrated customers for the last few years. Was this payback time? Was Datatronics going to bury them? Matt had seen this before: bigger competitors gobbling up smaller but better products and pulling the plug on them.

The little boxes on the PowerPoint slides weren't populated, of course, so Matt headed back to his office still not knowing where he stood, pleased at least that E-Z RP had a place on the map. It would be a huge change for customers, however. Now they'd be calling in to a major call center designed to deal with all Datatronics's products. The level of service and support customers had come to expect was bound to deteriorate. Matt spent some time chatting with his developers, encouraging them in the notion that the change would be for the better, although he could tell that some weren't convinced and would likely be polishing up their resumes and making the rounds—if they hadn't already done so. His staff had been carefully selected, not only for their skills but also for their interest in business and their ability to interact with both businesspeople and customers. Many of them had started in the E-Z RP Customer Service Center as new grads and had been promoted, first into maintenance and then development. They wouldn't relish being turned into back-room coders.

Back at his desk, Matt tried to interest himself in the latest project reports, until a small ping announced the arrival of an e-mail. It was a summons from Jennifer Merkley to meet with her at 5:00 that afternoon. "This is it," thought Matt. "I'm out, and they're going to do it after office hours." He spent the next hour tidying up his desk, getting rid of the junk and organizing it so it could be easily packed into a couple of boxes. He pulled out a slim file of letters—copies of glowing customer reviews that Bill had forwarded to him. After allowing himself a small moment of pleasure, he pitched it into the recycle bin, then thought better of it. Maybe these would be useful in a future portfolio of his accomplishments.

At 4:55 he headed off to Merkley's office and cooled his heels in the empty reception area for a good fifteen minutes. "Typical," he thought. "This company can't even fire you on time." Just then Merkley's door opened and out she came, accompanied by a neatly dressed, gray-haired man. "Matt, I'd like you to meet Victor Wang," she said as the two shook hands. "You two will be working together closely in the future."

"Oh," said Matt lamely, mentally switching gears. "Nice to meet you."

Merkley swept him into her office and motioned to him to sit down. "You're probably wondering about Victor," she began, and Matt nodded. "He's going to take over your E-Z RP team, starting tomorrow. We've decided to fully integrate the Datatronics and E-Z RP staff, which means mixing up the teams. Some of your staff will move to other products and vice versa."

"Oh," said Matt, again not knowing how to respond.

"You're also probably wondering what this will mean for your job," continued Merkley. Matt nodded again.

"Well, we want you to know that your work with the E-Z RP team has not gone unnoticed here at Datatronics."

"Thanks," spluttered Matt.

"We believe you have been instrumental in pulling together a highly customer-focused team that delivers." Matt sat up a little straighter, hope beginning to grow that this was not going to be the disastrous meeting for which he had steeled himself. "That's why we want you to take over our new combined Customer Service Center."

"WHAT the . . . ." An expletive almost escaped from his lips until he changed it to "Heck, what do I know about running a customer service center?"

Merkley almost smiled but then gave him a steely stare and said in a tone that brooked no opposition, "Look, Matt, you're a good development manager, and we know that, but we have a lot of them at Datatronics. What we don't have is someone who understands business and is customer focused. We need you in this role. You'll have a much larger staff and budget and a chance to prove yourself to senior management. I know it's a change, but if you're truly interested in being a manager, you will have to be flexible and go where we need you."

Matt gulped and gave her the only answer possible under the circumstances: "All right, I'll give it a shot." He was rewarded with a brisk handshake and a pile of manila folders.

"I was hoping you'd say that," she said. "So I took the liberty of asking the outgoing manager, Vish Singh, to pull together his plans for the group. He's heading off to India to start up our new Bangalore office." Reeling with too much information, Matt took the folders, thanked Merkley, and headed back to his office to consider this rather unexpected and not entirely welcome redirection of his career path.

Over the next few days and nights, Matt immersed himself in a whole new world. He watched harried CSRs take a continuous stream of calls. As soon as one ended, another would pop up. The E-Z RP service staff had been unceremoniously moved into the Datatronics call center, given a crash course in the company's other products, and cut loose. According to Vish's notes, cost seemed to be the driving force behind everything that was done. Customer service appeared to be under constant pressure to cut costs, and its budget had been routinely slashed by 10 percent a year over the past five years, despite the company's acquisition of several new products during this time. Everything ran by metrics—number of calls, call turnaround, cost per call, and so on. And the only new technology the center had acquired recently was a high-end, voice-activated IVR system, named Pamela. Its voice and features had been endlessly lampooned in the press, most notably when Datatronics had announced cutbacks and some wit had written to the paper hoping that Pamela was on the hit list. Although nothing had been said about outsourcing this function, Matt had his suspicions that when the new Bangalore office was up and running, he'd have some stiff competition from Vish to keep customer service in North America.

And the HR problems! The turnover was fierce. Unlike customer service at E-Z RP, there were few ways out and up the ladder at Datatronics. The company seemed to hire staff, work them hard, and then expect them to quit. Training was basic. Most staff learned on the job. Customers dealing with trainees on the line often ended up frustrated and confused. Sometimes the customer service reps seemed to be the last ones to know about new releases of products or new features. "We sure don't present a consistent face to our customers," Matt complained to his supervisory staff after receiving yet another complaint that different CSRs had provided contradictory advice. Second-level support was minimal because it cost more to provide.

Online data about products were available, but the search features were not strong and information about each product was presented in the format of the company that had originally developed it. Thus, the E-Z RP information looked different from the Web-Spider information and from the Delphi-Plus information, making it harder to flip from one call to the next. Even more frustrating for the CSRs was the fact that they had few mechanisms for feeding back common problems to the development teams. There was an online form for customer complaints but no means for the CSRs themselves to make suggestions and recommendations. On the surface, it seemed to Matt that the company didn't really care about customer service and was simply providing the minimum it could.

Matt raised this issue with his new boss, the CIO of Datatronics, in their first meeting after he'd been on the job about three weeks. "It seems to me that we see customer service as more of a cost center than as a means to learn more about our products and our customers' needs," he said. "Are we just giving lip service to the term *customer service*? Do our executives know how bad our service is?"

Joel McGivern had given him a quick, penetrating look as if he were wondering about Matt's motivation for the comment. "We care," said Joel drily, "about as much as it takes to keep our customers from switching to the other product. Our job is to find the right balance between saving money and saving our customers. If that seems harsh, it's the way of the world right now. We're in business to make a buck, not provide red-carpet service. It's dog-eat-dog out there, and our competitors are all looking for ways to beat our prices. Our efforts have to be focused on new products and new features, not on necessary evils like customer service."

"I suppose," said Matt dubiously. "But if we could delight our customers with our ability to assist them, if we could get to know their needs better so we could design a better product that wouldn't need as much support, and if we could use our center to develop business skills in our staff that we could use in the business, wouldn't that be worth something? And who says that customers don't want good service and might not be prepared to pay for it?"

"Absolutely no one wants to pay additional service fees," growled Joel. "We've tried that, and it doesn't work. Don't go there."

"Okay," said Matt. "But I worry that we're losing customers with this level of service. We certainly benefited from your attitude at E-Z RP, and I think our service was one of the reasons why you acquired us in the first place and why you wanted me in this job."

Joel looked thoughtful. "I'm not saying that there's no room for improvement," he said. "And if you make a good case for it, I might even be able to get you a little more money—on a project basis, not to increase our base operating costs. If you want to give it a go, give me your top ideas next week—with costs and time lines, mind you—and if I like them, I'm willing to take them to the steering committee for extra funding. In the meantime, however, I'd also like to know what you could do to improve things without any extra money." He paused and then smiled. "I hate those so-called 'customer help' lines as much as you do."

Discussion Questions

1. Outline the specific information that Matt should collect to build a case for improving customer service at Datatronics.
2. Describe your top ideas for Matt to present to Joel next week.
3. How would Matt get Joel to support his ideas?

17 Application Portfolio Management[1]

A ccording to many industry assessments, the typical IT organization spends as much as 80 percent of its human and capital resources maintaining an ever-growing inventory of applications and supporting infrastructure (Serena 2007). Although no one argues with the importance of maintaining applications (after all, they do run the business), everyone is concerned with rebalancing the IT budget allocation to increase the discretionary spend by decreasing the maintenance spend, ensuring that the set of applications is well aligned with business needs, and positioning the organization technologically to respond to future initiatives. Collectively, this activity has come to be known as "application portfolio management" (APM).

Formally, APM is the ongoing management process of categorization, assessment, and rationalization of the IT application portfolio. It allows organizations to identify which applications to maintain, invest in, replace, or retire, and it can have significant impact on the selection of new business applications and the projects required to deliver them. The overall goal of APM is to enable organizations to determine the best approach for IT to meet business demands from both a tactical and strategic perspective through the use of capital and operating funds allocated to building and maintaining applications. APM typically includes an analysis of operating and capital expenses by application, demand analysis (i.e., assessing business demand at the application level to determine its strategic and tactical business drivers), and application portfolio analysis (i.e., the current versus the desired state of the application portfolio in terms of both technology and business value).

Although APM is not a new idea, it may be one whose time has come. There are many espoused benefits of APM, including reduction of the cost and complexity of the applications portfolio, reduction or elimination of redundant functionality, optimization

---

[1] This chapter is based on the authors' previously published article, McKeen, J. D., and H. A. Smith. "Application Portfolio Management." *Communications of the Association for Information Systems* 26, no. 9 (March 2010): 157–70. Reproduced by permission of the Association for Information Systems.

of IT assets across different applications and functions, greater alignment with the business, better business decisions regarding technology, and an effective means of communicating the contribution of IT to the overall organization.

This chapter begins by examining the current status of IT applications in organizations. It then examines the notions of a portfolio perspective as it applies to applications (in contrast to a portfolio of financial assets) and outlines the specific benefits of such a perspective. Implementing a successful APM initiative requires three key capabilities—strategy and governance, inventory management, and reporting and rationalization—which are described in detail. The chapter concludes with some key lessons learned by organizations having invested in APM.

THE APPLICATIONS QUAGMIRE

Born of autonomous business-unit-level decision making and mergers and acquisitions, many IT organizations manage multiple ERP applications, knowledge management systems, and BI and reporting tools. All are maintained and periodically upgraded, leading to costly duplication and unnecessary complexity in IT operations. Left unchecked, the demands on the IT organization to simply maintain its existing inventory of applications threatens to consume the capacity to deliver new projects. (Serena 2007)

The proliferation of application systems within organizations is legendary. Built over time to serve an ever-changing set of business requirements, such systems span generations of technologies (e.g., hardware, software, systems, and methodologies), many of which are now obsolete and unsupported by the vendor community, are host to countless "workarounds," remain poorly documented, depend on the knowledge of a rapidly retiring workforce, and yet continue to support the key operations of the organization. Some (if not many) of these application systems have never been revisited to ascertain their ongoing contribution to the business. Based on decisions made by separate business units, many applications duplicate the functionality of others and are clearly redundant, and others have become unnecessary but have managed to escape detection. Accounts of organizations continuing to pay licensing fees for decommissioned software and supporting 27 different payroll systems all attest to the level of disarray that typically exists in large organizations. The full impact of such a quagmire becomes apparent either when virtually the entire IT budget is consumed by maintenance and/or when an organization attempts to integrate its suite of applications with those of an acquiring firm—whichever comes first.

Cause and effect are straightforward. The number of applications grows due to the practice of continually adding new applications without eliminating old ones. As it grows, the number of interfaces increases exponentially as does the number of complex and often proprietary enterprise application integration (EAI) solutions to "bridge" these disparate systems. The combined effect is to increase the frequency of (and costs of supporting) redundant systems, data, and capabilities across the organization. As their number and complexity grow, so does the workload and, without expanding IT budgets and headcounts commensurably, so does the portion of the IT budget devoted to maintenance and operations. From a management perspective, organizations are left with shrinking discretionary funds for new IT development and find themselves unable to assess the capability or measure the adequacy and value of current application support structures, track dependencies of business processes on applications, determine where money is being spent, and map IT investments to business objectives. Thus, in many organizations, the suite of IT applications has become unmanageable.

But while the cause and effect are identifiable, remedies are not easily obtained. The first obstacle is resources:

> The practice of continually adding to the IT burden while holding IT budgets and head counts relatively flat is obviously problematic. Yet that's exactly what many companies have done since the early 2000s. And this practice is one of the reasons why many CIOs feel that they simply don't have enough resources to meet internal demand for IT. (Gomolski 2004)

A second barrier is that few business managers want to give up any application once it's installed. In their minds, the agony of change is clearly not worth the rewards. "Some applications are so old that nobody remembers who ordered them" (Gomolski 2004, 29).

The third impediment, and perhaps the most severe, is the fact that IT often lacks the political clout to make business managers engage in an exercise to rationalize applications across the enterprise in order to decommission some applications.

THE BENEFITS OF A PORTFOLIO PERSPECTIVE

A part of the application dilemma is the lack of a portfolio perspective. Historically, organizations have opted to evaluate applications exclusively on their own merits—a practice that can easily promulgate unique systems across any business unit that can justify the expense. One manager claimed that this practice results in "a stream of one-off decisions... where each decision is innocent enough but, sooner or later, you are in a mess... sort of like walking off a cliff using baby steps."

In contrast, adopting a "portfolio" perspective means evaluating new and existing applications collectively on an ongoing basis to determine which applications provide value to the business in order to support decisions to replace, retire, or further invest in applications across the enterprise. The portfolio approach is universal in finance and provides a point of comparison. Boivie (2003) presents the following analogy:

> Just imagine you bought stock a decade ago for a lot of money, a good investment at the time, but then you did not review its value over the intervening years. Merely sitting on the stock may have been the right thing to do. Then again, you may have missed opportunities to invest more profitably elsewhere if the company was not doing well, or to invest more in the stock if it was profitable. Obviously this is not a wise way to handle your investment, but it's exactly what many companies are doing when it comes to investments in their IT applications!

TABLE 17.1	**Managing IT Applications as a Financial Portfolio**

Investment Portfolio Management	Application Portfolio Management
Professional management but the client owns the portfolio.	Professional management but the business owns the portfolio.
Personal financial portfolio balanced across investments in • equities • fixed income • cash	Application portfolio balanced across investments in • new applications • currency (maintenance, enhancements, upgrades) • retiring/decommissioning
Client directs investment where needed (e.g., 50% equities, 40% fixed, 10% cash).	Business directs investments where needed (e.g., 40% new applications, 30% currency, 30% decommissioning).
Client provides direction on diversity across investments (e.g., investment in one fund would exclude/augment investment in other funds).	Business provides direction on diversity of investment (e.g., investment in one business capability might exclude/augment investment in another).
Client receives quarterly updates on its portfolio health and an annual report.	Business receives quarterly updates on application portfolio health and an annual report.
New investments are evaluated on their impact on the overall portfolio as well as on their own merits.	New applications are evaluated on their impact on the overall portfolio as well as on their own merits.

Kramer (2006) concurs that application portfolio management is similar to the approach used by portfolio managers at money management firms where "investment officers continually seek to optimize their portfolios by assessing holdings and selling off assets that no longer are performing." It is suggested that "the same approach can be used by technology executives, especially when evaluating the applications in their portfolios and deciding which ones to continue funding, which to pull back on, and which to sunset or kill." One firm highlighted the similarities between investment portfolio management and applications portfolio management (see Table 17.1) in order to advocate for adopting a portfolio approach for IT applications.

The focus group suggested that the requirement for all new investments (i.e., IT applications) to be evaluated relative to all existing (i.e., past) investments within the portfolio is arguably the critical benefit provided by adopting a portfolio perspective. The group urged caution, however, due to the differences between a portfolio of financial assets (e.g., stocks and bonds) and one of IT applications. With the former, we assume a degree of independence among assets that rarely exists with applications. According to one writer (Anonymous 2008), "while financial planners can sell an underperforming stock, CIOs will likely find it far more difficult to dispose of an unwieldy application." Applications are rarely stand-alone; business functionality is often delivered by an integrated web of applications that cannot be separated piecemeal. As a result, diversification strategies can be difficult where IT assets are highly interdependent and deliver returns only collectively (Kasargod and Bondugula 2005).

A portfolio perspective forces the linkage between the set of existing applications (i.e., the applications portfolio) and the set of potential applications (i.e., the project portfolio). The linkage is bidirectional—that is, potential applications must be evaluated against existing applications and vice versa. Caruso (2007) differentiates these as follows:

- *Application portfolio.* The focus of the application portfolio is on the spending for established applications, trying to balance expense against value. These applications may be assessed for their contribution to corporate profitability and also on nonfinancial criteria such as stability, usability, and technical obsolescence.
- *Project portfolio.* Management of the project portfolio focuses on future spending, attempting to balance IT cost-reduction efforts and investments to develop new capabilities with technology and application upgrades.

The focus group suggested that organizations have focused most of their attention on new projects which has, in part, resulted in the applications quagmire previously described. The focus of this chapter is on application portfolio management. It argues that the effectiveness of the project portfolio can be enhanced substantially by managing the application portfolio much more judiciously. This linkage is made explicit later in the chapter.

The benefits to be realized by adopting an applications portfolio perspective are significant. The focus group was polled to solicit the benefits that their organizations had identified. These benefits were then grouped into the three categories, as suggested by Caruso (2007) and are presented in Table 17.2.

The list of benefits is impressive. To put them into perspective, a number of comments are in order. First, if the benefits to be realized are this substantial, why haven't organizations moved more aggressively to enact APM practices? The short answer is that APM has been difficult to fund and, once funded, represents an enormous management challenge. Second, the majority of these are "anticipated" benefits as they have yet to be reaped by focus group firms. Third, APM requires the development of a number of related activities (described in the latter sections of this chapter). Although benefits are realized during individual activities, the most significant benefits are not realized until most, if not all, of these capabilities have been completed. Finally, APM involves a different way of approaching IT investments—a collective view of all IT applications across the enterprise—which has cultural and political ramifications for organizations. The good news is that organizations that are well advanced in APM have realized significant benefits. We highlight one such firm in Table 17.3.

MAKING APM HAPPEN

Application portfolio management presents a significant management challenge and success requires the commitment of considerable organizational resources. The focus group suggested that APM involves the development of three interrelated capabilities. The first capability is the articulation of a strategy including goals, deliverables, and

TABLE 17.2	A List of APM Benefits

1. Visibility into where money is being spent, which ultimately provides the baseline to measure value creation
   a. Increasing the ease of determining which legacy applications are to be retired.
   b. Simplifying the technical environment and lowering operating costs.
   c. Reducing the number of applications and optimizing spending on application maintenance.
   d. Increasing the predictability of measuring service delivery for project selection.
   e. An enterprise view of all applications allowing for ease of reporting (e.g., How many applications use Sybase? How many systems support sales reporting?)
   f. A common view of enterprise technology assets improving reuse and sharing across the enterprise.
   g. Clarity over maintenance and support spending.
   h. Ability to manage and track business controls and regulatory compliance of all applications.

2. Prioritization of applications across multiple dimensions, including value to the business, urgency, and financial return
   a. Funding the right application effort by providing quick access to validated information in support of business cases for investment.
   b. Providing better project solutions by identifying available capabilities for reuse.
   c. Providing criteria to drive application rationalization and monitor impacts.
   d. Providing an "end state" view for all applications, which helps direct roadmaps and enables progress reporting.
   e. Expediting prioritization discussions and executive decision making.
   f. Driving IT refurbishment initiatives.

3. A mechanism to ensure that applications map directly to business objectives
   a. Aligning business and IT efforts with business processes by providing (1) clarity of the application landscape, leading to synergies across different business units, and the pursuit of a global systems architecture; and (2) insight into gaps or redundancies in the current portfolio, thereby enhancing the ability to manage risk effectively and efficiently.
   b. Enabling productive discussion with senior management regarding IT's contribution to business value.
   c. Identifying the strategic and high business value applications, thereby allowing the redirection of some of the funding previously used for nonstrategic applications.
   d. Enabling easy and effectively analysis of impacts to applications from changing business conditions.
   e. Improving the focus and direction of investments.
   f. Developing a vehicle to drive the technical portfolio to the "right" mix, based on strategy, architecture, TCO, and internal skill sets.
   g. Prioritizing efforts and focus for IT delivery—ensuring the right skills are in place to support business requirements.

a set of governance procedures to guide the management of the application portfolio. Next is the creation of an applications inventory to monitor key attributes of existing applications. The third capability involves building an analysis and reporting capability in order to rationalize the applications portfolio according to the strategy established.

TABLE 17.3	An APM Case Study

Vision

- Reverse the rising tide of application maintenance costs.
- Fund strategic development efforts from reduced support and maintenance costs.
- Align IT with business goals.

Challenge

- Assess current portfolio of applications.
- Establish targets, savings strategies, and supporting plans.
- Data currency and accuracy.

Solution

- Identify redundant or obsolete applications and set end-of-year targets for retiring a committed percentage of the total.
- Classify applications by their strategic value and shift maintenance support focus to highly strategic applications.
- Rank applications with a quality score; applications failing to meet a baseline are selected for preventive maintenance, code simplification, and maintainability.
- Migrate an increasing share of maintenance work to lower-case geographies.

Value

- Cut applications by 70%.
- Establish rigorous priorities—SLAs now vary based on objective business criteria.
- Reengineered applications—defects down 58% and maintenance costs down 20%.
- Relocated work—significant maintenance is now performed in countries with costs 60–70% lower than previously.

These capabilities (depicted in Figure 17.1), although distinct, are closely interrelated and work synergistically.[2] To deliver value with APM, organizations must establish all three capabilities. Experience suggests that organizations typically start by inventorying applications and work from the middle out to refine their APM strategy (and how it is governed) as well as to establish efforts to rationalize their applications portfolio. As such, APM represents a process of continual refinement. Fortunately, experience also suggests that there are real benefits to be reaped from the successful development of each capability. These capabilities are described in detail next.

Capability 1: Strategy and Governance

There are many different reasons to adopt application portfolio management. At one firm, the complexity of the IT application portfolio had increased to the point of becoming unmanageable. The firm viewed APM as the means to gain some measure of control over a burgeoning collection of disjointed IT applications. Another firm had set an architectural direction and established an IT roadmap and viewed APM as a way

---

[2] The focus group did not see APM as a "stage" model where organizations advance through a prescribed set of stages. Instead they identified three highly interrelated "capabilities" that organizations need to establish in order to advance their application portfolio management.

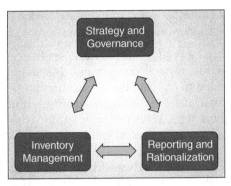

FIGURE 17.1 Key APM Capabilities

to "put some teeth" into the enforcement of these policies. At a third firm, the manager of a strategic business unit was frustrated over escalating annual IT costs and the "pile of applications" that seemed to have "little connection to actual business services." A simple poll of the focus group, however, suggested that APM tended to be an IT-led initiative as opposed to a business initiative—a fact that has implications for launching and funding APM.

To get an APM initiative underway, it is necessary to build a business case. How this is done depends on the firm's strategy. According to one manager, "[I]f APM is positioned as inventory management, you'll never get the business to pay for it." In his organization, APM was promoted as a cost-reduction initiative focused on the elimination of unused (or underused) applications, unnecessary software licenses, duplicated data, and redundant applications. The business case included an aggressive schedule of declining IT costs to the business. In another organization, the APM initiative is supported internally by the IT organization and driven largely by the enterprise architecture group. In fact, the business is unaware of its APM program. In a third organization, APM was couched within the overall strategy of transforming the business. The argument was that APM could "reduce ongoing support costs for existing applications in order to re-direct that IT spend into business transformation." The business case included metrics and a quarterly reporting structure to ensure that savings targets were obtained. The conclusion reached by the focus group was that each organization is unique and, given the wide variety of potential APM benefits, the best strategy is to attach APM to a broader enterprise goal. They felt that if APM is attempted solely within the IT organization without business backing, it is less likely to produce the full range of benefits.

The strategy selected to launch APM has direct ramifications for the information collected about each application (i.e., the second capability—inventory management) as well as what information is reported and tracked by senior management (i.e., the third capability—reporting and rationalization). In the next section of this chapter, we present a comprehensive set of information that could be collected for IT applications within the portfolio. Organizations, depending on their APM strategy, may focus on a subset of this information and develop a reporting and rationalization capability built on this information.

APM strategy and governance are linked; if strategy is the destination, then governance is the map. According to one manager, governance is "a set of policies, procedures, and rules that guide decisions and define decision rights in an organization." Application portfolio governance answers three questions:

1. *What decisions need to be made?* This addresses the types and/or categories of decisions often referred to as decision domains. It also links the decisions with the processes that are needed to manage the application portfolio.
2. *Who should make these decisions?* This addresses the roles and accountabilities for decision makers (e.g., who provides input, who approves and has final authority). This links the decisions to be made (the "what") with the decision makers (the "who").
3. *How are these decisions made?* This addresses the structures and processes for decision making (e.g., the architecture review board). This links the decisions to be made (the "what") with the people/roles (the "who") involved in decision making with the timelines and mechanisms for making those decisions (the "how").

On an ongoing basis, organizations introduce new applications and (infrequently) retire old applications. The key difference with APM is that these applications are managed holistically across the enterprise on a much more formalized and less piecemeal basis. The goal is to discover synergies as well as duplication, alternative (and less costly) methods for providing business services, and rebalancing (or rationalizing) the portfolio of applications with regard to age, capability, and/or technical health. This represents a significant organizational change that impacts governance procedures directly. According to one IT manager, "no longer can business units acquire an IT application that duplicates existing functionality without scrutiny by the APM police." With the adoption of APM governance procedures, such actions become visible at high levels within the organization.

How new governance procedures are actually implemented varies by organization. However, the focus group suggested that effective APM governance must be both freestanding (in order to have visibility and impact) as well as closely integrated within the framework of existing governance mechanisms (in order to effect the status quo). As an example, the IT project selection committee must consider the impact of prospective IT projects on the existing portfolio of enterprise applications if the organization is to achieve its APM rationalization goals regarding architecture and/or functionality. That is, the APM governance processes must leverage existing organizational governance processes, including architectural reviews, exception process handling, IT delivery processes, strategic planning and annual budgeting, and technology reinvestment and renewal. One manager shared his enterprise IT governance framework to demonstrate where and how APM was situated within other established processes (see Figure 17.2).

Effective governance starts with ownership, which entails responsibilities and accountabilities. At a tactical level, each IT application should have an owner. This individual is held responsible for the ultimate disposition of the application—that is, when it is enhanced, refurbished, or decommissioned. The sense of the focus group was that the application owner should be a business manager—except for internal IT applications. Each application should have a business owner, and it is common to also appoint a custodian whose key duty is to keep the information current. Given the technical nature of the application information (see Appendix A), the custodian is typically an IT employee, perhaps an account manager or someone within the enterprise architecture group.

With stewardship (i.e., owner and custodian) assigned for major applications, the next level of governance is the portfolio level. A management committee comprised

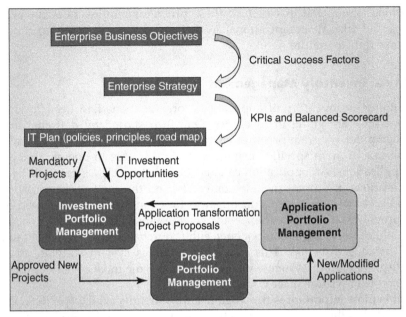

FIGURE 17.2   Positioning APM within an Enterprise IT Governance Framework

of application owners, senior enterprise architects, and IT planners/strategists should meet regularly, perhaps quarterly, to make decisions regarding the disposition of applications within the overall portfolio. This committee would report to the senior executive on portfolio activities, performance toward goal achievement, and establishment of linkages to fiscal planning and strategy. In very large organizations, an additional committee of portfolio owners might also be required.

Effective governance is critical for overcoming a number of problems common during the initial phases of APM. Some of the challenges experienced by the focus group included the following:

- Application owners are accountable to execute the process, but no one has defined who (or what body) is accountable for the process itself or what governance practices should be applied to make it happen.
- Managing applications requires additional maturity for defining a roadmap for the portfolio. Without this, some applications are well planned while the overall portfolio is not.
- The classification criteria for applications are in flux and lack an executive process for validating the ratings.
- Application assessments are not taken seriously by executive owners ("Everything is critical"), which erodes the credibility of the process and the overall value of the exercise of managing applications as a portfolio.
- Business managers lack awareness and accountability.
- There is difficulty from the "supply" side—for example, there is reluctance to take ownership of the data to ensure its integrity, quality, and timeliness.
- Demand-side aggression pushes for more and more application attributes.

The focus group felt that each of these problems requires effective governance procedures. But like all organizational initiatives, changes to existing routines and methods take time to mature.

Capability 2: Inventory Management

Before building an inventory of applications, organizations first need to know what applications they are going to inventory. One firm started by defining an application as a computer program or set of computer instructions that allows end users to accomplish one of more specific business tasks and is able to operate independently of other applications. An application can also be a distinct data store used by multiple other applications. Examples include commercial off-the-shelf packages, applications written in Excel that perform specific business functions, custom-developed computer software programs, a data warehouse and/or the reporting applications accessing it, and/or modules, services, or components, either purchased or custom built to perform a specific business function. This definition excludes system software or platform software (e.g., operating systems, device drivers, or diagnostic tools), programming software, and user-written macros and scripts.

What is most important is that organizations identify which specific applications will be included in the portfolio to be actively managed. One firm excluded all applications not explicitly managed by IT (e.g., Excel spreadsheets developed by managers for analytical purposes), another focused only on "major" applications according to size, and a third firm only included "business-critical" applications. This decision has direct implications for the size of the APM effort. The organization that limited its portfolio to business-critical applications reduced the portfolio to 180 applications from 1,200—a significant reduction in the amount of effort required. The organization's decision to limit (and therefore focus) its application portfolio depends on the strategy outlined in the first step.

With inclusion criteria established, organizations must then identify what specific information about applications will need to be captured. A list of possible information items gathered from the members of the focus group is presented in Appendix A. These items are categorized according to the following five headings:

- *General application information* is the information used to explicitly and clearly identify an application, distinct from all other applications, and provide a basic understanding of its functionality.
- *Application categorization* is the information providing criteria used to group applications for comparison and portfolio management purposes (e.g., business capability provided, life cycle status).
- *Technical condition* provides the overall rating of the technical quality of the application, including various elements of risk (e.g., development language, operating system, architecture).
- *Business value* provides an overall rating of the value of the application to the business (e.g., business criticality, user base, effectiveness).
- *Support cost* captures the order of magnitude of the overall cost of an application after deployment. It includes maintenance and support costs (including upgrades) but not the initial purchase, development, or deployment costs.

The focus group could not overstate the importance and criticality of selecting the information to be maintained as part of the application inventory as this information dictates the types of analyses that can be performed after the fact (as outlined in the next section). Once selected, the task of capturing application information and keeping it current is a monumental effort. Without clear ownership of the information and assigned responsibilities for a custodial function, attempts at application portfolio management typically falter. One of the key motivations for establishing a strict information regime is the delivery of demonstrable benefits from the exercise. These are discussed in the next section.

Capability 3: Reporting and Rationalization

With an application inventory established, a set of standard parameter-driven reports can be produced to monitor the status of all existing applications so management can readily ascertain the health of any specific application or the overall health of the portfolio of applications. One firm has a collection of standard reports that analyze the number of applications and their costs, how business capabilities are supported and where duplication exists, breakdowns of annual application costs, application life-cycle patterns, and reuse options for future projects. One widely adopted report compares applications on the basis of business value, technical condition, and cost (see Figure 17.3). As depicted, this chart helps organizations rationalize their IT application portfolio by tracking applications over time as they become less important to the business and/or lose technical currency. One organization found that eliminating those applications in the bottom left of the quadrant—which provide limited business benefit, often at a significant cost—can be a "combination of quick hits and longer-term initiatives." Even managers reluctant to retire a business application can be convinced with evidence of the full-support costs.

Once the application inventory is assembled, the number of ways to "slice and dice" the information is unlimited and the value obtained is commensurate. One

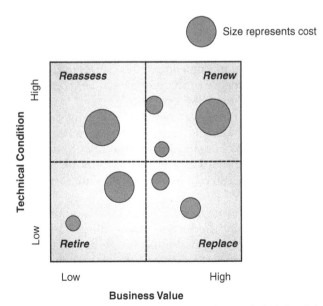

FIGURE 17.3 Application Portfolio Highlighting Business Value, Technical Condition, and Cost

manager claimed that for the first time her organization is able to answer questions such as "How many applications use Sybase?" and "How many systems support sales reporting"? The provision of ad hoc reporting capability is a quick way to discover the number of current licenses with a specific vendor and/or to assess the costs of providing specific business services. Ultimately, organizations need to know their true costs of doing business in order to explore options for providing different customer services. The information produced by analyzing the IT application portfolio takes organizations a huge step closer to this level of understanding and optimization.

The information needs supported by an application inventory vary by stakeholder. The IT organization wants to map business functionality against applications; the risk, audit, and security teams are most interested in regulatory compliance and a risk management perspective; and business teams are interested in understanding the costs and business value of the applications they use. Even within IT, different groups (e.g., solutions delivery, information security, production support, executive management, business continuity, regulatory compliance, infrastructure, architecture, and planning) have information needs that are unique from the application portfolio. For this reason, most firms mandate a single application portfolio capable of supporting many different views at different levels as well as a composite view of the entire portfolio. One manager explained this by claiming that although different views of the portfolio satisfy individual groups within her organization, the "consolidated view ultimately demonstrates the effectiveness of monitoring and tracking business performance of the assets across the entire IT application portfolio."

KEY LESSONS LEARNED

The following represent some of the lessons learned based on the collective experience of the members of the focus group:

- *Balance demand and supply.* Managers tend to push for the inclusion of more and different application attributes as well as more reports of infinite variety (the "demand" side) while balking at assuming ownership of this data in order to ensure its integrity, quality, and timeliness (the "supply" side). When launching an APM initiative, clear governance procedures should be established to govern regular enhancements and releases for APM reporting.
- *Look for quick wins.* Gaining awareness and acceptance of an APM initiative can be an uphill struggle. This effort is aided greatly by capturing a number of "quick wins" early on. For example, organizations should look carefully at the possibility of decommissioning applications as a ready source of immediate and visible wins that impact the bottom line directly. Reuse provides midterm wins, and rationalization provides longer-term wins.
- *Capture data at key life stages.* It is a mistake to wait to capture data when applications are already in production. Data should be captured at multiple stages—when the application is first approved, when in testing, when promoted to production, during significant modifications, and when retired. As soon as data are captured and made available, the organization can benefit. For example, knowing the attributes of applications under development can be valuable for planning/budgeting purposes and ultimately enables better project solutions.

- *Tie APM to TCO initiatives together.* If a total cost of ownership (TCO) initiative is underway, ensure that the APM is closely tied to the TCO initiative. Much of the information captured as part of the APM initiative will support the TCO initiative—and vice versa. Knowing this relationship in advance will ensure that the data are captured to facilitate both purposes. The long-term savings can be significant.
- *Provide an application "end-state" view.* It is important to provide current information about applications, but it is equally important to provide an end-state view indicating the application's future trajectory. This facilitates a planned and orderly evolution toward retirement for applications as well as key information for business planning (e.g., roadmaps, gap reporting, and progress reporting).
- *Communicate APM benefits.* Gaining awareness and acceptance of an APM initiative is a constant struggle. Organizations must seek opportunities to communicate why this initiative is underway, what results have been realized, and what the next stages to be accomplished are. Effective communication is even more important in situations where the APM initiative is being driven internally by the IT organization.

Conclusion

This chapter provides guidance to those investigating APM and/or planning to launch an APM initiative. Application portfolio management promises significant benefits to adopting organizations. Obtaining those benefits, however, requires the development of three mutually reinforcing capabilities. The first capability is the development an APM strategy buttressed with governance procedures, the second is the creation of an application inventory, and the third is a reporting capability built to align the application portfolio with the established strategy. Each of these capabilities provides stand-alone benefits, but together they enable an organization to optimize its IT application assets, reduce the cost and complexity of its portfolio, reduce or eliminate redundant functionality, facilitate better business decisions regarding technology, and effectively communicate the contribution of IT to the overall organization.

References

Anonymous. "Maximizing IT Investment." *Wall Street & Technology*, April 2008.

Boivie, C. A. "Taking Stock of Your Portfolio: Do You Have a Good Idea of the Value of Your IT Applications, Both Old and New?" *CIO Canada* 11, no. 10 (October 2003).

Caruso, D. "Application Portfolio Management: A Necessity for Future IT." *Manufacturing Business Technology* 25, no. 10 (October 2007): 48.

Gomolski, B. "Cleaning House." *Computerworld* 38, no. 51 (December 2004).

Kasargod, D., and Bondugula, K. "Application Portfolio Management." *Infosys* (April 2005): 1–8. Originally published in www.gtnews.com.

Kramer, L. "CIO Challenge: Application Portfolio Management." *Wall Street & Technology*, May 2006.

Serena Software Inc. "Application Portfolio Management (APM): Solving the Challenges of APM with Serena® Mariner®," 2007. www.serena.com/docs/repository/products/mariner/datasheet-apm-mariner.pdf (accessed March 12, 2011).

APPENDIX A

Application Information

A) *General application information* is the information used to explicitly and clearly identify an application, distinct from all other applications, and provide a basic understanding of its functionality.

- Name—the name that uniquely identifies the application
- Short name—an abbreviation or acronym that is likely a unique identifier of the application and is used for reporting when there is not room to use the application's full name
- Description—a more extensive description of the application typically focusing on its functional scope
- Portfolio owner—the title of the portfolio owner of the application and the name of the person currently filling that role (The portfolio owner is typically filled by someone at VP level or higher.)
- Stakeholders—key people (by name and title) that could have been identified as a portfolio owner if multiple portfolio owners were allowed
- Application owner—the title of the portfolio owner's delegate (if there is one) and the name of the person currently filling that role (The application owner is typically someone reporting to the portfolio owner and empowered to make decisions relating to the ongoing use and evolution of the application. The application owner role is typically filled by someone below the VP level.)
- Business consultant—the name of the IT–business liaison (This person is part of the IT organization but is responsible for the relationship with the business unit)
- Internally versus externally developed—states whether the application was developed internally (by any business or IT organization) or whether it was purchased from an external vendor
- Vendor—the name of the vendor that owns the application (For internally developed applications, this should be the business unit or IT unit that is responsible for maintaining the application, i.e., provides the resources and funding.)
- Product name—the name of the product (Only required when a product has an explicit name that is not the vendor name.)
- Version number—the complete version number of the application that is in production
- Current version—the most current version number in full release by the vendor
- Implementation date—the year and month that the solution went into production
- Last major upgrade—the year and month that the last major upgrade went into production (Major upgrades typically require a project approach, explicit funding, training, and planning to avoid downtime, etc. This field is blank if there has not been a major upgrade after the implementation date.)

- Last minor upgrade—the year and month that the last minor upgrade went into production (Minor upgrades are typically upgrades that can be performed during regularly scheduled maintenance windows and can be performed as part of routine application maintenance. This field is blank if there has not been a minor upgrade after the last major upgrade, e.g., point releases, security patches.)
- Next scheduled review—the year and month that the application profile should next be reviewed (By default, this should be one year from the current review, but will be updated as assessment schedules are developed.)

B) *Application categorization* is the information providing a variety of criteria/data used to group applications for comparison and portfolio management purposes.

- Application scope—identifies the breadth of use of the application across the organization (e.g., enterprise, multidivisional, divisional, multidepartmental, departmental, individual users)
- Life-cycle status—identifies the life-cycle stage that the application is in (e.g., emerging, standard, contained, retirement target, retired)
- SBUs used by—a choice of one or more business divisions that use the application
- SBUs used for—a choice of one or more business divisions that the application is used on behalf of
- Application capability—broad categories of capability that applications provide (e.g., supply chain management [SCM] planning, SCM execution, SCM procurement)
- Application subcapabilities—subcapabilities of functionality that applications provide (A single application will often provide functionality covering multiple subcapabilities.)
- Support organization—identifies the organizational support for the application (e.g., IT organization, third party, business unit)
- Recoverability—the requirement to be able to recover the application in the event of a disaster and the ability to perform that recovery
- Application type—a genera 1 categorization of the application's use of data (e.g., analytical/reporting, transactional, collaborative, hybrid)
- Application profile—a general categorization of the application's functional profile (e.g., suite, best of breed, in-house.)

C) *Technical condition* provides the overall rating of the technical quality of the application, including various elements of risk.

- Development language—the programming languages that the application is developed with (The language element should address programming code running on the server, client, database, middleware, etc.)
- Operation system(s)—the operating systems required for all layers of the application where there are application-specific requirements (This can be applied to the server, database, middleware, client, etc. This evaluation categorization does not address the Web browser in a Web-based application.)
- Hardware platforms—the hardware platforms required for all layers of the application where there are application-specific requirements (This can be applied to the server, database, middleware, client, etc.)

- Database/data model—the database platform and database model (i.e., data architecture) that the application is tied to (or built on)
- Integration—the integration tools and model used to integrate the applications with other applications (The "model" aspect of this criterion is closely related to the overall architecture of the systems but specifically looks at the framework/approach used for integration.)
- Architecture—the application architecture, technology patterns, and so on that define "how" different elements of technology were put together to create the application, for example, NET, J2EE, J2SE, OO, Client/Server, Web-based, and thin-client. (This criterion also addresses the extensibility of the application—the ability of the applications to be modified to meet future/changing functional requirements.)
- Security—the capability of the application to (1) limit access to data and functionality to specific users and/or groups and (2) provide audit information related to functions performed (or attempted to be performed) on the data viewed (or attempted to be viewed) by specific users (This metric addresses the application's native capabilities, the specific implementation/modification of those capabilities, and the security requirements of the organization.)
- Vendor viability—the likelihood that the vendor will remain strong in the relevant application market and industry vertical
- Vendor support—the ability and commitment of the vendor to provide support for the applications. (This includes the ability and commitment to provide new releases and patches to the application.)
- Key abilities—(1) availability of the application relative to user requirements identified in service level agreements (SLA), (2) scalability of the application to meet current and future user and transaction volumes, and (3) performance of the application in starting, retrieving information, and performing transactions
- User interface—the overall usability/intuitiveness of the application's interface (This is often reflected by training requirements, support requirements, online documentation, etc.)

D) *Business value* provides an overall rating of the value of the application to the business.

- Competitive advantage—the extent to which the application enables a capability that (1) increases revenue, (2) lowers cost, or (3) differentiates the company in the marketplace
- Business criticality—the extent to which the application materially affects the company's ability to conduct core business processes (i.e., sell, deliver, close financial books) (This includes the ability to meet regulatory requirements.)
- User base—the number and variety of users that use the application (This measure is adjusted to reflect the difference between causal/occasional users and power users, as well as internal versus external users. This measure also includes transaction volumes that the application performs to account for essential applications with few users but large transaction volumes that the business is dependent on.)

- Current effectiveness—ability of the application to meet current business requirements within the scope of the functionality it was intended to provide
- Future effectiveness—ability of the application to meet future business requirements within the scope of the functionality it was intended to provide and logical/reasonable extensions of that functionality.

E) *Support cost* captures the order of magnitude of the overall cost of an application after deployment. It includes maintenance and support costs (including upgrades) but not the initial purchase, development, or deployment costs.

- Elements included—license maintenance, other licensing fees, vendor/external support, internal support, and hardware
- Elements not included—PCs, network, telephony, or other shared services; end-user costs, such as time lost to support calls, downtime, and so on. (Typically these data are not readily available at the level of granularity required.)

CHAPTER

18 Managing IT Demand[1]

The need for demand management is well established in business. Gentle (2007) explains, "In order to manage planning, production, and delivery, any properly run business has to be able to balance orders for its products and services (i.e., demand) with its ability to produce them in terms of resource and scheduling constraints (i.e., supply). Otherwise it might produce too little of what is required, too much of what is not required, or deliver late, or have problems with product quality or customer satisfaction." Based on this, one might assume that IT organizations, being in the business of fulfilling organizational demand for their services, would have developed mature practices for managing IT demand. Nothing could be further from the truth. In fact, IT demand management has only recently been ranked as one of the top four priorities by IT leaders (Potter 2010).

This lack of attention is explained by the fact that IT managers have been preoccupied with the *supply* side; that is, delivering products and services faster, better, and cheaper. Concentrating on the supply side makes perfect sense for two reasons: first, it allows IT organizations to concentrate on the things that they can actually control; and second, most IT organizations interpret any role in manipulating IT demand as a political minefield to be conscientiously avoided. As a result, demand management practices have been underutilized. A study by the Hackett Group as reported by Betts (2009) concurs:

> IT has traditionally been more focused on how to meet ever-growing demand than on implementing processes to curb that demand and ensure that the highest value work gets done. As a result, demand management techniques are less mature than other cost control techniques.

What best explains the current interest is that IT demand management offers the means for IT organizations to work more effectively with their business partners. In fact,

---

[1] This chapter is based on the authors' previously published article, McKeen, J. D., H. A. Smith and P. Gonzalez, "Managing IT Demand." *Journal of Information Technology Management XXIII*, no. 2 (2012): 17–28. Reproduced by permission of the Association of Management.

some see demand management as the next frontier in IT cost efficiency (newScale 2010). They argue that focusing exclusively on the supply side of the equation without visibility into demand leaves IT organizations unable to perform effective capacity planning. The reality is that better demand management enables better supply management. In order to make good capacity plans, IT must understand the future needs of the business. According to newScale (2010),

> Demand management not only helps IT organizations to shape demand, it also helps them plan for demand and respond to changes in demand to meet business needs while controlling their IT budgets. This increased visibility into demand can help ensure more accurate and business-driven capacity planning.

So, after years of squeezing incremental costs out of the supply side of IT only to see those gains disappear into the vortex of mushrooming demands, perhaps it is time to turn attention to the demand side and tackle some key questions such as "How critical is the need for demand management?" If there is interest/pressure for demand management, where is this pressure coming from? What are the key drivers behind the demand for IT services? How does demand management impact the existing business–IT relationship? What are the key steps toward managing IT demand?

This chapter first examines the root causes of demand for IT services, the economics of demand management, and the importance of this issue. It then reviews a set of standard tools recommended for managing demand and concludes with identifying five key enablers vital for effective demand management.

UNDERSTANDING IT DEMAND

In order to better understand demand management, the focus group first discussed the root causes of IT demand. One manager suggested that IT demand is driven by two forces in her organization: "IT initiatives that deliver new capability to the business in support of the broader corporate strategy, and IT initiatives that are required from within to sustain IT's ability to deliver future work or new capabilities." She explained, "Although these drivers mostly represent market and investor pressures, IT is also driving change with its own renewal goals after years of underfunding." Another organization identified "historical autonomy, proliferation, lack of structured architecture and weak standards" as the key drivers of much of her organization's current demand for IT services. This particular organization was deluged with duplicate and, in some cases, redundant applications that collectively produced a "black hole" for IT resources.

Clearly IT demand needs to be considered from a development as well as an operational point of view. From an *operational* perspective, organizations need to "run" the business and this translates into baseline demand for IT. Organizations also need to "maintain" their IT assets and this too represents significant demand for IT resources. From a *development* perspective, IT is called upon to deliver new capability to enable the business to remain competitive in the marketplace. So, whether it is a "keep the lights on" or a "new channel to market" initiative, both place demands on (and compete for) available IT resources. One organization simply classifies IT demand as discretionary (i.e., strategic), maintenance (i.e., keep the lights on), and regulatory, which his organization light-heartedly refers to as "I want," "I need," and "I must," respectively.

IT demand management is best understood within an organizational context. First, the need to automate business processes and operations is unrelenting and, once automated, automated processes must be supported on an ongoing basis. Hence, the workload grows proportionally with the demand and increases year over year. Second, at any point in time, the level of IT capacity is relatively fixed, which limits IT's ability to satisfy demand (i.e., the supply side). Third, one way to increase capacity (again the supply side) is to offload certain tasks to third party suppliers (e.g., outsourcing network management). Most organizations exercise this option regularly in order to satisfy increased and increasing demand. Finally, the only way for organizations to "get ahead" of this dilemma is by proactively managing the demand for IT services. Ultimately this will do a better job of satisfying business needs for IT.

According to a Gartner survey (Potter 2010), 84 percent of IT organizations simply do not have the resources to meet enterprise expectations. This leaves only two possible responses. IT organizations can either "do more with less," which focuses on supply side activities (e.g., virtualization, data center consolidation, benchmarking, contract renegotiation) or they can "do less with less," which focuses on demand side activities (e.g., demand management, IT performance management, IT portfolio management, running IT like a business).[2] The first approach (i.e., doing more with less) is the quest for increased productivity and the reality is that IT organizations continually pursue enhanced productivity to remove costs from the business.

The second approach (i.e., doing less with less) differs dramatically from the pursuit of productivity and thus introduces a different set of challenges for IT organizations. Implicit within a strategy of "doing less with less" is the notion that perhaps not all of the requests for IT services are vital and that, by rationalizing these demands for IT services, the organization might benefit. So, where the goal of productivity is "doing things right" (i.e., internal efficiency), the goal of demand management is "doing the right things" (i.e., business effectiveness).

This helps to explain why IT organizations have preferred to address the supply side of the demand–supply gap. Certainly, it is much easier for IT organizations to exercise control over the supply side and, in fact, it is their prerogative to do so. But is IT in a position to shape the demand for IT services? According to Potter (2010), this "conjures up uncomfortable feelings among many IT leaders regarding the political process involved with chargeback and the behaviors created by approving or disapproving emotionally charged IT projects." So, perhaps the reason for the failure to address the demand side of the equation is a reluctance to say "no" to the business. The question is, after years of effort to support the business and to be seen as being accommodating, how does an IT organization tackle demand management whose goal is to question and ultimately rationalize the demand for IT services? As Cramm (2004) asks, "What right does IT have to tell the business what they can and cannot have?

---

[2] Gartner (Potter 2010) actually suggests four possible options. In addition to "doing more with less" and "doing less with less," IT organizations can "do more with more" and/or "do less with more." These two latter strategies, however, are only available within expanding economies or growing markets, respectively.

THE ECONOMICS OF DEMAND MANAGEMENT

The field of economics has used the concept of demand management for years. In its most elemental form, demand management is the "art or science of controlling economic demand to avoid a recession" (Wikipedia 2014a). The notion of demand management has also been focused to control consumer demand for environmentally sensitive goods. The economic notions of demand management that are most applicable for IT organizations, however, are those that apply to the "management of the distribution of, and access to, goods and services on the basis of needs" (Wikipedia 2014a). Here the tools are *policies* that allocate existing resources according to a hierarchy of neediness and the underlying idea is for "the government to use tools like interest rates, taxation, and public expenditure to change key economic decisions like consumption, investment, the balance of trade, and public sector borrowing resulting in an 'evening out' of the business cycle" (Wikipedia 2014a).

This latter view suggests how to approach demand management. Instead of asking IT organizations to act as "traffic cops" and/or imposing sanctions on capital spending to artificially curtail demand, the economics approach is to create a system of policies and procedures coupled with adequate governance to ensure that the allocation of scarce IT services goes to the highest-value opportunities (Cramm 2004). The goal is to capture and prioritize demand, assign resources based on business objectives, and engage in projects that deliver business benefits. But, as is frequently the case, what appears simple conceptually in reality presents a formidable set of challenges. To address these challenges, the focus group discussed three commonly used tools for demand management and identified what they considered to be five key organizational enablers for the effective management of IT demand.

THREE TOOLS FOR DEMAND MANAGEMENT

Most articles (e.g., Betts 2009) advocate the use of tools for managing the organizational demand for IT resources, including project portfolio management, service catalogs, and chargeback. These are described briefly with an accompanying explanation of how they work to shape demand.

- *Project portfolio management (PPM)*—These are processes designed to rationalize and prioritize IT investment decisions based on objective criteria. PPM allows an organization to understand and quantify business needs and the investments needed to deliver software to achieve those benefits (Hotle et al. 2010). With effective PPM, demands for IT resources are vetted in accordance with governance procedures that result in a justified list of IT investments that satisfy the needs of business leaders. IT demand is limited and shaped to the extent that only those projects that succeed in passing through the PPM process are funded. According to Cramm (2004), PPM results in a "multi-year forecast of IT spending that constrains overall demand and results in increased project scrutiny."
- *Service catalog*—Here, discrete IT service offerings are associated with a price per unit. As an example, hardware services might include costs for a standard desktop/laptop/tablet configuration and a standard smart phone configuration; application services might include costs for developing a business case, designing a solution, building a solution, and/or implementing a solution. According to Young (2011), a service catalog is a "service order- and demand-channeling mechanism intended to make it easier for end consumers to request and buy

things from IT." Knowing what is available and what it costs allows business managers to make informed demands for IT services and, to the degree that these services are standardized, shapes this demand appropriately. According to one manager, this clarification of IT services affects demand by "allowing managers to order from a menu rather than saying I'm hungry."

- *Chargeback*—This is a financial management technique that charges consumers according to the volume of IT services consumed (i.e., operations) or work done on their behalf (i.e., new development). Thus, IT demand is controlled through direct price-based allocation to business consumers as motivation to act rationally and to discourage unnecessary demands. This approach to demand management results in a set of IT investments that are justifiable and affordable by business managers.

The adoption of these strategies appears to be widespread. As a case in point, the organizations in the focus group have long deployed chargeback and PPM and most are in the process of building service catalogs. The benefits of these three strategies, according to newScale (2010), accrue independently and collectively:

> Best practices for demand management start with defining standardized services, exposing those services to customers via an IT service catalog, controlling and shaping demand through guided self-service, and providing cost transparency through showback or chargeback. The results: great adoption of cost-effective service options, consumption choices that result in lower IT costs, and effective planning to meet business needs and minimize over-capacity.

While acknowledging the usefulness of these three tools, the focus group characterized them as "necessary but insufficient." They argued that the benefits derived from these tools are often more IT-related than business-related. Focusing on lowering IT costs through self-guided service and minimizing overcapacity makes sense from an IT-perspective but neither of these guarantees that IT investments are focused on the "highest value" opportunities—the ultimate goal of demand management. In order to manage IT demand effectively, these tools must be accompanied by mechanisms that the group referred to as organizational enablers.

KEY ORGANIZATIONAL ENABLERS FOR EFFECTIVE DEMAND MANAGEMENT

Members argued that IT demand management is not a single process that an organization can identify. That is, in response to the question "How do you manage demand?," no organization could say "We use this process." Instead, the group suggested that demand management is a *developed organizational capability* that results from five key organizational enablers: strategic initiative management, application portfolio management, enterprise architecture, business-IT partnership, and governance and transparency. These key factors work synergistically with the tools previously described to enable effective demand management (see Figure 18.1). Having a successful application portfolio management (APM) initiative, for example, does not guarantee effective IT demand management but the absence of APM would definitely jeopardize the efficacy of demand management. Each of these key organizational enablers is described next.

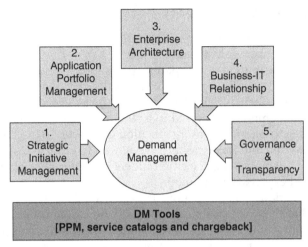

FIGURE 18.1 Tools and Key Enablers of Demand Management

Strategic Initiative Management

Strategic initiative management is the organizational mechanism for prioritizing and funding IT investments at the *enterprise* level. Although the focus is primarily on large discretionary/strategic investments, as the name implies, this process also adjudicates large infrastructure projects. One organization established a strategic project office (SPO) with a mandate to provide "governance and direction over enterprise-wide project approvals and planning to ensure these investments are aligned with the organization's core strategies." With a membership consisting of the head of each line of business plus the head of technology, the SPO meets monthly to review all projects that exceed $1 million, that are unplanned,[3] or whose incremental annual operating expenses exceed $500M. The SPO, not only approves these projects, but also directly governs them through their life cycle.

The effective management of strategic initiatives is a crucial step for overall demand management. Without this capability, organizations are left with no structure for prioritizing IT funding opportunities at the enterprise level that leaves them unable to align their IT investments with corporate strategy. According to one manager, the absence of a strategic initiative management initiative is a "siloed approach which results in ad-hoc decisions, increased cost and complexity, and redundancy of applications all of which increase the overall demand for IT services." The cost of the legacy environment this creates further restricts the investment in new IT capabilities and innovation. The absence of an effective strategic initiative management capability is a double-edged sword: it drives up the demand for IT resources while reducing the ability to conduct capacity planning to take advantage of a rationalized demand.

---

[3] According to Gentle (2007), unplanned demand "corresponds to the huge amount of unpredictable work that IT does which is not contained in well-defined project structures. These include things like change requests, feature requests and bug fixes which arise from changing business and regulatory environments, changes in strategy, company reorganizations, mergers and acquisitions, and insufficiently tested systems."

Application Portfolio Management

Unlike PPM that deals with future projects, APM focuses on existing applications, trying to balance expense against value (Caruso 2007). These applications may be assessed for their contribution to corporate profitability, and also on nonfinancial criteria such as stability, usability, and technical obsolescence. McKeen and Smith (2010) provide strategies for effectively implementing an APM initiative. The existing portfolio of applications (sometimes referred to as the asset portfolio) must be continually maintained in order to support the organization effectively. This need for continual maintenance creates demand for IT resources. Allowed to grow in response to the needs of separate lines of business, a legacy environment soon becomes highly complex, difficult to change, and expensive to maintain.

In one organization, it was not until they had instituted an APM initiative that they discovered that they had significant overlap and duplication across applications (e.g., 70 management information systems, 51 order management applications, and 27 regulatory reporting systems). The costs of maintaining this environment were driven up substantially and needlessly. Furthermore, their ability to deliver new applications was jeopardized due to the inherent complexities within the application portfolio itself.

With an effective APM initiative now in place, this same organization has reduced its technology-related operating costs and realized significant business value through reduced staff and maintenance requirements, reduced cycle times for process execution, a thorough rationalization of their application portfolio with a 40 to 50 percent reduction in size, and realized technology cost improvements through application retirement. Furthermore, the organization was able to re-orient their technology cost profile to value creating activities and away from maintenance. Most significantly, resultant savings were applied to new initiatives without increasing the overall IT budget. This example demonstrates how APM can be effective at reducing overall demand as well as reshaping it.

Enterprise Architecture

According to Wikipedia (2014b), enterprise architects (EA) "work with stakeholders, both leadership and subject matter experts, to build a holistic view of the organization's strategy, processes, information, and information technology assets. The enterprise architect links the business mission, strategy, and processes of an organization to its IT strategy, and documents this using multiple architectural models or views that show how the current and future needs of an organization will be met in an efficient, sustainable, agile, and adaptable manner. Enterprise architects operate across organizational and computing silos to drive common approaches and expose information assets and processes across the enterprise. Their goal is to deliver an architecture that supports the most efficient and secure IT environment meeting a company's business needs."

In this role, an EA is strategically placed to bridge the two worlds of business and technology. According to McKeen and Smith (2008), EAs are "able to take a view across business change programs, assessing their combined business and technical risk, overlap/dependencies and business impact on the staff and customers of an organization." Over the years, the role of enterprise architecture has become even more business focused and this has drawn EAs into increasingly senior management discussions. The organizational advantages of this are immediate. It has enabled EAs to influence the demand for IT resources by vetting strategic choices in light of what is possible from a business and technical solution perspective. According to one manager, this allows his enterprise architecture group to "get ahead of the business which helps them to manage IT demand proactively."

The ability of EAs to shape demand depends on two leverage points. The first is the establishment of a "future state architecture blueprint" (see McKeen and Smith 2006) that identifies the current architecture, the future architecture, and outlines a current-to-future transition plan. Combined with effective governance and transparency, this mechanism is highly effective at shaping IT demand by ensuring that everything aligns with the architectural plan. At one organization, it was their adoption of a common enterprise architecture that tightly integrated business and technology that enabled "informed enterprise-wide transformation planning to drive effective development across all business units."

The second key leverage point provided by enterprise architecture is the ability to promote enhanced business capability from a top-down perspective. Rather than depending solely on "bottom-up" demand from the lines of business, the enterprise architecture team at one organization was able to identify and champion enhanced business capabilities because of their ability to link the organization's technical architecture to business strategy. Deploying these two leverage points allows the IT organization to shape demand by aligning new initiatives with the architectural plan and by highlighting enhanced capabilities enabled by the same architectural plan.

Business–IT Partnership

Managing IT demand runs counter to the well-ingrained role of IT—to be an order taker—to do whatever the business needs and whatever is sent its way (Morhmann et al. 2007). For years, the accepted wisdom has been that if the business wants it and is willing to pay for it, then it is not the role of the IT organization to question these decisions. The members of the focus group debated this issue. It was evident that no organization represented within the focus group subscribed faithfully to the "order-taker" role for IT; everyone felt that their IT organization needed to be more proactive in order to be most effective within their organizational service role. However, lively disagreement with regard to the degree of IT "proactiveness" emerged.

On one side of the issue, a manager adamantly stated, "IT should definitely take a leadership position in managing demand...and that IT was well positioned to identify, analyze and recommend potential applications of IT to the business." At her organization, the IT executive team had built strong relationships with their business partners over time especially at the highest levels of the organization. Their CIO was a valued member of the executive committee, was requested to present to the board at every meeting for ten minutes (previously the CIO had presented once a year), and carried substantial influence in terms of the future application of IT in discussions about how best to leverage the business.

At another organization, the relationship between IT and the business was not nearly as well established and lacked the requisite foundation of mutual trust (Smith and McKeen 2010). According to this manager, their IT organization was "struggling with the business to close knowledge gaps in terms of what the business was asking for and what IT was able to deliver." Some newly formed committees were in the "process of aligning IT with the business to enable prioritization of work across the different business units." A lack of business strategy and/or a clear understanding of business requirements had led to a vacuum that IT was attempting to fill. Demand management was described as the oscillation between "technology push" and "business pull," which produced a lot of business resentment. The lack of a mutual trusting relationship clearly hampered the effectiveness of their demand management initiative.

A third organization suggested that value was driven at many levels within the enterprise requiring alignment between IT and the business leadership on objectives, investments, and outcome. Her organization had articulated three levels of partnership required to effectively shape demand.

- The first level is as a *utility* partner focusing on table stakes; that is, keeping operations running as effectively as possible. The goal is competitive cost alignment and containment, where IT partners with the business to reduce the operating costs through such means as labor arbitrage and competitive sourcing.
- The second level is as a *technology* partner. The goal here is continuous improvement such as accelerated time to market through new or enhanced processes.
- The third level is a *business* partner. This type of partnership is focused on business results through such mechanisms as improved market share, revenue growth, profit improvement, and cycle time reduction.

The group agreed that demand for IT resources does originate at different levels within the organization and therefore IT organizations must be effective at each of these different levels. In addition to senior IT executives, other key relationship players are business analysts, account/relationship managers, and business architects.

One organization mapped out a set of generic attributes for an effective IT–business partnership capable of shaping demand for IT resources. According to this manager, effective demand management requires the following:

- *Relationship management*—Where collaboration and partnership are key to identifying business capabilities and requirements. Continuous communication is essential. In fact, some have argued that relationship management has to transform into the role of demand management (Cameron 2006).
- *Leadership*—A technology manager's leadership style has significant implications for the success of the partnership; for example, is he or she driven by collaboration? Is the business a key partner or kept at arm's length?
- *Clear business requirements*—Without clear business requirements, the technology group will struggle. Even under the best of cases, high-level requirements may drastically change when digging into the details of business needs.
- *Marketing skills*—With the ever-changing technology landscape, marketing technology capabilities becomes critical. Thus, instead of talking about technology, the conversation should be about business capability.

These partnership traits would take on different degrees of importance depending on whether the relationship called for a business partner, technology partner, or a utility partner.

Governance and Transparency

It is customary for organizations to have a process for vetting IT project proposals (i.e., a business case[4]). Furthermore, the business is normally expected to pay for new development as well as a pro rata share of the technology costs to run the business (i.e., chargeback). Together these two forms of governance shape the demand for IT resources. They do this by encouraging and/or sanctioning investment behavior on the part of the business. For example, we would expect that business managers would be reluctant to request and pay for anything nonessential. Nevertheless, organizations find themselves having to manage IT demand. As a result, are we to conclude that these governance mechanisms are inadequate? The focus group made two arguments: First, they suggested that IT demand will always exceed supply due to the myriad potential applications of information technology in the workplace; and second, they felt that existing governance structures were indeed lacking. We explore the latter of these two issues next.

Business managers continuously seek to leverage their business with technology whether that happens by streamlining processes, offering self-serve options, implementing enhanced information/reporting systems, or implementing dynamic pricing systems. Provided they have the money, their only challenge is to win approval for the requisite IT resources. IT managers are equally motivated to provide such systems as are desired by the business. Specifically, delivering systems on time and within budget rewards IT managers. In sum, both parties are highly motivated to deliver new capabilities to the business. The resulting effect, according to members of the focus group, is encouragement to overstate the short-term benefits of delivering the desired capability and to understate the long-term costs of maintaining it. Without a countervailing governance structure to reinforce different behavior, IT demand expands to overwhelm supply.[5]

Recognizing the need for a remedial governance mechanism, two separate organizations adopted similar approaches. Both mandated the adoption of a standard business case template combined with compulsory training for all business managers in business case development. Both organizations also mandated that the finance organization must sign off on the acceptability of benefits proposed in all business cases. The third and arguably most important process change was to track the delivery of project benefits following implementation in order to hold business managers accountable for realizing anticipated benefits. The combination of these three initiatives produced significant behavioral changes.

- Training business managers in the process of preparing business cases had the immediate effect of raising the overall quality of submitted business cases and sharpened the focus on benefits identification.
- Assigned accountability for realizing benefits countered the tendency to overstate benefits and understate costs.

---

[4] Typical business cases require a business sponsor, risk analysis, architectural plan, business requirements, detailed design, project management plan, vendor RFP (if applicable), work schedule, and project manager.

[5] From an economics point of view, a potential countervailing strategy would be a pricing mechanism. That is, demand could be curbed by increased pricing of IT services. Although this might dampen demand in the short run, according to the focus group, such a strategy would introduce so many new and different impediments to the adoption of IT that it would be difficult to predict what long-term effects it might have on IT demand.

All in, these governance procedures reduced overall demand for IT resources but more importantly, focused limited IT resources on the "right" systems. Both firms expressed confidence that these were effective strategies for managing IT demand.

Transparency goes hand-in-hand with governance. A well-articulated process that is understood by everyone and adhered to by all managers is the goal. Information needs to be understood, consistently interpreted, and applied correctly for there to be any hope of effective decision making. A byzantine chargeback allocation algorithm, for example, provides little guidance in terms of appropriate action and usually fails to produce its intended behavioral effect. In like fashion, allowing "unplanned" or "off-plan" activity to enter the service queue undermines even the best demand management initiatives. One manager claimed that unplanned demand is like "getting bitten to death by ducks"—no single bite will kill you but one thousand bites later and you are dead! As mentioned earlier, the solution adopted by one organization was to shuttle off all unplanned activity to their strategic project office in order to make it visible and force it to compete with other demands for IT resources thereby ensuring an open and transparent process.

McKeen and Smith (2010) argue that effective application portfolio management can impact demand management due to the increased transparency provided by accurate information. In fact, providing information can on occasion make governance unnecessary. A vivid example of this was provided by one organization. Having made a significant investment in an application portfolio initiative to track IT expenditures, senior IT executives were able to present the following information to their senior business partners:

- The annual investment in systems designated as surplus[6] by the business.
- All investments to enhance these surplus systems.
- Annual investment in systems misaligned with overall strategy. For example, it was discovered that only 20 percent of their IT investment was directly focused on "improving the customer experience" and "driving revenue" despite the fact that these two areas were designated as the enterprise's top priorities.
- Investment in systems at odds with future state architecture.

Highlighting these expenditures resulted in almost immediate managerial action—something that had been lacking previously. Redundant systems were retired and investments in surplus systems were stopped. Of particular note is that these significant savings were obtained without the introduction of any additional governance mechanism. According to the focus group member, what called business executives to action was seeing these numbers on the charts denoting unnecessary expenditures. She claimed that business executives simply "did not want to have their stuff in the red boxes."

---

[6] This organization identifies all applications as "buy," "hold," or "sell." Surplus systems are those marked as "sell."

Conclusion

While attention on supply side issues will continue (i.e., to ensure that the IT organization is run as efficiently as possible), future management activity must increasingly focus on the demand side to ensure that IT investments are made as effectively as possible. IT demand management, however, is not a single process but rather a "developed organizational capability." This capability requires basic tools (e.g., service catalog, chargeback, and project portfolio management) working in concert with five key organizational enablers (strategic initiative management, application portfolio management, enterprise architecture, business–IT relationship, and governance and transparency). Together these mechanisms enable organizations to allocate capital and human resources to the highest-value IT opportunities. Of equal if not greater benefit is that active demand management enables IT organizations to forge more effective working partnerships with the business. Instead of being relegated to the role of order-taker, IT organizations can now engage in proactive discussions with their business partners to establish a future agenda for IT. And because the supply side works in unison with the demand side, this enables enhanced capacity planning of benefit to both. For the first time, many IT organizations will be able to get a step ahead of the business and build capability to enable new strategic business initiatives with shortened time to market. This has been a prized but elusive goal of IT. In organizations where IT is recognized for its strategic importance and/or IT processes have reached a high level of maturity, managing IT demand has likely begun; for others, the time to manage IT demand has arrived.

References

Betts, M., "Business Demand for IT is Outstripping the Budget," *Computerworld Blogs*, May 2009, *http://blogs.computerworld.com/business_demand_for_it_is_outstripping_the_budget*.

Cameron, B., "From Relationship to Demand Management: IT's Relationship Managers Will Be Focus for Aligning Business and IT." *Forrester Research*, October 2006.

Caruso, D., "Application Portfolio Management: A Necessity for Future IT." *Manufacturing Business Technology* 25, no. 10 (October 2007): 48.

Cramm, S., "Managing IT Demand 101." *CIO*, article 32222 (April 2004), *www.cio.com/article/32222*.

Gentle, M., *IT Success: Towards a New Model for Information Technology*, Hoboken, NJ, USA: John Wiley & Sons, October, 2007.

Hackett Group Inc., "New Hackett Research Quantifies Growing IT Services Gap; Demand to Increase by 17% through 2010 as Budgets Remain Flat." Research Alerts #05122009, May 2009, *www.thehackettgroup.com/about/alerts/alerts_2009/alert_05122009.jsp*.

Hotle, M., J., Duggan, and J., Woods, "Drive Application Overhaul Efforts with a Portfolio Approach." Gartner Research Inc., ID Number: G00205640, July 2010.

McKeen, J. D., and H. A. Smith, "Creating and Evolving a Technology Roadmap," *Communication of the Association of Information Systems* 20, no. 21 (September 2006): 451–63.

McKeen, J. D., and H. A., Smith, "The Emerging Role of the Enterprise Business Architect." *Communications of the Association for Information Systems* 22, no. 14 (February 2008): 261–74.

McKeen, J. D., and H. A., Smith, "Application Portfolio Management." *Communications of the Association for Information Systems* 26, no. 9 (March 2010):157–70.

Morhmann, G., Schlusberg, C., and Kropf, R., "Demand Management in Healthcare IT: Controlling IT Demand to Meet Constrained IT Resource Supply." *Journal of Healthcare Information Management* 21, no. 3 (Fall 2007): 56–63.

newScale, *http://www.newscale.com/solutions/IT_demand_management*, April 2010.

Potter, K., "IT Cost Optimization Round 2: Strategic Shifts and Doing Less with Less." Gartner Research Inc., ID Number: G00205937, August 2010.

Smith, H. A., and J. D., McKeen, "Building a Strong Relationship with the Business." *Communications of the Association of Information Systems* 26, no. 19 (April 2010): 429–40.

Wikipedia, definition of demand management, http://en.wikipedia.org/wiki/Demand_management, June 2014a.

Wikipedia, definition of enterprise architect, http://en.wikipedia.org/wiki/Enterprise_architect, June 2014b.

Young, C., "ITSM Fundamentals: How to Construct an IT Service Catalog." Gartner Research Inc., ID Number: G00210792, March 2011.

19 Creating and Evolving a Technology Roadmap[1]

If you don't know where you are going, any road will get you there.

LEWIS CARROLL (1865)

The preceding quote applies rather well to technology roadmaps. In the past, companies have followed a number of different technology paths that have not always led to the "promised land" despite conscientious effort. There are many reasons for this. First, the target evolves, which means that development of a technology roadmap should be an ongoing process. To continue the analogy, we are forever "traveling" but never "arriving." Second, technology has many different masters. Vendors, trade associations, standards-setting boards, alliance and/or trade partners, mergers and acquisitions, growth and expansion, strategic directional change, new technological development, and economic shifts (e.g., price performance, adoption patterns, and obsolescence) are all continuously influencing where companies want to go with technology. Third, unexpected roadblocks occur (e.g., the company that produces the application platform that runs your business declares bankruptcy). If building and evolving a technology roadmap were easy, it would always be done well.

Why do we need a technology roadmap? IT managers believe that without the guidance of a roadmap, their companies run the risk of making suboptimal decisions—technology choices that make sense today but position the company poorly for the future. There is also a strong sense that the exercise of developing a technology roadmap is valuable even if the actual roadmap that is developed is subject to change. Another adage that applies is, "Plans are nothing; planning is everything." It is through the articulation of a technology roadmap that you learn what you did well, where you failed, and how to improve the process. Finally, a technology roadmap limits the range of technology options and reduces the decision-making effort compared to facing one-off

---

[1] This chapter is based on the authors' previously published article, McKeen, J. D., and H. A. Smith, "Creating and Evolving a Technology Roadmap." *Communication of the Association for Information Systems* 20, no. 21 (September 2006): 451–63. Reproduced by permission of the Association for Information Systems.

decisions repeatedly over time. Because a roadmap has cast the evolution of technology on a defined path, it means that an organization can simply accept this decision and not revisit it continuously. Thus, a technology roadmap reduces the organization's cognitive workload.

This chapter begins with a general discussion of technology roadmaps and presents a model to explain various input factors. It then describes each of the components of a technology roadmap and offers advice derived from the shared experiences of the focus group.

WHAT IS A TECHNOLOGY ROADMAP?

It is important to develop an understanding of what a technology roadmap actually is. To do so, we can build on the analogy of a travel map. A travel map is a guide that tells you where you are now by positioning you within the greater environs and highlights existing options to get you where you want to go. In offering directions, it can suggest travel times, routes, scenic alternatives, and perhaps points of interest. A technology roadmap differs. Unlike a travel map, it is difficult to purchase a technology "map" for the simple reason that organizations all have uniquely different starting points, different goals, and, therefore, different destinations. Travel maps accommodate travel regardless of destination or purpose. Technology roadmaps must also entertain external factors such as industry trends, the competitive landscape, and vendor strategies and offerings (Chang 2010). Finally, alternative technology options are not self-evident and must be identified through research and exploration (and sometimes experimentation). Thus, each option bears a different cost and time structure. As an analogy, the travel map provides an excellent starting point, but when creating a technology roadmap, more is needed. The first step is to develop a common understanding of what exactly is meant by the term *technology roadmap*.

In the group, every participant used a different definition of the term. On analysis, we reached consensus on aspects of the definition. It was clear that the main purpose of a technology roadmap is to establish the technology direction for the organization. It has two objectives. The first is to articulate how technology will support the enterprise's overall vision, strategy, and objectives. This was evident in the definition used at one company:

> Our technology roadmap is the collective vision of the opportunities for technology to serve the business.

The second goal is to frame and constrain technology solutions to provide coherence and integration among those solutions across the enterprise and to define target architectures for implementers. These dual objectives simply recognize the need for IT to forge a relationship between IT and the business while, at the same time, serving the unique internal needs of IT. After some discussion, the group agreed on the following definition:

> A technology roadmap is a mechanism for the identification, justification, planned evolution, and orchestration of technologies to enhance business performance.

THE BENEFITS OF A TECHNOLOGY ROADMAP

That every participating organization has a technology roadmap suggests that there are perceived benefits in building and evolving one. These benefits fit into two categories—external and internal—reflecting the dual purpose of the technology roadmap as described previously.

External Benefits (Effectiveness)

External benefits relate to aligning IT with the business, result in IT *effectiveness*, and include the following:

- *Achieving business goals.*   A technology roadmap compares the business plan with the current technological environment to identify gaps. To the extent that the technology roadmap effectively addresses these gaps, business goals should be supported by technology.
- *Reducing complexity.*   The technology environment is highly complex due to the degree of interaction among systems. The adoption of a technology roadmap typically reduces the number and variety of technological choices, thereby simplifying things. Just getting to single versions of applications, such as one e-mail program, greatly reduces complexity.
- *Enhancing interoperability of business functionality across lines of business (LOBs).*   Identifying the technology that supports different LOBs is the first step toward integration. The degree of integration and interoperability is first and foremost a business decision. The technology should be designed to support this vision.
- *Increasing flexibility.*   This begs the question of whether differentiation or integration enables flexibility. With respect to technology, the argument is usually won by commonalities.
- *Increasing speed of implementation.*   Common standards, methodologies, and technology platforms relieve the learning burden and, thereby, increase the time to market with new systems.
- *Preserving investments in new and existing systems.*   Mapping technologies on an evolutionary trajectory means that IT investments are based on long-term considerations.
- *Responding to market changes.*   Having an up-to-date technology roadmap means that IT can respond accurately and appropriately to market changes. Organizations without the benefit of a technology roadmap are forced to make decisions "from the ground up" as opposed to building from an established framework.
- *Focusing investment dollars.*   Having a technology roadmap means that investments in IT can be much more focused. Fewer dollars, better targeted, produce-enhanced results.
- *Responding to new legislation.*   Compliance with new legislation (e.g., privacy, environmental programs) is greatly simplified with a rationalized technology roadmap.
- *Reducing difficulties associated with deployment of new technologies.*   New technologies require learning and change. Therefore, fewer technologies, common platforms, and similar approaches effectively relieve this burden.

Internal Benefits (Efficiency)

Internal benefits attribute to IT directly and result in IT *efficiency*, including the following:

- *Providing a common design point.*   This facilitates the end-to-end integration of reusable components and applications.
- *Building a consistent and cohesive technology base.*   Without the proliferation of haphazard technology, one can create a critical mass of skills dedicated to select technologies.
- *Ability to move forward in planned phases.*   With technologies mapped onto a life cycle, there is an orderly evolution for each technology, which creates synergies.
- *Consolidating global solutions.*   For global companies, the local in-country technologies are synched to the global technology roadmap, which introduces even greater consistency across business processes, reducing overall IT expenditure.
- *Lowering the cost of development and maintenance.*   Technology roadmaps provide an inventory of technology, and thus they make it possible to increase the reusability of system components, leverage commodity components available in the marketplace, standardize techniques across multiple applications, and prevent the "disintegration" and proliferation of execution, development, and operations architectures.

It is interesting to note that no companies in the group were able to demonstrate the *financial* impacts attributable to their adoption of a technology roadmap. Perhaps more surprising was the fact that the companies had not been asked by senior management to produce such a benefit statement. The initial development of a technology roadmap is typically an initiative of the IT department. This suggests that IT departments understand the benefits of a technology roadmap and appear not to question the value of committing resources to this activity. Perhaps the internal benefits of building a technology roadmap—which are significant, judging from the preceding list—justify the exercise all by themselves. These benefits appear to be more tangible and immediate than external benefits.

ELEMENTS OF THE TECHNOLOGY ROADMAP

The process of developing a technology roadmap is depicted in Figure 19.1. It hinges on a gap analysis to assess the extent to which the current state of technology supports the current and forecasted needs of the business. From this are derived the organization's future technology requirements, which, coupled with a migration strategy, constitute the core of a technology roadmap. Participants identified seven important activities in developing and maintaining a technology roadmap. These are described below and are interspersed with strategies suggested by the group, based on their experiences. At the outset, it is important to dispel the notion that the development of a technology roadmap is a "once every five years" undertaking. Instead, there was strong consensus that a technology roadmap should constitute a working instrument to be updated and revised annually. Otherwise it becomes inflexible, perhaps dated, and, as a result, unresponsive to the business.

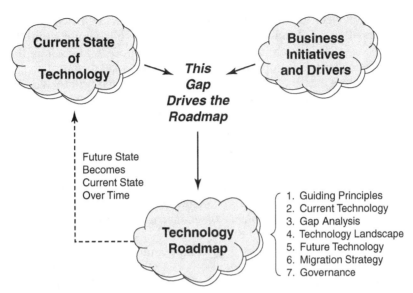

FIGURE 19.1   The Process of Developing a Technology Roadmap

Activity #1: Guiding Principles

When launching a technology roadmap, it is important to establish a set of principles that will guide its development and enhancement. First and foremost, this is a statement about the role and purpose of technology within the business that should clearly convey aspirations and purpose. It outlines how technology will support the business, stipulating the envisioned role for technology to play. This roadmap should be a statement about the *type* of technology support to be delivered to the business with a sense of performance. For example, contrast the following two statements: "We will provide technology that is proven, reliable, and cost effective" and "We will provide leading-edge technology."

In addition to establishing the role and purpose for the technology roadmap, it is important to outline its goals. One company's goal for its technology roadmap was "to increase the speed of developing, deploying, and productively executing future business models." It then outlined three strategies to accomplish this:

1. Decouple the business processes from the underlying IT applications.
2. Decouple business applications from the infrastructure.
3. Establish a new collaboration environment that supports the rapid introduction and productive use of the new business processes.

This signaled to the organization that IT was adopting a service-oriented architecture (SOA). Because SOA was not well understood by the business, the technology roadmap spoke to the desire to identify components of the business model, which could be designed as reusable software services; to adopt integrated and standardized processes for optimizing cost; to accelerate integrated data/information architecture to enable horizontal integration across the enterprise; and to provide a stable, secure, and ubiquitous workspace for employees to be more effective in their roles and efficient in their jobs by delivering information, applications, and people to easily collaborate within the context of business processes. This established the mandate, purpose, and goals of the technology roadmap, using language appropriate for the organizational context.

With the purpose and goals established, guiding principles can then be articulated to explain other key factors and decisions that would impact technology and, therefore, have a bearing on the technology roadmap. The following statements are examples of key principles used by focus group members:

- *Establish investment boundaries.* "We will invest in technology at a rate necessary to sustain our business growth."
- *Outline the role of technology for the organization.* "We will adopt a 'fast follower' strategy, aggressively adopting proven, architecturally compliant technologies."
- *Outline the role of technology within the industry.* "Technology is a core business competency."
- *Reinforce the role of standards.* "All components will adhere to open industry standards."
- *Specify the role of support.* "We will assist employees with technology problems that occur via call centers, desktop support, self-help, and/or service-level agreements."
- *Specify the impact on resident IT skills.* "We will draw technology expertise from our existing large skill base."
- *Outline development preference.* "We will buy first, build second."
- *Establish expectations.* "Service levels and availability are outlined for all production systems."
- *Adherence to regulatory standards.* "We will be security and privacy compliant."
- *Specify timeframe.* "The 'future' in our technology roadmap has a three- to five-year horizon."

Activity #2: Assess Current Technology

This is basically an inventory. It should outline what technologies the business currently has and describe their status (e.g., standard, unsupported, discontinued). The first task is to develop a classification scheme to assist in managing the inventory. For each type of technology domain (e.g., operating systems; hardware, desktops, servers, and storage; telecommunications and networks; applications; and databases), members recommended recording the following minimum information: business process area, platform, vendor, level of support, dependencies (products, applications), critical versus noncritical, and life cycle.

The next step is to assign a technology custodian/owner, so someone within the firm is responsible for each technology domain. At one company, these individuals are referred to as technology "domain architects." Typical duties of such individuals include acquiring the technology, maintaining the relationship with the vendor, updating and enhancing the technology, facilitating in-house training for those working with the technology, accreditation regarding the technology, recording all applications of the technology, maintaining documentation (e.g., licensing; financing; and establishing service levels, guarantees, and warranties), and retiring the technology when appropriate.

This is a major responsibility particularly when individuals will have more than one domain assigned to them.

One of the key tools in managing the technology inventory is a framework to classify technologies. One such tool, the Application System Asset Management (ASAM) Decision Chart (Mangurian 1985), assesses the business importance (i.e., the application's overall value to the business), functional support (i.e., how well the system meets the business requirements), and technical support (i.e., the system's efficiency and effectiveness). This particular tool has been used successfully over a number of years by one firm. On an annual basis, all application systems are evaluated against these three criteria, leading to one of the following actions: maintain, renovate, replace, augment, or eliminate.

Another company uses a two-by-two matrix that evaluates applications on the basis of their criticality to the business (i.e., whether or not they support business processes deemed critical to the business units) and their strategic importance (i.e., those providing global functions that will not be replaced over the next two years). Placement within this matrix (i.e., maintenance classification) dictates service levels: strategic/critical applications receive "gold" service; critical/nonstrategic applications receive "silver" service; strategic/noncritical applications receive "bronze" service; and nonstrategic/noncritical applications receive "blue" maintenance. Yet another company uses the "WISE" chart to evaluate technologies on the basis of their strategic value and longevity, yielding four life cycle stages: *Watch, Invest, Support,* and *Eliminate* (McKeen and Smith 2003).

The focus group agreed that the specific classification scheme matters less than the fact that a company has a scheme to manage its technology inventory. The technology inventory also provides input to other processes such as risk management, team development, and skills planning.

Activity #3: Analyze Gaps

With a technology inventory in place, organizations can perform a gap analysis between the technology that is currently available and that which is required. The first step is to identify the required technology. This ties the technology roadmap directly to the business and is perhaps the most crucial step in developing an effective plan. One manager made this point rather emphatically by saying, "Get this wrong, and the roadmap is junk." Others suggested that simply asking business leaders for their future requirements will not work for a number of reasons. First, business leaders do not think in terms of requirements; they think in terms of growth, customers, sales, markets, costs, suppliers, and shareholders. It takes a lot of work and skill to translate this view of the business into technology requirements. Second, the roadmap has to be ahead of the business—that is, it must reflect the fact that because business changes faster than technology, you have to build technology in anticipation of business change and growth. A technology roadmap cannot afford to be reactive; it must be proactive regardless of whether the technology vision is "quick second" or "late adopter." Third, business is driven by innovation and differentiation, while IT benefits from standards, common features, and universality. This will always put IT at odds with the business. According to one participant, it boils down to the question, "When is a line of business so different that common systems don't make sense, and what criteria do you apply to test this?"

Eliciting business drivers and building a composite picture of the technology required to support the business vision is more art than science. It requires close cooperation between IT and the business. This cooperation happens at many levels within the organization and should be an ongoing activity. The annual IT planning cycle articulates the applications to be introduced over the next year, but attempting to derive a technology roadmap from this activity is a case of "too little, too late." IT has to be working with the business closely enough to be well ahead of the annual planning cycle. At one company, the domain architects are being reoriented to align them closely with the business units to create a better early-warning system for application needs driven by growth and changes to the business model. Its manager stated the following:

> *The enterprise has a vision, and each line of business has a vision, and the job of the domain architect is to put all these visions on the table to expose gaps. To do this, architects need to be 75 percent business and 25 percent technology. Today they are the reverse.*

At another company, business analysts work together with enterprise architects to "get a fix on future business directions." We tend to think of architects and technical experts as playing the key roles, whereas the focus group pointed out that the best vantage point for performing a gap analysis between the existing technology and emerging business drivers is the CIO office, due to the fact that the CIO sits at the same table as other senior executives to set the strategy for the business. The focus group pointed out that having the CIO at these sessions provides a significant advantage in terms of forecasting the future for technology within the company.

With a "line of sight" to the business strategy, coupled with an accurate technology inventory, all the tools to perform a gap analysis are in place. The outcome of the gap analysis is an articulation of the technology required to support the business's vision and strategy. Unfortunately, a technology roadmap cannot be simply created from this analysis because it must also be governed by trends in the external environment.

Activity #4: Evaluate Technology Landscape

The group was unanimous in its recommendation that firms must continuously invest in research and development (R&D) if they are to keep abreast of technology. The size of this investment, however, differs depending on how critical IT is to a firm. The roadmap should articulate how large this investment will be, how it will be enacted, who is responsible, and what guidelines are in place to assist this initiative. Setting these structures in place is the easy part; knowing when enough is enough is more difficult.

In the past much of a company's technology was dictated by its choice of vendor; if asked what its technology roadmap was, a firm could simply reply by naming a single vendor. Today's lock-in by vendors is much reduced, particularly with the widespread adoption of open standards, interoperability among various platforms, Web, and cloud services. As a result, vendors must enact different strategies to win over clients as they seek new footholds in industry sectors, opportunities to showcase emerging technologies, and ways to gain entry into new markets. Many times, this is accomplished by partnering with willing organizations in R&D initiatives. As a result, organizations should be leveraging their vendor communities aggressively. One focus group member had only used a portion of her R&D budget because a key vendor had provided all the technology and most of the support free of charge.

Focus group members shared a number of different approaches to R&D, but all shared a common challenge: capital funding. At some companies R&D flies "below the radar" as "skunkworks." Here the IT department uses its own money that it has squirreled away over time, treating R&D similar to a cost of doing business. In others, R&D is financed by a technology investment fund (i.e., a tax to the business levied as a percentage of technology usage). This fund is governed by a committee composed of senior managers who guide the investment in R&D. In another firm, IT maintenance is reduced by 10 to 15 percent per year, and the dollars are reallocated to strategic IT investments, much of which are funneled to a "technology adoption program" described as a "sandbox where new technologies are tried, improved, tested, scaled, and assessed for business value." These latter approaches are preferable because they don't attempt to hide R&D. In fact, they make R&D transparent to the organization. Business leaders understand the need for reinvestment in the physical plant; IT is no different.

Activity #5: Describe Future Technology

This part of the IT roadmap should contain a description of the technologies to be adopted in the future. These future technology roadmaps should not be simple lists. They should also include the *logic* that was used in the decision to follow a certain path. If, for instance, the technology roadmap depicts a preferred vendor strategy, equally if not more important is the reasoning that underpins this strategy. Making this explicit within the roadmap permits others to challenge the logic without challenging the decision. This is essential, particularly if you wish to obtain constructive input from business managers when creating your technology roadmap.

Equally important are the assumptions built into the roadmap. IT professionals are frequently guilty of assuming that it is obvious to others why a certain strategy has been adopted. Hence, there is value in making all embedded assumptions explicit. These assumptions may reflect trends in the competitive marketplace (e.g., vendor A will continue to dominate with its software offerings), the general environment (e.g., the adoption of open standards will accelerate), specific technologies, or general trends (e.g., new development will increasingly adopt Agile practices). This exposure provides the basis for meaningful conversation to help clarify the roadmap's dependence on widely accepted (but perhaps not articulated) assumptions.

The group felt that describing the technology was fairly straightforward, using major technology domains such as hardware, software, applications, and networks. The difficulty often is in regard to the granularity of future technology. The question is, how do you decide the level of detail in future technology platforms? According to one manager, "If your roadmap is severely impacted by business change, your roadmap is probably too granular." The opposite, creating a technology roadmap that is too high level, is equally inadequate. The goal is to find the "sweet spot" between the two extremes, which is "more art than science," he said.

Activity #6: Outline Migration Strategy

A technology roadmap should also outline a migration strategy to get you from today's technology platforms to tomorrow's. At first glance, the implementation of a technology roadmap appears similar to the accomplishment of other major IT initiatives. The focus group, however, was quick to point out the differences. Of these, the primary one is that a technology roadmap is not a self-contained project; it affects *every* project as technologies are embedded within the entire spectrum of applications, many of which cross lines of business, geography, and generations. By positioning each technology domain on a life cycle (e.g., watch, invest, support, eliminate), two dominant migration strategies emerge—"gradual" and "big bang."

The gradual strategy focuses on the application (i.e., as new applications are implemented or reworked, their technology is updated to fall in line with the dictates of the roadmap). The big bang strategy emphasizes the technology (i.e., all instances of a given technology are updated across all applications). The choice is not an either–or situation, nor is it a "technology only" decision. Rather the choice should be dictated by the business. There are few situations where the big bang approach is absolutely necessary simply because there are always means of staging the conversion over time, applications, business lines, and/or platforms. As one participant noted, "Even large architectural builds/deployments are typically done within a program across several phases." Sometimes, though, the big bang is a business necessity due to the need to reap advantages in a reduced timeframe.

A major challenge facing the migration strategy is the need to assign priorities to the various technology components that need to be changed. One organization uses the following criteria to assess the criticality of migration in order to assign order of execution:

- Technology elements that are inflexible
- Elements that do not meet the strategic direction
- Components that are expensive to maintain
- Components that do not meet nonfunctional requirements (e.g., scalability, extensibility)
- Architectural designs built to reflect obsolete business strategies (e.g., segmentation silos, line-of-business silos).

Once priorities are assigned, timelines can be established for the migration of various technologies.

A migration strategy should explicitly recognize a number of dominant trends within technology, such as the movement toward cloud-based services and big data. Although such trends provide useful high-level guidance, they need to be augmented by more tactical guidelines (see Appendix A). Of particular interest here is the need for a migration strategy to explicitly plan for the migration of *people* skills in alignment with the future technology demands.

Activity #7: Establish Governance

Every organization should have an established process in place to articulate who is responsible for creating the technology roadmap, how and on what basis, by whom it is updated and enhanced, and finally who approves the technology roadmap. Most organizations in the group felt that the technology roadmap was legitimately the responsibility of the enterprise architecture function, which is responsible for mapping out the architectural platforms to support the various lines of business. The majority of companies recognized the need for two distinct levels of architecture governance within their organizations:

- *Strategic.*   Individuals and groups at this level (typically, senior executives from IT and the business) set the overall architecture direction and strategy and ensure alignment with business objectives. They set standards and approve deviations from these standards. In addition, they monitor the overall attainment of the goals as articulated within the technology roadmap.
- *Tactical.*   Members of this tactical group tend to be from the IT ranks, including architects, analysts, and managers. They typically work across lines of business as well as within lines of business with responsibility for the execution of the strategy (as opposed to its development). A key role is the provision of architecture consulting services to project teams.

At one company the key personnel of the tactical group are domain architects who have responsibility for broad categories of technology (e.g., server platforms), subdomain architects who have responsibility for technologies within a larger domain (e.g., tablets), and product stewards who have responsibility for specific products (e.g., mobile OS). Accountability cascaded down this hierarchy with domain architects responsible for setting strategy, understanding the marketplace, and controlling proliferation of technology and product stewards responsible for new releases and versions of technologies as well as troubleshooting. At this organization, ultimate accountability rests with the executive architecture review board—a committee composed of senior business and IT architects—that ratifies the technology roadmap and makes final decisions regarding proposed deviations to the roadmap. If a need arises for an "off-profile" (i.e., "noncompliant") technology, it comes before this architecture review board for an "opinion." According to the manager, this is a very effective deterrent because "most people don't want their project elevated to the executive architectural review board!" The other important deterrent is the tax levy (i.e., elevated chargeback costs) imposed on adopters of noncompliant technology.

A major part of governance is enforcement. Effective enforcement requires IT to develop a new breed of "corporate" architect who is business focused and businesscentric. According to one member, "Techcentric architects tend to be seen as police officers…there to enforce the law." It is better to have a businesscentric architect who can entertain business solutions that violate the preferred technology direction in light of increased technology risk (i.e., the risk of doing it) and business risk (i.e., the risk of not doing it) and arrive at a decision that best suits the business. The difference in approach is one of accommodation, as opposed to denial and prevention.

At one company the IT group did not want to ever have to "tell a business unit that they could not buy a specific package." The trade-off was to let the business specify the application's requirements and to let IT choose the product. Another firm tackled this problem by charging the business for the additional costs of a noncompliant application, such as extra in-house skills, application integration, conversions, and interfacing software. The overriding goal in all these firms was to achieve optimal decisions for the business, not rigid adherence to a technology roadmap.

A repository can be an aid to tracking decisions as well as a means of listing assigned responsibilities. At one company this "architecture library" lists all technology domains (e.g., hardware, applications) and all products within each domain. Product metadata include the following:

- Status (i.e., emerging, contained, mainstream, declining, retirement, obsolete)
- Proposed replacement product
- Name of product steward, subdomain architect, and architect
- Business impact analysis
- Interdependencies
- Total cost of ownership

Knowing that a specific product is "declining," who the product steward is, the name of the replacement product, and the business impact analysis demonstrating exactly where and how this product affects business processes all provide extremely valuable information to the organization. Such a resource requires a significant amount of work to build but, once built, greatly reduces the complexity of maintaining and evolving a technology roadmap.

PRACTICAL STEPS FOR DEVELOPING A TECHNOLOGY ROADMAP

As part of the meeting, focus group members were asked the following question: "If you were a 'roadmap consultant,' what advice would you offer to management?" When their suggestions were combined and analyzed, the collective wisdom reduced to the following five recommendations. Interestingly, this advice would arguably apply to many, if not most, IT initiatives.

1. *Be bold and innovative when planning the roadmap.*
   - What you have done should not be the gauge by which you determine what you should do.
   - Innovation is key; start with a blank piece of paper.
   - Invent your future. Inspire others to help you build it.

2. *Align technology with the business.*
   - Determine what role technology will play in satisfying the business vision.
   - Focus on using technology to solve business problems and deliver business value.
   - Know when it is appropriate to choose leading-edge technology over being a late adopter/quick second.
   - Ensure that the roadmap is flexible, extensible, and attainable to change with the business.
   - Ensure that the organizational structure supports the delivery of a technology roadmap.

3. *Secure support for the roadmap.*
   - Ensure that the funding model supports a technology roadmap.
   - A migration strategy and roadmap require an executive sponsor, ownership, and accountability. Ensure that strategic decisions are made at the right level.
   - Stay the course!

4. *Don't forget the people.*

- Every technology change requires changes in people's skills.
- Map new technologies to required skill acquisition and/or development.
- Take steps to ensure that IT personnel understand the technology roadmap and its logic, ramifications, and time frame.

5. *Control, measure, and communicate progress.*

- Measure progress along the way; use leading indicators.
- A successful roadmap must be measurable and updated at appropriate checkpoints.
- Communication of the roadmap is essential to success.
- Establish a governance process to manage technology and vendor choices.

Conclusion

The purpose of a technology roadmap is to guide the development of technology in an organization. But as pointed out in this chapter, it serves a much greater purpose for a business. It communicates the role that technology will play in advancing business goals. It outlines the explicit assumptions on which the roadmap is based and describes how these assumptions directly affect the rate and order of attainment of goals. It suggests the impact of future technology on the set of required in-house skills for the IT department. And it provides a vehicle for explaining the logic of technology-related decisions to business managers who otherwise may interpret such decisions as overly rigid and unproductive. As such, a technology roadmap should be viewed as an important opportunity for IT to engage the business in meaningful and productive dialogue focused on furthering business goals. To limit this activity to simply forecasting technology is to miss a significant opportunity.

References

Carroll, L. *Alice's Adventures in Wonderland.* London: MacMillan & Co., 1865.

Chang, Hsin-lu. "A Roadmap to Adopting Emerging Technology in E-Business: An Empirical Study." *Information Systems and eBusiness Management* 8, no. 2 (March 2010): 103–30.

Mangurian, G. E. *Alternative to Replacing Obsolete Systems.* Cambridge, MA: Index Systems Inc., 1985.

McKeen, J. D., and H. A. Smith. *Making IT Happen.* Chichester, England: John Wiley & Sons, 2003.

APPENDIX A

Principles to Guide a Migration Strategy

One focus group organization adopted the following four key principles to guide its migration strategy:

1. Migrate from product-centric to process-centric applications architecture using a service-based architecture that is grouped into layers such as presentation, business process, and data.
   - Maintain a sourcing strategy to develop strategic systems with competitive advantage in-house. Nonstrategic systems will be sourced through packages and services as available.
   - Maintain a technology skills base for critical technologies.
   - Utilize strategic partnerships to bring in leading-edge technology skills to accelerate implementation while, at the same time, transferring knowledge to your staff to permit in-house support and future development.

2. Deploy modular or component-based applications to minimize test and utility life cycle costs.
   - Adhere to a component-based and layered architecture with standardized, generic interfaces.
   - Ensure conformance of application development initiatives to the logical architecture specifications in order to engineer quality into the applications.
   - Build flexibility into the application components by allowing end users to establish and change business rules.

3. Utilize components based on industry standards as the building blocks of architecture services.
   - Adhere to (or adopt) industry-accepted standards and methodology to promote ease of integration.
   - Minimize the complexity of application interfaces by adopting flexible data interface standards—for example, extensible markup language (XML).
   - Adhere to corporate technology and application development standards in order to improve the efficiency, effectiveness, and timeliness of application development initiatives.

4. Insulate applications from being affected by changes in other applications through middleware.
   - Use enterprise application integration (EAI) middleware services to integrate application services across and within business domains.
   - Define and document application interfaces well in a metadata repository that includes interface methods, purpose, and terms of usage.
   - Include in EAI services application interface services and work flow integration services, both within the department and in the extended enterprise.
   - Increase the degree of information and work flow integration across customer- and vendor-facing processes.

20 Enhancing Development Productivity[1]

Poor development productivity has been a perennial problem for IT (Brooks 1975; McKeen and Smith 2003; Oman and Ayers 1988). "IT takes too long to deliver" is a common complaint among today's business leaders (Luftman and Zadeh 2011; Overby 2005). Over the past three decades (or more), a considerable number of panaceas have been proposed for helping organizations to get the systems and IT functionality they need better, faster, and cheaper. Structured approaches to programming and design and the introduction of systems development life cycle methodologies were first. Then came automated systems development tools, attempts to measure productivity (e.g., function points), and new development approaches such as rapid application development (RAD). More recently, organizations have sought to buy off-the-shelf software, use middleware to integrate it, introduce enterprise resource planning systems (ERPs), or adopt software-as-a-service in order to deliver more functionality at a lower cost. Companies have also realized that the processes *around* systems development, such as system prioritization and enterprise architecture, can have a significant impact on development timelines and most now have procedures in place to manage these activities. Finally, many organizations have turned to contract or outsourced staff (often in other countries) to help them with extra resources during high-demand periods or to provide a large group of qualified development personnel at a lower overall cost (Han and Mithas 2014; Lacity and Willcocks 2001).

Nevertheless, over the past decade the situation has gotten worse in many ways. Changes in technology, connectivity and collaboration, and the introduction of open standards has meant that the IT function is sitting at the intersection of two powerful and rapidly changing forces—technological innovation and globalization—and IT has become absolutely critical to effective business strategy. Furthermore, development teams are becoming increasingly complex to manage, incorporating people and partners from different companies and locations. And development activities are more challenging, involving many regulatory, architectural, business, financial, HR, security, and risk

---

[1] This chapter is based on the authors' previously published article, Smith, H.A., J.D. McKeen and W.A. Cram, "Enhancing Development Productivity," *Journal of Information Technology Management*, XXXIII, no. 3, September 2012. Reproduced by permission of the Association of Management.

management hoops that have little to do with the traditional design and coding of the past but that need to be orchestrated to deliver a coherent, viable service. Unfortunately, new systems development techniques have not always kept pace with these changes. Many that have promised, such as service-oriented architecture (SOA), software-as-a-service, and agile development, still have not displaced traditional approaches. At the same time, the new technical and managerial practices needed to support them have not been fully introduced. In short, improved development productivity is still long on promises and short on delivery.

This chapter explores improving development productivity from a number of perspectives. It begins by examining the problem of IT development productivity and how system development practices are changing. It then explores the key obstacles involved in improving development productivity and outlines practices that are proven to work. It concludes with recommendations for managers about how to create an improved environment for systems development productivity.

THE PROBLEM WITH SYSTEM DEVELOPMENT

In the past, the focus group explained that "system development" largely meant creating customized software applications for an individual organization. Today, it still means custom building but development also includes selecting, implementing and integrating packaged software solutions, and increasingly, integrating smaller, reusable software components with existing legacy applications across a variety of platforms with a variety of development tools. However, although systems development has changed over time, many of the problems associated with it have not changed; that is, there are still very high failure rates with development projects and they are still perceived to take too long, cost too much, and deliver limited business value (Korzaan 2009).

Research has not been particularly helpful in providing ways to improve on any of these fronts. There have been few studies of actual development practices to determine what works and under what circumstances and there is thus very little on which to base guidelines for different types and sizes of development (Dyba and Dingsoyr 2009). In short, "we need to know more about what we know and don't know about software development" (Adams 2009). One study noted that improvement in software development models and best practices has been a "long slog" since the 1980s and using the traditional "waterfall" model of systems development[2] has "continued to fail in delivering acceptable measures of software development performance" (Royce 2009). The Standish Group's ongoing study of software development success rates shows that in 2009 only 32 percent were considered successful (that is, on time, on budget and with the required features and functions), while 24 percent were considered failures (i.e., they were cancelled or never used). The remaining 44 percent either finished late, were over-budget, or had fewer than required features or functions (Levinson 2009). While these measures have improved somewhat since 1994, progress has been agonizingly slow.

Although IT practitioners and consultants have worked hard to define a strict set of rules to guide and govern software development, and have seen some modest gains

---

[2] By this we mean a system development life cycle (SDLC) approach in which all requirements are first defined, and then an application is designed, developed, tested, and implemented with few changes.

from such factors as improved governance, project management offices, and better methodologies, many believe that "rules don't work and haven't since 1967" (Berinato 2001). These ongoing problems have meant that system development has long "suffered from way too many management fads and silver bullets *du jour*...and [left managers prey to] consultants and sellers of 'software oil'" (Adams 2009).

Finally, system development continues to be plagued by the difficulty of measuring "productivity." What exactly is a successful systems development project? Many companies define it as meeting schedules and budgets and by the functionality delivered (Levinson 2008). Yet, these common metrics typically "do more harm than good" (Cardin et al. 2008). While they are easy for business people to understand, they perpetuate a "myth" that these are the only three factors that make a project successful. Furthermore, they take no account of some major elements that are often responsible for project failure, such as changes in requirements or scope, unreasonable deadlines, project dependencies, and lack of business accountability (Levinson 2008). "We still have no formal productivity metrics," said one IT manager, "and it's not a priority for us." Nevertheless, said another, summarizing the challenge faced by everyone in the focus group, "we are still expected to deliver business value with increasing speed and efficiency."

TRENDS IN SYSTEM DEVELOPMENT

For many years, system development has been conceptually seen as a functional, engineering project, similar in nature to building a bridge (Chatterjee et al. 2009). Unfortunately, efforts to develop methodologies that embody software engineering principles designed to lead to consistent performance outcomes, while resulting in some improvements, have not been as successful as predicted (Chatterjee et al. 2009; Royce 2009). Therefore, in the past two decades, numerous efforts have been made to address system development productivity shortcomings in other ways, including the following:

1. *Adopting new development approaches.* There are a significant number of new development approaches that their proponents believe address some or all of the problems with the traditional waterfall development method. While a comprehensive assessment of these approaches is beyond the scope of this chapter, they can be classified into three major types:
   - *Agile.* Introduced in the 1990s, this approach encompasses a variety of "anti-waterfall" methods of system development, such as spiral, incremental, evolutionary, iterative, and RAD. They stress the need to incorporate flexibility into system development by breaking up a large project into smaller pieces that can be developed in overlapping, concurrent phases to rapidly deliver business value in a series of short increments. Speed and agility are achieved by collapsing or compressing one or more phases of the waterfall method and by incorporating staged delivery or incremental implementation (Jain and Chandrasekaran 2009).
   - *Composition.* This approach models and develops generic components comprising data, processes, and services that can be reused in different development efforts (Plummer and Hill 2009). Based on detailed analysis and architecture, components (e.g., acquire customer name and address) can be plugged into any system without being reprogrammed. Initially called "object

oriented programming" in the 1990s (McKeen and Smith 1996), and "service oriented architecture" (SOA) more recently, composition has been difficult to achieve because of the intensive modeling and architecting required and the IT organizational changes require to adapt to them (Blechar and Norton 2009; Plummer and Hill 2009). With this approach, system development becomes process orchestration, combining various software components into an "application container" (Blechar 2010).

- *Integration.*   The 1990s also saw the widespread introduction of packaged software to the marketplace that could be purchased and implemented rather than developed in-house. As a result, many companies, including most of those in the focus group, adopted a "buy don't build wherever possible" philosophy for their generic applications, such as accounting, human resources, or customer relationship management. More recently, this marketplace has begun to evolve so that companies can purchase software-as-a-service from the cloud, rather than implementing it within their own organizations. Although preprogrammed, such services or packages still require various amounts of effort to select and then integrate them into an organization's existing processes, platforms, and data (Mahoney and Kitzis 2009; Plummer and Hill 2009).

However, for most companies, adopting new development approaches still involves using them only selectively and change has been agonizingly slow as a result.

2. *Enhancing the waterfall methodology.*   Although new development approaches are gaining ground in organizations, the waterfall remains the predominant system development process for large-scale, industrial strength projects (Royce 2009; Schindler 2008). The waterfall method is still considered most practical for large system development projects because the engineering principles implicit in it involve formal coordination strategies, centralized decision making, formal communication, and prescribed controls, which help to offset the challenges caused by the increased complexity and interdependencies and reduced communications opportunities on large projects (Xu 2009). The focus group's presentations concurred with this assessment. "While we are trying to introduce new and more flexible approaches to development, our senior management is not committed to them and are resisting them," said one manager. "We're doing lots of experimentation with different development approaches but these are done within our standard methodology," said another. Improving the waterfall development process is therefore still a high priority for most companies. In recent years, organizations have attempted to improve the "maturity" of their traditional software development processes using Capability Maturity Model Integration (CMMI) to move them from ad hoc activities to more managed, better defined, quantifiable processes, so they yield standardized, replicable results (Chatterjee et al. 2009; Hanford 2008). For example, one focus group company has created an enhanced delivery framework complete with a process map, detailed activities, templates, inputs, outputs, entry and exit criteria, artifacts, roles, and links to standards. Another manager stated, "We have well-defined SDLC methodologies and standards and procedures are enforced...[But] we are always looking for applications development best practices to improve them."

3. *Improved governance.* It has also been accepted that there are a number of factors other than the development process itself that will affect the quality and the effectiveness of systems development. Today, in spite of a persistent engineering mind-set that permeates system development practices, there is also growing acceptance that building systems can be more of an art than a science. "Systems are a unique and complex web of intellectual property bounded only by vision and human creativity...They are more similar to movie production [than bridge-building] where no laws of physics or materials apply...most quality is subjective [and] anything can change" (Royce 2009). To deal with these conditions, some organizations are beginning to adopt governance mechanisms based on economic disciplines that accept the uncertainties involved in systems development—especially at the beginning—and adapt and steer projects through the risks, variances, and moving targets involved (Royce 2009). Thus, many focus group companies have adopted different governance practices for different stages of the development life cycle, such as staged estimates of cost and time, "gating reviews," and quality assessments at different life cycle phases. Other governance mechanisms, such as those used in Sweden, also consider the social and cultural implications involved (Chatterjee et al. 2009). Still others govern by a set of software outcomes, including flexibility, responsiveness, operational efficiency, quality of interaction, learning, product performance, and benefits achieved (Liu et al. 2009; Smith et al. 2010). In the focus group, most managers stressed that compliance with all legislation and regulations has become a further significant governance issue for all their systems initiatives. Some also stressed the need for better governance of the processes that "touch" and impact systems development activities, such as quality assurance, architecture, security, and testing. In short, governance at a variety of levels is becoming more important to ensure productivity in systems development (Plummer and Hill 2009).

4. *Changing resourcing strategies.* One trend in systems development that is very clear is the widespread use of contractors and outsourced developers to supplement in-house development staff. A major driver behind improved governance, methodologies, standards, and componentization of software is the desire to use cheaper development labor, often located in other countries. This globally dispersed development, however, increases the need for new internal business and technical skills. New resourcing strategies increase the need for better business, technical and data architecture, improved business analysis, IT strategy that is more closely linked to business, and project managers who can coordinate and leverage the efforts of a diverse group of internal and external, IT and business staff to deliver consistent and effective IT products (Blechar 2010; Plummer and Hill 2009). At present, only 28 percent of CIOs believe that they have the right skills in their IT organizations to support these changes (Mahoney and Kitzis 2009). The group agreed that development skills are changing. "Our focus is on improving project management, business analysis and quality assurance staff," said one manager. "We're stressing the development of relationship management, analysis and consulting skills," said another. "Improved resource allocation is also essential," said a third, "because there are only so many staff with the necessary skills. In the past, each business unit had dedicated resources; now they all work for the enterprise."

OBSTACLES TO IMPROVING SYSTEM DEVELOPMENT PRODUCTIVITY

It is clear from the earlier mentioned trends that systems development *is* changing and has changed to address complaints of poor productivity. However, it is also clear that these changes are still not adequately addressing the problem. There are several reasons why improvements in development productivity have been difficult to achieve. While many of them may not be surprising to long-time IT managers, they bear repeating since they pose significant barriers to success in this area.

First, there is still a need for a more holistic understanding of system development, both within IT and within the business. As already noted, development is a much more complex and uncertain process than was first understood. Too often, our mental models of development appear to be dated—locked into a time in the past when the problem being addressed was straightforward and the programming effort significant. Today, the programming is straightforward, while the problems are highly complex, typically involving many parts of the business and many IT functions and requiring significant business knowledge, technical skill, relationship and communications abilities, and conceptual understanding (Chakraborty et al. 2010). In an earlier look at this subject we noted that *all* activities impacting system development should be considered when trying to improve productivity. "There is a need to ensure that everything works together to further the overall goal. It makes no sense to improve one part of the process if it doesn't accomplish this" (McKeen and Smith 1996). Members of the focus group identified three primary areas where there are currently significant bottlenecks in the development process:

- *Business involvement.* This can be an obstacle to development success at several levels. At the highest level, it is well-known that business sponsorship is essential to ensure that the right projects are developed (Hanford 2008). While many organizations have addressed this problem through their governance processes, the focus group stressed that many business leaders still pay only lip service to their responsibilities. This impacts the system development process in several ways. "Our business users take forever to complete their parts, such as agreeing to a proposed solution or signing off on key phases of a project," said a manager. "They don't see how this affects our work, which can't proceed without it." The focus group felt strongly that business users needed more education about their roles in (and impact on) every level of the system development process, including governance, analysis, testing, and change management, in order to make development more productive.
- *Analysis.* "We were very surprised to find that analysis takes about 30 percent of the elapsed time of development," said one manager. "Business analysis is not at the same level of maturity as other parts of development," said another. Analysis can be an obstacle to productivity and effectiveness in many ways, in addition to the time it takes. Significant problems can be caused by failing to clearly define the scope of a project, to understand the dependencies between projects, to identify the changes that will need to be made to business processes when a system is implemented, or to recognize and incorporate the needs of multiple stakeholders in system requirements (Lemmergaard 2008; Levinson 2008).
- *Testing.* Several companies are focusing on testing, which they have found takes between 20 and 40 percent of development effort and resources. "We are spending

increasing amounts of money on testing; it's a growing job," said one manager. "It's extremely complex and expensive to set up and maintain test environments," said another. In system development, testing is typically done by three groups—the development team itself; quality assurance; and business users. Delays often occur with the last two groups, who focus on their own needs and optimize their own processes with little regard for their impact on the progress of an individual project or the business as a whole.

Second, the systems development process itself continues to be problematic. Today, many organizations try to force fit all projects to a single development approach, often with disastrous results (Norton and Hotle 2010). If there's one thing that practitioners and managers agree on, it's that whatever development approach is used, it should be appropriate for the project being undertaken. Typically, small projects suffer from too much process when a full-scale, CMMI-style methodology is used, while large projects cannot coordinate all their variables using an agile development approach (Adams 2009). Agile approaches are useful when requirements are not fully known or in rapidly changing business conditions. Yet, "for most organizations, [agile development] should be known by the acronym BDSF (delivering bad software fast)" (Norton and Hotle 2010). Conversely, too much process makes a project inflexible and adds layers of red tape that causes a project to bog down (Levinson 2009). Not using a methodology is not the answer as this can increase the risk that important tasks will fall through the cracks or that a project won't be completed on time (Levinson 2008). Members of the focus group were finding resistance to an overabundance of methodology from within IT as well as from the business. Thus, the ongoing challenge for IT managers is to find the right balance between structure and consistency and speed and flexibility.

Third, poor communication on the part of both IT and business tends to create misunderstandings and conflicts that can inhibit projects. One of the major goals of a good development methodology is to mediate between all stakeholders to prevent the changes in requirements and scope that result from problematic communication. But communications issues cannot be fully dealt with by a methodology (Liu et al. 2009). "Most of the project management mistakes IT departments make boil down to either a lack of adequate planning or breakdowns in communication (either among the project team or between the project team and the project sponsors. These mistakes can be fatal" (Levinson 2008). While much of the blame for ineffective communication tends to be placed on IT (Smith and McKeen 2010), there is considerable evidence that business people do not take the time or make the effort to understand what is being said to them (Liu et al. 2009). "Our business doesn't want to hear about what we must do," said a focus group manager. Too often, executives rely on simplistic metrics, such as progress against schedule and budget, because they are easy to understand. These in turn perpetuate the perception of poor development productivity (Royce 2009). "Project sponsors latch on to initial estimates…and because [they] don't understand project complexity and other factors influencing cost and timelines…they may see a project as a failure…even if changes resulted in improved value…" (Levinson 2008). Improved communication about changes in requirements, cost estimates, and schedules is therefore critical to improving perceptions of development productivity and success (Cardin et al. 2008).

IMPROVING SYSTEM DEVELOPMENT PRODUCTIVITY: WHAT WE KNOW THAT WORKS

There is still a lot that we don't know about improving system development productivity and members of the focus group were actively experimenting with a wide variety of initiatives in this regard, which may or may not be successful. However, they identified five sets of practices that they believed clearly made a significant difference:

1. *Optimize the bigger picture.* System development should be seen as only one part of an overall business and technical effort to deliver value to the enterprise. This starts at the top with a clearer understanding of the IT value proposition: delivering strategic insight and leadership; understanding business needs and designing solutions; and sourcing solutions implementation (Mahoney and Kitzis 2009). This bigger picture has a number of implications for both business and IT. First, IT and business strategy must be closely aligned to ensure IT is working on the right things and in the right order, said the focus group. Business and technology architecture functions, combined strategic governance, roadmaps, and improved business and IT relationships should all be designed to deliver *enterprise* value (not IT or business unit value). Second, all aspects of the earlier stages of development need to be reassessed and streamlined, including governance activities around project approvals, prioritization and funding; managing demand; educating business people in their roles and responsibilities in system development and holding them accountable; improving business casing; information and solutions architecture; use of proofs-of-concept, prototypes, and use cases; and developing strong project managers with excellent communications skills. Finally, resource management and sourcing strategies must be developed to ensure staff with the right skills are available when needed; applications development best practices need to be monitored and implemented; and testing and quality assurance should be centralized to eliminate duplication of effort.

   However, although each of these activities is important, none should be optimized at the expense of delivering overall value. All too often, individual functions seek to do the best job possible but forget how their work affects the overall goal. It is therefore important for senior IT leaders to ensure that this goal is kept in mind by all groups involved in delivering solutions to the enterprise. One company has had significant success—reducing cycle time by 30 percent—through such holistic process improvements. Another noted, "Becoming more outcome-focused, optimizing the whole development process and developing a shared business/IT agenda has led to substantial productivity improvements for us."

2. *Adopt more flexible processes.* While not all companies are willing to give up on the waterfall development methodology, they all recognize that "just enough" process should be the goal. Ideally, a development approach should be matched with the deliverables involved and the level of compliance required (Hotle 2009). Focus group companies were actively exploring ways to accomplish this goal. One company has developed a methodology tailoring tool that helps determine the levels of oversight and control that are needed by outside groups (i.e., security, architecture, operations) according to the level of risk involved. Another company ranks its development projects into three tiers. "Tier 1 is very visible and requires a higher level of formality and governance; Tier 3 projects are encouraged to adopt more

agile approaches," said the manager. A third is encouraging "smarter execution choices" from a full range of development approaches by enabling teams to choose from a variety of methodologies depending on business needs. Finally, one manager noted that his organization uses a little bit of everything when it comes to its efforts to improve its productivity. "We have adopted a 'buy vs. build' approach and have packaged ERP systems in several divisions; we use composition services for data capture, transformation, and delivery between systems—to take the burden away from the system developers; and we use a combination of agile and waterfall methods for new development."

3. *Reduce complexity.* It is widely accepted that complexity is a major cause of slow system development (Chakraborty et al. 2010). Standardization wherever possible therefore reduces complexity and makes development more straightforward (Royce 2009). While aiming for flexibility, the focus group was therefore also trying to reduce complexity in a number of ways. One organization has cut back on the reporting it requires, for example limiting the paperwork for its Project Management Office to just a few short questions. "This has helped us a lot," said the manager involved. Standards are a key way most companies are using to limit technological complexity. "Multiple technologies, platforms, languages and tools mean more complex software engineering," said a manager. Finally, several companies are trying to increase reuse of software components. "We're actually tracking the amount of reuse in each system; doing this has led to a 50% increase in reuse and a corresponding 20% reduction in defects," said a manager, noting that making reuse a performance metric for systems has been an important factor in its success.

4. *Enhance success metrics.* Success is a multidimensional concept depending as much on perceptions as on objective reality. While, as noted earlier, metrics of progress against schedule and budget are too simplistic for the current development environment, it is also true that IT can overdo the metrics it provides (Levinson 2008). Metrics for system development should be designed to accomplish four goals and used selectively for different audiences:

   • *Increase buy-in.* System development is a team activity, with business and other parts of IT playing key roles on the team. It is therefore essential that all team members be committed to achieving the same goals. In fact, the more people are committed to a goal, the more likely they are to contribute toward its outcomes (Korzaan 2009). Thus, metrics that clearly link a project and its component parts (e.g., architecture, testing, change management) with delivering well-articulated strategic business value are most likely to ensure a coherent and consistent effort to deliver. Such metrics are usually developed in a business case but may also be part of an overall business or technical roadmap and should be kept front and center throughout system development (Smith and McKeen 2010).

   • *Promote desired behavior.* Measuring something is an important way to promote behavioral change (Kaplan and Norton 1996). Members of the focus group had therefore developed scorecards to track desirable new development behaviors, such as reuse, quality, and collaboration. These metrics are often designed to change perceptions within IT, regarding what management values in systems development.

   • *Educate perceptions.* Perceptions can be "educated, trained and controlled" (Gladwell 2005) and business perceptions of system development productivity need management, transparency, and clear communication. Metrics therefore need to be interpreted for them by IT in light of business conditions and individual situations (Levinson 2008; McKeen and Smith 2009).

- *Monitor performance.* Finally, system development performance should be tracked to determine the actual results delivered rather than the progress of the various activities of the software development process (Royce 2009). "We need to become more outcome-oriented so that we don't get bogged down in process," agreed a focus group manager. "This is a fundamental change in IT's mind-set." Such a new mind-set also supports the shift to newer development approaches, such as agile, package implementation, reuse, and delivery of software-as-a-service.

5. *Create a smarter development environment.* Getting "smarter" about development involves improving collaboration, knowledge sharing and capabilities, and finding new opportunities for leveraging the work that is done. With the boundaries between business and IT becoming increasingly blurred and larger numbers of stakeholders involved in the process (both within IT and in business), development has become both a much more social and multidisciplinary process, while at the same time teams are becoming increasingly dispersed geographically (Chakraborty et al. 2010; Mahoney and Kitzis 2009). Collaboration and knowledge sharing initiatives can enhance traditional forms of communication, facilitate relationship building, and ensure that there is a single version of the "truth" available to everyone on a project team. Several companies in the group have implemented collaboration and document sharing tools with considerable success. "Our top priority is promoting collaboration with the business," said one manager. Another is implementing knowledge repositories and document-sharing software to enable better access to work that has already been done. Improved search capabilities are also a top priority for companies seeking to improve reuse. Another focus group company is stressing improving its capabilities by creating communities of practice around its four main technology disciplines (i.e., project management, business analysis, development, and quality assurance) to create thought leadership that is "more than the sum of its parts" and drive change throughout the IT organization. One has identified the key gaps in capabilities for its major functional areas and is developing learning paths to close them. Finally, companies are becoming smarter about how they handle requests for compliance projects, for example, gathering all compliance requirements together in planning to ensure that they are dealt with "once for all."

NEXT STEPS TO IMPROVING SYSTEM DEVELOPMENT PRODUCTIVITY

Although these five general trends in systems development are working well in the focus group companies, their breadth and the integration and behavior change required is daunting. While keeping these "big picture" initiatives in mind, the managers in the group identified five "quicker fixes" that were likely to have an immediate impact on productivity, while furthering these larger goals:

- *Look for and address bottlenecks.* Assessing the entire system development process for bottlenecks in an organization can yield surprising results. One company had no idea how long it took business sponsors to complete sign-offs; another found that cumbersome governance processes took inordinate amounts of time to resolve simple conflicts. With time pressures extreme these days, it makes sense to identify and speed up such bottlenecks first rather than increasing pressure on the core members of the development team.

- *Focus on outcomes.*   As already noted, IT metrics have typically measured elements of the process, such as consumption of resources, rather than value delivered. With the development world changing rapidly due to the advent of software services and application assembly, it is essential to refocus both business and IT on *what* functionality is being delivered, not *how* it is delivered. Making the shift to a more dynamic, innovative, and effective IT organization means changing what is measured. One firm now undertakes a quarterly assessment across its entire IT organization of the seven key capabilities it wants to develop: community participation, collaboration, transparency, innovation, agility (i.e., time to value), component-based development, and asset management and reuse. It believes encouraging these behaviors will promote faster time to market for all its development initiatives.

- *Clarify roles and responsibilities.*   Several firms have seen commitment to development projects increase, both from internal IT groups and from business sponsors and users when their roles and responsibilities were clarified. For example, one company clearly explains where IT architecture is accountable in system development, when it should be consulted, and when it should merely be informed. Another provides clarity about who is responsible for resolving development problems. "This has helped us to stop churning and increase motivation," said the manager. Another manager, who had overseen a transition from a traditional waterfall IT development organization to an SOA function, stated, "Making change is *all* about clarity of roles and responsibilities."

- *Simplify the development environment.*   All companies in the focus group had some initiatives to decommission or replace end-of-life or duplicate technologies and applications. Some are attacking this type of complexity more vigorously than others. One firm had slashed its legacy applications by one-third over the past three years. The benefits of a simpler environment are numerous—speed of implementation, flexibility, more investment dollars, and easier new technology deployment. In particular, one firm that had mandated a single desktop and common infrastructure found it dramatically increased its time to market for new development initiatives.

- *Simplify testing.*   Testing has long been seen as a system development bottleneck (McKeen and Smith 1996), and with the addition of more complex technological environments and more stringent compliance regulations, requiring separate groups to perform different types of testing, the situation has become much worse in recent years, said the focus group. Therefore, they have each put much effort into streamlining and automating this activity. Many companies have created a centralized test environment with automated scripts and standard tests that dramatically increase throughput. "With these you are not starting from scratch each time," said a manager. Testing tools and methods, including automated regression testing, risk assessments, and analysis of defects have helped both to speed up the process and provide the necessary documentation of results.

Conclusion

Much has improved in the practice of system development over the past two decades and if the development environment had stayed static, it is likely that productivity would also have been perceived to have improved dramatically. Instead, systems have become increasingly complex at every level so process improvements have barely made a dent in the dilemma of development productivity. This chapter has addressed the ongoing nature of the productivity problems facing IT managers in systems development and how the field is changing. It has examined some of the serious systemic barriers to fundamental change in how systems are developed and documented best practices for dealing with them. There is unfortunately no silver bullet when it comes to improving system development productivity, in spite of much effort to find one. While a few organizations are "pushing the envelope" in an attempt to radically change how systems are delivered, for most, improvements are more likely to come as a result of persistent and iterative analysis of what works and what doesn't in their particular organizational context.

References

Adams, W. "An Agile Cure for All Ills?" *IEEE Software* 26, no. 6 (November/December 2009): 8.

Berinato, S. "The Secret to Software Success." *CIO Magazine*, July 1, 2001.

Blechar, M. "Why You Should Coordinate Your SODA, MDM and Business Process Improvement Initiatives." Gartner Group, ID Number: G00175167, March 24, 2010.

Blechar, M., and D. Norton. "Trends in Model-Driven Development, 4Q09-3Q10." Gartner Group, ID Number: G00169442, August 27, 2009.

Brooks, F. *The Mythical Manmonth: Essays on Software Engineering*. Reading, MA: Addison-Wesley Publishing, 1975.

Cardin, L., A. Cullen, and T. DeGennaro. *Debunking IT Project Failure Myths*. Cambridge, MA: Forrester Research, July 28, 2008.

Chakraborty, S., S. Sarker, and S. Sprateek. "An Exploration into the Process of Requirements Elicitation: A Grounded Approach." *Journal of the Association for Information Systems* 11, no. 4 (April 2010): 212–49.

Chatterjee, S., S. Sarker, and M. Fuller. "Ethical Information System Development: A Baumanian Postmodernist Perspective." *Journal of the Association for Information Systems* 10, no. 11 (November 2009): 787–815.

Dyba, T., and T. Dingsoyr. "What Do We Know about Agile Software Development?" *IEEE Software* 26, no. 5 (September/October 2009): 6–9.

Gladwell, M. *Blink: The Power of Thinking without Thinking*, New York: Little Brown and Company, 2005.

Han, K., and S. Mithrs. "The Real Saving from IT Outsourcing." *MIT Sloan Management Review* 55, no. 2 (Winter 2014).

Hanford, M. "The CMMI for Development Value Proposition for the PMO." Gartner Group, ID Number: G00158078, May 21, 2008.

Hotle, M. "'Just Enough Process' Is Built on Deliverables." Gartner Group, ID Number: G00168230, September 22, 2009.

Jain, R., and A. Chandrasekaran. "Rapid System Development (RSD) Methodologies: Proposing a Selection Framework." *Engineering Management Journal* 21, no. 4 (December 2009): 30–35.

Kaplan, R., and D. Norton. *The Balanced Scorecard*, Boston, MA: Harvard University Press, 1996.

Korsten, P. "The Essential CIO." *IBM Institute for Business Value*, Somers, NY: IBM Global Business Services, 2011.

Korzaan, M. "The Influence of Commitment to Project Objectives in Information Technology (IT) Projects." *Review of Business Information Systems* 13, no. 4 (Fourth Quarter 2009): 89–97.

Lacity, M., and L. Willcocks. *Global Information Technology Outsourcing: In Search of Business Advantage,* Chichester, England: John Wiley and Sons, 2001.

Lemmergaard, J. "Roles in the ISD Process: A Collaborative Approach." *Journal of Enterprise Information Management* 21, no. 5 (2008): 543–56.

Levinson, M. "Common Project Management Metrics Doom IT Departments to Failure." *CIO Magazine,* August 1, 2008.

Levinson, M. "Recession Causes Rising IT Project Failure Rates." *CIO Magazine,* June 18, 2009.

Liu, J, G. Klein, J. Chen, and J. Jiang. "The Negative Impact of Conflict on the Information System Development Process, Product and Project." *Journal of Computer Information Systems* 49, no. 4 (Summer 2009): 98–104.

Luftman, J., and H. S. Zadeh. "Key Information Technology and Management Issues 2010–11: An International Study." *Journal of Information Technology* 26, no. 3 (2011): 193–204.

Mahoney, J., and E. Kitzis. "Integrating the Transformation of Business and IT." Gartner Group, ID Number: G00167927, May 15, 2009.

McKeen, J., and H. Smith. *Management Challenges in IS: Successful Strategies and Appropriate Action.* Chichester, England: John Wiley and Sons, 1996.

McKeen, J., and H. Smith. *Making IT Happen: Critical Issues in IT Management.* Chichester, England: John Wiley and Sons, 2003.

McKeen, J., and H. Smith. *IT Strategy in Action.* Upper Saddle River, New Jersey: Pearson Education, 2009.

Norton, D., and M. Hotle. "Best Development Methods: A Scenario View." Gartner Group, ID Number: G00171772, March 18, 2010.

Oman, R., and Ayers, T. "Productivity and Benefit-Cost Analysis for Information Technology Decisions." *Information Management Review* 3, no. 3 (Winter 1988): 31–41.

Overby, S. "Turning IT Doubters into True Believers: IT Value." *CIO Magazine,* June 1, 2005.

Plummer, D., and J. Hill. "Composition and BPM Will Change the Game for Business System Design." Gartner Group, ID Number: G00173105, December 21, 2009.

Royce, W. "Improving Software Economics: Top 10 Principles of Achieving Agility of Scale." *IBM White paper,* May 2009.

Schindler, E. "Getting Clueful: 7 Things CIOs should Know About Agile Development." *CIO Magazine,* February 6, 2008.

Smith, H. A., and J. D. McKeen, "How to Talk so Business Will Listen…And Listen so Business Can Talk." *Communications of the Association of Information Systems* 27, no. 13 (August 2010): 207–16.

Smith, H., J. D. McKeen, C. Cranston, and M. Benson. "Investment Spend Optimization: A New Approach to IT Investment at BMO Financial Group." *MIS Quarterly Executive* 9, no. 2 (2010): 65–81.

Xu, P. "Coordination in Large Agile Projects." *Review of Business Information Systems* 13, no. 4 (Fourth Quarter 2009): 29–43.

21 Information Delivery: IT's Evolving Role[1]

It wasn't so long ago that IT was called "data processing" (DP) and information delivery consisted of printing out massive computer listings full of transaction data. If DP was particularly enlightened, business got summary reports, which might or might not contain useful information. The advent of online systems made data marginally easier to use, but it was still mostly data—that is, facts with very little context or analysis applied to them. "Usability" was talked about, but this aspect of information delivery was largely ignored. As a result, it was not unusual to find customer service representatives switching between ten or more different "screens" (each representing a different organizational data silo) to get the information they needed to do their job. But with the advent of the Internet, organizations realized that—despite the fact that they could force their employees to wend their way through an enterprise's Byzantine organizational structure and bits and bytes of data—customers were not going to go searching for the data they needed. Data had to be meaningful, provide an integrated picture of their interactions, and generally be significantly easier to interpret and understand. In other words, data had to become information, and it had to be delivered in ways customers could use.

While information delivery channels and practices were evolving, so too were organizations' needs for information. Many firms now realize that rather than simply processing transactions, they can "mine" what they collect to uncover new insights, often leading to substantial savings and/or revenue growth opportunities. Until recently, however, investments in information analysis and decision support languished as companies undertook higher-priority projects with more direct and immediate impact on their bottom lines. Today the success of how some companies use information for competitive advantage and operational effectiveness is causing business leaders to look more carefully at how well their firms are leveraging information (Lavalle et al. 2011).

Both the Internet and cloud technologies have dramatically changed the ease with which information can be stored, integrated, and delivered on an ad hoc basis.

---

[1] This chapter is based on the authors' previously published article, Smith, H. A., and J. D. McKeen. "Information Delivery: IT's Evolving Role." *Communications of the Association for Information Systems* 15, no. 11 (February 2005): 197–210. Reproduced by permission of the Association for Information Systems.

Today it is both technically and financially feasible to deliver literally millions of pages of text to data delivery devices (i.e., personal computers, tablets, and smartphones) as needed. As well, the technologies available to manage different types of information are improving rapidly and converging. Traditionally, different software has been used to manage documents, records, and other information assets (Kaplan 2002). Now the lines of demarcation between them are blurring. Software, although still imperfect, is opening the door to a host of new possibilities for information management and delivery. All these factors are placing new pressures on IT to focus more thoughtfully on the *information* component of its function.

This chapter first surveys the expanding world of information and technology and why information delivery has become so important so rapidly. Then it discusses the value proposition of information in organizations. Next it describes the important components of an effective information delivery function in IT. Finally, it looks at how information delivery will likely evolve over the next five to ten years and what this will mean for IT and organizations.

INFORMATION AND IT: WHY NOW?

In the late 1990s, information management and delivery were barely on the radar screens of most IT managers (McKeen and Smith 2003). Today it is consuming a considerable amount of IT effort and has blossomed into a number of multifaceted, high-value IT activities (Laney and White 2014). Of course, IT organizations have had some data management functions for many years, but these have been largely limited to data warehouse and database design and administration. As one participant claimed, "We've been talking around the subject of information for a long time, but it hasn't really been critically important until recently."

A number of reasons account for this new attention to information. First, there is no doubt that organizations are overwhelmed by all sorts of information. The number of documents, reports, Web pages, data items, and digital assets has literally grown exponentially in recent years. Unfortunately, our ability to store and protect information has far outstripped our ability to extract and present it (Beath et al. 2012). Research shows that the average knowledge worker now spends about a quarter of his or her day looking for information either internally or externally (Kontzer 2003).

Second, companies are now recognizing that information and how it is used has considerable value. Almost all organizations believe they could be doing more with the information they already have (Korsten 2011; Kruschwitz 2011). This is coupled with a new understanding of how value is derived from IT. Traditionally, organizations have expected to deliver value from their information systems alone (often through greater efficiencies in transaction processing), yet research shows that improved information stemming from good information management practices, *in combination with excellent systems,* is a stronger driver of financial performance (Kettinger and Marchand 2011). Participants noted that information is being used in their organizations for much more than transactional decisions. "We are using all sorts of information in new ways," said one. "We are trying to understand the data drivers of our business and use it to manage our processes more effectively. We are also using data analytics to uncover strategic new business opportunities." Another noted, "In the past we sent reports to executives who would consider the information they contained and issue directives to their staff. Now we are sending information directly to frontline staff so they can take action immediately."

In addition to recognizing the value of transactional, operational, and strategic information, companies are also coming to realize that embedding information in their workflows—including information from external sources—can be extremely valuable. A firm's ability to extract and leverage explicit knowledge from its employees by formalizing it in systems and procedures directly contributes to its structural capital (Holmes 2011; Smith et al. 2009). Some companies have already realized significant benefits from standardizing their information as structural capital and distributing it appropriately (Kettinger et al. 2003; Ross 2012).

Third, new laws governing what can and cannot be done with information are also leading to greater awareness in IT about what information is collected and how it is used and protected. Addressing privacy concerns, for example, requires the development of more sophisticated methods of user identification and authorization, permission management, controls over information flows, and greater attention to accuracy and analysis of where and how individual items of information can be used (McKeen and Smith 2012). No longer can huge customer records be sent from system to system, for example, simply because some of their data elements are needed. Companies risk not only contravening the law but also embarrassment in the marketplace. Financial accountability legislation is also driving greater attention to the integrity of information at every step in its collection. Requiring senior officers to *guarantee* the accuracy of the firm's financial statements is changing many previously *laissez-faire* attitudes toward information.

Finally, information possibilities are rapidly expanding. New technologies are creating different types of information, opening up innovative channels of information delivery, and providing new ways of organizing and accessing information. Just a few years ago, e-mail, social media, mobile computing, texting, and the Internet simply didn't exist. Today they are all major sources of new information *and* new delivery channels. Navigation tools, mobile technology, and vastly improved storage media (to name just a few) are driving new information applications that were not possible in the recent past. As the pace of new technology innovation ramps up, information delivery challenges and possibilities are, therefore, also escalating. In short, today IT personnel are finding that information delivery is a key element of almost every aspect of their work as well as a fundamental part of their ability to derive value from technology.

DELIVERING VALUE THROUGH INFORMATION

Information delivery plays a critical role in several new areas in delivering value in organizations:

- *More effective business operations.*   Although information has long been used to run organizations, in the past it was largely paper and transaction based. Today executives have access to online "dashboards" that combine a wide variety of transaction, process, and supply-chain metrics to give them a much broader and more detailed picture of their operations. Typically, dashboards are designed differently for different needs (e.g., sales, logistics), functions (e.g., HR, accounting), and/or processes (e.g., inventory management) and for different spans of control. They usually include drill-down capabilities, highlight problem areas, and integrate information from several systems. Other types of operational information that are available to organizations include predictive analysis (e.g., trends, timelines), benchmarks (both internal and external), quality measures (e.g., defects, stock-outs), and "scorecard" information (e.g., financial, internal business, customer, and learning and growth). What's also significant is that these types of information are now being given to frontline staff so they can better manage their own areas of responsibility, identify and avoid exceptions, and take action before problems arise. Operational information may be integrated with guidelines that direct courses of action so staff will better understand how to use it effectively.

- *Mobile and E-business (Virtual Business).*   These new virtual channels are having considerable impact on how organizations present information about their products and services to customers. In the past, customers would often get conflicting information depending on which "door" they entered (i.e., which part of the business they contacted). Virtual business has forced organizations to confront their own internal inconsistencies, identify information gaps and inaccuracies, and deal with inadequacies in their offerings, which are much more apparent when presented in these mediums. IT and senior executives often have to take a hard line with line-of-business leaders who tend to have a function-specific perspective on information. As one manager noted, "Taking the customer's point of view in virtual business development cuts across our established lines of business and organizational distinctions. Often there are political issues about information ownership, organization, and presentation. These must be nipped in the bud and everyone forced to put the customer's needs first."

  These channels have also become a significant driver of interactions among companies, enabling them to transact business in new ways, manage their roles in different supply chains, and offer new services to business clients that didn't previously exist. In both the B2C and B2B spheres, virtual business is largely about how information is integrated and presented to improve products and services. However, these are also changing the competitive landscape by making it considerably easier to comparison shop online. In the past, companies were able to be competitive by offering complex combinations of products and services, which discouraged one-to-one comparisons. Today, whole new businesses have grown up to facilitate comparison shopping. These firms are placing themselves as intermediaries between a company and its customers (e.g., online travel, insurance quotes). Thus, companies that continue to use information to obfuscate their services, rather than inform their customers, could easily find themselves disintermediated and at a strategic disadvantage.

- *Internal self-service.*   Virtual information channels are driving significant internal change as well. They are being used to simplify employee access to human resources materials and procedures, streamline procurement, manage approvals, provide information on benefits and entitlements, and maintain telephone numbers, to name just a few types of information that are now routinely accessible online. Companies now make millions of documents available to their staff through content management systems. As with virtual business, however, internal self-service is driving a complete reanalysis of what information is collected and how it is presented, navigated, and used. "Portals and online self-service make administrative problem areas more visible. They also force managers to simplify policies and procedures," said one manager.

- *Unstructured information delivery.*   Increasingly, organizations want to be able to access *all* their information online, including that which has traditionally been retained as paper documents. New software, navigation, and storage technologies are leading to the convergence of the records management, library management, and electronic document management functions in organizations (Kaplan 2002; Laney and White 2014). In the past IT has had very little to do with unstructured information. Now IT must develop taxonomies, navigation, and access methods for unstructured information and even to integrate structured and unstructured information into work processes delivered where needed.

  Another major source of unstructured information in which IT is involved is e-mail, video, text messaging, and social media comments. These technologies have captured the organizational imagination so rapidly that policies and best practices in this area are still catching up. Jurisprudence has recognized that these interchanges are corporate records. In response, organizations are developing procedures for managing these more effectively. The barrage of messages from outside corporate boundaries in combination with personal use of corporate e-mail and the vulnerability of corporate information to external hackers are giving IT managers severe migraines. Archiving e-mail, filtering spam, coping with viruses that tag along with messages, building sophisticated firewalls, and creating business cases for messaging technologies are all new IT activities that have sprung up to better manage these new forms of wanted and unwanted information.

  IT is also working to incorporate collaborative technologies that help capture and leverage the work of teams and groups. These technologies are being effectively used in such endeavors as providing the means whereby knowledge workers can share information about what they are doing, capturing best practices, brainstorming, tracking key decisions, and documenting a project's history. Often IT workers themselves are the first users of these technologies, bearing the brunt of the learning involved before they are rolled out to the rest of the organization.

- *Business intelligence.*   This is a function that is currently well developed in some organizations and not in others. However, the arena of business intelligence is growing rapidly in importance in organizations due to increased competition and the speed with which organizations must respond to competitive threats. Business intelligence includes both internal intelligence gathering (often known as data mining) and external intelligence gathering about trends, competitors, and industries. IT organizations are, at minimum, expected to design an effective internal information environment (aka a data warehouse) developed from their business information systems, within which users of a variety of skill levels can operate. Typically this requires an understanding of the context in which information will be used, modeling how data will be represented, and providing appropriate tools for different types of users. End users can access this information in a variety of ways ranging from ad hoc queries to generating predesigned reports. More sophisticated organizations have full-time data analysts on staff whose jobs can range from answering questions for users to exploring the data in order to uncover new opportunities (Brohman and Boudreau 2004; Marchand and Peppard 2013).

A key IT concern in the design and management of internal data warehouses is the speed with which inquiries can be answered. It is not unusual for a user to build an inquiry that will bring a modern computer system to its knees. Therefore, protecting operational systems and optimizing routine queries is of paramount importance. Many IT organizations design parallel universes in which data warehouses can operate without affecting the production environment.

External business intelligence gathering is a relatively new field. For some companies, this simply means providing access to news wires and online "clipping services." Other organizations, however, are designing sophisticated criteria that can be used to "crawl" the Internet, monitor external data feeds from social media and other sources, and organize information about competitors' products and services. In companies where product innovation is an important function, access to external research services is important. Many IT organizations now have librarians whose job is to assist users to find external information electronically. However, the future ideal will be to integrate external information more seamlessly into work processes and present it to users when needed.

• *Behavior change.*   Organizations already recognize that people pay more attention to what is measured. As a result, organizations have become increasingly more sophisticated about designing the metrics and scorecards they use to monitor both individual and corporate performance (see Kaplan and Norton 1996). It is less well recognized that information can both drive and inhibit certain behaviors in individuals. One participant explained, "More and more, our job is less about technology and more about behavior change. How we present information plays a big part in driving the behaviors the organization is looking for."

Promoting information-positive behavior means ensuring the information that is available is trustworthy and of high quality and information about the business is widely available to all levels of employees to help shape their behavior (Kettinger and Marchand 2011):

> People can sense information effectively only when they understand a company's business performance and how they personally can help to improve performance.... This common sense of purpose fosters an environment in which people begin to look beyond their own jobs and become concerned about the information needs of others. Sensing is enhanced and information valuation assessments become more precise. (Marchand et al. 2000)

Some companies have begun to use greater information transparency to modify and guide staff behavior with extremely positive results (Smith et al. 2009), but organizations have just scratched the surface of what is possible in leveraging the complex linkages between information and behavior. In general, information transparency highlights both strengths and weaknesses, successes and failures. Identifying key information helps staff to focus their efforts in areas that are of concern to management. For example, publishing infection statistics by specialty unit in a hospital can change staff hand-washing habits. Similarly, stressing overall "file completion" information can help customer service staff solve holistic customer problems, rather than processing the individual transactions involved, and thus provide more effective customer service.

EFFECTIVE INFORMATION DELIVERY

The explosion of new information delivery opportunities in organizations has left IT departments scrambling to organize themselves appropriately and develop new skills, roles, practices, and strategies. Even more than with systems development, effective information delivery involves careful attention to the social and behavioral dimensions of how work is done. "Politics is a huge dimension of information delivery," said a participant. "Defining data means establishing one version of the truth and one owner. As we move to standardized definitions, single master files for corporate data items, and common presentation, we get into major battles. In the past we have had ten systems for ten nuances of information. Everyone built their own thing." Another said, "Information integration is very difficult to achieve on a large scale. This problem becomes even more difficult and important in global enterprises and with strategic alliances."

New Information Skills

Better information delivery means clarifying and making visible the knowledge frameworks and mental models that have been applied to create both data and information (Li and Kettinger 2004). Business and IT practitioners must recognize the existence of these frameworks and make appropriate judgments about how they affect the information that is delivered. Although IT staff have been doing this for years when designing reports and screen layouts, the organization's increasing reliance on structured information for decision making means that it is critical to consciously make appropriate decisions about how information is designed and presented. IT staff, therefore, not only need new skills in thinking about information, but they also need better training in analyzing how it will be accessed and used. Furthermore, with more integrated data, it is now essential that business rules be applied to who gets to see what information. "Our systems serve a number of different types of users," said an IT manager at a major pharmaceutical firm. "It is essential that we know who they are. Salespeople, doctors, pharmacists, hospitals, regulatory agencies, and patients all have different information needs and rights. We cannot afford to put the information into the wrong hands." Finally, as already pointed out, navigation and usability have long been afterthoughts of systems analysis and design. Today this must be an integral part of every IT deliverable.

New Information Skills Within IT

- Political judgment
- Information analytics
- Workflow analysis
- Information access
- Business rules for information use
- Usability
- Information navigation

New Information Roles

IT has a number of new or enhanced roles for managing the logistics of information delivery as well. IT's information responsibilities now include the following:

- Data custodianship
- Storage
- Integration
- Presentation
- Security
- Administration
- Personalization and multilingual presentations
- Document indexing and searching
- Unstructured content management and workflow
- Team and collaboration software
- Network and server infrastructure for information hosting/staging.

In addition, IT often hosts several key information management functions. Examples include library and information services, records and information management (e.g., archiving, regulatory compliance), information solutions delivery (including portal design), and data architecture and modeling.

Business responsibilities for information include ownership, quality, and currency. However, even here IT must sometimes establish and enforce the procedures and policies within which business will exercise these responsibilities. For example, some organizations have a formal system of information "expiry dates" for non-system-generated information, and reminders are sent to owners to ensure appropriate review and updating.

New Information Practices

Effective information delivery involves developing practices to manage different forms of information over their life cycles (see Figure 21.1). For each type of information, strategies, processes, and business rules must be established to address each of the four life cycle stages.

1. *Capture.* This includes all activities involved in identifying (i.e., analyzing and integrating) information for possible use. Typically, gaps appear at the borders between silos of information and when trying to connect structured and unstructured information. Capture may also involve digitizing information that is currently in paper format (e.g., documents). At present few organizations formally capture external business intelligence information such as economic, social, and political changes; competitive innovations; and potential problems with partners and suppliers, although many have begun to capture social media content. In the future, however, such information will be captured from an increasingly wide range of sources from both outside and inside the organization (Kettinger and Marchand 2011). Furthermore, users will increasingly demand real-time or near-real-time information, and this will require further refinement of information-capture practices.

2. *Organize.* Organizing information involves indexing, classifying, and linking together sources. At the highest level, this involves creating a taxonomy—that is, a systematic categorization by keyword or term (Corcoran 2002). This provides an

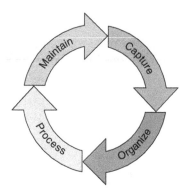

FIGURE 21.1   The Information Management Lifecycle

organizing framework for information that facilitates ease of access. A second layer of organization involves creating metadata—that is, information about content and location. Metadata provide a roadmap to information, much as a card catalog points to the location and information about a book (Lee et al. 2001). Metadata are especially important for workflow design, the overall management of information, and information exchange among enterprises or different software applications. A third layer of organization is provided by processes that identify information ownership and ensure that it meets the necessary corporate, legal, and linguistic standards. These processes also manage activities such as authorship, versioning, and access. A final component of organization involves information presentation. Many organizations have developed a common look and feel for their materials, such as mobile, Internet, or portal pages, to enable ease of navigation and interoperability among platforms.

3. *Process.*   As already noted, organizations have only begun to leverage the value of their information. New information-delivery technologies and channels as well as the recognition of the business value of information are driving the development of new organizational capabilities based on information and technology. IT plays a significant role in the analysis of information and its capture in the form of structural capital. However, organizations also need businesspeople with deeper analytic skills who can combine their knowledge of business with knowledge of data. Statistical modeling and analytic skills will also be increasingly needed to identify opportunities and make sense of huge amounts of data.

4. *Maintain.*   Different types of information must be maintained differently (Williams 2001). For unstructured content, such as documents, social media content, and Web sites, maintenance involves keeping information up to date. All information needs to be regularly assessed as to how well it is meeting the business's needs. Finally, principles and standards must be established for information retention and preservation and for its disposal.

New Information Strategies

A final element of effective information delivery involves strategy. All organizations have a generic vision of delivering the right information to the right person at the right time. However, achieving this goal involves careful consideration of what an

Information Delivery Best Practices

- Approach information delivery as an iterative development project. No one gets it right the first time.
- Separate data from function to create greater flexibility.
- Buy data models and enhance them. This will save many person-years of effort.
- Use middleware to translate data from one system to another. This is especially important for companies using several different packaged systems, each of which contains its own embedded data model.
- Evolve toward a real-time customer information file. These files are notoriously difficult to build all at once; however, having a single source of customer information makes managing customer privacy much easier and also makes it possible to offer new integrated products and services.
- Design information delivery from the end user (whether external customer, employee, or supplier) backward. This substantially reduces internal infighting and focuses attention on what is really important.

organization wants to accomplish with information and how it proposes to derive business value from it. Interestingly, many organizations are currently placing their highest priority on using information for internal management and administration. Employee self-service cuts out much administrative overhead in human resources management, procurement, and accounting. "There are huge savings to be gained by delivering better information on our operational processes and using information to better manage workflows and approvals," said a participant.

Some firms are also developing *microstrategies* for particular areas of the business or types of user. These small-scale initiatives often involve giving users subsets of data containing the specific information they need and appropriate analysis tools. One company has developed an information-access architecture that provides different types of tools to users depending on their abilities to use them to "mine" data. Basic users are given canned inquiries with drill-down capabilities and the ability to export information into an Excel spreadsheet. More skilled users are given basic analytic tools and access to metadata, and expert users are given professional analytic tools.

At the other end of the strategy scale are companies such as UPS, CEMEX, and Monsanto that have made information a strategic priority. Each of these companies has an enterprisewide strategy for using information. UPS collects information about every element of the delivery process (Watson et al. 2010). CEMEX uses information to control every aspect of its cement production and delivery logistics worldwide (Kettinger and Marchand 2004). Monsanto improved the accuracy of its sales forecasting by routinely testing assumptions about prices and trends (Holmes 2011).

THE FUTURE OF INFORMATION DELIVERY

Organizations have begun to discover the power of information, but they have barely scratched the surface of what will be possible over the next decade. Already new technologies are beginning widespread implementation that will have as big an impact on information delivery as the Internet has had over the past decade. These technologies will not only change what is possible to do with information, but they will also change how we view the world of information delivery and how organizations and individuals behave with respect to information. Some of the most important future directions for information delivery include the following:

- *The Internet of things.* Wireless communications and radio frequency identification (RFID) product tags will soon enable organizations and industries to track individual physical objects (e.g., cans of beans, car parts) as they move through the supply chain. Already, Walmart is conducting large-scale trials of this technology with two hundred of its major suppliers. Within a few years, many predict that RFID will replace the Universal Product Code (Langton 2004). And this is just the beginning. As these technologies become more sophisticated, organizations will be able to track and remotely monitor the status of everything from the freshness of lettuce between the field and the store to the location of hospital supplies. Even though this technology is almost ready for prime time, most organizations are nowhere near ready to cope with making sense of such a large influx of information. This will be one of the biggest challenges of the future (Smith and Konsynski 2003).

- *Networkcentric operations.* The growth of standardized communication protocols, network devices, and high-speed data access will soon make it possible to collect, create, distribute, and exploit information across an extremely heterogeneous global computing environment in the near future. Value will be derived from the content, quality, and timeliness of the information moving across the network. Three critical elements must be in place to achieve this goal:

  1. *Sensor grids.* These are coupled with fast and powerful networks to move raw data. Small sensory devices and computers will be connected to other machines to evaluate and filter a wide variety of information, highlighting areas and anomalies to which the organization should pay attention (Watson et al. 2010).
  2. *High-quality visual information.* Along with sophisticated modeling and simulation capabilities and display technology, high-quality visualized information will provide dramatically better awareness of the marketplace, operations, and environmental impact. This will enable more targeted strategies, support more focused logistics, and provide full-dimensional understanding of the business environment at a variety of locations and levels.
  3. *Value-added command and control processes.* Superior information will make the loop of control shorter, effectively taking decision rights away from competitors and providing rapid feedback to frontline workers.

  These new capabilities will be developed to achieve information advantage (i.e., to know more) and execution advantage (i.e., to produce less friction between parts) over competitors.

- *Self-synchronizing systems.* Traditionally, leaders have worked from the top down to achieve synchronization of effort. When decisions are made in this way, each iteration of the "observe-orient-decide-act" (OODA) loop takes time to complete with the front line passing information up the hierarchy until enough is accumulated to make a decision, which is then passed back down the organizational levels to the front line to take action. In contrast, we know that complex processes organize best from the bottom-up (e.g., markets, the Internet, and evolutionary processes), and they are efficient and can allocate resources without high overheads. Such self-synchronization eliminates the lags in the OODA loop and accelerates responsiveness.

In the future, information in organizations will be used to promote self-synchronization to enable a well-informed workforce to organize and coordinate complex activities from the bottom up without management involvement. (Crowdsourcing is an early application of this concept.) Systems themselves will be designed to self-monitor and self-correct in a similar way. This will dramatically change the role of management and how organizations operate. Leaders will set the "rules of engagement" but be much less involved in the day-to-day running of their organizations (Smith and Konsynski 2003).

- *Feedback loops.* A central feature of self-synchronization is the creation of closed feedback loops that enable individuals and groups to adjust their behavior dynamically. Researchers have already demonstrated the power of feedback to change behavior (Zoutman et al. 2004). Feedback mechanisms built into systems will require the creation of new metrics for monitoring such individual behavioral factors as transparency, information sharing, and trust. Similarly, organizations will incorporate feedback loops into their operations, continually scanning and evaluating and adapting strategies, tactics, and operations. With the right technology and infostructure (i.e., appropriately organized and managed information), different views can be brought to bear on a situation and adjustments made on an ongoing basis.

- *Informal information management.* Finally, organizations have a significant unmined resource in the informal information kept by knowledge workers in their own personal files. Information-delivery mechanisms of the future will look for opportunities to organize and leverage this information in a variety of ways. For example, software exists today that "crawls" people's address books to find who in an organization knows people whom others in the organization want or need to contact. Other types of software analyze personal files to compile an expertise profile of individual employees. The field of informal information management is still in its infancy, but it is certainly one to which IT managers should pay attention because it represents a huge, untapped pool of information.

Conclusion

Information delivery in IT is an idea whose time has finally come. IT practitioners and experts have been talking about it for years, yet only recently has the business truly begun to understand the power and the potential of information. New technologies and channels now make it possible to access and deliver information easily and cheaply. As a result, information is now being used to drive many different types of value in organizations, from business intelligence to streamlined operations to lower administrative costs to new ways to reach customers. The challenges for IT are huge. Not only does effective information delivery require IT to implement new technologies, but it also means that IT must develop new internal nontechnical and analytic capabilities. Information delivery makes

IT work much more visible in the organization. Developing standard data models, integrating information into work processes, and forcing (encouraging) business managers to put the customer/employee/supplier first in their decision making involve IT practitioners in organizational and political conflicts that most would likely prefer to avoid. Clearly, IT managers are front and center of an information revolution that will completely transform how organizations operate. The changes to date are just the tip of the information iceberg. In the not-so-distant future, new streams of information will be flooding into the organization, and IT managers will be expected to be ready with plans for its use. For the first time, senior business executives are ready to hear about the value of information. IT managers should take advantage of this new openness to develop the skills and capabilities they will need to prepare for the coming deluge.

References

Beath, C., I. Bercerra-Fernandez, J. Ross, and J. Short. "Finding Value in the Information Explosion." *MIT Sloan Management Review* 53, no. 4 (Summer 2012).

Brohman, K., and M. Boudreau. "The Dance: Getting Managers and Miners on the Floor Together." Proceedings of Administrative Sciences Association of Canada, 2004.

Corcoran, M. "Taxonomies: Hope or Hype?" *Online* 26, no. 5 (September/October 2002): 76–78.

Holmes, B. "What's IT's Role in Analytics Adoption?" *MIT Sloan Management Review*, Reprint No. 52301 (January 2011).

Kaplan, R., and D. Norton. *The Balanced Scorecard.* Boston: Harvard Business School Press, 1996.

Kaplan, S. "Emerging Technology." *CIO Magazine*, January 15, 2002.

Kettinger, W., and D. Marchand. "Working an Informated Opportunity Zone." Unpublished case study prepared for the Society for Information Management's Advanced Practices Council, Chicago, May 2004.

Kettinger, W., and D. Marchand. "Information Management Practices (IMP) from the Senior Manager's Perspective: An Investigation of the IMP Construct and Its Measurement." *Information Systems Journal* 21 (2011): 385–406.

Kettinger, W., K. Paddack, and D. Marchand. "The Case of Skandia: The Evolving Nature of I/T Value." Unpublished case study prepared for the Society for Information Management's Advanced Practices Council, Chicago, January 2003.

Kontzer, T. "Search On." *Information Week* 923 (January 20, 2003): 30–38.

Korsten, P. "The Essential CIO." *IBM Institute for Business Value*, Somers, NY: IBM Global Business Services, 2011.

Kruschwitz, N. "First Look: The Second Annual New Intelligent Enterprise Survey." *MIT Sloan Management Review* 54, no. 1 (Summer 2011): 87–89.

Laney, D., and A. White. "Agenda Overview for Information Innovation and Governance 2014." Gartner Inc., ID Number: G00259582, January 10, 2014.

Langton, J. "Wal-Mart Tests Alternative to Bar Code." *Globe and Mail*, June 3, 2004.

Lavalle, S., E. Lesser, R. Shockley, M. Hopkins, and N. Kruschwitz. "Big Data, Analytics and the Path from Insights to Value." *MIT Sloan Management Review* (Winter 2011).

Lee, H., T. Kim, and J. Kim. "A Metadata-Oriented Architecture for Building Datawarehouse." *Journal of Database Management* 12, no. 4 (October–December 2001): 15–25.

Li, Y., and W. Kettinger. "A Knowledge-Based Theory of Information: Clarifying the Relationship between Data, Information, and Knowledge." Draft paper, Management

Science Department, Moore School of Business, University of South Carolina, Columbia, 2004.

Marchand, D., W. Kettinger, and J. Rollins. "Information Orientation: People, Technology and the Bottom Line." *Sloan Management Review* (Summer 2000).

Marchand, D., and J. Peppard. "Why IT Fumbles Analytics." *Harvard Business Review* 91, no. 1–2 (January/February 2013): 104–12.

McKeen, J., and H. Smith. *Making IT Happen*, New York: John Wiley and Sons, 2003.

McKeen, J., and H. Smith. *IT Strategy: Issues and Practices*, 2nd ed. Upper Saddle River, NJ: Pearson Education, 2012.

Ross, J. "Do You Need a Data Dictator?" *MIT Sloan Management Review*, Reprint No. 54123 (August 2012).

Smith, H., and B. Konsynski. "Developments in Practice X: Radio Frequency Identification (RFID)—An Internet for Physical Objects."

Communications of the Association for Information Systems 12, no. 19 (September 2003).

Smith, H. A., J. D. McKeen, and T. A. Jenkin. "Exploring Strategies for Deploying Knowledge Management Tools and Technologies." *Journal of Information Science and Technology* 6, no. 3 (2009): 3–24.

Watson, R. T., J. W. Boudreau, and S. Li. "Telematics at UPS: Energy Informatics in action." *MISQ Executive* 9, no. 1 (2010): 203–13.

Williams, S. "The Intranet Content Management Strategy Conference." *Management Services* 45, no. 9 (September 2001): 16–18.

Zoutman, D., D. Ford, A. Bassili, M. Lam, and K. Nakatsu. "Impacts of Feedback on Antibiotic Prescribing for Upper Respiratory Tract Infections." Presentation available from the authors (zoutman@cliff.path.queensu.ca), Queen's University, Kingston, Ontario, 2004.

MINI CASE

Project Management at MM[2]

"We've got a real 'warm puppy' here," Brian Smith told Werner McCann. "Make sure you make the most of it. We could use a winner."

Smith was MM's CIO, and McCann was his top project manager. The puppy in question was MM's new venture into direct-to-customer marketing of its *green meters*, a product designed to help better manage electrical consumption, and the term referred to the project's wide appeal. The strategy had been a hit with analysts ever since it had been revealed to the financial community, and the company's stock was doing extremely well as a result. "At last," one had written in his popular newsletter, "we have a company that is willing to put power literally and figuratively in consumers' hands. If MM can deliver on its promises, we fully expect this company to reap the rewards."

Needless to say, the Green project was popular internally, too. "I'm giving it to you because you have the most project-management experience we've got," Smith had said. "There's a lot riding on this one." As he walked away from Smith's office, McCann wasn't sure whether to feel complimented or terrified. He had certainly managed some successful projects for the company (previously known as ModMeters) over the past five years but never anything like this one. *That's the problem with project management,* he thought. *In IT almost every project is completely different. Experience only takes you part of the way.*

And Green was different. It was the first truly enterprisewide project the company had ever done, and McCann was having conniptions as he thought about telling Fred Tompkins, the powerful head of manufacturing, that he might not be able to have everything his own way. McCann knew that, to be successful, this project had to take an outside-in approach—that is, to take the end customers' point of view on the company. That meant integrating marketing, ordering, manufacturing, shipping, and service into one seamless process that wouldn't bounce the customer from one department to another in the company. MM had always had separate systems for each of its "silos," and this project would work against the company's traditional culture and processes. The Green project was also going to have to integrate with IT's information management renewal (IMR) project. Separate silos had always meant separate databases, and the IMR project was supposed to resolve inconsistencies among them and provide accurate and integrated information to different parts of the company. This was a huge political challenge, but, unless it worked, McCann couldn't deliver on his mandate.

Then there was the issue of resources. McCann groaned at the thought. MM had some good people but not enough to get through all of the projects in the IT plan within the promised timelines. Because of the importance of the Green project, he knew he'd get good cooperation on staffing, but the fact remained that he would have to go outside for some of the technical skills he needed to get the job done. Finally, there was the schedule that had to be met. Somehow, during the preliminary assessment phase, it

---

[2] Smith, H. A., and J. D. McKeen. "Project Management at MM." #1-L05-1-009, Queen's School of Business, November 2005. Reproduced by permission of Queen's University, School of Business, Kingston, Ontario.

had become clear that September 5 was to be the "hard launch" date. There were good reasons for this—the fall was when consumers usually became concerned with their energy consumption—but McCann worried that a date barely twelve months from now would put too much pressure on his team. "We've got to get in there first, before the competition," Smith had said to him. "The board expects us to deliver. You've got my backing and the support of the full executive team, but you *have* to deliver this one."

SIX WEEKS LATER

It was full steam ahead on the Green project. It's *amazing* what a board mandate and executive sponsorship can do for a project, thought McCann, who knew how hard it usually was to get business attention to IT initiatives. He now had a full-time business counterpart, Raj Sambamurthy. Samba, as he was known to his colleagues, had come out of Tompkins's division and was doing a fantastic job of getting the right people in the room to make the decisions they needed to move ahead. The Green steering committee was no Mickey Mouse group either. Smith, Tompkins, and every VP affected by the project were meeting biweekly with him and Samba to review every aspect of the project's progress.

McCann had pulled no punches when communicating with the committee. "You've given me the mandate and the budget to get this project off the ground," he had told them. "But we have to be clear about what we're trying to accomplish." Together, they had hammered out a value proposition that emphasized the strategic value of the project and some of the measures they would use to monitor its ultimate success. The requirements and design phase had also gone smoothly because everyone was so motivated to ensure the project's success. "Linking success to *all* our annual bonuses sure helped *that!*" McCann had remarked wryly to Samba.

Now McCann was beginning to pull together his dream team of implementers. The team had chosen a package known as Web-4-U as the front end of the project, but it would take a lot of work to customize it to suit their unique product and, even more, to integrate it with MM's outmoded back-end systems. The Web-4-U company was based in Ireland but had promised to provide 24/7 consultation on an as-needed basis. In addition, Samba had now assembled a small team of business analysts to work on the business processes they would need. They were working out of the firm's Cloverdale office, a thirty-minute drive from IT's downtown location. (It was a shame they couldn't all be together, but space was at a premium at headquarters. McCann made a mental note to look into some new collaboration software he'd heard about.) Now that these two pieces were in place, McCann felt free to focus on the technical "guts" of the system. "Maybe this will work out after all," he said.

THREE MONTHS TO LAUNCH DATE

By June, however, McCann was tearing out what little hair was left on his head. He was seriously considering moving to a remote Peruvian hamlet and breeding llamas. "*Anything* would be better than this mess," he told Yung Lee, the senior IT architect, over coffee. They were poring over the project's critical path. "The way I see it," Lee stated matter-of-factly, "we have two choices: We can continue with this inferior technology and meet our deadline but not deliver on our functionality, *or* we can redo the plan and go back to the steering committee with a revised delivery date and budget."

McCann sighed. Techies *always* saw things in black and white, but his world contained much more gray. And so much was riding on this—credibility (his, IT's, the company's), competitiveness, and stock price. He dreaded being the bearer of this bad news, so he said, "Let's go over this *one* more time."

"It's not going to get any better, but here goes." Lee took a deep breath. "Web-4-U is based on outmoded technology. It was the best available last year, but *this* year the industry has agreed on a new standard, and if we persist in using Web-4-U, we are going to be out of date before Green even hits the street. We need to go back and completely rethink our technical approach based on the new standard and then redesign our Web interface. I know it's a setback and expensive, but it has to be done."

"How come we didn't know about this earlier?" McCann demanded.

Lee replied, "When the standard was announced, we didn't realize what the implications were at first. It was only in our quarterly architecture meeting that the subject came up. That's why I'm here now." The architects were a breed apart, thought McCann. All tech and *no* business sense. They'd lost almost three months because of this. "By the way," Lee concluded, "Web-4-U knew about this, too. They're scrambling to rewrite their code. I guess they figured if you didn't know right away, there would be more chance of you sticking with them."

The chances of *that* are slim to none, thought McCann. His *next* software provider, whoever that was, was going to be sitting right here under his steely gaze. Seeing an agitated Wendy Chan at his door, he brought the meeting to a hasty close. "I'm going to have to discuss this with Brian," he told Lee. "We can't surprise him with this at the steering committee meeting. Hang tight for a couple of days, and I'll get back to you."

"OK," said Lee, "but remember that we're wasting time."

Easy for *you* to say, thought McCann as he gestured Chan into his office. She was his counterpart at the IMR project, and they had always had a good working relationship. "I just wanted to give you a heads-up that we've got a serious problem at IMR that will affect you," she began. Llamas began prancing into his mind's eye. "Tompkins is refusing to switch to our new data dictionary. We've spent months hammering this out with the team, but he says he wasn't kept informed about the implications of the changes, and now he's refusing to play ball. I don't know *how* he could say that. He's had a rep on the team from the beginning, and we've been sending him regular progress reports."

McCann was copied on those reports. Their pages of techno-jargon would put *anyone* to sleep! He was sure that Tompkins had never got past the first page of any of those reports. His rep was a dweeb, too, someone Tompkins thought he could live without in his daily operations.

"Damn! This is something I *don't* need." Like all IT guys, McCann *hated* corporate politics with a passion. He didn't understand them and wasn't good at them. Why hadn't Samba and his team picked up on this? They were plugged into the business. Now he was going to have to deal with Chan's problem as well as his own if he wanted to get the Green project going. Their back-end processes wouldn't work at all unless everyone was using the same information in the same format. Why couldn't Tompkins see that? Did he *want* the Green project to fail?

"The best way to deal with this one," advised Chan, "is to *force* him to accept these changes. Go to John Johnson and tell him that you need Tompkins to change his business processes to fit our data dictionary. It's for the good of the company, after all." Chan's strong suit wasn't her political savvy.

"You're right that we need Tompkins on our side," said McCann, "but there may be a better way. Let me talk to Samba. He's got his ear to the ground in the business. I'll speak with him and get back to you."

After a bit of chitchat, Wendy Chan left McCann to his PERT chart, trying again to determine the extra cost in time if they went with the new technology. Just then the phone rang. It was Linda Perkins, McCann's newly hired work-at-home usability designer. She was one of the best in the business, and he was lucky to have snagged her just coming off maternity leave. His promise of flexible working hours and full benefits had lured her back to work two months before her year-long leave ended. "You've *got* to do something about your HR department!" Perkins announced. "They've just told me that I'm not eligible for health and dental benefits because I don't work on the premises! Furthermore, they want to classify me as contingent staff, not managerial, because I don't fit in one of their petty little categories for employees. You promised me that you had covered all this before I took the job! I gave up a good job at LifeCo so I could work from home."

McCann had indeed covered this issue in principle with Rick Morrow, IT's HR representative, but that had been almost eight months ago. Morrow had since left the firm. McCann wondered if he had left any paperwork on this matter. The HR IT spot had not yet been filled, and all of the IT managers were upset about HR's unreceptive attitude when it came to adapting its policies to the realities of today's IT world. "OK, Linda, just hang in there for a day or two and I'll get this all sorted out," he promised. "How's the usability testing coming along?"

"That's *another* thing I wanted to talk with you about. The team's making changes to the look and feel of the product without consulting me," she fumed. "I can't do my job without being in the loop. You *have* to make them tell me when they're doing things like this."

McCann sighed. Getting Perkins on the project had been such a coup that he hadn't given much thought to how the lines of communication would work within such a large team. "I hear you, Linda, and we'll work this out. Can you just give me a few days to figure out how we can improve things?"

Hanging up, he grabbed his jacket and slunk out of the office as quickly as he could before any other problems could present themselves. If he just kept walking south, he'd make it to the Andes in three, maybe four, months. He could teach himself Spanish along the way. At least the llamas would appreciate his efforts! MM could take its project and give it to some other poor schmuck. *No way* was he going back! He walked furiously down the street, mentally ticking off the reasons he had been a fool to fall for Smith's sweet talk. Then, unbidden, a plan of attack formed in his head. Walking always did the trick. Getting out of the office cleared his head and focused his priorities. He turned back the way he had come, now eager to get back in the fray. He had some things to do right away, and others he had to put in place ASAP.

Discussion Questions

1. Some organizational factors increase a project's likelihood of success. Identify these "facilitators" for the Green project.
2. Other organizational factors decrease a project's likelihood of success. Identify these "barriers" for the Green project.
3. Outline the things that McCann needs to do right away.

MINI CASE

Working Smarter at Continental Furniture International[3]

Joel Parsons hurried down the hall to the monthly executive committee meeting doing a mental checklist of all the things he was responsible for: sales analysis—check; marketing stats—check; quarterly and YTD financials—check; operating statistics—check; trends in each of these areas—check. Parsons was right hand man to the President of Continental Furniture International (CFI) and his primary job was to collect, analyze, and interpret any and all information the president needed to run the company. Joel had joined CFI a year ago from a similar job as manager of Data Analysis, assisting the vice president of Operations at UPS, where he had been involved in implementing some of the world's most sophisticated delivery scheduling and package flow technology. "I could use a bright young MBA here with me to shake things up at CFI," the president, Alan Chambers, had told him during his interview. "We need better business intelligence if we're going to be better than our competition."

"*That* was a laugh," thought Joel as he took his place beside Chambers and flipped open his laptop. These days his lived on Excel. This company thrived on its spreadsheets and Joel was responsible for digesting everyone else's data and packaging it for the President so he was always up to speed. Sure, they also had computer reports and even a financial "dashboard," thanks to the company's new ERP system, but the business world was changing and these canned reports only scratched the surface of what the president needed to know.

The next hour was a typical executive meeting, with each VP reporting on his or her progress and the president grilling them on *exactly* what was going on. To keep everyone on their toes, he always liked to have a few facts at his fingertips. At this meeting, there seemed to be a theme. "How much do we spend to heat our Andover warehouse?," he inquired of the VP of Operations. "Why are our delivery costs rising so quickly?" "What are we doing to make sure our drivers are following all our safety protocols?" Occasionally, he would turn to Joel to check a fact or a trend, but he had done his homework and wanted everyone to know it. Joel watched the VPs squirm with discomfort as they tried to dig through their own spreadsheets to find the information Alan was demanding.

As they moved through the agenda, Joel was happy he wasn't on the hot seat. The last to report was the CIO, Cheryl Drewry. A long-serving executive, Drewry was tough, spoke her mind, and delivered what she promised; it was the reason she'd been around so long. After listening to Cheryl's report on the progress of their major IT projects, Alan paused and all heads looked up expectantly.

---

[3] Smith, H. A., and J. D. McKeen. "Working Smarter at Continental Furniture International." #1-L10-1-002, Queen's School of Business, February 2005. Reproduced by permission of Queen's University, School of Business, Kingston, Ontario.

"I asked you all to clear an extra hour for this meeting for a reason," he stated. "We're doing well as a company but we need to do better. Our ERP system has got us part of the way. We now have good, common processes and some common data and consistent functionality. In short, we've picked all the low-hanging fruit. Now I'm worried about what's next. We can't afford to be complacent. *Everyone* has an ERP these days—even those guys at WWF. Everyone grinned at the nickname of World Wide Furniture, CFI's archrival for many years. The two companies had seesawed back and forth at the No. 1 and 2 positions in the furniture industry. Right now, CFI was No. 1 and it was Alan's job to keep it that way.

Alan continued, "What we now need is a way to work *smarter*—a way to leverage the information we've got and use it more effectively. There are lots of things that we could do but my first priority is to use information to enable CFI to *Go Green!*" He paused dramatically, while the VPs took a deep breath wondering what it was going to mean for their divisions. "Cheryl and I have discussed this and we feel there is enormous potential to use information, IT systems, and our great people to become more productive, more profitable and to reduce costs, while saving energy. This is truly a win-win for everyone!"

The room burst into sustained applause. The idea was a winner to be sure. How could you not like it? But Joel knew the hard work that it took at UPS and he wondered if these guys knew what they were in for. Alan turned the floor over to Cheryl who gave a brief overview of what they were planning.

"First, we are going to give each of you a set of data analytics tools so that you can explore our data warehouse yourselves. We want you to start thinking about ways you can use data differently. Second, we are going to establish an energy informatics team, composed of some business and IT people. They are going to examine any and all opportunities for using information to save energy anywhere in our company by working smarter. Third, we want your ideas and support to make this a corporate showcase."

Alan stood up. "This is an exciting and very strategic initiative for our company. It's a chance to be both socially and fiscally responsible and to lead in our industry. The energy Informatics function is going to be crucial to its success so I'm personally going to be monitoring our progress by having this team report directly to me, with a dotted line to Cheryl. And fortunately, we've got just the right person to lead it...." He gestured at Joel.

"Joel Parsons has several years' experience doing just this type of work at UPS. He helped them implement package flow technology which enabled the company to shave 30 million miles off its daily delivery driving two years' ago. This has saved over 3 million gallons of fuel annually—benefiting both the company and the environment. Take a bow, Joel."

Totally dumbfounded, Joel stood up and bowed dramatically and the meeting broke up a minute later, with everyone shaking his hand and congratulating him on his new appointment. Gathering his papers and laptop, he felt a hand on his shoulder. It was Alan.

"Sorry for the surprise Joel but this was super secret and I knew you would love a chance at this job. You've been suggesting we improve our analytic capabilities ever since you got here."

That was true, but delivering these capabilities was going to be a serious challenge. While he knew what the goal was, getting there was going to be a project of a nature few companies had tried. It was going to take it all—business smarts, technology, data, people's commitment at every level, and processes. Somehow, they ALL had to tie together effectively to deliver real business and environmental value.

"I'll do my very best for you sir," he replied. Give me a few weeks to get my thoughts together and to speak with Cheryl and the other VPs and I'll outline how I suggest we implement this strategy. With a curt nod of his head, and a clap on his back, Alan left the room leaving Joel with a million thoughts swirling in his head.

Over the next few weeks, Joel had meetings with every one of the VPs to assess the scope of the opportunities involved, identify issues, concerns and potential obstacles, and to quietly evaluate who was *really* on board with the Green strategy.

In addition, he met individually with the two IT members of his team, who had been hand-picked by Cheryl. She had chosen good people, Joel thought. Susan Liu was a data warehouse specialist. She understood what data the company was already collecting from its various systems, how "clean" it was, and what types of analyses were being done at present.

Mario Fortunato was an analyst who had helped implement the company's ERP system, which was now its processing backbone. He was a good choice, thought Joel, because he had an excellent overview of the entire company's operations from suppliers to consumers. Joel had asked Alan to hold off appointing the last business member of the team until he better understood the business expertise that might be needed.

In their first team meeting, Joel outlined their mandate as he saw it. "Going green is both a huge opportunity and a huge challenge. So far, we've never used our data and systems to help us use energy more effectively. While we've had some energy-saving initiatives at CFI, these have been entirely initiated by our building maintenance group doing generic things like installing energy-efficient light bulbs and such. What we need first is a 'quick hit' so that everyone in the company can see what we're trying to do and why."

Susan jumped in. "We could start with our data centers. There seem to be lots of ways to save energy there."

"You're right of course Susan," said Joel. "We should be doing this and I'll make sure that Cheryl has this in her plans. But what we need here is a much more visible way to demonstrate the business value and energy efficiency of this initiative."

Mario looked thoughtful. "I'm not sure if this is what you mean but we know how much each of our buildings, offices and warehouses across the continent use in electricity, water, and heating and cooling. Our ERP system gathers this information from the utility bills that are sent to us electronically. Each building is considered a separate unit for billing purposes and has a separate set of metering. Could we run a contest that would post each building's energy usage each month and provide prizes when they reduce their usage relative to their previous three year average?"

"*That* is an absolutely brilliant idea, Mario!" Joel exclaimed. "It's quick—at least I think it is; it's visible; it uses data we already have; and it involves everyone. And best of all, we can run with it while we work on a more comprehensive energy informatics strategy."

Joel was right on all counts. Three months later, the team launched the "Great Green Challenge" with an energy utilization dashboard on everyone's desktop as well as on special monitors in the warehouses. This showed each building's utilization of the three main resources and enabled staff to understand their usage not only in comparison to previous years but also by time of day and month. They could also compare their usage against other similar buildings. Each building had a "green committee," which collected employee suggestions and worked with the appropriate people to implement them. Prizes would be awarded in various categories, such as biggest percentage monthly decline in usage, most innovative suggestion, and largest annual cumulative percentage decrease. The team also posted the most effective ideas on its collaboration site so others could see them. Prizes were small—coffee and donuts for all staff, movie passes, and virtual gold stars—but the contest gave the whole company a focus for its efforts to reduce its carbon footprint and its staff clear information about how they could work to save energy. Everyone was motivated by this program and within a few months after the launch, utility bills were reflecting small, but significant declines. Alan even dropped by to congratulate the team on its success.

Success gave the team, which had now grown by two new members, further ideas for other energy informatics projects, so Joel called a strategy meeting to help chart out their next move.

"What if we were to tap into the computers in our trucks?," asked Menakshi Deena, who had joined them from the Operations Division. "They collect lots of data about everything from seatbelt use to oil pressure to the amount of time spent idling. Since we have thousands of trucks, we could really save a bundle if we could figure out how to use them more efficiently and safely."

They hashed the idea around, growing more and more positive about it as they did. "I like it!" Joel said at last. "Let's make Energy Telematics our next major Green team initiative."

After running the idea by Alan, who gave it the go-ahead, the team started into the project in earnest. Sue and Menakshi were put in charge of data collection.

"We can get over 200 vehicle-related elements from every truck," Sue reported. "If we put a GPS chip in each truck, we can collect data on what the trucks and the drivers are doing at every stop in their route. We can then use this data to optimize all sorts of energy use."

"But we're going to need to develop some software to help us analyze and report all this data," said Mario doing some rapid calculations. "There will be literally thousands of data points every day for every truck."

It took a lot of work to figure out all the technical details. The company's trucks had a variety of different hardware and software platforms in its various vehicles and daily data collection and standardization routines had to be developed. Then, the team had to develop algorithms to analyze what was collected in order to determine where problems were occurring. Ted Prior, from Logistics, helped design a pilot test with 50 trucks in their Omaha depot, flying out personally to be there when the data receivers were installed.

"They work great," he reported Friday afternoon just before flying home. "We only had a few glitches but otherwise, when the trucks pull in at the end of the day, the drivers simply push a transmit button on their dashboards and all the data is transmitted. We're going to be up and running in no time!"

Monday morning Joel arrived bright and early to find an urgent voice mail from Alan's EA. "He wants to see you *immediately!*" said the message. Hurrying up to the executive suite, Joel wondered what the problem could possibly be. Everything was on track and running smoothly as far as he could tell. Alan's face told a different story. "Sit down," he barked when Joel peered in the doorway. "I've just heard that our drivers in

Omaha are threatening to strike," he said as Joel took his seat. "They think you're going to use your system to monitor their behavior. What's going on?"

"I have no idea sir," Joel stammered. "We've just done a technical pilot."

"Well, I've told them out there that the pilot has been suspended indefinitely," Alan said. "Clearly, you haven't been careful about the impressions you're giving so you'd better go back to the drawing board."

Back in the team room, Joel called an urgent meeting to explain the situation. "We've done a lot of work to collect this data and it could have a huge impact on our costs, energy efficiency and safety record," he noted. "But we will not get a chance to prove this if we don't figure out how to get the drivers onside. We didn't need to 'sell' the Great Green project, but this hostile reaction suggests that we may have some selling to do with other parts of the organization as well as our truck drivers. Anybody got any other ideas about what could go wrong?"

"Well, our front-line operations managers are super busy," said Menakshi. "We'd better be careful how we present this program to them or it could be seen as a lot of extra work."

"Our mechanics should be involved as well," said Ted. "They seemed quite interested in the information we could pull off the trucks. They could be quite helpful if we get them involved."

"We've got all this great data," said Sue, "but how are we going to get the drivers to *act* on it? Just collecting this information isn't enough."

"We've also got to consider how to roll this project out across the company," said Mario. "If the drivers can get this upset about a simple technical pilot, what are they going to do when they see the information we're planning to collect!"

The team fell silent and Joel turned all these thoughts over in his mind. He knew his future at CFI depended on what they did next. They'd barely started this project and it was already in trouble.

"Okay," he said. "We've hit a snag so now we've got to find a way to get Energy Telematics back on track. I told Alan we'd work up a plan and, if he likes it, he'll unsuspend the project. Who's got some ideas?"

Discussion Questions

1. Why was Joel's team caught off guard by the hostile reaction of the truck drivers to "technical" pilot of the Energy Telematics project at the Omaha depot?
2. Why did the "Great Green Challenge" succeed while the Energy Telematics project hit road bumps right out of the gate? What are the lessons learned for Joel and his team?
3. Develop a plan for Joel and his team to get the Energy Telematics project unsuspended. The plan will need details of who, what, when, where and why.

MINI CASE

Managing Technology at Genex Fuels[4]

"You have got yourselves into a terrible predicament," said V. R. "Sandy" Sandhuramen, his soft Indian accent belying the gravity of his words. "You are incredibly lucky you have managed to do business as well as you have, but this situation cannot be allowed to carry on." Sandy, a high-priced technology consultant, had been hired by Genex Fuel's new CIO, Nick Devlin, to review the company's technology portfolio and help him and his newly appointed IT architect, Chuck Yee, get a handle on the firm's technology needs.

Genex, a major producer of crude oil and natural gas, is the largest marketer of petroleum and petroleum products in the region. It is structured into three distinct business divisions, each comprising a number of functional segments. Until recently, IT had been decentralized into the three divisions, each with its own director of IT who reported to the divisional executive vice presidents (EVPs). Devlin, formerly the director of the corporate division, had been appointed CIO and given the specific mandate to bring in SAP as the primary technology platform for all the divisions.

"We have to start behaving like we're one business," said the CEO when he appointed Devlin. "I want a much more agile and responsive IT organization than we've had in the past. It seems to me that every time I ask IT to look into something I've heard or read about, they always come up with a thousand and one reasons why it *won't* work. We need to be able to use technology competitively, and that won't happen unless you can get ahead of the curve."

Devlin's excitement about his new mandate had lasted just about a week, until the true scope of the challenge became clear. He had asked each divisional IT director for an inventory of hardware and software currently in place and to briefly outline the work that was in their plans for the coming year. "We must have one of every piece of hardware and software ever produced," Devlin marveled as he scanned their reports. On the one hand, there was a new customer management system called COMC, which had been implemented to improve real-time information exchange between the company's 135 bulk fuel sites and Genex headquarters. On the other hand, IT was still running an archaic DOS-based marketing system called MAAS to provide customer service and reports. "And they want to bring in SAP!" he groaned. "We need a plan, and we need it soon."

That was when Devlin had engaged Sandy to work with Yee. "First, I want a no-holds-barred assessment of our current situation," he had said, and now they were in his office, outlining the "terrible predicament."

---

[4] Smith, H. A., and J. D. McKeen. "Managing Technology at Genex Fuels." #9-L05-1-004, Queen's School of Business, February 2005. Reproduced by permission of Queen's University, School of Business, Kingston, Ontario.

"The biggest problem you face at present," said Sandy, "is the fact that you have absolutely no standards and no integration, as you discovered for yourself, Nick." There was a lot of technology out there—both old and new—and it was a political hot potato. Almost every system had its group of advocates, some very senior in the company. All the EVPs had invested their individual technology budgets in the hardware and software that they felt could best support their work. The problem was that maintaining this mishmash was now costing an arm and a leg. And it was highly doubtful that the company was getting true value for its technology investment.

"We should be able to leverage our existing investments so we can invest in new technology," said Yee. "Instead, almost all our budget is taken up with holding these systems together with toothpicks and tape."

"One of the most challenging situations," Sandy went on, "is Price One."

Obsolete but absolutely essential, Price One is the fuel-pricing system that stores the pricing algorithms for all fuels marketing functions, including aviation, marine, retail, branded associates, and industrial and wholesale. Although pricing is an integral part of marketing, Price One cannot communicate with COMC and is not easily adaptable to changes in the business environment. Price One perfectly reflected the business and technology that existed ten years ago, but this has now become a real drawback. To get around these limitations while continuing to use Price One, staff manually feed information from pricing requests in COMC to Price One to get approval because both systems use different terminology in coding products for different pricing methods.

Price One also lacks the ability to link information from different systems to ensure data integrity. As a result, Price One has accumulated some irrelevant data groups under pricing for products, and such corrupted data can be detected only by an experienced individual who has been dealing with that product group for decades and who would know at a glance the validity of the data. One of Price One's critical flaws is its inability to link with other systems, such as COMC, and to pick up competitive market information in order to approve price. Previous plans to rewrite this system have been resisted strenuously by management because of the expense. Now the system is on its last legs.

"And like most oil and gas companies," Sandy observed, "you have automated very few of your information assets as other types of organizations have done." Typically for the industry, Genex had grown by acquiring other, smaller firms and had inherited an enormous amount of physical data. It now has more than two million items of paper and microfilm. It has one hundred twenty thousand tapes of data. Some items date back to the 1940s and came from numerous sources. The company's seismic assets, on which it bases many of its decisions and which has a replacement cost estimated at more than two billion dollars, are stored on a wide variety of media from analog tapes, magnetic reels, and cartridges to optical discs to paper, film, and microfilm. They are spread out across five conventional physical warehouses.

This system of data management is problematic for two main reasons. First, with land sales occurring every two weeks, it is extremely difficult to make timely decisions based on all known information about a property. Clearly, the more seismic information a company can bring to bear on its decisions, the better it can decide where it wants to do further work. Second, the company's data assets, on which its future depends, are extremely vulnerable. There is no backup. When needed, the only copy of the information requested is physically transported to Genex's offices. The tapes on which the data reside deteriorate further with each reading. Furthermore, much information resides on obsolete forms of media and is getting increasingly difficult to access.

"Finally, IT is getting a lot of pressure from the executive office," reported Sandy. "These guys have seen what's going on in other companies, and they want to see Genex move into the twenty-first century. Staff at Genex cover vast territory and must work from home, from local facilities, or on the road. Not only does Genex need to provide a virtual working environment for these workers, but it also needs to consider how they can work together as a team without having physical colocation for communication."

"Well, I guess we have it all," said Devlin. "Integration problems, outdated hardware and software, inconsistent data, expensive workarounds, pressure to modernize, and substantial budget limitations." Turning to Yee and Sandy, he smiled. "Now what are we going to do about it? Where do we start?"

Discussion Questions

1. What evidence is the CEO using to suggest that Genex is not using technology competitively?
2. Did Devlin need to hire Sandy, a "high-priced technology consultant," to tell him that technology at Genex was a mess?
3. Devise a strategy to successfully implement enterprisewide systems (such as SAP) at Genex.

INDEX

L

Leadership in IT
  challenges, 177–178
  changing role of IT leader, 65–67
  changing the culture, 191–192
  create sustainable process, 178
  development of, 70–73
  first steps, 192–193
  provide adequate resources, 178
  qualities of good leader, 67–68
  reassess process and practice, 178
  resources, 190–191
  short business horizons, 190
  strike correct balance, 178
  styles of, 69
  value proposition for, 73–74
Life cycle stages of technology, 289, 292
Lines of business (LOBs), 176, 285
LOBs. *See* Lines of business

M

Management
  advice to, 35–36
  in aligning strategies, 19
  involvement in decision making, 19
  modeling of IM value by, 153
  support of IT, 5, 12, 24
Management of portfolio, 11
Managing IT demand
  economics of, 273
  key organizational for effective, 274–280
  organizational context, 272
  portfolio management, 280
  supply management, 271
  "technology push" and "business pull", 278
  three tools, 273–274
  ultimate goal, 274
  understanding, 271–272
Mass collaboration, 223
Maturity model for IT function delivery, 101–105
Measurement. *See also* Business metrics;
    Dashboards, digital
  as component of value realization, 9–10
Memoranda of understanding (MOUs), 106
Metrics, business. *See* Business metrics
Migration strategies, 292
  principles to guide, 296
Misperceptions of IT. *See* Perceptions of IT's
    value/effectiveness
Motivation. *See* Incentive systems
MOUs. *See* Memoranda of understanding

N

National Institute of Standards and
    Technology, 137
Negative perceptions of IT. *See* Perceptions
    of IT's value/effectiveness

O

Object oriented programming, 300
"Observe-orient-decide-act" (OODA)
    loop, 320
Obstacles to effective communication
  attitude, 57–58
  business organizations structure, 57
  changing nature of IT work, 56
  frequency, 57
  hiring practice, 57
  nature of, 57
"Off-profile" ("noncompliant") technology,
    293
OLAP. *See* Online analytical processing
Online. *See* Internet
Online analytical processing (OLAP), 208
OODA loop. *See* "Observe-orient-decide-act"
    loop
Operations costs
  defined, 119, 120
  separated from innovation costs, 127
Opportunities
  experimental initiatives, 21
  for investments in IT, identifying, 7–8, 11
  leveraging others' ideas, 21
  prioritizing, 23
Outsourcing. *See* Sourcing

P

Partnership
  between IT and business, 19–20
  as sourcing option for IT functions, 105–108
"Peeling the onion," 3–6, 27
People. *See* Employees
Perceptions of IT's value/effectiveness
  conflicts in, 4–5
  time as factor in, 5
Performance, business. *See* Business
    performance
Pilot studies, value of, in diminishing risk, 12
"Placeholders" in budgets, 126
Planning and budget process, 123–126
Policy for IM, 145
Portfolio value management process, 11
PPM. *See* Project portfolio management